Lecture Notes in Computer Science 5310

Commenced Publication in 1973
Founding and Former Series Editors:
Gerhard Goos, Juris Hartmanis, and Jan van L

Henning Schulzrinne   Radu State
Saverio Niccolini (Eds.)

Principles, Systems and Applications of IP-Telecommunications

Services and Security for Next-Generation Networks

10th International Workshop, IPTComm 2008
Heidelberg, Germany, July 1-2, 2008
Revised Selected Papers

 Springer

Volume Editors

Henning Schulzrinne
University of Columbia
Department of Computer Science
1214 Amsterdam Avenue
New York, NY 10027-7003, USA
E-mail: hgs@cs.columbia.edu

Radu State
INRIA-LORIA
615, rue du Jardin Botanique
54602 Villers-les-Nancy, France
E-mail: state@loria.fr

Saverio Niccolini
NEC Laboratories Europe
Network Research Division
Kurfürstenanlage 36
69115 Heidelberg, Germany
E-mail: Saverio.Niccolini@nw.neclab.eu

Library of Congress Control Number: 2008937990

CR Subject Classification (1998): C.2, E.3, E.4, B.4, K.6.5

LNCS Sublibrary: SL 5 – Computer Communication Networks and
Telecommunications

ISSN   0302-9743
ISBN-10   3-540-89053-X Springer Berlin Heidelberg New York
ISBN-13   978-3-540-89053-9 Springer Berlin Heidelberg New York

Springer is a part of Springer Science+Business Media

springer.com

© Springer-Verlag Berlin Heidelberg 2008
Printed in Germany

Typesetting: Camera-ready by author, data conversion by Scientific Publishing Services, Chennai, India
Printed on acid-free paper   SPIN: 12542239   06/3180   5 4 3 2 1 0

Preface

These are the proceedings of IPTComm 2008 – the Second Conference on Principles, Systems and Applications of IP Telecommunications – held in Heidelberg, Germany, July 1–2, 2008. The scope of the conference included recent advances in the domains of convergent networks, VoIP security and multimedia service environments for next generation networks. The conference attracted 56 submissions, of which the Program Committee selected 16 papers for publication. The review process followed strict standards: each paper received at least three reviews. We would like to thank all Program Committee members and external reviewers for their contribution to the review process. The conference attracted attendees from academia and industry. Its excellence is reflected in the quality of the contributed papers and invited talks. Additional industry talks and applied demonstrations assured a synergy between academic and applied research. We would also like to acknowledge and thank our sponsors, many of whom supported the conference generously: NEC, AT&T, Codenomicon, IPTEGO, EADS, Cellcrypt, MuDynamics, SIP Forum and EURESCOM, Finally, we would like to thank all the researchers and authors from all over the world who submitted their work to the IPTComm 2008 conference.

August 2008
Henning Schulzrinne
Radu State

Organization

Executive Committee

Conference Chairs	Saverio Niccolini (NEC Laboratories) and Pamela Zave (AT&T Labs Research)
Program Chairs	Henning Schulzrinne (Columbia University, USA) and Radu State (INRIA-LORIA, France)
Publicity Chair	Gregory W. Bond (AT&T Labs Research, USA)

Program Committee

Gregory W. Bond	AT&T Labs Research, USA
Sapan Bhatia	Princeton University, USA
Marcus Brunner	NEC Laboratories Europe, Germany,
Gonzalo Camarillo	Ericsson, Sweden
George Carle	University of Tuebingen, Germany
Eric Chen	NTT Information Sharing Platform Laboratories, Japan
Charles Consel	INRIA, France
Tasos Dagiuklas	TEI of Mesolonghi Nafpaktos, Greece
Ram Dantu	University of North Texas, USA
Carol Davids	Illinois Institute of Technology, USA
Rosario Garroppo	University of Pisa, Italy
Vijay K. Gurbani	Bell Laboratories, Alcatel-Lucent, USA
Luigi Logrippo	Université du Quebec en Outaouais, Canada
Thomas Magedanz	Fraunhofer FOKUS, Germany
Evan Magill	University of Stirling, UK
Saverio Niccolini	NEC Laboratories Europe, Germany
Calton Pu	Georgia Tech, USA
Stefano Salsano	University of Rome "Tor Vergata", Italy
Gunter Schafer	University of Ilmenau Germany
Henning Schulzrinne	Columbia University, USA
Jan Seedorf	NEC Laboratories Europe, Germany
Dorgham Sisalem	Tekelec, Germany
Radu State	INRIA-LORIA, France
Simon Tsang	Telcordia, USA
Xiaotao Wu	Avaya, USA
Pamela Zave	AT&T Labs Research, USA

Table of Contents

A SIP-Based Programming Framework
for Advanced Telephony Applications

Wilfried Jouve[1], Nicolas Palix[1], Charles Consel[1], and Patrice Kadionik[2]

[1] INRIA / LaBRI
{jouve,palix,consel}@labri.fr
[2] IMS / University of Bordeaux,
351 cours de la Libération, F-33405 Talence Cedex, France
kadionik@enseirb.fr

Abstract. The scope of telephony is significantly broadening, providing users with a variety of communication modes, including presence status, instant messaging and videoconferencing. Furthermore, telephony is being increasingly combined with a number of non-telephony, heterogeneous resources, consisting of software entities, such as Web services, and hardware entities, such as location-tracking devices. This heterogeneity, compounded with the intricacies of underlying technologies, make the programming of new telephony applications a daunting task.

This paper proposes an approach to supporting the development of advanced telephony applications. We introduce a declarative language to define the entities of a target telephony application area. This definition is passed to a generator to produce a Java programming framework, dedicated to the application area. The generated frameworks provide service discovery and high-level communication mechanisms. These mechanisms are automatically mapped into SIP, making our approach compatible with existing SIP infrastructures and entities. Our work has been validated on various advanced telephony applications.

1 Introduction

In recent years, telephony has dramatically broadened its scope by integrating a variety of forms of communications, including video, text, and presence events. This broadened scope has also created a need for telephony applications to invoke ever more heterogeneous, non-telephony resources such as Web services, calendars, and databases. This situation changes significantly the programming of telephony applications: it now consists of coordinating heterogeneous entities and exchanging arbitrary types of values. These entities may either be hardware, like a phone terminal, or software, like a Web service. Because telephony applications involve an increasingly wide range of potential entities, selecting the appropriate ones is becoming a real challenge. To take up this challenge, programmers are forced to encode properties, like location or functionalities, in the entity references, using error prone, ad hoc techniques [25].

To address the extended scope of telephony applications, platforms based on SIP (Session Initiation Protocol) have, by definition of the protocol, the potential

H. Schulzrinne, R. State, and S. Niccolini (Eds.): IPTComm 2008, LNCS 5310, pp. 1–20, 2008.

to provide a rich range of communication forms, namely, instant messaging [9], events [29] and sessions [33]. More specifically, instant messaging is a one-to-one interaction mode; it can, for example, be used to display information about missed calls. Event is a one-to-many interaction mode; it is the preferred mechanism to propagate information such as presence status. Finally, session is a one-to-one interaction mode with data exchanged over a period of time; it is typically used to set up a multimedia stream between users.

Software layers have been added on the top of SIP in an attempt to facilitate the development of applications (*e.g.*, JAIN [37], SIP Servlets [17] and Parlay [14]). However, these layers provide a limited level of abstraction in that they require programmers to have an extended expertise in the underlying building blocks, including the signalling protocol, the API to the protocol-support layer, network protocols and distributed system programming. Going beyond software layers, other approaches have introduced programming languages dedicated to telephony service creation. However, languages such as CPL [31], LESS [40] or VisuCom [23] have a scope limited to end-user services. Others approaches, like SPL [8], propose scripting languages that are restricted to express routing logic.

This Paper

This paper proposes an approach to covering the broadened scope of telephony applications and raising the abstraction level for programming these applications. To do so, we provide the programmer with a declarative language, named *DiaSpec*, to define the entities involved in a telephony application area. An entity is characterized by its interaction modes, consisting of the SIP-native interaction modes, namely, messages, events and sessions. However, to cope with non-telephony resources, our approach also provides a command mode, that is an RPC-like mechanism, to invoke entity operations (*e.g.*, a database look-up operation). Entity declarations are passed to a generator, called *DiaGen*, that produces a programming framework in Java dedicated to the target application area. This framework provides the programmer with a discovery service for entities and programming support dedicated to interact with the declared entities. The programmer writes telephony applications using high-level, automatically generated methods, that are mapped into SIP-compliant operations.

The contributions of this paper are as follows.

- We introduce a discovery service integrated into a SIP-based programming framework, making explicit the properties needed to select the relevant entities for an advanced telephony application.
- We provide the programmer with high-level interaction modes, raising the abstraction level of SIP-native operations and introducing a uniform mechanism to invoke non-SIP resources.
- We have developed DiaGen, a generator of programming frameworks for advanced telephony applications that is SIP compliant, enabling applications to abstract over heterogeneous entities.

Outline

The rest of this paper is organized as follows. Section 2 introduces an example to motivate and illustrate our approach. Section 3 presents a methodology, and supporting declaration language, for the development of advanced telephony applications. In Section 4, we describe how our development methodology, and high-level programming support, are automatically mapped into a SIP infrastructure. Section 5 examines the tool chain implementing this mapping. We discuss the related works in Section 6 and conclude in Section 7.

2 Working Example

To motivate our approach, we consider an application that prevents close collaborators from missing each others calls. Currently, a call has to be repeated until the callee answers the phone. When the missed call is returned, the original caller may not be available anymore. To address this situation, our advanced service queues a call between close collaborators when the callee is unavailable and calls back both parties as soon as they become available. We name this application *presence-based automatic callback*. The key interest of our working example is to motivate the need to coordinate a variety of building block services and to illustrate how this need is addressed by the high-level programming support provided by our approach.

Let us now introduce the building block services of presence-based automatic callback. A location manager keeps track of the location of users and publishes this information. A presence manager updates the status of the users depending on their location and activities (*e.g.,* busy on the phone). A virtual phone manages the incoming calls of a user depending on its status: when available, the user gets forwarded a call, otherwise a call from a close collaborator is sent to the *pending call manager*. When both collaborators are available the pending call manager initiates a call between them. A virtual phone provides a useful mediator between the telephony platform and the user; it can serve other purposes beyond presence-based automatic callback. For example, it could define routing logic with respect to a user, regardless of his terminals.

For the sake of simplicity, we do not further detail the presence manager in the remainder of this paper. As a result, the user status is treated by the location manager. Figures 1 and 2 present use cases of presence-based automatic callback. In Figure 1, Bob calls Alice while she is out of her office. His call gets queued in the pending call manager. As shown by Figure 2, when Alice comes back to her office, both Bob and her are invited to initiate a conversation on the phone.

Although conceptually simple, the presence-based automatic callback application relies on (1) SIP events to manage user presence, (2) SIP signalling to forward and initiate calls, and (3) a real-time transport protocol for multimedia sessions. The nature of these operations require programmers to dive into the API of the SIP platform. For example, SIP Servlet provides support for SIP methods and SIP dialog management but it offers low-level interface to manipulate message headers and body. JAIN SLEE supports a high-level interface to

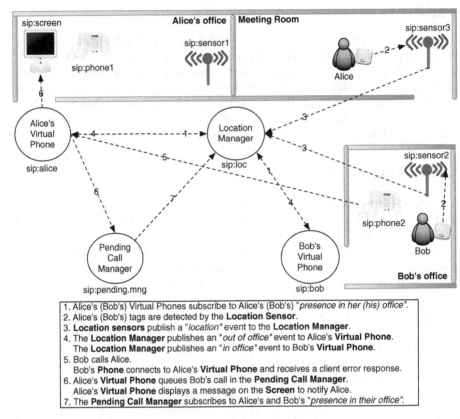

Fig. 1. Presence-based Automatic Callback: initial process

a telephony platform. However, because it is protocol agnostic, it introduces an overly generic interface to cover a range of protocols besides SIP.

Programming advanced telephony applications also involves interacting with heterogeneous SIP entities; in our working example, these entities are hardware (*e.g.,* a phone terminal), software (*e.g.,* a virtual phone), and non-telephony (*e.g.,* a location sensor). Not surprisingly, this heterogeneity is often reflected in the application code impeding future evolutions.

3   The DiaGen Programming Framework

Our approach is based on the notion of *taxonomy* that describes the distributed entities that are relevant to a given application *area* in the telephony *domain*. This description is enriched by attributes that further characterize possible variations. An area is introduced by an architect, whose task is to identify what kinds of entities are relevant and how they should interact. Application programmers then use the area definition to guide and structure the implementations of the services provided by the various entities. A DiaSpec area specifies not only what

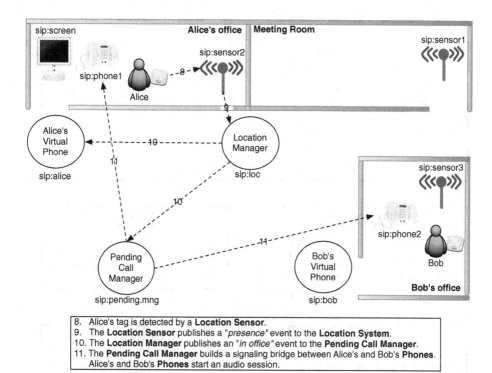

8. Alice's tag is detected by a **Location Sensor**.
9. The **Location Sensor** publishes a "*presence*" event to the **Location System**.
10. The **Location Manager** publishes an "*in office*" event to the **Pending Call Manager**.
11. The **Pending Call Manager** builds a signaling bridge between Alice's and Bob's **Phones**.
    Alice's and Bob's **Phones** start an audio session.

Fig. 2. Presence-based Automatic Callback: a scenario

kinds of data can be exchanged between entities, as is declared by an interface, but also which kinds of entities can participate in a given interaction, and the mode by which the interaction should be carried out. DiaGen, the compiler for DiaSpec, translates these declarations to Java code that is constructed such that many of the expressed constraints are checked statically by the Java type checker. The generated Java code relies on SIP to carry out interaction between entities, as detailed in Section 4.

3.1   The DiaSpec Specification Language

A DiaSpec area is expressed as a collection of *service classes*, each of which represents a set of entities sharing common functionalities. We refer to these entities as *services*. Associated with each service class is a collection of *attributes*, characterizing the non-functional properties of the associated services, and a collection of *interaction modes*, specifying how the associated services may interact with other entities. Finally, service classes and attribute values are organized hierarchically, permitting more specific instances to be used where less specific instances are required, thanks to polymorphism. In the rest of this section, we describe the declaration of the attributes, interaction modes, and hierarchical relationships in more detail, using the fragments of our application area shown in Figure 3 and Figure 4.

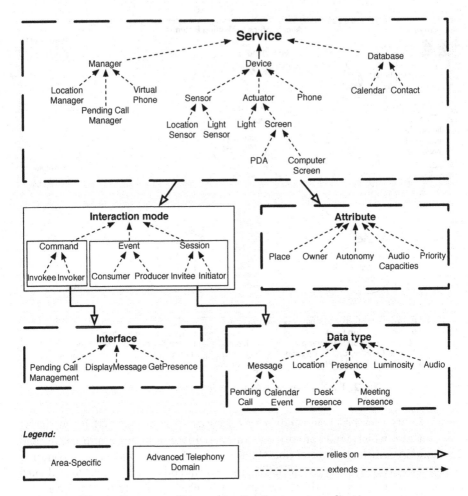

Fig. 3. Excerpts of hierarchies for the target application area

Attributes. The attributes of a service class describe the range of entities that the service class corresponds to, in terms of their non-functional properties (*e.g.,* location). Attributes are specified in a parenthesized list following the name of the service class. For example, in Figure 4, the service class `Phone` introduces the specified attribute `AudioCapabilities`. An attribute is a Java data type, allowing sub-classing between attribute values according to the Java class hierarchy. Figure 3 shows various hierarchies extracted from our application area. Attributes are used within a service implementation, in the service discovery process, both to characterize the implemented service and to specify the set of entities with which the service needs to interact.

Interaction modes. The interaction modes associated with a service class describe how its services produce or consume data. DiaSpec supports three kinds of interaction modes: *commands*, *events*, and *sessions*. A command interaction amounts to a Remote Procedure Call (RPC), allowing a one-to-one interaction between distributed entities. An event interaction implements the standard publish/subscribe paradigm [27], in which an event publisher broadcasts an event notification to a collection of subscribers. A session interaction natively supports negotiation of session parameters and exchange of a stream of data. The declared interaction modes strictly define how an entity can interact with other entities.

A interaction mode declaration specifies the interaction mode and indicates whether a service provides or requires the interaction. Such a declaration has either of the following forms:

provides *interactionMode*
requires *interactionMode*

In the former case, the service, acting as a server, must implement the interaction mode. In the latter case, the service, acting as a client, may use the required interaction mode.

```
service  Service(Owner) {
}
service  Device(Location, Autonomy) extends  Service {
}
service  LocationSensor() extends  Sensor {
  provides event Location
}
service  Calendar() extends  Database {
  provides event Info
}
service  Phone(AudioCapacities) extends  Device {
  provides session Audio
  requires session Audio
}
service  Screen() extends  Device {
  provides command DisplayMessage
  requires command PendingCallManagement
}
service  Manager(Priority) extends  Service {
  provides command StartStop
}
service  VirtualPhone() extends  Manager {
  requires session Audio
  requires event DeskPresence
  requires command PendingCallManagement
  provides session Audio
}
service  LocationManager() extends  Manager {
  requires event Location
  provides command GetPresence
  provides session Presence
  provides event Presence
}
service  PendingCallManager() extends  Manager {
  requires event DeskPresence
  requires command DisplayPendingCall
  provides command PendingCallManagement
  binds session Audio
}
```

Fig. 4. Excerpts of an application area in DiaSpec

The sub-term *interactionMode* specifies the mode of a given interaction. A mode is either `command`, `event`, or `session` combined with the name of a Java type characterizing the interaction. For a command, the Java type is an interface listing the relevant methods (*e.g.*, `DeskPresence`). For an event or session, the Java type indicates the type of the data that are exchanged. These Java types are, like the attributes, organized into a hierarchy. For example, Figure 3 presents the data type hierarchy, containing two sub-nodes to `Presence`, namely, `DeskPresence` and `MeetingPresence`. A service could subscribe to either event type or to the generic `Presence` event type.

To illustrate these declarations in more detail, we consider the `Location-Manager` and `LocationSensor` service classes, shown in Figure 4. The `Location-Sensor` service class provides a single event functionality and then, produces `Location` event (*i.e.*, Cartesian coordinates), to the `LocationManager` service class. The `LocationManager` service class in turn requires `Location` events. Based on this location, the `LocationManager` service can then provide information about user presence in a predefined set of places (*e.g.*, office rooms, meeting rooms or corridors), as a command (*i.e.*, `getPresence`), as a session of `Presence` data or as a `Presence` event (*e.g.*, `DeskPresence`).

Hierarchical Relationships. The DiaSpec description of a distributed environment of entities is structured as a hierarchy, as illustrated by Figure 3 for the definition of our application area. In a service class declaration, a sub-class relationship is specified using the `extends` keyword. Starting at the root node, the hierarchy breaks down the set of possible entities of this area into increasingly specific service classes. Each successive entry adds new attributes and interaction modes that are specific to the service class it represents. A service class furthermore inherits all the attributes and interaction modes of its ancestors.

In our approach, inheritance plays a decisive role in service discovery. Conceptually, a developer who wants access to a service class designates the corresponding node in the service hierarchy, and receives all of the services corresponding to the service classes contained in the sub-tree. This strategy implies that code that implements a service class should be associated with a node as low as possible in the hierarchy, to most precisely expose to users the variety of functionalities provided by the service. Yet, code that uses a service class should choose the least detailed class of services that meets its needs. In doing so, (1) a service discovery request is more likely to be successful and to return a larger number of entities; (2) the resulting application only exposes the functionalities it requires, thus improving its portability, and making it forward compatible with future or refined versions of the requested service class.

3.2 Developing Advanced Telephony Services

To develop a new service in our approach, the programmer first determines the service class it should belong to. The declarations of the selected service class then provide the programmer with an area-specific design framework for implementing all the facets of the service, ranging from its operations to its deployment. This design framework is supported by a programming framework that is automatically generated from the DiaSpec specification. We assume that code is implemented in Java.

The Interface Provided to Programmers. For each DiaSpec specification, the generated framework provides an abstract class that contains methods and instance variables, corresponding to interaction modes and attributes, respectively. Definitions are generated for methods that solely depend on the information provided by the DiaSpec specification. For example, a method for publishing an event only depends on the type of the event, and thus is defined in the abstract class, whereas commands are represented by abstract methods that the programmer must implement in the service. This organization implies that the programmer can focus his development effort on the application logic. This use of abstract classes also triggers the generation of programming support in an Integrated Development Environment (IDE), such as Eclipse.

Definition of Services. To create a service, the programmer first extends the abstract class corresponding to the selected DiaSpec service class. In an IDE such as Eclipse, this action triggers the creation of a class skeleton (or class stub in Eclipse parlance) that the programmer must then fill in with the service code. We now describe the subsequent programming process, and the support that Eclipse provides.

Interaction modes. The interaction modes are represented by the methods and abstract methods of the abstract class. As examples, we use the implementation of a `PendingCallManager` service (Figure 5 and Figure 6).

Command. Commands are represented by abstract methods in the abstract class. From these declarations, Eclipse generates method stubs[1] for all of the commands that need to be implemented. As shown in Figure 5, for the pending call manager, these methods are `addPendingCall`, `deletePendingCall`, `start` and `stop` declared by the DiaSpec nodes `PendingCallManager` and `Manager` (`PendingCall-Management` and `StartStop` interfaces in Figure 4).

When a service needs to invoke a command from another service, it calls the associated method of this service, which embeds an RPC call. For example, the `MyPendingCallManager` service shown in Figure 6 may need to display a notification message on a screen. Line 22 of this service invokes the `display` method of a previously obtained screen.

Event. For a DiaSpec service class that provides an event interaction mode, the corresponding abstract class defines a `publish` method for each declared type of output event. Services implementing the interface definition invoke these `publish` methods to publish the corresponding event. In our Location Manager example, the produced event is a Presence event. Consequently, the Location Manager publishes an event whenever the location of a contact changes. This event will be received via an event channel by all services that have subscribed to it.

---

[1] We refer to *method stubs* as methods generated by an IDE, whereas stubs refer to client stubs created using an IDL compiler.

```
public class MyPendingCallManager extends PendingCallManager {

  public MyPendingCallManager(String uri) {
    super(uri);
    // TODO Auto-generated constructor stub
  }

  public void receive(DeskOffice event, Service source) {
    // TODO Auto-generated method stub
  }

  public void addPendingCall(Person caller, Person callee) {
    // TODO Auto-generated method stub
  }

  public void deletePendingCall(int pendingCallID) {
    // TODO Auto-generated method stub
  }

  public void start() {
    // TODO Auto-generated method stub
  }

  public void stop() {
    // TODO Auto-generated method stub
  }

}
```

Fig. 5. The MyPendingCallManager class skeleton (from Eclipse)

For a DiaSpec specification that provides an event interaction mode, the corresponding abstract class also defines a receive abstract method for each declared type of input event. Such a method has an argument of the corresponding event type. From this declaration, Eclipse generates a method stub, which is to be filled in by the programmer. Lines 13-16 of Figure 6 show the method definition provided by the programmer for MyPendingCallManager, which implements the PendingCallManager service class that can receive DeskPresence events. The pending call manager may then subscribe to DeskPresence events from various sources. In Figure 6, line 11, it subscribes to all available LocationManager services in the building A by invoking subscribe.

Session. The code relevant to a session is similar to that of an event: services declared as session invitee lead to the creation of the connect and disconnect method stubs, whereas services in service classes declared as session initiator invoke these methods to receive a stream of data. Services in service classes declaring session binder use the bind method to establish a session between two services that have session capabilities. In our example, the Phone services are invitees and the PendingCallManager service is an audio session binder. As such, the pending call manager can establish a session between the caller's Phone and the corresponding callee's Phone (line 15 of Figure 6).

Attributes. The programmer must initialize the values of the attributes in the constructor of the service. In doing so, the service is characterized, enabling other services to discover it. Such properties (*i.e.*, priority and owner) are initialized in the constructor of the pending call manager as shown in lines 5-6 of Figure 6. This constructor first invokes the constructor of the abstract class, via a call to **super**, to register the service in the SIP registrar. In our approach, this constructor always requires a URI as an argument, as this information is necessary to identify the service.

```
1.  public class MyPendingCallManager extends PendingCallManager {
2.    private LinkedList<LocationManager> myLocManagers;
      [...]
3.    public MyPendingCallManager(String uri) {
4.      super(uri);
5.      priority.setValue(Priority.HIGH);
6.      owner.setValue(Owner.ADMIN);

7.      LocationManagerFilter filter = LocationManager.getFilter();
8.      filter.location.setValue(Location.BuildingA);
9.      myLocManagers = LocationManager.getServices(filter);
      [...]
10.     for (LocationManager myLocManager:myLocManagers)
11.        myLocManager.subscribe((IDeskPresenceEventInput)this);
12.   }

13.   public void receive(DeskPresence event, Service source) {
14.     PendingCall pendingCall = updatePendingCalls(
            event.getPerson(),
            event.isInOffice()
        );

15.     AudioSession session = bind(
          pendingCall.getCalleePhone(),
          pendingCall.getCallerPhone()
        );
      [...]
16.   }

17.   public void addPendingCall(Person caller, Person callee) {
18.     PendingCall pendingCall = addPendingCallToDB(caller, callee);

19.     ScreenFilter filter = Screen.getFilter();
20.     filter.location.setValue(callee.getDeskLocation());
21.     Screen calleeScreen = Screen.getService(filter);

22.     calleeScreen.display(pendingCall);
23.   }

24.   public void deletePendingCall(int pendingCallID) {
      [...]
25.   }

      // Updates pending calls with caller/callee presence.
      // Returns the next pending call where caller and callee
      // are in their office.
26.   private PendingCall updatePendingCalls(Person person, boolean isInOffice) {
      [...]
27.   }

      // Stores pending calls.
28.   private void addPendingCallToDB(Person caller, Person callee) {
      [...]
29.   }
      [...]
30. }
```

Fig. 6. A Pending Call Manager

Service Discovery. The programming framework that is generated from a DiaSpec specification provides the programmer with methods to select any node in a service class hierarchy. The result of this selection is a set of all services corresponding to the selected node and its sub-nodes, which we refer to as a *filter*. From a filter, the programmer can further narrow down the service discovery process by specifying the desired values of the attributes. Eventually, the method getServices or getService is invoked to obtain a list of matching services or one service chosen at random from this list, respectively.

Although a DiaSpec specification characterizes a telephony application area statically, our approach still permits services to be introduced dynamically within a filter. In doing so, we offer an alternative to the string-based discovery process by supplying selection operations generated from the DiaSpec specification, making the discovery logic safe with respect to the service class hierarchy.

As an example, consider the MyPendingCallManager service that should get the presence of people at their desk, in the building A. It obtains a filter by selecting the LocationManager node (line 7) and then sets the location attribute to limit the scope of Location Manager to those that are in the BuildingA (line 8). The operation getServices (line 9) then returns the location managers corresponding to this request, including its sub-nodes, if any. Finally, lines 10-11 iterate over all of the obtained location managers to subscribe to each DeskPresence event.

4   Mapping DiaGen into SIP

Despite the rich features of SIP, there is still a gap to fill between this protocol and the level of abstraction provided by DiaSpec. For example, SIP does not support an RPC-like mechanism, which is critical to command a wide range of entities like Web services. For another example, multimedia support mainly addresses major audio and video formats. However, advanced telephony applications involve other kinds of streams like locations and luminosity measurements.

In this section, we propose directions to extend the scope of SIP, leveraging on existing mechanisms and standards. The goal of the proposed extensions is to provide the programmer with dedicated programming support by introducing service discovery and high-level interaction modes, consisting of command, event and session.

4.1   Message Bodies

Targeting advanced telephony applications requires to keep pace with a constant flow of new devices and formats of exchanged data. To cope with this situation, SIP message bodies need to include data of arbitrary types. A number of proposals has been made to describe message body types for SIP messages. These proposals include body types for service description (*e.g.*, SDP [15]), service functionality invocation (*e.g.*, DMP [20]) and exchanged data (*e.g.*, CPIM [21]). Unfortunately, these proposals are not interoperable and force developers to create and manipulate numerous libraries to marshal and unmarshal message bodies.

Our approach abstracts over these issues by directly relying on the programmers' Java declarations. More specifically, Java *data types* are processed by the

DiaGen compiler to automatically produce marshaling and unmarshaling support. DiaGen uses the SOAP protocol to encode values in SIP messages. This format is standardized, XML-based and widely used. Although verbose, SOAP is increasingly supported by embedded systems (*e.g.*, XPath offers an API for manipulating XML in embedded systems). Furthermore, some implementations are now written in C, providing high performance and low memory footprint. A key advantage of our approach is that we can develop new back-ends to DiaGen to target other data formats (*e.g.*, the eXternal Data Representation (XDR) data format [11]).

4.2   Service Discovery

In the advanced telephony domain, new services appear and disappear over time (*e.g.*, SIP phones are switched on/off). Fortunately, SIP provides a way of handling this dynamic behavior via the registration process that supports mobility. To do so, SIP entities register their SIP URI with the registration server. This server associates SIP URIs and network addresses of the entities (*i.e.*, IP address and port). When communicating, SIP entities have their network address looked up from their URI by the proxy server. Although the SIP URI is a useful building block to provide service discovery, it does not take into account attributes that are needed to refine entity selection (*e.g.*, a device location or its rendering capabilities).

To circumvent this limitation, approaches consist of associating the characteristics of an entity with its SIP URI. This is either done by introducing parameters to the SIP URI [39] or by directly encoding characteristics of an entity in the string of its URI [25]. These approaches lack abstraction and are error-prone.

To solve this issue, our approach provides the programmer with an abstraction layer over SIP URIs. This layer corresponds to the hierarchy of service classes introduced earlier; this hierarchy characterizes the entities of an application area. To discover one or more entities of a service class, the programmer makes a request consisting of the service class name, refined by values assigned to attributes. The discovery process produces a list of SIP URIs that matches the request.

To map our discovery process into SIP, we introduce a service broker. This component is notified by the registration server every time a REGISTER request is received. When notified, the service broker sends an OPTIONS request to the newly registered service to collect the name of its service class and its attributes. The service broker is also invoked when an application requests services. To do so, a request consists of the name of the service class and attribute values. When issued by the operation `getServices`, all registered services matching the request are returned. Alternatively, the operation `getService` can be used to obtain a unique, randomly chosen, service from services matching the request.

4.3   Interaction Modes

Once discovered, a service is invoked to perform specific tasks. To do so, our approach provides the programmer with dedicated programming support and high-level interaction mechanisms. It extends and builds upon SIP operations.

Session. SIP supports multimedia sessions that are described using SDP. Negotiation of SDP session parameters is based on the offer/answer model [32]. Once negotiated, the session is launched and a stream of data gets transmitted. To deliver multimedia streams, the Real-time Transport Protocol (RTP) is widely used [34]. Today, the combination of SDP and RTP is widely used to deal with multimedia sessions from negotiation to streaming. However, this combination falls short of addressing other kinds of streams. Yet, emerging applications combine telephony with sensors streaming a variety of measurements to track people's location, to detect intrusion, to remotely monitor devices, *etc.*

To address these new situations, our approach consists of generalizing SDP to any Java data type, while re-using its negotiation model. Specifically, Java data types are used by DiaGen to generate a codec that takes the form of a serializer, allowing RTP to transmit streams of any data type. In doing so, our approach leverages existing technologies and APIs such as JMF [4].

Event. SIP event notification is mostly used for presence [29,30,36]. DiaSpec helps specifying a wide variety of event types that are not supported by available packages. To do so, we do not create a new event package for each new event type. Instead, we define a unique *generic* event package that supports arbitrary data types. As described previously, new message body types are automatically introduced by DiaGen.

The implementation of this event package is compliant to the event framework defined in existing protocol specifications [28,26]. Using the SUBSCRIBE request, event consumers subscribe to both a service class and a data type (*e.g.*, Location event of location sensors). A notification server manages these subscriptions. Event producers publish events to the notification server that notifies corresponding event consumers using respectively the SIP methods PUBLISH [26] and NOTIFY [28].

4.4   Interoperability with External Services

Any SIP-compliant resource is natively supported by DiaGen generated programming frameworks. However, extended forms of telephony application rely on increasingly many non-SIP resources. To integrate these resources, the programmer mixes SIP with other technologies, complicating the development process. To resolve this issue, we propose a uniform SIP-centric development approach to interoperating with external resources. In this approach, non-SIP resources are wrapped to become SIP compliant. For example, we developed a X10 gateway to convert SIP messages, representing commands to appliances, into X10 commands [5]. For another example, we wrapped a MySQL database to convert commands to MySQL requests.

Wrapping non-SIP Compliant Services. A great number of services from databases, to lights, to cameras is interfaced via the command interaction mode; it is used to control or query the status of these entities. Examples of commands include databases accessed via Web Service invocations, lights via X10 primitives and cameras via UPnP operations. However, despite various attempts (*e.g.,* the DO message [38]), SIP does not propose a standardized format to represent and transport commands.

The DiaGen framework extends the use of the standardized SIP MESSAGE request, initially defined for instant messaging, to handle RPC-like interactions [7,22]. To differentiate instant messaging exchanges from DiaGen commands, we use the content type header whose value is set to application/soap+xml. The return value of a command is included in the response message. Both command invocation and returned value are represented as SOAP messages. Existing tools are used to automatically generate (un-)marshaling procedures for Java data types.

The key benefit of our approach is that SOAP is a de facto standard, making our generated programming frameworks inherently interoperable with existing Web services, without requiring a dedicated gateway [24,10].

Interoperability with Existing SIP Services. Our generated programming frameworks supports native SIP entities, ranging from SIP phones to instant messaging clients. Because of its momentum, SIP should soon be spreading to other areas, making SIP-compliant devices that are not directly related to telephony (*e.g.,* SIP webcams and displays). This situation should motivate further the need for dedicated programming support.

To deal with native SIP entities, DiaGen needs to convert SIP message body types into Java data types, and conversely. These conversions concern the SDP format for service registration and session establishment, the Presence package for events, the CPIM message body for instant messaging, and DTMF digits contained by INFO messages. The DiaSpec specification imports these SIP native message bodies as data types to either create richer data types or reuse them directly. Then, developers manipulate these legacy bodies as any other new data types. The DiaGen framework provides automatic conversion to interact with native SIP services. The service broker annotates these services as legacy services at registration time. From these annotations, a dedicated service proxy is generated; it performs the appropriate conversion automatically.

5   Implementation

The information provided in a DiaSpec area has been designed to enable verifications and programming support generation, throughout the life-cycle of a telephony application: from design, to development, to deployment, to run time. To do so, we have developed DiaGen, a tool chain that processes DiaSpec declarations and telephony applications.

5.1   The DiaGen Compiler

Figure 7 shows the main processing steps of our approach: area compilation and service compilation. Initially, a DiaSpec area specification is passed to the area compiler, which (1) verifies the consistency of the area, (2) generates an area-specific programming framework. Using the generated framework, programmers

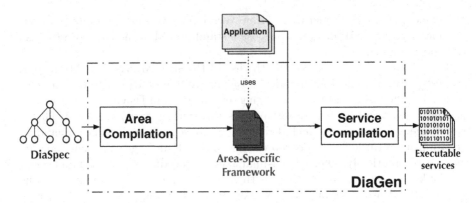

Fig. 7. Overview of our processing chain

then develop various services forming the telephony application. Each service is then passed to the service compiler, which (1) checks that Java classes implementing the service conform to the DiaSpec specification and (2) invokes a Java compiler to generate a class file.

DiaGen parses and analyzes a DiaSpec specification, and generates Java code. To do this processing, we use the tools JastAdd [13,16] and JastAddJ [12]. JastAdd is a meta-compiler providing advanced support for constructing modular and extensible compilers. JastAdd has been used to develop an extensible Java 5.0 compiler named JastAddJ. JastAddJ makes it possible to easily introduce new language constructs into Java, and to implement new static analyses. We use JastAddJ to introduce DiaSpec declarations, to analyze them, and to generate Java classes and interfaces.

5.2   The DiaGen Architecture

The OpenSER SIP server is used as a SIP proxy server, a SIP registration server and a SIP location server [3] in the DiaGen architecture. The DiaGen services, the service broker and the notification server act as SIP entities. As such, they register to the OpenSER server. OpenSER is configured to send a raw copy of every REGISTER message to the service broker (except its own) to notify it of a newly registered service. Upon receipt of this message, the service broker sends a OPTIONS request, as described in Section 4, to collect the service class and its attributes. DiaGen services, the service broker and the notification server use the Java API of Jain-SIP for signalling purposes [1]. Java data types are serialized in SOAP using kSOAP [2]. kSOAP is a SOAP Web service library for resource-constrained Java environments such as J2ME applications.

5.3   Scenarios

We are collaborating with a telecommunications company on a project aimed to develop scenarios combining telephony with home automation. This project uses an ADSL modem as a gateway to enable homeowners to control their home remotely and to allow home residents to interact with heterogeneous services. The first step of this project was to characterize the set of entities (*e.g.*, devices and servers) that would be required to carry out a number of existing and future scenarios. This phase led to an environment description written in DiaSpec, enabling this knowledge to be shared among area experts and application programmers. DiaSpec was then passed to DiaGen to generate a framework customized with respect to home automation. Various scenarios are now being developed to validate the approach, involving entities such as SIP phones, entry phones, PDAs, video cameras, lights, doors, luminance sensors, Web services, Google calendar and digital media receivers. These scenarios include the Entrance Manager and the Surveillance Manager. The Entrance Manager connects entry phones to homeowners' cell phones for an audio session and allows the homeowners to remotely open the door using their cell phones. When an intrusion is detected, the Surveillance Manager sends a text message via SMS to the homeowner, sends an audio message to the police phone, records the intrusion scene using video cameras and sends the recorded video to the homeowner via email.

6   Related Work

Several research projects have used SIP beyond the telephony domain. TinySIP is a modified version of SIP for use by wireless sensors in a hospital environment [22]. Berger *et al.* leverage the SIP event model to determine user location in ubiquitous computing environments [7]. However, their approach has a limited scope. Moyer *et al.* argue for the use of SIP in wide-area secure networked devices [25]; however, this proposal has not been studied further. In contrast with our approach, these works rely on existing, low-level programming frameworks (*e.g.*, JAIN SIP, SIP Servlet). As a result, the programmer needs to manage the intricacies of the underlying technologies, such as protocols, network layers, and signalling.

SPL is a domain-specific language (DSL) whose goal is to ease the development of robust telephony services [8]. Although SPL provides high-level programming abstractions, it is still close to SIP and only addresses the routing logic.

Rosenberg *et al.* have emphasized the need for programming support that is dedicated to Internet telephony services [31]. They propose CPL, an XML-based scripting language for describing and controlling call services. Wu *et al.* propose another XML-based language, LESS, to program end-system services [40]. Services written using CPL and LESS scripting languages are mostly limited to coarse-grained processing and dedicated operations. VisuCom is an environment to graphically create telephony services [23]. It support the development of routing services with respect to non-telephony resources like agendas and phone directories. VisuCom includes various verifications. Examples of errors detected in services include call loss, incorrect state transitions, and unbounded resource usage.

These high-level languages target non-programmers and provides static verifications. However, they focus on end-user services and call processing. As a consequence, they lack expressivity to program advanced telephony applications as targeted DiaSpec.

Existing, general-purpose middlewares (*e.g.*, CORBA, DCOM) are highly flexible and support a large number of features to ease the development of distributed applications in a wide range of application areas. This genericity can, however, be a burden when it comes to address requirements from specific domains such as telephony, as adaptation code must be developed to match the application's needs [6,19]. Moreover, associated programming frameworks force developers to use unsafe and generic structures of code. In contrast, the DiaGen approach, by generating programming support, provides developers with structures of code typed with respect to the target area, as captured by the DiaSpec specification.

CINEMA is a SIP-based infrastructure that enables multimedia collaboration via IP phones, instant messaging and e-mail, among other forms of communication [18]. In CINEMA, service development relies on low-level programming support (*e.g.*, SIP Servlet) or end-user oriented languages (*i.e.*, CPL and LESS). In contrast, our approach provides high-level programming support and targets a wide range of applications involving a variety of telephony and non-telephony resources. Continuing the work on CINEMA, Shacham *et al.* address the use of heterogeneous devices in ubiquitous environments [35]. They introduce location-based device discovery and customization for session interactions using SIP. Unlike DiaGen, they focus on a single interaction mode (*i.e.*, session). Moreover, they do not show how to interface and integrate these devices in distributed applications.

7 Conclusion

In this paper, we argued that the broadened scope of the telephony domain makes the development of services an overwhelming challenge. To take up this challenge, we proposed a two-step approach to developing applications. First, declarations define the entities involved in a telephony application area and how they interact with each other. Then, these declarations are processed by a generator to produce a programming framework dedicated to the target application area. Generated frameworks provide high-level programming support, including service discovery and communication mechanisms. They are SIP compliant and are automatically mapped into a SIP infrastructure. A generated framework forms a programming layer, abstracting over underlying technologies.

Our approach has been implemented and validated on advanced telephony applications, running over a SIP infrastructure and invoking SIP entities. Currently, we are extending the scope of our approach to a wide variety of devices and software components, to assess the generality of SIP as a general-purpose *software bus* to coordinate distributed entities.

Acknowledgement

This work has been partly supported by France Telecom and the Conseil Régional d'Aquitaine under contract 20030204003A.

References

1. JAIN-SIP, JAVA API for SIP Signaling, https://jain-sip.dev.java.net
2. kSOAP 2, http://ksoap2.sourceforge.net
3. OpenSER - the open source SIP server, http://www.openser.org
4. SUN microsystems, Java Media Framework API (JMF),
   http://java.sun.com/products/java-media/jmf/
5. X10 communication protocol, http://www.x10.org
6. Apel, S., Bohm, K.: Towards the development of ubiquitous middleware product
   lines. In: Gschwind, T., Mascolo, C. (eds.) SEM 2004. LNCS, vol. 3437, pp. 137–
   153. Springer, Heidelberg (2005)
7. Berger, S., Schulzrinne, H., Sidiroglou, S., Wu, X.: Ubiquitous computing using SIP.
   In: NOSSDAV 2003: Proceedings of the 13th international workshop on Network
   and operating systems support for digital audio and video, pp. 82–89. ACM, New
   York (2003)
8. Burgy, L., Consel, C., Latry, F., Lawall, J., Palix, N., Réveillère, L.: Language technology for Internet-telephony service creation. In: IEEE International Conference
   on Communications (June 2006)
9. Campbell, B., Rosenberg, J., Schulzrinne, H., Huitema, C., Gurle, D.: Session initiation protocol (SIP) extension for instant messaging. RFC 3428, IETF (2002)
10. Chou, W., Li, L., Liu, F.: Web service enablement of communication services. In:
    ICWS 2005: Proceedings of the IEEE International Conference on Web Services,
    Washington, DC, USA, 2005, pp. 393–400. IEEE Computer Society Press, Los
    Alamitos (2005)
11. Eisler, M.: XDR: External Data Representation Standard. RFC 4506, IETF (May
    2006)
12. Ekman, T., Hedin, G.: The JastAdd extensible Java compiler. In: OOPSLA 2007:
    Proceedings of the 22nd annual ACM SIGPLAN conference on Object oriented
    programming systems and applications, pp. 1–18. ACM Press, New York (2007)
13. Ekman, T., Hedin, G.: The JastAdd system – modular extensible compiler con-
    struction. Science of Computer Programming 69(1-3), 14–26 (2007)
14. Glitho, R., Poulin, A.: A high-level service creation environment for Parlay in a SIP
    environment. In: ICC 2002. IEEE International Conference on Communications,
    vol. 4, 4:2008–2013 (2002)
15. Handley, M., Jacobson, V.: SDP: Session Description Protocol. RFC 2327, IETF
    (1998)
16. Hedin, G., Magnusson, E.: JastAdd: an aspect-oriented compiler construction sys-
    tem. Science of Computer Programming 47(1), 37–58 (2003)
17. Java Community Process. SIP Servlet API (2003),
    http://jcp.org/en/jsr/detail?id=116
18. Jiang, W., Lennox, J., Narayanan, S., Schulzrinne, H., Singh, K., Wu, X.: Integrat-
    ing Internet telephony services. IEEE Internet Computing 6(3), 64–72 (2002)
19. Jouve, W., Ibrahim, N., Réveillère, L., Le Mouël, F., Consel, C.: Building home
    monitoring applications: From design to implementation into the Amigo middle-
    ware. In: ICPCA 2007: IEEE International Conference on Pervasive Computing
    and Applications, pp. 231–236 (2007)
20. Khurana, S., Gurung, P., Dutta, A.: Device Message Protocol (DMP): An XML
    based format for wide area communication with networked appliances. Internet
    draft, IETF (2000)

21. Klyne, G., Atkins, D.: Common Presence and Instant Messaging (CPIM): Message format. RFC 3862, IETF (2004)
22. Krishnamurthy, S., Lange, L.: Distributed interactions with wireless sensors using TinySIP for hospital automation. In: PerSeNS 2008: The 4th International Workshop on Sensor Networks and Systems for Pervasive Computing, Hong-Kong, China. IEEE Computer Society Press, Los Alamitos (2008)
23. Latry, F., Mercadal, J., Consel, C.: Staging Telephony Service Creation: A Language Approach. In: Principles, Systems and Applications of IP Telecommunications, IPTComm, USA. ACM Press, New-York (July 2007)
24. Liu, F., Chou, W., Li, L., Li, J.: WSIP - Web service SIP endpoint for converged multimedia/multimodal communication over IP. In: ICWS 2004: Proceedings of the IEEE International Conference on Web Services, Washington, DC, USA, p. 690. IEEE Computer Society Press, Los Alamitos (2004)
25. Moyer, S., Marples, D., Tsang, S.: A protocol for wide area secure networked appliance communication. Communications Magazine, IEEE 39(10), 52–59 (2001)
26. Niemi, A.: Session initiation protocol (SIP) extension for event state publication. RFC 3903, IETF (2004)
27. Oki, B., Pfluegl, M., Siegel, A., Skeen, D.: The information bus: an architecture for extensible distributed systems. In: SOSP 1993: Proceedings of the fourteenth ACM symposium on Operating systems principles, pp. 58–68. ACM Press, New York (1993)
28. Roach, A.B.: Session Initiation Protocol (SIP)-specific event notification. RFC 3265, IETF (2002)
29. Rosenberg, J.: A presence event package for the session initiation protocol SIP: Session Initiation Protocol. RFC 3856, IETF (2004)
30. Rosenberg, J.: A watcher information event template-package for the Session Initiation Protocol (SIP). RFC 3857, IETF (2004)
31. Rosenberg, J., Lennox, J., Schulzrinne, H.: Programming Internet telephony services. IEEE Internet Computing 3(3), 63–72 (1999)
32. Rosenberg, J., Schulzrinne, H.: An offer/answer model with the Session Description Protocol (SDP). RFC 3264, IETF (2002)
33. Rosenberg, J., et al.: SIP: Session Initiation Protocol. RFC 3261, IETF (June 2002)
34. Schulzrinne, H., Casner, S., Frederick, R., Jacobson, V.: RTP: A transport protocol for real-time applications. RFC 3550, IETF (2003)
35. Shacham, R., Schulzrinne, H., Thakolsri, S., Kellerer, W.: Ubiquitous device personalization and use: The next generation of IP multimedia communications. ACM Trans. Multimedia Comput. Commun. Appl. 3(2), 12 (2007)
36. Sugano, H., Fujimoto, S., Klyne, G., Bateman, A., Carr, W., Peterson, J.: Presence Information Data Format (PIDF). RFC 3863, IETF (2004)
37. Sun Microsystems. The JAIN SIP API specification v1.1. Technical report, Sun Microsystems (June 2003)
38. Tsang, S., Moyer, S., Marples, D.: SIP extensions for communicating with networked appliances. Internet draft, IETF (May 2000)
39. Vaha-Sipila, A.: URLs for telephone calls. RFC 2806, IETF (2000)
40. Wu, X., Schulzrinne, H.: Programmable end system services using SIP. In: Proceedings of The IEEE International Conference on Communications 2002. IEEE, Los Alamitos (2003)

An IMS Based Mobile Podcasting Architecture Supporting Multicast/Broadcast Delivery

Rodolfo Cartas, Markus Kampmann, Heiko Perkuhn,
and Juan Miguel Espinosa

Ericsson Research,
Ericsson Allee 1, 52134 Herzogenrath, Germany
Communication and Distributed Systems, RWTH Aachen, Templergraben 55,
52062 Aachen, Germany
{heiko.perkuhn,markus.kampmann}@ericsson.com
rodolfo.cartas@gmail.com, espinosa@nets.rwth-aachen.de
http://www.ericsson.com

Abstract. Podcasting is an automatic content distribution mechanism that has gained popularity in the last couple of years. It differs from traditional vertical integrated media distribution such as Radio and Television in that 1) content is periodically made available over the Internet; and 2) media consumption takes places in computers or digital media players. This allows users to escape from the established schedule-based media experience and linear structure of broadcast programs. Content aquisition through podcasts can lead to scalability problems, when the number of subscribers grows quickly. The reason is that each client polls periodically for new content, usually about once per hour. It is expected that with the transformation of cell phones into portable information devices, this kind of services will be also used in mobile networks. This becomes a problem as bandwidth resources in these networks are scarce. In this paper we present an Advanced Podcasting Service that aims to reduce bandwidth usage maintaining an actual podcast subscription inside the network and reducing podcast distribution impact by selecting an appropriate delivery mechanism, such as multicast, while transparently supporting existing podcasting applications. To do so, the proposed architecture uses the IP Multimedia Subsystem (IMS) and the Multimedia Broadcast/Multicast Service (MBMS), both born from the efforts of the Third Generation Partnership Project (3GPP). Finally, the proposed architecture was implemented and evaluated in a local testbed.

1 Introduction

Podcasting refers to the automatic distribution of media files using standard web technologies. Its origins can be traced back to the early attempts to publish news headlines in a syndicated manner. That is, make short summaries of web content available to other web sites or consumers. It was only till 2005 that this technology started to be widely used to indicate the online availability of prerecorded multimedia files. Initially, podcasts used to deliver audio files only, but

H. Schulzrinne, R. State, and S. Niccolini (Eds.): IPTComm 2008, LNCS 5310, pp. 21–44, 2008.

nowadays many different types of media files are distributed in such a fashion. According to Forrester Research, at least 25% of users online have shown interest in podcasts [14]. This study also predicted that the number of households consuming podcasts in the United States will grow from 700,000 in 2006 to about 12 million in 2010. Content producers and providers can certainly benefit from this growth. The report also highlighted the fact that the diversity of content available in podcast format had exploded over a two year period. This explosion was also reflected in popular culture. In 2005, the *New Oxford American Dictionary* selected the word 'podcast' as Word of the Year [16]. In a very short term, Podcasting grew from an exotic technology employed mainly by hobbyists to a technology widely used by mainstream media producers.

In order to acquire content, a user 'subscribes' to a content channel or web feed made available over the Internet. The web feed is an XML document that contains information that references the media files belonging to the podcast. The web feed document is updated every time new content is published. A subscription to a web feed means that a podcast aggregation software or 'podcatcher' will periodically poll the feed document, and in case that updates are found, it will proceed to download the referenced media file. After downloading, the podcatcher informs the user that it has retrieved new content, making it appear as a push service. This content distribution model is shown in Figure 1.

The fact that podcasting follows a periodical polling model, by means of establishing unicast connections for each poll attempt and further download, implies that the service does not scale well with a growing customer base. Once a content provider makes her content available through a web feed, her bandwidth costs can grow very quickly [11]. First, due to the fact that content availability check patterns of podcatchers are different from that of human users, and second,

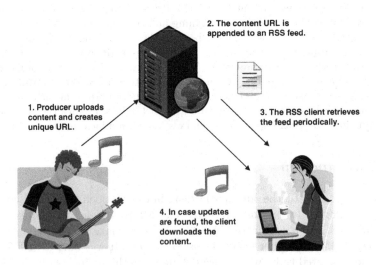

Fig. 1. Podcasting model

content transfer uses considerable amounts of bandwidth when delivered in a point-to-point fashion.

In 2007, a survey [24] found out that almost half of the content available as a podcast is consumed in the users' computers and not in mobile devices, because they do not synchronize their devices frequently. One way to overcome this is allowing users to subscribe to podcasts and get content directly from a mobile device. Podcast distribution might represent a new revenue generating service for network operators, but such a service would shift the problems inherent to podcasting to the mobile network and one of the operators' main concerns is the efficient use of network resources. This paper presents an Advanced Podcast Delivery Service Architecture acting inside an operator's domain to efficiently distribute podcast content while keeping the already familiar podcasting end user experience.

The proposed architecture monitors subscription aggregates and schedules the use of resources in order to minimize its impact on the network operation. Subscription aggregates provide a direct tool to measure this impact of the distribution of a certain file. The use of enablers in the operator domain could also mean revenue opportunities, like charging for premium podcast subscriptions. The service uses the IP Multimedia Subsystem (IMS), to maintain user subscriptions, and the Multimedia Broadcast/Multimedia Service (MBMS), to efficiently distribute content with high subscription rates. IMS offers a control layer over fixed and mobile networks based on IP that allows the provision of rich multimedia services. MBMS is a multicast/broadcast service for 3G mobile networks based on IP multicast that offers resource sharing at core and radio networks. This solution breaks traditional podcast retrieval dynamics while keeping legacy podcasting software intact. Other approaches to solve bandwidth strain, such as centralized aggregation and peer-to-peer have been proposed for a traditional podcast distribution. In the former, a third-party hosts the feed and content on behalf of its customers. Although content producers may reduce their bandwidth consumption, but it makes little difference in case of access and distribution networks. In the latter, a peer-to-peer network overlay cooperatively polls and distributes web feeds. However, in a mobile operator network this translates into more processing on relatively low processing power terminals and has an associated impact on scarce radio resources The remainder of this paper is structured as follows. Section 2 and Section 3 present the principles of the IP Multimedia Subsystem and of the Multimedia Broadcast/Multicast Service (MBMS). Section 4 introduces a survey of podcasting exploring the dynamics that cause its inefficiency and presents measurements from the Internet. Section 5 presents the proposed Service Architecture. Section 6 presents the evaluation carried out on a proof-of-concept prototype. Finally, Section 7 presents the conclusions and future lines of development.

2   IP Multimedia Subsystem

The IP Multimedia Subsystem (IMS) is the 3GPP proposal for a Next Generation Network core. It defines a control layer over fixed and mobile networks based on IP allowing the provision of rich multimedia services. Its specification

was introduced in UMTS Release 5 and it was refined in releases 6 and 7. The
IMS specification enforces the use of Internet protocols and open standards. Its
main signaling protocol is the Session Initiation Protocol (SIP). Functionally,
the IMS is organized in planes in charge of providing different service aspects:
the Access and Transport, Control, and Service Plane. The Access and Transport Plane provide a mechanism to access the IMS core through a wide range
of network technologies. The Control Plane comprises functions for reliably establishing multimedia sessions. There are functions for authorization, location,
negotiation, routing, and charging. Two functions are the heart of this plane: the
Home Subscriber Server (HSS) and the Call Session Control Function (CSCF).
The HSS is the master user data repository inside an IMS domain. The CSCF
controls and oversees the establishment of sessions. Media control is a responsibility of the Media Resource Function Controller (MRFC), whereas signaling
to switched networks is a responsibility of the Border Gateway Control Function, further divided into a Signaling Gateway and a Media Gateway Control
Function. The Application Plane comprises application and content servers in
charge of implementing the business logic of a service. An Application Server
is a SIP-capable entity in the network that serves SIP requests [3] and accesses
the CSCF by the IMS Service Interface (ISC). Application Servers may opt to
include other protocols to offer converged services. Figure 2 depicts the IMS
reference architecture.

The Session Initiation Protocol (SIP) [20] is an application layer protocol
designed by the Internet Engineering Task Force (IETF) whose main goal is
the management of rich interactive sessions. It provides mechanisms to create,
modify, and end a session between two or more parts. Designed as a signaling
protocol, SIP operates independently of the transport protocol and of the types
of sessions established with it. Hence, SIP is used in conjunction with several

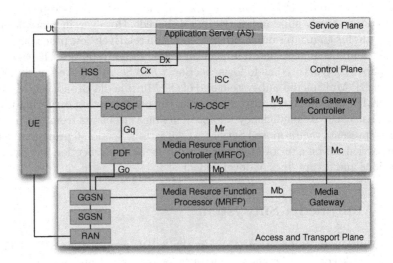

Fig. 2. IMS Architecture

other protocols in a multimedia system. Additionally, SIP extensions have been introduced to support instant messaging and subscription to events, to name a few. SIP is a text based protocol that follows a request-response transaction paradigm. A transaction is generated when a client issues a request that invokes a particular method on the server causing the second to generate at least one response. The most salient point of this protocol is its provision of building blocks to assemble services, meaning that SIP does not provide services *per se*. Rather than that, the protocol primitives are only used to transfer opaque objects needed for the provision of a specific service. Hence, all these features make SIP easy to extend, debug, and useful for building services [6].

3   Multimedia Broadcast/Multicast Service

The Multimedia Broadcast/Multicast Service (MBMS) is a unidirectional point to multipoint bearer service allowing the transmission from a single source entity to multiple recipients [1] standardized by the 3GPP. It provides a broadcast and multicast delivery mechanism for 2.5G and 3G networks. that enable a point to multipoint service: Cell Broadcast Service (CBS) and IP Multicast. CBS allows broadcast transmission to all subscribers in a given service area over a shared channel; however, it only supports low bit rates and small amounts of data. This technology is commonly used to transmit general interest messages. support for IP multicast for mobile subscribers, the service uses point to point tunneling for transport, thereby making it hard to save resources at radio and core networks. Transmitting data over MBMS bearers allows sharing resources in the core and radio networks, thus making a more efficient use of them. Its architecture is based on IP Multicast and retains compatibility with it at the gateway level (Gateway GPRS Support Node, GGSN). The MBMS realization [4] requires the modification of several elements in the packet switched domain of the UMTS architecture, namely the User Equipment (UE), the radio access network, the Serving GPRS Support Node (SGSN), and the Gateway GPRS Support Node (GGSN). A new functional entity, the Broadcast/Multicast Service Center (BM-SC), provides functions for different MBMS User Services in the Service Layer. Its interfaces to the GGSN represent the boundaries of the MBMS Bearer Service. Thus, it serves as an entry point for content provider transmissions. This entity is in charge of several service provision aspects: it authorizes, starts, schedules, announces, and delivers MBMS transmissions. Towards the core network, it establishes and controls MBMS transport bearers [10].

The MBMS bearer service provides a new point-to-multipoint transmission bearer, which may use common radio resources in cells of high receiver capacity [10]. Bearers transport IP data and provide two modes of operation: Broadcast and Multicast. The Broadcast mode is a unidirectional point-to-multipoint transmission of data from a single source entity to all users in a broadcast service area [1]. There is no specific requirement to activate or register to a particular broadcast service. services. Broadcast with counting represents an enhanced delivery method[]. The Multicast mode is a unidirectional point-to-multipoint

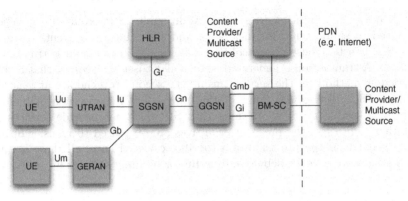

Fig. 3. MBMS Architecture

transmission of data from a single source entity to all users in a multicast group [1]. In order to receive a particular multicast service, the UE requires joining the multicast group.

On top of the bearer service, MBMS defines two User Services to facilitate applications, namely, the Download and Streaming Services. A User Service is associated with metadata that specifies how to access the service. This metadata is acquired before joining a specific service. The Streaming service delivers multimedia data, and it uses RTP [22] as a transport protocol. The Download service pushes discrete binary data files over an MBMS bearer. Due to the nature of the MBMS radio channel, the goal of this method is file transmission reliability. To do so, data transmission is protected using FEC coding and an off-band file repair service. The download delivery method uses the FLUTE protocol [17] to transfer content.

In 3GPP Release 6, UTRAN MBMS channels can operate with different data rates ranging from 64kbps up to 256kps. The MBMS service could comprise several channels, for instance using WCDMA MBMS technology. Furthermore, MBMS services can use only a portion of available cell bandwith, so parallel services such as voice are not disturbed.

3.1 IMS-MBMS Integration

The original IMS specification only targets the management and establishment of conversational services transported over unicast bearers and, currently, the IMS and the MBMS are two separate subsystems in the 3GPP network architecture. However, the IMS can take advantage of a multicast bearer service to offer non conversational services. In releases 7 and 8, 3GPP included the integration between these subsystems as a study item [2]. The first approach add small modifications both to IMS and MBMS nodes. MBMS services controlled by the IMS core are realized by adding SIP signaling to the BM-SC, replacing the Home Location Register (HLR) with the Home Subscriber Server (HSS) as the central user data repository, and adding an interface between the Gateway GPRS Support Node (GGSN) and the Policy and Charging Rules Function (PCRF).

This proposal is regarded as a short-term solution, as many of the functionalities in both subsystems overlap [13]. The second approach involves the partition of the BM-SC functionality into several enhanced IMS entities, such as Application Servers and the MRF. This approach avoids the dependence of a deployed BM-SC in the network, as its functions are implemented elsewhere. Additionally, an MBMS session establishment is negotiated directly between an Application Server and the GGSN according to the procedures of the Gmb interface. The last proposal is further explored by the C-Mobile Project [5].

4   Podcasting Characteristics

Podcast services today do not scale very well. The reason lies in their inherent dynamics that are explored in the following paragraphs.

4.1   The RSS Format

A Really Simple Syndication (RSS) document is a structured list of items contained in an XML document that is made available over the web. An item is the basic unit of syndication and it may contain structured metadata representing a blog entry or a news article summary. The RSS 2.0 format includes a mechanism to retrieve related media files through the use of a special tag describing content metadata, the `<enclosure>` tag. Clients retrieve the feed periodically, look for updates, and in case enclosures are present, proceed to download the referenced material.

4.2   Impact on Bandwidth

When the syndication technology started to become widespread, growing concerns related to the strain on servers and network bandwidth were reported [11]. Many providers chose to offer only summaries or limit the number of items in a feed. Bandwidth usage concerns are inherently associated with the nature of the RSS format and its polling dynamics. Detailed behaviors are identified in [21] [25].

   In the case of podcasting, another issue that largely increases bandwidth consumption is the distribution of large media files. Although clients should download media only when they identify a podcast update, the aggregate bandwidth usage can grow very quickly, especially when a podcast becomes popular. The problem relies on the fact that a unicast transmission session, an HTTP session, must be established by each client that is interested in acquiring the content. The uncoordinated update and content retrieval effort can thus cause surges in a mobile operator network.

4.3   Characterization of Podcasting Feeds

In order to picture the characteristics of the network workload produced by podcasting feeds and their referenced content, a passive study was carried out. Previous studies focused on general RSS feeds [15]. The study included the size

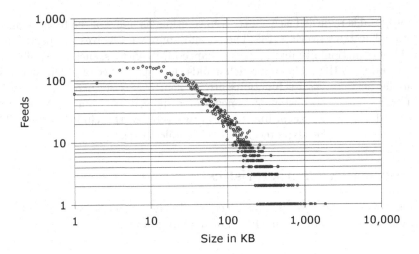

Fig. 4. File size distribution of feed documents

of the feed documents, the length of feed <item> elements, the size of enclosed media files, and their publication frequency. To do so, we obtained the URIs of 8,889 feeds listed in PodcastAlley[1], a content guide and podcast directory. A web crawler was written in order to fetch feed snapshots and treat the RSS documents to obtain the information of interest. The feed documents weigh 690 MB and comprise 286,509 episodes.

Feed Size. In the podcasting distribution approach, new content and references to media files are contained in <item> elements that form a feed document. Figure 4 plots results of the survey and indicates that: 1) feeds have a size similar to those of most web accessible objects [7]; and 2) although most feeds are smaller than 100 KB, a behavior close to that of a long tail distribution is observed. The minimum observed feed size is 748 bytes, the median is 37.57 KB, the average is 73.48 KB. The ninth decile is found at 180.7 KB, but the maximum feed size is 1,867.62 KB.

The presence of very long feeds is explained either by the fact that these usually contain all the episodes from long running shows, or because they contain complete articles along with enclosures that reference media files. In order to save bandwidth, most content providers cut the number of available episodes in the feed to reduce the feed size.

Item Length. Another feed characteristic of interest is the length of <item> elements contained in web feeds. This variable is measured because an <item> represents the basic unit of content syndication, and the fact that clients already have most of the feed content can be exploited to reduce sent information. To evaluate this variable, the <item> elements of all the feed snapshots were extracted and their length was measured. A long tail distribution is confirmed by the plot in

---

[1] http://www.podcastalley.com

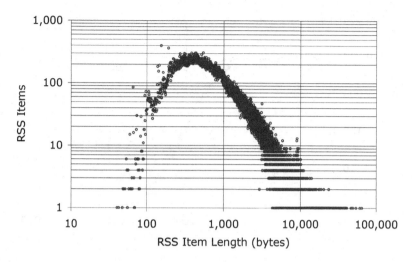

Fig. 5. Length distribution of `<item>` elements

Figure 5. The minimum observed `<item>` length is 41 bytes, enough to send only an enclosed url, while the maximum length is 62 KB, an `<item>` that contains a complete article together with an enclosed media file. The median is 866 bytes and the average is 1,439 bytes, 90% of the items are shorter than 3,132 bytes. This suggests that sending recently appended items only offers bandwidth savings.

Enclosure Size. The size of files referenced by `<enclosure>` tags in podcast feeds is by far the factor that affects bandwidth usage the most. It is true that efficient distribution of RSS updates is desirable, but feeds are small when compared to the average media file sizes. In many cases, podcast content is taken from content produced for other media distribution schemes such as radio or television, therefore making large media file sizes when the content is compressed with standard codecs. The enclosure size was taken directly from the `<enclosure>` tag, and when it was not included, an HTTP connection was set up to obtain its value from response headers. Figure 6 plots the results of this process. The minimum observed file size was 98 KB while the maximum file size was 1,146 MB. The median is 16.16 MB, the average 24.1 MB, and the ninth decile is found at 52.93 MB. As in the previous two cases, the behavior of this variable approaches that of a long tail distribution. This data indicates that the distribution of podcast content can consume large portions of network bandwidth.

Publication Frequency. The last variable under study is the publication frequency of new content. Figure 7 shows the distribution of update interval of podcasts as reported by the collected feeds. In contrast to feeds carrying web syndication such as news or blogs, whose update intervals fall mostly within one hour, podcasting updates tend to be more sporadical due to the complexity of producing media content. Most podcasts are published in a weekly fashion, and followed by those published within a day. The median is 6.06 days while the mean is 7.41 days.

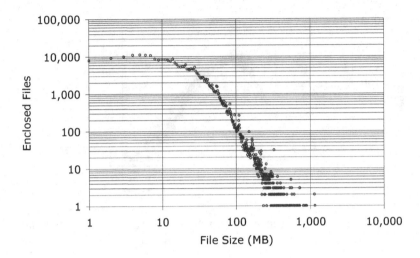

Fig. 6. File size distribution of feed documents

Discussion. The results presented so far show that enhancements in the distribution of podcast feeds and content can alleviate possible traffic surges. Possible enhancements are, on the one hand, sending feed updates only, and on the other, multicast/broadcast distribution of content with high subscription rates within an operator domain. This is not realizable in the traditional podcasting architecture, as there is no real subscription between consumer and provider. An architecture that brokers this liaison is hence introduced.

5 Mobile Podcasting Architecture

In this section we present an Advanced Podcast Delivery Service Architecture that uses a podcast subscription signal to the application server in the operator's domain taking care of content delivery. The service uses subscription aggregates and operator's policies to efficiently deliver content.

5.1 Requirements

Taking into account the scenario previously described, a mobile podcasting service would satisfy the following requirements:

- **Efficient Resource Utilization:** The distribution of very popular content tends to cause traffic surges both at the distribution and access networks. The mobile operator can efficiently save resources by introducing a file distribution strategy to reduce such surges. Given that podcasts are distributed in a 'subscription' fashion, such information gives operators an indicator to alleviate their impact on the network. Hence, popular content must be distributed using shared resources, *i.e.*, through multicast or broadcast bearers.

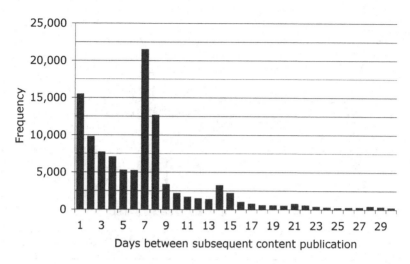

Fig. 7. Publishing Frequency

An entity in the network decides which content to send over these bearers assessing the amount of users interested in the content.

- **Leverage of existing Podcast Applications:** There is already a wide selection of podcasting software available. In order to use the mobile podcasting service, all these programs would need modifications. Therefore, the solution must be backwards compatible with existing RSS clients. Furthermore, the leverage of existing software should not alter the end user experience.
- **Break RSS Dynamics:** The inherent dynamics of RSS strain resources both at the network and at the servers. The service must then avoid unnecessary requests especially at the radio access network.
- **Efficient Content Monitoring:** The service must reduce the amount of outgoing bandwidth required to extract content from podcast sources. This reduction can be achieved by a mechanism that monitors content sources and later pushes content notifications and the content itself to service subscribers.
- **Leverage IMS enablers:** Use the existing IMS enablers to support service related functions, such as service triggering and charging.
- **Media Adaptation:** Available podcast content is encoded in a wide variety of formats, whereas mobile terminals can only play a reduced set. The service should provide a mechanism to re-encode content into mobile terminal friendly and transport efficient formats.

5.2   Components

Figure 8 shows the Architecture of the proposed Podcasting Service. The service uses both the IMS and the MBMS subsystems as building blocks. The BM-SC Service entity in Figure 8 comprises most of the standard BM-SC functionality Components at the user equipment and at the network domain are in charge of the service provisioning.

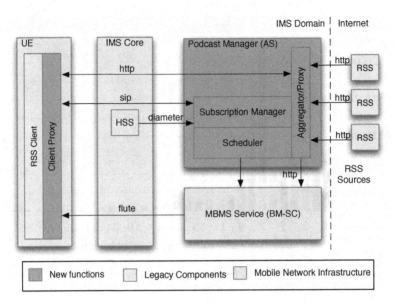

Fig. 8. Service Architecture

The service takes advantage of the measurement of subscription aggregates. This measurement translates into a "popularity" distribution that allows the system to preempt possible traffic surges by selecting an appropriate file distribution scheme. The solution is based on a signaling mechanism that explicitly indicates the user interest in a content feed.

The service relies on the IMS infrastructure to trigger the procedures at the application level and to route service signaling. Instead of delivering content metadata by HTTP, content metadata notifications are transported using SIP in case of content whose subscription rates are low. In such a scenario, clients start procedures to retrieve new content upon notification reception. The service sends podcasts with high subscription rates over multicast bearers, as this makes a better utilization of network resources.

In order to maintain backwards compatibility with current podcasting clients and servers, the solution uses a hierarchy of augmented proxy caches. These proxies break RSS dynamics, first at radio level and then at outbound link level, while avoiding the introduction of changes to the user experience. Although feeds may be marked as not cacheable, the decision to cache feeds was taken after observing large feed update intervals, and because the Application Server periodically refreshes them. Signaling and the functions of each component are discussed below.

Signaling. The SIP Event Notification Framework [18] defines a mechanism to convey changes on the state of a given resource. It defines two SIP methods: SUBSCRIBE and NOTIFY. The SUBSCRIBE method requests the current state and future changes on a resource whose information is collected by a remote node, the notifier. The notifier issues NOTIFY messages that contain the full or partial information on changes suffered by the resource. Although RFC 3265 restricts their usage to notifications related to SIP state, they can be easily adapted to notify events related to other domains [9].

Update notification is carried out by the specification of an *event package*, as defined in [18]. The name of this event package is rsssubnot; all requests conforming to this package specification must set their Event header to this value. To create a podcast subscription, the subscriber identifies the web feed URI and sends a SUBSCRIBE request to a feed monitoring agent. The feed monitoring agent tracks the state of the feed by frequently polling it. In case the monitoring agent finds a new <item> element within the recently polled feed, it extracts the recent update and wraps it in a NOTIFY message. The subscriber receives the notification and reconstructs the web feed. This mechanism indicates the availability of new content and allows the network operator to differ its delivery, but does not help to alleviate surges caused by popular content. In the same event package, a NOTIFY that includes information to join an MBMS service is also defined.

Client Proxy. The Client Proxy is a software agent residing at the user equipment mediating between a standard podcatcher or RSS client and the applications inside the IMS domain. The use of an augmented proxy makes it possible to keep the inner workings of podcatching software untouched. This component receives signaling from applications inside the network and manages multicast transfer sessions.

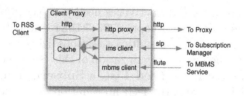

Fig. 9. Client Proxy Process Organization

Figure 9 presents the process organization of this component. The Client Proxy is composed of a **cache** to store web feeds and media files; an **HTTP proxy** that serves client requests; an **IMS client** to register, subscribe and receive notifications from the IMS domain; and an **MBMS client** to receive content sent over multicast download services. For its correct operation, the user equipment must be registered and authenticated in the IMS domain.

The **HTTP proxy** process is in charge of receiving RSS client requests and possibly retrieve them from a local cache, thus easing bandwidth usage and breaking periodical feed polls. When the resource is not available in cache, the proxy forwards the request to a domain proxy. Upon the response arrival, the proxy inspects the HTTP header fields suggesting the presence of a feed document. For instance, the MIME type application/rss+xml entails the presence of an RSS feed contained in the response body. This procedure spots a feed "subscription" at the application level. When the test is positive, the proxy triggers an actual SIP subscription. Hence, feed maintenance is delegated to the IMS client process.

The **IMS client** process maintains connectivity with the IMS domain. It registers, authenticates, and manages SIP transactions. Upon feed detection by the HTTP proxy, the IMS client generates a SUBSCRIBE request to the feed according to the guidelines given previously. It expects to receive NOTIFY requests with updates or multicast indications. Upon an update notification, the IMS client might indicate the MBMS client to activate a multicast/broadcast service, or it might incorporate the new <item> elements detected by the service into the appropriate web feed. A unicast download session is triggered to download content referenced by the update and store it in cache. The local *HTTP proxy* serves the newly updated feed and content when receiving requests from the RSS client.

The **MBMS client** is in charge of initiating a multicast/broadcast service transmitting podcast content. The session is triggered when the IMS client receives NOTIFY requests containing service bundles for the MBMS client to wait for an MBMS session start. Content is then received and stored in the local cache. The steps depicted in the figure are performed per every HTTP and SIP request. An *enhanced RSS client* could incorporate subscription and multicast/broadcast download procedures, hence reducing extra processing induced by the presence of an HTTP proxy.

Subscription Manager. The Subscription Manager is the part of the Application Server in charge of offering the podcasting service signaling interfaces to the IMS core and users. The Subscription Manager keeps the state of the current user subscriptions and coordinates the activities needed to accomplish service provision. The Subscription Manager accepts SUBSCRIBE requests from clients and informs them of possible updates or multicast sessions using NOTIFY requests.

Figure 10 presents the process organization of this component. The Subscription Manager is composed of a **Feed List**, a **Subscription List**, and a **SIP servlet**. The **Feed List** stores the feed information of all the unique feeds the system monitors. The **Subscription List** maintains the information related to active SIP subscriptions. The **SIP servlet** process inside this component accepts and generates SIP requests that trigger the service logic.

The **SIP servlet** process is responsible of processing incoming SUBSCRIBE requests. It can also communicate with the HSS to generate charging records, as per subscription for example. Once a SUBSCRIBE request arrives, the SIP servlet

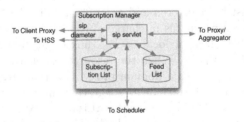

Fig. 10. Subscription Manager Process Organization

extracts user information and the feed URI carried by it. This information is stored in the appropriate data entities. If the feed is new, the SIP servlet requests the registration of the feed to the Proxy/Aggregator module; the registration is necessary to poll feeds and detect updates. It also requests the assistance of the Scheduler (see Section 5.2) to create an MBMS channel to transfer the feed and its referenced content in case it becomes popular. The SIP servlet then proceeds to send the first NOTIFY request in the dialog that includes an MBMS Service Description Bundle.

When the Proxy/Aggregator signals the detection of changes in a web feed, the Subscription manager issues a scheduling request to the Scheduler component to deliver the new content. The Scheduler then informs about the selected transport mechanism. When this mechanism is unicast, the SIP Servlet sends NOTIFY requests containing only the feed updates to the subscribed users. The Subscription Manager may delay the notification of updates if indicated to do so by the Scheduler. The Subscription manager takes no further action if the chosen delivery mechanism is multicast/broadcast.

Scheduler. The Scheduler is the component in the Application Server whose responsibility is to decide the best content delivery strategy of podcast content upon its detection. The Scheduler makes this decision based on subscription aggregates and on operator policies. When the content proves to be popular, an MBMS session is established to transmit it. In contrast, the update of content with low subscriptions is notified to the clients using unicast bearers. This notification may be delayed to times of low network congestion, as podcast content has soft time constraints.

Figure 11 shows the internal process arrangement of this component. The Scheduler is composed of **Operator Policies** and **Subscribtion List** data entities, plus a **Distribution Decision** process. The **Operator Policies** entity stores all the network provider preferences related to efficient content distribution. The Subscribtion List entity is shared with the Subscription Manager and its data indicates how many users are interested in a particular podcast media file. When content is not popular enough to be transfered over multicast/broadcast bearers, the service delegates content acquisition through unicast bearers to the client processes running at the user equipment.

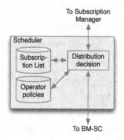

Fig. 11. Scheduler Process Organization

The Scheduler distribution decision process is fired when the Subscription Manager requests content scheduling. The **distribution decision** process will take as input the content, the number of subscribers, and parameters such as preferred distribution times, operator policies, and network load, in order to choose the best distribution method. When selecting unicast, the Subscription Manager becomes responsible for delivering the updates. The Scheduler may instruct the Subscription Manager to delay the delivery of updates to avoid network congestion. In case of multicast, the Scheduler instructs the Proxy/Aggregator component to acquire the content referenced in the feed update. Once the content has been downloaded, the Scheduler negotiates with the domain BM-SC service entity the transmission of the recently downloaded content. The negotiation process includes the scheduling of the transmission start and the transfer of contents from the Application Server to the BM-SC service entity. It will take responsibility of the actual multicast/broadcast transmission to the final recipients. Additional associated delivery procedures, such as file repair, might also be included in the negotiation. This component also assists the Subscription Manager in the establishment of a multicast group dedicated to transmit the feed and its referenced content.

Aggregator/Proxy. The Proxy/Aggregator is the component in the Application Server whose responsibility is to serve and store both feeds and content. It breaks outbound traffic to the content provider by storing HTTP accessible feed resources. The Proxy/Aggregator accepts the initial HTTP requests and responds with a copy stored in cache. It also checks the availability of new content retrieving feeds periodically. The central feed monitoring process reduces the amount of outbound traffic that would lack coordination and control in a scenario where multiple clients poll RSS resources. An algorithm to efficiently broker the RSS polling process by a central aggregator is presented in [23].

Figure 12 shows the internal process organization of the Proxy/Aggregator. It is composed of an **HTTP proxy** serving client requests, a **Feed/Podcast retriever** to monitor and download content, and a **Re-encoder** to convert content to terminal friendly formats. This processes make use of a **Cache** and a **Feed List**. The former stores feeds and content, whereas the latter keeps track of the subscribed feeds.

The **HTTP proxy** process is responsible of serving HTTP requests done by Client Proxies. When a request is received, the request URI is looked up in the

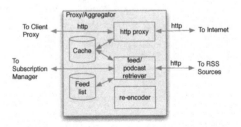

Fig. 12. Proxy/Aggregator Process Organization

local cache and it is locally served in case it is found. When the requested resource is not contained in the cache, the *HTTP proxy* forwards it to the actual server. The response is cached and then forwarded to the requester. The deployment of such a proxy diminishes the amount of outbound bandwidth necessary to distribute podcast content.

When the Subscription Manager indicates the registration of a feed, the **Feed/Podcast retriever** process sets a timer to fetch the feed. Once this timer expires, the Feed/Podcast retriever will request the feed to the content provider and examine it for content updates. If updates are found, the new feed is cached and updates are signaled to the Subscription Manager. This component can also explicitly download content when indicated to do so. The content is downloaded, possibly re-encoded, and cached.

6 Evaluation

This section presents the performance evaluation conducted on a basic deployment of the proposed architecture. A series of experiments to assess the bandwidth savings that the proposed approach introduces was carried out. The first set evaluates the notification mechanism of RSS updates, while the second set evaluates media distribution with unicast and multicast bearers.

To evaluate the proposed solution, a proof-of-concept prototype was implemented. The prototype includes a converged Application Server and a Client Proxy that implement the components described earlier with the exception of a media re-encoder module. These components were later deployed in a wireless network emulating a mobile network. A traffic shaper limiting the available local bandwidth to 2 Mbps was installed. IP Multicast distribution was fulfilled with a FLUTE protocol implementation and its rate was set to 256 kbps, the highest rate available in UTRAN MBMS bearers in Release 6. The traffic shaper treats unicast and IP multicast content differently to avoid losses that might affect IP multicast traffic.

6.1 Notification Mechanisms

To measure the impact of RSS update notifications, the Client machine issued subscriptions to 35 RSS feeds. These feeds were taken from Bloglines[2], an RSS web aggregator, and represent the most popular feeds monitored by the site. The Application Server monitored all these feeds during 5 days with a polling period of 30 minutes. As a well behaved RSS aggregator, the Application Server issues feed requests with the ETag request header to retrieve the whole feed only when it has been modified. To send SIP NOTIFY requests, the server compares the previous feed copy with the newest one, and creates the body of the request only if new items are found. Finally, the server measures and records the length of both the feed and the NOTIFY requests. The amount of data used by these mechanisms is recorded on a per user basis, that is, these numbers would increase linearly in a scenario where many users are subscribed to the same feeds.

---

[2] http://www.bloglines.com

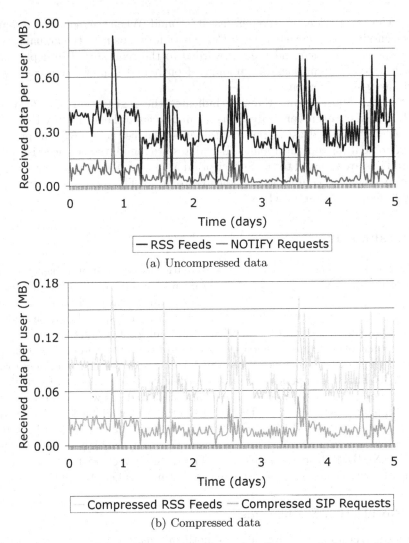

(a) Uncompressed data

(b) Compressed data

Fig. 13. Amount of data delivered to subscriber per scheduled poll

Figure 13 illustrates the results of the aggregate notification process throughout the five days of evaluation. It shows the total amount of data that the server
sends after polling all the RSS sources. The measurements take into account four
cases, for uncompressed (a) and compressed (b) data: 1) Traditional delivery of
RSS feeds, that is, a client would receive a replica of the document from the
original RSS source; 2) Notification of changes using the SIP NOTIFY method; 3)
Traditional delivery of compressed RSS feeds using the GZIP algorithm; 4) Notification of changes using the SIP NOTIFY method with compressed body using
the GZIP algorithm.

The plot shows that the transmission of complete RSS documents is the most expensive in terms of bandwidth. Then comes the transmission of compressed documents, which clearly diminishes the bandwidth usage, and even shows better results than the uncompressed notification of new items during peak times, that is, when updates occur the most. This is because XML documents, being plain text, keep good compression properties. Although the transmission of uncompressed SIP NOTIFY requests behaved well, it provided average bandwidth savings of approximately 85% when compared to uncompressed RSS, its compression offered even further improvements. In addition, its compression smoothened the peaks observed earlier. When comparing both the transmission of whole RSS documents and the notification of compressed updates, savings of nearly 95% are observed. Table 1 summarizes the behavior of each notification mechanism.

Table 1. Significant statistical values for RSS distribution

	Average	St. Dev.
RSS Feeds	0.32 MB	0.137
SIP NOTIFY Requests	0.06 MB	0.049
Compressed RSS Feeds	0.07 MB	0.028
Compressed SIP NOTIFY Requests	0.02 MB	0.01
SIP Notification savings	84.83%	8.445
Compressed SIP Notification savings	94.77%	1.81

6.2   Content Distribution

For this experiment podcast feeds and their referenced content were served by the local Application Server and several clients were instantiated at the Client machine. Additionally, a traffic shaper limiting the bandwidth to 2 Mbps at the Application Server network interface was set up to create a bandwidth bottleneck to emulate strain on bandwidth caused by podcast distribution. The throughput measurement was carried out at the client machine. Table 2 shows the podcasts, the information of the file they reference, and the number of subscribers assigned to them.

Table 2. Feeds, Files, and Number of Subscriptions

Feed	File	File Size	Subs.
BBC	newspod.mp3	16.9 MB	32
Dixo.com	tao.mp3	22 MB	16
Deutsche Welle	artsandideas.mp3	20 MB	8

Unicast Delivery Results. Figure 14 shows the throughput progression of the traffic aggregates that deliver the three files. The reactive mechanisms incorporated into the TCP protocols try to maximize the volume of data transfer while being fair to other applications competing for bandwidth resources [12].

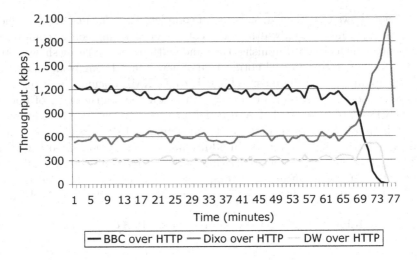

Fig. 14. Throughput progression for unicast delivery

Table 3. Unicast Delivery Statistics

	Transfer Time		Throughput	
Aggregate	Average	Stdev	Average	Stdev
BBC	68.5 min	2.271	34.0 kbps	1.162
Dixo	76 min	0.482	40.1 kbps	0.342
DW	73.5 min	1.239	37.5 kbps	0.776

However, this notion of fairness can be seen by a transport protocol only in terms of fairness between end-to-end flows [8]. That is, in terms of bandwidth, podcasts with high subscriptions rates will tend to grab a larger share of resources. As it can be appreciated in Figure 14, the delivery of BCC content to all its subscribers used most of the available bandwidth. This usage is in line with the Subscription distribution parameters introduced earlier, that is, more than half the available bandwidth was allocated to it. During the transmission of BBC, the rest of the traffic aggregates reach an amount of bandwidth proportional to the distribution of their subscribers. Towards the end of the capture, the Dixo traffic aggregate monopolizes the bandwidth, since the other two aggregates have concluded their transmissions. Due to the reduced transfer capacity and the large amount of users competing for resources, individual throughputs tend to be low, around 40 kbps for each client, and thus transfer time is considerable. Table 3 summarizes the behavior of the clients.

Multicast Delivery Results. The second experiment evaluates a scenario where only IP multicast distribution is allowed, thus a delivery queue for both popular and unpopular content is formed. Pure IP multicast transmission frees network resources, but generates delivery delays, since no parallel bearers are assumed. In the case of this testbed, subscribers see higher throughputs because

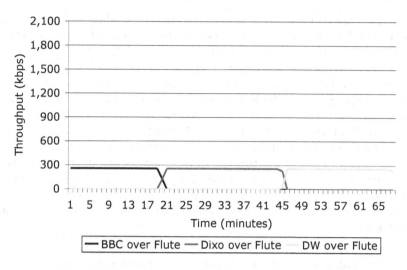

Fig. 15. Throughput progression for multicast delivery

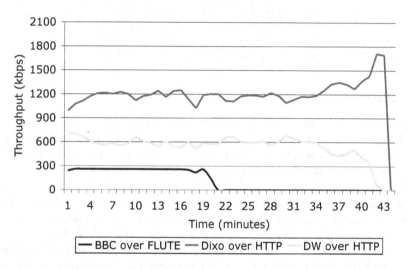

Fig. 16. Throughput progression for combined unicast-multicast delivery

no competence between adaptive traffic takes place, but it translates into longer waiting times as only one MBMS channel is available. The delivery times for the BBC, Dixo, and DW content are 19.5 minutes, 23 minutes, and 25.36 minutes, respectively. The total delivery time is 68 minutes.

Combined Unicast-IP Multicast Delivery Results. The third experiment evaluates a scenario in which a multicast session is initiated to deliver the most popular content. Figure 16 shows the throughput progression of the HTTP and FLUTE aggregates. Due to the FLUTE transmission, which transfers content to 32 users, more bandwidth for unicast transfer is available. As a consequence, transfer times for less popular content benefits from less bandwidth competition. Additionally, the plot shows that multicast transfer of data is more efficient, as transfer time is reduced and content is received by all subscribers.

A comparison between multicast and unicast distribution is drawn using the transfer time gain G_t [19]. It depends on the unicast transfer time T_{uc}, on the multicast transfer time T_{mc}, and is defined as $G_t = \frac{T_{uc}-T_{mc}}{T_{uc}}$. In the pure unicast scenario total transfer time takes about 77 minutes, whereas in the combined scenario, total time is about 43 minutes. The transfer time gain yields a value of $G_t = 0.44$. As the unicast transfer time is a variable directly proportional to the number of users receiving content, higher gains are possible in case of large multicast groups. Compared to the pure multicast scenario, the time gain equation yields a value of $G_t = 0.36$. Table 4 gives a summary of transfer times and throughputs.

Table 4. Combined Unicast-Multicast Delivery Statistics

	Transfer Time		Throughput	
Aggregate	Average	Stdev	Average	Stdev
BBC	19.5 min	-	256 kbps	-
Dixo	41.4 min	1.726	74 kbps	3.568
DW	38.6 min	2.632	72 kbps	5.083

6.3   Discussion

These experiments focused on measuring the savings introduced by the proposed architecture. The first experiment compared a traditional RSS polling scenario with the proposed asynchronous notification mechanism. It clearly shows that the proposed solution offers a considerable improvement on bandwidth usage by avoiding the transmission of duplicate information already stored at the client. Furthermore, the ability to control when to deliver updates given by the Application Server allows to delay RSS update notification to avoid straining network resources. A second set of experiments contrasted distribution of content using only unicast sessions with the proposed combined unicast-multicast, and with a pure multicast distribution scheme. These experiments show that the best mechanism to reduce transfer time is a combined unicast-multicast scenario, as it reduces intensive resource competition by adaptive unicast flow and avoids long queues in a pure multicast scenario.

7   Conclusions

This paper presents a service architecture that uses explicit signaling mechanisms to indicate podcast subscriptions and content retrieval by unicast or MBMS transfer sessions. Signaling was addressed by a new event package for the SIP notification infrastructure, while multicast delivery is modeled by an

IP Multicast scheduler. The proposed signaling allows resource savings at the radio level as the user equipment avoids issuing frequent feed requests. Content distribution is coordinated by a central entity measuring subscription rates that suggest the popularity of a given podcast. The evaluation results show that this design improves bandwidth usage. Furthermore, the proposed service can allow operators to control podcast delivery, as updates and content delivery can be scheduled according to their policies.

The future work comprises an analytical model considering user subscriptions, content production, and available delivery resources to validate the benefits of the proposed architecture. Such a model would also hint at further bandwidth optimizations. Additionally, one of the main concerns of an operator is how to gain revenue from the services introduced in its network, a model to charge for content is required.

References

1. 3GPP. 3GPP TS 22.146 v7.2.0; Multimedia Broadcast/Multicast Service; Stage 1 (Release 7) (October 2006)
2. 3GPP. 3GPP TR 23.847 v1.3.0; Study on Enhancements to IMS Service Functionalities Facilitating Multicast Bearer services (Release 8) (October 2007)
3. 3GPP. 3GPP TS 23.228 v7.9.0; IP Multimedia Subsystem (IMS); Stage 2 (Release 7) (September 2007)
4. 3GPP. 3GPP TS 23.246 v7.4.0; Multicast Broadcast/Multicast Service (MBMS); Architecture and functional description (Release 7) (September 2007)
5. C-Mobile Project. C-Mobile WP4.1. Detailed Research Objectives and Requirements for the Core Network Enhancements and New Entities (September 2006)
6. Camarillo, G., García-Martín, M.A.: The 3G IP Multimedia Subsystem (IMS), 2nd edn. Wiley, Chichester (2006)
7. Crovella, M.E., Taqqu, M.S., Bestavros, A.: Heavy-tailed probability distributions in the World Wide Web, pp. 3–25. Birkhauser Boston Inc., Cambridge (1998)
8. Ford, B.: Directions in Internet Transport Evolution. IETF Journal, 3(3) (December 2007)
9. Garcia-Martin, M., Schulzrinne, H.: Notification of General Events Using the Session Initiation Protocol (SIP) Event Notification Framework. Internet Draft draft-garcia-sipping-general-events-00 (work in progress) (May 2007)
10. Hartung, F., Horn, U., Huschke, J., Kampmann, M., Lohmar, T., Lundevall, M.: Delivery of Broadcast Services in 3G Networks. IEEE Transactions on Broadcasting 53(1, Part 2), 188–199 (2007)
11. Hicks, M.: RSS Comes with Bandwidth Price Tag (September 2004), http://www.eweek.com/article2/0,01759,1648625,00.asp
12. Jacobson, V.: Congestion Avoidance and Control. In: ACM SIGCOMM 1988, Stanford, CA, pp. 314–329 (August 1988)
13. Knappmeyer, M., Al-Hezmi, A., Ricks, B., Tönjes, R.: Advanced Multicast and Broadcast Content Distribution in Mobile Cellular Networks. In: 50th IEEE Global Communications Conference (2007)
14. Li, C.: Podcasting hits the charts (April 2006), http://www.forrester.com/Research/Document/Excerpt/0,7211,38761,00.html

15. Liu, H., Ramasubramanian, V., Sirer, E.G.: Client behavior and feed characteristics of RSS, a publish-subscribe system for web micronews. In: IMC 2005: Proceedings of the Internet Measurement Conference 2005 on Internet Measurement Conference, p. 3. USENIX Association (2005)
16. Oxford University Press. "Podcast" is the Word of the Year (December 2005), http://www.oup.com/us/brochure/NOAD_podcast/?view=usa
17. Paila, T., Luby, M., Lehtonen, R., Roca, V., Walsh, R.: FLUTE - File Delivery over Unidirectional Transport. RFC 3926 (October 2004)
18. Roach, A.B.: Session Initiation Protocol (SIP)-Specific Event Notification. RFC 3265 (June 2002)
19. Rodriguez, P., Biersack, E.: Continuous multicast push of web documents over the Internet. IEEE Network Magazine 12(2), 18–31 (1998)
20. Rosenberg, J., Schulzrinne, H., Camarillo, G., Johnston, A., Peterson, J., Sparks, R., Handley, M., Schooler, E.: SIP: Session Initiation Protocol. RFC 3261 (June 2002)
21. Sandler, D., Mislove, A., Post, A., Druschel, P.: Feedtree: Sharing web micronews with peer-to-peer event notification. In: International Workshop on Peer-to-Peer Systems (2005)
22. Schulzrinne, H., Casner, S., Frederick, R., Jacobson, V.: RTP: A Transport Protocol for Real-Time Applications. RFC 3550 (July 2003)
23. Sia, K., Cho, J.: Efficient Monitoring Algorithm for Fast News Alert. IEEE Trans. on Knowl. and Data Eng. 19(7), 950–961 (2007)
24. Webster, T.: The Infinite Dial: The Podcast Audience Revealed (March 2007), http://www.edisonresearch.com/home/archives/2007/03/the_podcast_aud.php
25. Wyman, B.: If you must poll, at least poll well. September 2004 [cited January 10, 2008], http://web.archive.org/web/20060206020914/bobwyman.pubsub.com/main/2004/09/if_you_must_pol.html

Generalized Third-Party Call Control in SIP Networks

Eric Cheung and Pamela Zave

AT&T Laboratories—Research, Florham Park, New Jersey, USA
cheung@research.att.com, pamela@research.att.com

Abstract. Third-party call control (3PCC) is essential to implementing advanced services in Voice-over-IP (VoIP) networks. It allows intermediary applications to control how the media streams of endpoint devices are connected together. However the Session Initiation Protocol (SIP), the widely adopted open standard for VoIP signaling, presents a number of challenges that make 3PCC in SIP complex and prone to errors. Previously proposed solutions only address operations under ideal conditions and thus are incomplete. Furthermore, the problem of compositional 3PCC by multiple applications has not been addressed. In this paper, we propose a general solution for robust and comprehensive media connectivity control. The solution has been verified, and allows multiple applications operating concurrently in a call path to interoperate successfully.

1   Introduction

The widespread adoption of Voice-over-IP (VoIP) creates an opportunity for innovations in new voice, multimedia, and converged (with web and data) services. The Session Initiation Protocol (SIP) is currently the most commonly used open standard for establishing voice and multimedia media sessions. In addition to being an end-to-end signaling protocol, SIP is also useful for invoking intermediary application servers that provide advanced features to the endpoints. For example, at the architectural level the IP Multimedia Subsystem (IMS) is a widely-adopted standard defined by the 3rd Generation Partnership Project (3GPP)[1] for wireless and wireline communications. In the IMS architecture, multiple application servers are invoked one by one based on the profiles of the subscribers, thereby forming a chain of applications between the endpoints. At the level of the application developers, the SIP Servlet Java API (application programming interface) [2] is an emerging standard for programming SIP and converged applications. Within a SIP Servlet container, an *application router* component selects multiple applications to service a call, forming a chain of applications within the container. In both examples, this application chain model may offer several advantages over implementing all applications in the endpoints:

– New applications can be developed as independent modules with standard SIP interfaces, and added incrementally.

H. Schulzrinne, R. State, and S. Niccolini (Eds.): IPTComm 2008, LNCS 5310, pp. 45–68, 2008.
© Springer-Verlag Berlin Heidelberg 2008

- Endpoints only need to support baseline SIP, and do not increase in complexity as more applications are deployed.
- No software installation or upgrade is required at the endpoints. Endpoints may not support such software installation, or it may be operationally undesirable.
- For some applications, executing from the endpoints may impose complex trust and security requirements.
- Endpoints may be turned off or become disconnected from the network. It is easier to maintain centralized servers in the network to be accessible continuously.

One of the key requirements of this model is the ability to control media sessions independently of the media endpoints that actually transmit and receive the media content. Third-party call control (3PCC) refers to this capability. The key characteristics of 3PCC include:

1. An entity that is distinct from the media endpoints can initiate, manage (which may include changing connectivity amongst multiple endpoints, changing media types selection, changing codec selection, and so on), and terminate the media sessions. In this paper, this entity is referred to as the third-party call controller or simply the controller.
2. The third-party call controller has a signaling relationship with each endpoint involved in the media sessions using a standard signaling protocol. The media endpoints do not need to establish and maintain direct signaling relationships amongst themselves, but only indirectly via the controller. Furthermore, from the perspective of each media endpoint the controller appears as a regular peer endpoint, just as in a point-to-point relationship.
3. The media streams flow directly between the media endpoints. The third-party call controller does not access or relay the media streams.

A canonical example of 3PCC is the click-to-dial application. Unlike a regular point-to-point call where the caller initiates the session from his/her endpoint device, click-to-dial allows the caller to initiate the call by clicking on a link on a web page. For example, a company's products page may contain such a link for a potential customer to talk to a sales representative. The HTTP request is translated into a request to a third-party call controller to establish a SIP call to the caller and the callee, and then to set up a media session between them.

Another key requirement of the application chain model is that the 3PCC mechanism must be composable. i.e. the system behavior must be correct even if multiple controllers are in the signaling path, and they operate concurrently. This is crucial to support the goal of modularity.

Third-party call control in SIP has received a significant amount of attention and is recognized as an important call control model. In particular the click-to-dial use case has been cited extensively (e.g. [10], [6], [9]). However, thus far the literature has only included limited example call flows under ideal conditions. Moreover, the click-to-dial use case is relatively simple as the endpoints involved are restricted by the SIP protocol to only a small number of possible actions during call setup time, and only two endpoints are involved. More complex scenarios, for example cases where a controller and the endpoints simultaneously take action causing race conditions, have not been studied in depth. No general and robust solution that can handle error or race conditions has been proposed. Furthermore, composing multiple third-party call controllers have not been studied.

This paper proposes a general solution for third-party call control involving multiple media endpoints at any call states, taking into account race and transient conditions. The solution also supports compositional media control by any number of controllers. Its contributions are twofold: (1) It specifies the correct SIP protocol behavior of a controller under all conditions in order to fulfill the above goals. (2) It divides the functions of a controller into three logical components: the media port, the Hold program and the Flow program, and provides a high-level API for developers to build 3PCC applications that behave correctly and compositionally.

This paper also presents verifications of the safety and correctness properties of the proposed solution. Recommendations on the SIP standard and implementations to facilitate 3PCC are also discussed.

2 The Challenges Presented by SIP

2.1 Summary of SIP Operation

For this paper, we only consider the baseline SIP standard as defined by [13] and any necessary supporting standards, most notably the offer-answer exchange [11]. All other extensions to SIP are excluded and left for future work.

As implied by its name, SIP is primarily designed as a signaling protocol for establishing media sessions. A point-to-point call begins when the caller sends an INVITE request to the callee. The callee can send multiple provisional responses until if it decides to accept the call, it sends a 200 OK response. The caller then sends an ACK message to acknowledge the receipt of the 200 OK response. This INVITE-200-ACK sequence thereby establishes (1) a *SIP dialog* at the signaling level, and (2) a *media session* at the media level, as an offer-answer exchange is conveyed by these messages. The offer-answer exchange reflects the media capabilities of the endpoints, as well as the list of media types the users wish to communicate with. The SIP dialog and the media session persist over the lifetime of the call. Should either party desire to modify the properties of the media session, for example to add video or to temporarily put the other party on hold, it may send a new INVITE request to initiate a new offer-answer exchange. Such mid-call INVITE requests are called re-INVITE requests to distinguish them from the first INVITE that establishes the dialog. Finally, either party may send a BYE request to terminate both the dialog and the media session.

The INVITE-200-ACK messages may convey the offer-answer exchange in one of two ways: (1) INVITE conveys offer, and 200 OK conveys answer (ACK does not contain any session information); and (2) INVITE does not contain offer or

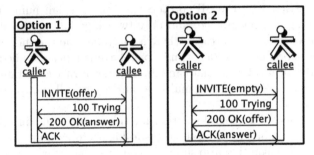

Fig. 1. Two options for media offer-answer exchange in point-to-point SIP calls

answer, 200 OK conveys offer, and ACK conveys answer. These two options are illustrated in Figure 1. In the first option, the initial caller is also the media offerer. In the second option, the initial caller, by not including a media offer in the INVITE, is establishing a SIP dialog but soliciting the callee to make a media offer.

A media offer lists the media streams the offerer wishes to include in this media session. The description of each media stream comprises the type of media (e.g. audio or video), the directionality of the stream, and media format information. The media format includes the codecs and other parameters associated with the codec such as video resolution or framerate that the offerer is capable of sending and/or receiving (depending on the directionality). The answerer must send an answer that contains its own media format in response to each media stream in the offer. It cannot include any additional media streams in the answer. The directionality of each media stream must also be compatible with the directionality in the offer. Subsequently, either side may send a new offer that contains additional media streams or change the directionality. The format of the offer and answer conforms to the Session Description Protocol (SDP)[7].

Note: For simplicity, media answers conveyed in provisional responses are not discussed in this paper. As the subsequent 200 OK response must contain the same answer, this omission does not impact generality. Also, for brevity the rest of the paper will omit provisional responses, including the 100 Trying response.

2.2   Issues That Affect 3PCC

A third-party call controller must use the same two options of conveying offer-answer exchange in the INVITE-200-ACK sequence to establish and control the media session between the two actual media endpoints. A click-to-dial call flow is shown in Figure 2, based on 'Flow I' in [10]. Note that there are two distinct SIP dialogs—a dialog between the controller and party1, and another dialog between the controller and party2. The controller uses option 2 to set up the dialog with party1, and uses option 1 to set up the dialog with party2. By relaying the offer-answer exchange end-to-end, the controller establishes one media session directly between the two parties.

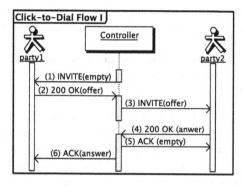

Fig. 2. Example click-to-dial call

There are several issues with third-party call control in SIP. They are discussed below.

Offer-answer Exchange Closely Linked to Signaling Protocol. In the signaling layer, the INVITE-200-ACK messages forms a three-way handshake designed for unreliable transports such as UDP. If the callee does not receive the ACK message after sending 200 OK response, it must assume that the response did not reach the caller and retransmit the 200 OK until it receives the ACK. If it does not receive the ACK after a certain timeout (default to 32 seconds), it must consider the dialog and session terminated.

On the other hand, in the media layer if the 200 OK contains an offer, the ACK must contain an answer. However, the answer may not always be immediately available. Consider the click-to-dial call flow in Figure 2. After the controller receives message (2) 200 OK(offer) from party1, it must relay the offer to party2, and wait for the answer before it can send (6) ACK together with the answer to party1. If party2 is not an automated system but a real person, it may take up to a few minutes for it to send (4) 200 OK(answer). Therefore, this delay may result in unnecessary retransmission of messages, or in the worst case lead to failure to establish the media session.

Offer can only be Answered Once. There are many use cases where a controller first connects the caller to one party, then after a period of time connects the caller to a second party. For example, in a calling-card application the controller may first connect the caller to a prompt-and-collect media server to authenticate the caller and to obtain the destination. When that is completed the controller calls the destination. It is natural that the media offer from the caller is applicable equally to the offer-answer exchange with the media server, and the offer-answer exchange with the final destination. A naive controller may store the offer from the caller, and send it to the final destination after the prompt-and-collect phase is completed. However, in SIP offer-answer, it is not possible to send more than one answer to an offer. Another naive solution is to send the second answer to the caller as an offer. However, if the answer from the caller is different from the initial offer, the controller must then again send this answer as an offer to the final destination. This may result in an infinite offer-answer spiral.

As a result, once the controller has sent an answer to an offer, it cannot reuse the offer and send it to another endpoint because there is no way to send an answer to the initial offerer.

Reduced Media and Codec Choices. When an endpoint responds to a media offer, the answer must correspond to the offer and cannot add new media streams. While it may add codec choices to streams already present in the offer, or subsequently send a more full-featured offer to add media streams or include additional codecs for existing streams, the answerer usually would not do so. After all, the offerer has already indicated the media types and codecs it desires to communicate with. As a result, the answerer usually does not have an opportunity to make a unilateral declaration of its full capabilities and desires.

Another common situation is that after the initial offer-answer exchange is completed, the two endpoints may perform another offer-answer exchange to narrow down the media or codec choices. For example, many endpoints support a multitude of codecs, but can only handle one codec at a time. Such an endpoint would send an offer listing the supported codecs. Once the peer endpoint has indicated the codecs it can support in the answer, the first endpoint would then send another offer with just one codec to lock it down.

These two properties of the offer-answer exchange affect 3PCC. When a controller connects two endpoints together, even if it has an outstanding unanswered offer from one endpoint, it must not send it to the other endpoint as a fresh offer. Doing so may restrict the codec and media choices that the two endpoints may communicate with.

One Outstanding INVITE Transaction at a Time. The SIP protocol dictates that after a UA has sent a re-INVITE request, it must wait for the transaction to complete before it can send another re-INVITE request. Similarly, the offer-answer protocol dictates that an offerer after sending an offer must wait for the answer before sending another offer. This means that if a controller performs media connectivity switching in a state where a re-INVITE or an offer has been sent, it must wait for the answer to return before proceeding. This asynchrony adds complexity and additional states to the application logic of the controller.

Re-INVITE Request Glare. When two SIP user agents (UAs) are in an established dialog, both of them may send mid-dialog re-INVITE requests. If they send re-INVITE requests at the same time, a glare condition arises. The SIP protocol dictates that each UA must then reject the re-INVITE request with a 491 Request Pending response. Each UA may try to send the re-INVITE request again, but if the UA is the original initiator of the dialog (i.e. the initial caller), then it must do so after waiting 2.1-4 seconds. If the UA is initially the callee, then it must do so after waiting 0-2 seconds([13] Section 14.1). Thus if both UAs decide to retry, the initial callee would be able to do so first, and the second attempt should not result in glare.

The possibility of re-INVITE glare creates additional complexity for a third-party call controller. When in the middle of a media switching operation the controller sends a re-INVITE request, it may be rejected. Even when the controller is not in the middle of media switching but is simply acting as a relay, the two endpoints may send re-INVITE at the same time, causing glare at the controller.

In our experience, the re-INVITE glare causes significant difficulties and complexity to a robust 3PCC design.

SDP Manipulation. The third-party call controller connects two previously unconnected endpoints together by causing a media offer-answer exchange to occur between the two endpoints. However, the SIP protocol mandates that the session descriptions in an offer-answer exchange within a SIP dialog must conform to certain restrictions. Firstly, the answer must contain the same media streams as the offer. Secondly, any new offer must retain the number and order of media streams from the previous exchanges, although new streams may be added. Thirdly, the origin line in the SDP sent to an endpoint must remain unchanged, except for the version number which must be incremented by one in each successive SDP sent.

While this manipulation is not technically hard, it requires the controller to constantly parse, modify and format SDP in SIP messages as they are relayed between endpoints.

2.3   Existing Solutions in SIP Community

The SIP community has worked on 3PCC since the early days of the protocol. The often cited Best Current Practice document [10] is the culmination of at least four years of work by the IETF SIP and SIPPING working groups. Its main focus is on how a third-party call controller can initiate a call to two parties as in the click-to-dial use case. It studies four candidate call flows, and recommends two of the flows for different circumstances. It also suggests a call flow that switches one party in a two-party call to a mid-call announcement while putting the second party on hold, and then reconnects the two parties after the announcement is completed.

However, this document falls short of offering a complete solution. In all the call flow examples, the endpoints are quiescent and the controller is the only SIP entity that initiates signaling transactions, and thus all the call flows may proceed in an orderly fashion. This is helped by the fact that for the click-to-dial use case endpoints are not allowed to send any requests until a SIP dialog is established. However, in general and especially for mid-call 3PCC, the controller may receive SIP messages at inconvenient times and must be able to handle them. For example, the endpoints can send re-INVITE messages on their own. Thus when the controller is triggered to perform mid-call 3PCC operations, it may be in the middle of re-INVITE transactions with one or more of the endpoints. The document addresses one such case but the proposed handling of the scenario is potentially problematic (see "Generate dummy offer or answer" section in 3.1). Furthermore, the document only discusses cases where there is only one controller in the call path. It does not address how the media controlling actions from multiple controllers can be composed in a correct manner such that the desired end result may be achieved. In general, the controllers operate independently of each other, and thus they are likely to perform media action at the same time, causing various race and glare conditions.

Nonetheless, [10] provides many useful ideas and strategies. The authors have made use of and expanded many of these ideas in formulating our generalized solution.

3   Proposed Solution

3.1   General Strategy

This section can be viewed as a collection of basic tools that a third-party call controller may make use of. Then in the following section, a more structured design of the controller is proposed, making use of many of the same tools.

Solicit an Offer with Empty INVITE Request. This technique is based on 'Flow I' in [10], and solves the second and third problems discussed in Sections 2.2. The controller can solicit a media offer from an endpoint by sending an INVITE request that contains no SDP. This is a basic pattern in most 3PCC call flows. In Figure 2, messages 1, 2 and 6 represent this pattern. Note that there is a dependency on the endpoint to send its full set of media capabilities and the user's desired set of media streams in the offer conveyed in the 200 response, even if it is already in the middle of a SIP dialog and there is a media session established. Its offer cannot be restricted by the offer-answer exchange that has already taken place. This dependency is discussed in Section 7.1.

Create a No-media SIP Dialog First. In the first issue discussed in Section 2.2, the dual-purpose of the ACK message to acknowledge receipt of 200 OK and to convey an media answer causes a dilemma of having to send the ACK quickly, and having to wait for the media answer. This problem is solved by a new call flow called Flow IV in [10], and which is illustrated in Figure 3. The controller first establishes a SIP dialog and a session with zero media streams with the first party (messages (1) to (3)). Once the dialog is established, the controller can use the same call flow in Figure 2 (but exchange party1 and party2). Because party1 has already answered the initial INVITE request, it is assumed that it will respond to (6) re-INVITE and provide an answer in (7) 200 response immediately. Therefore the controller can send (9) ACK to party2 quickly to avoid excessive retransmission or timeout. Note there is dependency on the endpoint to respond quickly to mid-dialog re-INVITE requests. Section 7.2 discusses this dependency in full.

Flow I shown in Figure 2 is still useful in cases where the second party is known to respond quickly, for example if it is an automaton like a media server. In such cases, it is not necessary to create the no-media SIP dialog first.

Generate Dummy Offer or Answer. As discussed in Section 2.3, if the endpoints are not quiescent, the controller must handle situations where the endpoint sends a re-INVITE request in the middle of the controller's operation. One instance of this occurrence is discussed in [10]. Consider the call flow in Figure 4: after controller sends (4) INVITE, party2 may take some time to respond. In the meantime, party1 sends a re-INVITE with a new offer. How should the controller respond so it can proceed with its operation when party2 responds with the answer? The recommendation in [10] is to send a 491 Request Pending response to reject the re-INVITE. However, this approach may cause a situation where both sides repeatedly resend re-INVITE requests, all of which could then be rejected by the other side, causing an infinite retry loop. Thus the controller will fail to complete the call flow and to connect the two parties together. This is particular problematic if party1 is in fact another controller.

We propose that a better alternative is to send an answer which disables each offered media stream by setting the port in the answer to zero. This is appropriate as the controller is not ready to connect party1 to any media endpoint yet.

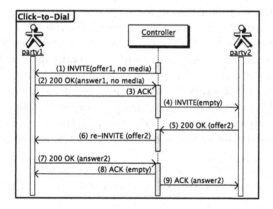

Fig. 3. Click-to-Dial SIP call, revised (Flow IV)

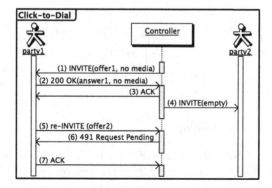

Fig. 4. Click-to-Dial Flow IV rejecting unexpected re-INVITE

Similarly, if party1 sends a re-INVITE with no SDP to solicit an offer, the controller can send a dummy offer that is a SDP with no media stream.

Handle re-INVITE Glare. A similar situation arises when the controller and an endpoint send re-INVITE at the same time, creating the glare condition discussed in Section 2.2. The controller must follow the retry strategy according to the SIP specification. If the controller is the initiator of the SIP dialog, it may receive a retry of the re-INVITE before it is allowed to retry its own. In this case, the controller may have to respond with 200 OK with a dummy offer or answer as discussed in the previous section.

It is important that the controller does not create a re-INVITE glare knowingly. For example, if it has received a re-INVITE from an endpoint and has not responded to it yet, the controller must not send a re-INVITE to that endpoint. Instead, it must respond to the re-INVITE first before starting a new transaction.

Maintain State of Offer-answer Exchange. As discussed in Section 2.2, if the controller is in the middle of a re-INVITE transaction and the associated offer-answer exchange, it must wait for it to complete before it can initiate another one. For example, if it has sent an offer in a 200 OK response, it must wait for the answer in the ACK. This necessitates tracking the state of the offer-answer exchange in the SIP dialog with each endpoint. For the purpose of storing the media state of a SIP dialog, we do not use the actual SIP message names. Rather, we use abstractions of the messages that indicate their media-related content. This affords the advantage that the abstraction can still apply when in the future we consider other SIP extensions that may also convey media offer-answer exchanges, for example the reliable provisional response extension [12].

Within the baseline SIP protocol, the two ways in which the INVITE-200-ACK messages can convey media offer-answer exchange can be abstracted as follows:

Table 1. Abstract media protocol messages

Option 1		Option 2	
INVITE(sdp)	offer	INVITE	solicit
200 OK(sdp)	answer	200 OK(sdp)	sol_offer
ACK	–	ACK(sdp)	answer
491 Request Pending			error

3.2   Design of the Controller

At the high level, a third-party call controller manages the media connectivity amongst a set of endpoints. There is a SIP dialog between each endpoint and the controller. We shall refer to the controller end of such a dialog as a *media port* or simply a *port*. Depending on application logic, the controller may isolate an

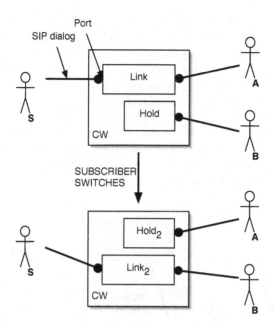

Fig. 5. 3PCC in a call-waiting application

endpoint (put on hold), or link two endpoints together in a media session. This suggests that its operation may be divided into two functional programs: the *Hold* and the *Link* programs. As the controller changes the way endpoints are connected, it puts their corresponding media ports into the appropriate Hold and Link programs. The Hold and Link programs examine the states of the media ports, and send SIP requests and responses accordingly to achieve the goal of the programs.

As an example, Figure 5 shows a call-waiting application (CW) where subscriber S is in two separate calls with A and B. At the top of the figure, the subscriber is connected to A, and B is put on hold. CW puts the ports for S and A in a Link program, and the port for B in a Hold program. When the subscriber signals to CW to switch the lines (e.g. by a flash signal), CW puts the port for A in a new Hold program, and puts the ports for S and B in a new Link program.

A media port is responsible for tracking the state of the offer-answer exchange in its corresponding SIP dialog. A state transition occurs whenever a SIP message that contains media semantics is received or sent on the port.

Each media port is always in a Hold or Link program. When a port receives a SIP message that contains media semantics, it passes the message to the program it is in. When the program wishes to send a SIP message to the endpoint, it passes the message to the port to send out. The Hold and Link programs may decide to send more than one message at a time. In the case of the Link program, it may also decide to send one or more SIP messages on the other port.

The following sections discuss the details of the media port and the Hold and Link programs.

Media Port Finite State Machine. As the controller exchanges SIP messages with an endpoint, the state of the corresponding media port changes. This is represented by the finite state machine (FSM) shown in Figure 6. The abstract media protocol messages in Table 1 are used. The state names that start with C_ refer to states in which the port is acting as UA client in the current transaction, i.e. it has sent the INVITE or re-INVITE. Conversely, the state names that start with S_ refer to states in which the port is acting as UA server in the current transaction. A state transition that is labeled !message means the port is sending the message, and a state transition that is labeled ?message means the port has received the message. When either the endpoint or the controller terminates the SIP dialog by sending a BYE request, the FSM is destroyed.

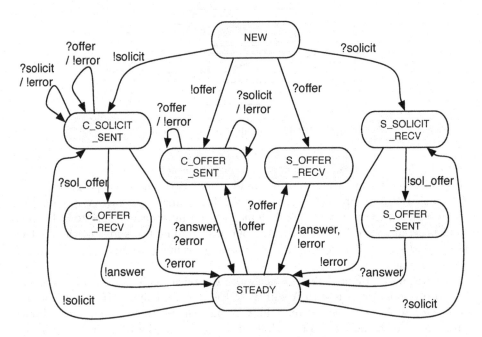

Fig. 6. Finite state machine of a media port

While most of the FSM should be self-explanatory, a few details are worth discussing. When the media port is in the C_SOLICIT_SENT or C_OFFER_SENT state, it may receive a solicit or offer from the endpoint due to re-INVITE glare. The media port always sends an error response (denoted for example by ?solicit/!error in the state transition). Typically the media port will then receive an error response from the endpoint, and transition to the STEADY state.

From the S_OFFER_RECV or S_SOLICIT_RECV state, the Link program may decide to send an error on this port because it has received an error from the other port. The port transitions to the STEADY state. This case will be discussed in the Link program section below, and illustrated in Figure 7(b).

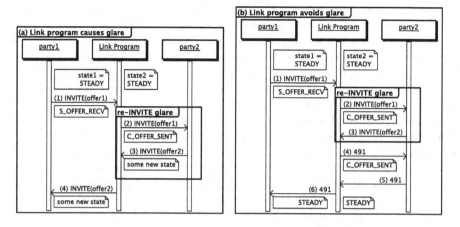

Fig. 7. Re-INVITE glare in Link program

The Hold Program. The Hold program operates on a single media port. Its function is relatively simple—to stop the endpoint from transmitting media. If there is an established SIP dialog, the Hold program must send a re-INVITE to disable all existing media streams by setting the port number of each media stream to 0. If the endpoint sends a new offer, the Hold program must generate an answer that disables all media streams. Finally, if the endpoint sends a solicit, the Hold program must send an offer that disables all media streams.

If upon entry the port state is such that the Hold program cannot send a re-INVITE request (e.g. C_OFFER_SENT), it must wait until a response is received at the port and the state transitions to STEADY before sending the re-INVITE request. On the other hand, if upon entry the media port is in certain states, the Hold program can take short-cut. For example, from S_OFFER_RECV the Hold program can send an answer that disable all media streams immediately.

After sending a re-INVITE request, the request may be rejected if the endpoint is also sending a re-INVITE causing a glare condition. If the incoming re-INVITE contains an offer, the Hold program can simply sends an answer that disables all media streams, instead of sending its own media offer.

The Link Program. The Link program operates on a pair of media ports, thus its function is much more complex. The Link program operates in two phases: (1) the matching phase, and (2) the transparent phase.

Upon entry, the Link program begins operation in the matching phase, the goal of which is to match the media states of the two ports. First, it examines the states of the ports. If both ports are in the NEW state, the Link program immediately enters the transparent phase. Otherwise, depending on the port state the controller may have to send the appropriate dummy offer or answer to complete any outstanding transactions. For example, if a port is in the C_OFFER_RECV state, the Link program can send a dummy answer and transition to the STEADY state. It may also need to wait for a message to arrive at a port. For example from the C_OFFER_SENT state the Link program must wait for an answer to arrive and transition to the STEADY state.

Once the states of the two ports are suitable, the Link program can send a solicit message on one port to start the basic end-to-end offer-answer exchange call flow. As above, this solicit message may be rejected due to glare. If the Link program loses the re-INVITE retry then it must handle the incoming re-INVITE and wait till the media states are suitable again.

Similar to the Hold link, if upon entry one of the ports is in certain media states the Link program can take shortcuts. For example, if the state of port1 is C_SOLICIT_SENT upon entry, then the Link program does not need to send a solicit because one is already sent. The Link program will need to make sure that port2 is in STEADY or S_SOLICIT_RECV state, then upon receipt of an sol_offer on port1 it can send an offer or sol_offer respectively on port2.

Once the Link program has solicited and relayed end-to-end a fresh offer-answer exchange (because the offer is solicited, it contains full media capabilities) between the endpoints, it enters the transparent phase. In the transparent phase, the Link program passes media offers and answers transparently between the endpoints in most cases. However, it is important that the Link program does not create glare by sending a re-INVITE to an endpoint after it has received a re-INVITE from that endpoint. This is illustrated in Figure 7. In (a), the Link program passes re-INVITE from party1 to party2 (message 1 and 2). At the same time, party2 sends re-INVITE (3). If Link program simply passes it to party1 (4), it would create a glare in the dialog with party1. Furthermore, this creates new media states in both dialogs, which adds significant complexity to both the Hold and the Link programs as they will now need to handle these new states on entry. In contrast, the handling shown in (b) is simpler. The Link program rejects the re-INVITE (3) with a 491 Request Pending response (4), and keep the media state in C_OFFER_SENT. If subsequently party2 sends a 491 response (5), the Link program can pass it to party1 (6), returning both dialogs to the STEADY state.

If a re-INVITE is rejected for reasons other than glare, the Link program must notify the application logic. For example, an endpoint may reject an offer because it cannot accept any of the media streams. How such error conditions should be handled depends on the specification of the application. For example, the application may decide to abandon the switching operation and return to the media connectivity prior to the operation. In other cases, the application may decide to tear down the call altogether.

Because with 3PCC the two endpoints may both be initial callers or initial callees, they may retry the re-INVITE within the same time interval (i.e. 2.1–4 or 0–2 seconds respectively). The SIP specification suggests that the UA wait a random time inside the specified interval, but we have encountered UA implementations that always retry after a fixed interval. This issue is discussed in Section 7.3.

3.3   Detailed Operation

The call-waiting scenario shown in Figure 5 will be used to demonstrate some of the operations of the Link and Hold programs. A message sequence diagram

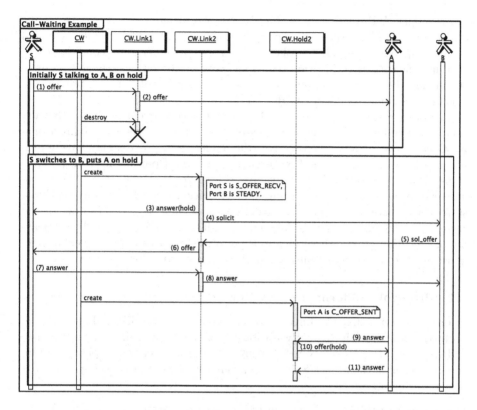

Fig. 8. Message sequence diagram of a call-waiting scenario

is shown in Figure 8. Initially ports S and A are in Link1. S's endpoint sends a
re-INVITE with an offer (1). As Link1 is in transparent phase, it relays the offer
from S to A (2). At this point the subscriber signals CW to switch to B. CW
destroys Link1, and creates Link2 and Hold2. Ports S and B are put in Link2
in S_OFFER_RECV and STEADY states respectively. The Link program sends
(3) answer to S to respond to the pending offer and put S on hold, and sends (4)
solicit on port B to get a fresh offer. An end-to-end offer-answer exchange then
takes place from (5) to (8), and Link2 reaches transparent phase. At the same
time, port A is put in Hold2 at C_OFFER_SENT state. The Hold program must
wait for (9) answer before sending (10) offer to put A on hold.

4 Formal Verification

In order to verify the correct behavior of the proposed solution, we have developed a model of the controller in the specification language Promela. This
model includes the Hold program, the Link program and the media port. The
abstracted media messages, i.e. solicit, offer, sol_offer, answer, and error, are used

in the model. A Promela model of a SIP UA was also developed to serve as the environment in which the controller operates. The UA model is cooperative, and always responds positively to solicit or offer except under glare conditions. We then use the formal verification tool Spin [8] to verify various configurations of the models. For brevity, we only discuss the verification of the Link program as it is more complicated than the Hold program.

The Link program and the UA are modeled as concurrent processes that execute independently. Messages are passed between processes via unidirectional FIFO *channels*. At any given state of the model, each process may have multiple possible execution steps. Spin executes one step from amongst all possible steps in all the processes, and advances the model to a new state. This stepwise execution is repeated, resulting in an execution *trace*. If the trace reaches a state where there are no possible execution steps, the execution stops at an end state. In an exhaustive search, Spin explores all traces, i.e. all possible interleaving of execution steps. All verifications performed for this paper are exhaustive searches. They are divided into two parts as discussed below.

4.1 Protocol Conformance and Correctness

In order to verify that the Link program conforms to the SIP and offer-answer protocols, and that it correctly establishes a media session between the two endpoints, we use the safety test features of Spin coupled with appropriate instrumentation in the model. Spin raises an error if one of the following conditions occurs during a search:

Invalid end states. An execution trace must not terminate when a UA is in the middle of an offer-answer exchange. The UA model defines a valid end state as one where there is no pending offer or answer.

Assertions. Numerous assertion statements are included in the models. When a media port sends or receives a message it asserts that it is allowed in the current state. When a UA sends a media offer, it includes a new version number. When it subsequently receives an answer, it asserts that the version number matches that in the offer. When the Link program enters the transparent phase, it asserts that it has relayed an end-to-end offer-answer exchange between the two UAs.

Non-empty channels. An execution trace must not stop when there are still unhandled messages in the FIFO channels. This is an indication that a message arrives when the model does not expect it.

In addition, Spin also performs coverage analysis and lists statements unreached in any of the traces.

The first configuration connects two UA models directly. This is shown in Figure 9(a). Each UA model can send any one of all allowable messages at a given state. For example, initially a UA has the option to send either solicit or offer, or do nothing. This purpose of this analysis is to validate the UA model. The coverage analysis also verifies that all statements in the model are reached, indicating that all possible UA actions are modeled.

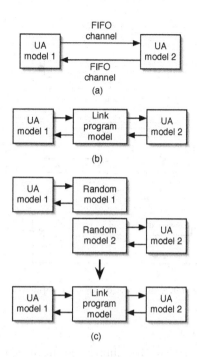

Fig. 9. Configurations of Promela models for Spin verification

In the next configuration in Figure 9(b), two UA models are connected to the Link model. At the beginning of execution, both media ports are in NEW state, thus the Link program enters the transparent phase immediately. This configuration validates that the Link program in the transparent phase conforms to protocols, and that it correctly relays the offer-answer exchange between the two UAs, allowing them to establish a media session.

To validate the entire Link program, we first develop a Random program. The Random program operates on one port, and is connected to a UA model. From each port state, the Random program either sends out one of the allowable messages or does nothing. The configuration in Figure 9(c) first connects each UA to a Random program and allows some execution to occur. This causes the media port to reach any one of its states. Then the UAs are connected to the Link program. Thus the Link program starts operation when the two media ports and the messaging channels are in arbitrary but legal states. The coverage analysis verifies that across the traces the Link program is entered with all combinations of port states.

In general, the Link program begins in the matching phase. Through the use of assertion statements, it is verified that when the Link program progresses to the transparent phase it has solicited an offer from one of the UA models, and has completed an end-to-end exchange of that offer and corresponding answer between the two UA models.

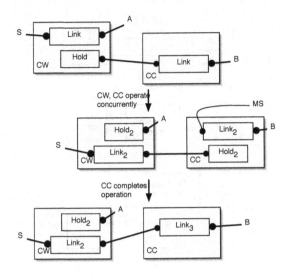

Fig. 10. Composition of two applications

4.2 Liveness Property

We have not yet verified that the Link program always succeeds in reaching the transparent phase. In order to verify this property, a linear-time temporal logic (LTL) verification is used. The LTL formula that expresses this property formally is:

$$\Box\,(isLinked \rightarrow \Diamond\ isTransparent)$$

where *isLinked* is set to true when the UA models are connected to the Link model, and *isTransparent* is true when the Link program enters the transparent phase. This formula says that in any verification trace, it is invariantly true ($\Box$) that connecting the two UAs to the Link program implies ($\rightarrow$) that eventually ($\Diamond$) the Link program will reach transparent phase.

The UA model must be modified for the liveness verification. If a UA, upon receiving solicit or offer from the Link program, always sends its own solicit or offer to cause a glare, the Link program will be flooded and can never reach transparent phase in such a hostile environment. Therefore, the UA model is modified to send only a finite number of offer or solicit messages. However, after the UA has received an offer or solicit message from the Link program and has sent a positive response, the count is reset so it can send those messages again.

A successful Spin exhaustive search verifies that in a non-flooding environment the Link program always reaches the transparent phase.

5   Compositional Media Control by Multiple Controllers

An important goal of this work is to support multiple controllers in the call path between the media endpoints. This is a very common scenario, and often the

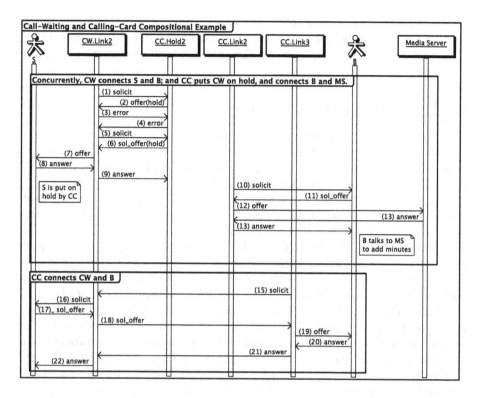

Fig. 11. Message sequence diagram of a call-waiting and calling-card scenario

controllers belong to different administrative domains and as such there cannot be any overarching framework that coordinates their operations. For example, consider again the call-waiting example but this time B subscribes to a calling-card (CC) application. As shown in Figure 10, while CW is triggered to connect S and B, CC may also operate at the same time to connect B to a media server to request payment.

Such simultaneous operations must not lead to deadlocks, infinite loops, or incorrect end states. Rather, the controllers must cooperate to arrive at the correct media connectivity of the endpoints. The Hold and Link programs are designed to support compositional 3PCC by multiple controllers. Figure 11 shows a message sequence that the programs might generate while implementing this scenario. The glare caused by the concurrent CW and CC operation and its resolution are shown by messages 1 to 9. In this case because CW was the initial callee in the CW–CC dialog, CW can retry sending the solicit message first. At the same time, CC connects B with a media server. When the payment collection is completed, CC reconnects B to the call towards S. Because CW has entered transparent phase past message 9, it simply relays the offer-answer exchange between CC and S.

It is impossible to use Spin to verify configurations of all possible number of controllers in a chain because the problem is unbounded. Instead, we are working on a proof by induction to shown that the proposed solution converges with any number of controllers.

6   Application of the Solution

The generalized solution presented in the paper offers a concrete blueprint for SIP developers when programming 3PCC applications. With the correct placement of media ports in Hold and Link programs, applications can correctly perform media control operations under any transient or race situations.

The structure of this approach lends itself to familiar software development goals of modularity, abstraction and reuse. Clearly the media port FSM and the Hold and Link programs can be implemented as reusable software libraries or objects. Application developers would then have a high-level, *goal-oriented* API for safe and robust media connectivity control. The media-affecting SIP messages and the state of each port can be abstracted and hidden from the programmer (although the programmer can still have visibility to them if necessary because sometimes application logic depends on them). In most use cases, the application logic is triggered to alter the media connectivity by an asynchronous event, for example a user action or a timer expiry. When this occurs, the programmer can express the new media connectivity goal by putting the appropriate ports into newly created Hold and Link program objects. The programmer may do so without being concerned with the current port states. The program objects will then perform their tasks to fulfill the goals expressed by the programmer. This may take some time but their operation can be hidden from the programmer.

The authors and their colleagues are currently working on implementing this solution using the open source ECharts for SIP Servlets development kit [14]. ECharts for SIP Servlets is a state-machine-driven programming environment for the SIP Servlet API. In this environment, the media state FSM and the Hold and Link programs can be implemented as *machine fragments* that can be re-used by other higher-level ECharts for SIP Servlets machines.

7   Recommendations for the SIP Community

This generalized 3PCC solution has a few dependencies on SIP UA behavior that are not currently mandated by the SIP specifications. These dependencies have been pointed out in Section 3, and will be discussed fully in this section. The authors propose that the SIP community consider these issues and their impact on correct 3PCC operations, and if deemed appropriate establish best current practices for UA implementations or modify the SIP specifications.

7.1   Solicited Offer Contains Full Media Capabilities

In order to achieve full media capability exchange, 3PCC has a dependency on UA behavior. When a UA receives a mid-dialog media solicit (i.e. re-INVITE request with no SDP), it should send an offer (i.e. 200 OK response to the re-INVITE) that reflects its full set of media capabilities and the user's desire. This is a SHOULD strength specification in [13] Section 14.2: "A UAS providing an offer in a 2xx (because the INVITE did not contain an offer) SHOULD construct the offer as if the UAS were making a brand new call, ... Specifically, this means that it SHOULD include as many media formats and media types that the UA is willing to support."

Implementers of SIP UAs should be aware of the impact if an implementation deviates from this behavior. It may lead to inability to establish media connection with the new UA to which the controller connects it due to lack of common codecs. It may also lead to reduced media type even though both UAs support it, for example if a UA does not offer video because the UA it was previously connected to only supports audio.

7.2   Delayed Response to Re-INVITE

This solution has a dependency on a UA to respond to mid-dialog re-INVITE requests quickly. In Figure 3, party1 must respond to (6) re-INVITE(offer2) quickly. Otherwise, the controller cannot send (9) ACK to stop party2 from retransmitting (5) 200 OK(offer2). If party2 does not receive an ACK after it completes all its retransmissions (by default after 32 seconds), [13] section 14.2 suggests that it should terminate the dialog: "If a UAS generates a 2xx response and never receives an ACK, it SHOULD generate a BYE to terminate the dialog." Therefore, the results may range from increased network traffic due to retransmissions, to users being disconnected.

We have tested several UA implementations and they do not alert the user of the new offer in the re-INVITE, and do respond quickly. However, it seems reasonable that some implementations may elect to consult the user, especially if the offer adds a new media type. Indeed, [13] suggests in section 14.2: "If the session description has changed, the UAS MUST adjust the session parameters accordingly, possibly after asking the user for confirmation."

If the user does not respond quickly, then this problem will be exposed. We propose that this should be a subject for discussion within the SIP community on how this may be resolved.

7.3   Re-INVITE Glare Retry Timer

This dependency affects how two UAs connected through a controller handle the re-INVITE glare condition. The glare resolution mechanism in [13] is based on a backoff-retry strategy. However, the randomness of the retry timer is not mandated. Section 14.1 says: "If a UAC receives a 491 response to a re-INVITE, it SHOULD start a timer with a value T chosen as follows: ... If the UAC is not the owner of the Call-ID of the dialog ID, T has a randomly chosen value of between 0 and 2 seconds in units of 10 ms."

We have encountered UA implementations that use a fixed timer value. Such implementations are still compliant because this is a SHOULD strength clause, and also the clause does not specify that a new random value must be generated every time. If a click-to-dial application connects two such implementations, and subsequently they simultaneously send re-INVITE, then the glare will not be resolved as they will retry at the exact same time.

We propose that the SIP specification strengthen this clause, or establish best current practices for UAs to calculate a new random timer value every time.

8   Related Work

The work in the SIP community on 3PCC is mainly documented in [10]. Its contributions and limitations have already been discussed throughout this paper. The authors are not aware of any previous published work on compositional 3PCC by multiple SIP-based controllers, perhaps because the problem is not yet widely recognized. Therefore we have to look beyond SIP for relevant related work.

In the public switched telephone network (PSTN), a telephone call typically traverses multiple telephone switches. Each of them may perform media switching. However, in the PSTN the signaling and media travel along the same path and media switching is performed locally within each switch. Therefore compositional control is straightforward.

Distributed Feature Composition (DFC) is an architecture for composing feature logic modules (*feature boxes*) in a pipe-and-filter manner. An IP-based implementation of DFC [4] addresses compositional media control by using a central media-control module [5]. The central media-control module maintains a graph that represents media connectivity amongst the external endpoints and the feature boxes. When a feature box performs media switching, it sends commands to the central media-control module, which in turn updates the graph. Based on the graph, the media-control module can then determine how endpoints are connected to each other. This implementation has been deployed as the advanced feature server for a nationwide consumer VoIP service [3]. However, this approach has two obvious deficiencies: (1) the centralized algorithm is a performance bottleneck, and (2) if the feature modules reside in multiple administrative domains, they must have a signaling and trust relationship with the central media-control module.

In order to improve on the central graph-based algorithm approach, the authors have successfully developed a comprehensive solution for distributed control [16]. This solution includes an architecture-independent descriptive model, a new media-control protocol, a set of high-level programming primitives, a formal specification of their compositional semantics, and an implementation. This solution has been partially verified for correctness, and analysis shows that it offers better performance than a comparable SIP-based solution. However, because the solution relies on a new, non-SIP protocol designed specifically for compositionality, it is not directly usable in existing SIP networks.

The work presented in this paper draws heavily on the experience and insights gained while working on the previous solutions. Comparing the solution reported in [16] to the solution for SIP here, the SIP solution is more complex. It is also less efficient in the sense that it requires more message exchanges to accomplish the same media switching operation, especially under glare conditions. However, it can be applied directly to SIP deployments in the many service provider networks and enterprises today.

Moving to a higher level of abstraction, the Parlay Group [15] specifies the Parlay/OSA and the Parlay X APIs for IT developers to access multimedia communication networks such as SIP. The Parlay/OSA API supports 'multiparty call control', which covers click-to-dial and more generally managing multiple parties and changing the media connectivity amongst them. The Parlay X API supports 'third party call' which is a subset of the Parlay API capabilities. These are high-level, protocol-agnostic APIs. A SIP network may expose these APIs to applications via a Parlay gateway. As such, the Parlay standards do not specify how these media control operations in the APIs may be supported at the SIP level, but leave the details to each Parlay gateway implementation. The solution presented here is well-suited for implementing correct 3PCC behavior in Parlay gateways.

9   Conclusion and Future Work

In this paper, we have presented a comprehensive and generalized solution for third-party call control in SIP networks. The solution enables endpoints to establish maximum media capabilities and types, and it can also handle transient states and race conditions that can occur in the SIP protocol. The solution supports compositional control whereby multiple third-party call controllers are in the call path and perform media control operation simultaneously. Finally, the solution has been verified for correctness and liveness properties with a model checking verifier when a single controller is involved.

This solution has several dependencies on SIP UA behavior that are not strictly mandated by the SIP specification, although they are commonly adhered to by existing UA implementations. These dependencies have been identified and recommendations are made for their resolution.

Some ongoing and future works include the proof by induction discussed in Section 5, and adding support for selected SIP extensions, for example the reliable provisional response RFC [12]. Work is also underway to implement the solution using the ECharts for SIP Servlets development environment. When completed this will greatly facilitate developing SIP Servlet-based third-party call controllers.

Acknowledgments. Michael Jackson made important contributions to our earlier work on media control. This work has also benefited from our long-term collaborations with Greg Bond, Hal Purdy and Tom Smith.

References

1. 3rd Generation Partnership Project. TS 22.228: Service requirements for the Internet protocol (IP) multimedia core network subsystem. Technical report, 3GPP, V8.3.0 (December 2007)

2. BEA. SIP servlet API version 1.1. Java Community Process JSR 289 (2008), http://jcp.org/en/jsr/detail?id=289
3. Bond, G.W., Cheung, E., Goguen, H.H., Hanson, K.J., Henderson, D., Karam, G.M., Purdy, K.H., Smith, T.M., Zave, P., Ramming, J.C.: Experience with component-based development of a telecommunication service. In: Heineman, G.T., Crnković, I., Schmidt, H.W., Stafford, J.A., Szyperski, C.A., Wallnau, K. (eds.) CBSE 2005. LNCS, vol. 3489, pp. 289–305. Springer, Heidelberg (2005)
4. Bond, G.W., Cheung, E., Purdy, H., Zave, P., Ramming, J.C.: An open architecture for next-generation telecommunication services. In: ACM Transactions on Internet Technology, vol. IV, pp. 83–123 (February 2004)
5. Cheung, E., Jackson, M., Zave, P.: Distributed media control for multimedia communications services. In: IEEE International Conference on Communications, vol. 4, pp. 2454–2458 (2002)
6. Chiang, T.-C., Gurbani, V.K., Reid, J.B.: The need for third-party call control. Bell Labs Technical Journal 7(1), 41–46 (2002)
7. Handley, M., Jacobson, V.: SDP: Session description protocol, IETF RFC 2327 (April 1998)
8. Holzmann, G.J.: The Spin Model Checker: Primer and Reference Manual. Addison-Wesley Publishing Company, Reading (2004)
9. Mahy, R., Sparks, R., Rosenberg, J., Petrie, D., Johnston, A.: A call control and multi-party usage framework for the session initiation protocol (SIP). IETF Internet-Draft draft-ietf-sipping-cc-framework-09 (November 2007)
10. Rosenberg, J., Peterson, J., Schulzrinne, H., Camarillo, G.: Best current practices for third party call control (3pcc) in the session initiation protocol (SIP), IETF RFC 3725 (April 2004)
11. Rosenberg, J., Schulzrinne, H.: An offer/answer model with the session description protocol (SDP),IETF RFC 3264 (June 2002)
12. Rosenberg, J., Schulzrinne, H.: Reliability of provisional responses in the session initiation protocol (SIP). RFC 3262 (June 2002)
13. Rosenberg, J., Schulzrinne, H., Camarillo, G., Johnston, A., Peterson, J., Sparks, R., Handley, M., Schooler, E.: SIP: Session initiation protocol, IETF RFC 3261(June 2002)
14. Smith, T.M., Bond, G.W.: ECharts for SIP Servlets: a state-machine programming environment for VoIP applications. In: IPTComm 2007: Proceedings of the 1st International Conference on Principles, Systems and Applications of IP telecommunications, pp. 89–98. ACM, New York (2007)
15. The Parlay Group. Homepage, http://www.parlay.org/
16. Zave, P., Cheung, E.: Compositional control of IP media. In: IEEE Transactions on Software Engineering (to appear, 2008)

Automatic Adaptation and Analysis of SIP Headers Using Decision Trees

Andrea Hess, Michael Nussbaumer, Helmut Hlavacs, and Karin Anna Hummel

Department of Distributed and Multimedia Systems
University of Vienna, Austria
Lenaugasse 2/8, A-1080 Vienna
{andrea.hess,karin.hummel,helmut.hlavacs}@univie.ac.at,
michael.nussbaumer@ani.univie.ac.at
http://www.cs.univie.ac.at/

Abstract. Software implementing open standards like SIP evolves over time, and often during the first years of deployment, products are either immature or do not implement the whole standard but rather only a subset. As a result, messages compliant to the standard are sometimes wrongly rejected and communication fails. In this paper we describe a novel approach called Babel-SIP for increasing the rate of acceptance for SIP messages.

Babel-SIP is a filter that is put in front of a SIP parser and analyzes incoming SIP messages. It gradually learns which messages are likely to be accepted by the parser, and which are not. Those classified as probably rejected are then adapted such that the probability for acceptance is increased. In a number of experiments we demonstrate that our filter is able to drastically increase the acceptance rate of problematic SIP REGISTER and INVITE messages. Additionally we show that our approach can be used to analyze the faulty behavior of a SIP parser by using the generated decision trees.

Keywords: Protocol adaptation, Decision tree based learning, SIP.

1   Introduction

One of the success factors of the Internet and of many of its applications is the openness of its protocols. Thousands of protocols are described in the form of request for comment (RFC), some being simple and described by one single RFC, some being spread over several RFCs, where each RFC might either describe one important aspect of the protocol, or even comprise a suit of closely related protocols rather than one single protocol. Due to the complexity of many protocols, it is often not possible to create suitable protocol stacks from scratch which implement the open standards completely and flawlessly right from the start. Rather, it is often better to first implement a subset of the most important features of a protocol, then before shipping the product, to try to run as many test runs as possible for debugging. After the first release, software producers then

H. Schulzrinne, R. State, and S. Niccolini (Eds.): IPTComm 2008, LNCS 5310, pp. 69–89, 2008.
© Springer-Verlag Berlin Heidelberg 2008

try to gradually implement missing features and continuously run debugging and compatibility tests. Since many companies develop their products like this, and also since many complex standards do leave some questions unanswered, it regularly may happen that devices adhering to the same protocol standard are unable to communicate with each other.

Consider SIP [1] for instance, which will be introduced in more detail in Section 3. SIP is a protocol for call session establishment and management, on which voice over IP (VoIP), for instance, is based. It is thus the glue binding together phones on the one side, and telephone infrastructure like proxy servers on the other side. Due to the multitude of products around SIP, in the recent years, many incompatibilities between phones and proxies have been observed (despite events like SIPit[1]). For testing compatibility, commercial VoIP proxy vendors usually purchase a set of hard and soft phones, and then test them against their product (of course many other software and conformance tests are run as well). Together with the proxy software, vendors then often specify a list of hard phones or soft phones which are known to work with their product. Proxy customers are in turn advised to use phones from this list. For instance, for the commercial proxy considered in this work, during the recent versions, several hard phones were known which would not be able to register themselves to the proxy. In case incompatibilities arise, proxy customers usually must wait until the proxy vendor acknowledges and removes the observed incompatibilities in the next patch or proxy release, something which might take weeks or even months.

In the long run, products get more and more robust, and compatibility issues are gradually removed. However, in the transient phase of initial deployment, usually during the first years of a newly proposed protocol, such incompatibilities may cause a lot of despair.

In this paper we present Babel-SIP, a novel SIP translator that is able to improve the situation significantly. Babel-SIP can be plugged in front of a proxy, and automatically analyzes incoming SIP messages. It gradually learns, which kind of SIP messages are likely to be accepted by the proxy SIP parser, and which are likely to be rejected because of the above described incompatibilities. The same learning concept can then be used to pro-actively adapt incoming SIP messages which are likely to cause trouble in such a way that the new version of the SIP message is likely to be accepted by the SIP parser.

We consider our approach to be generic in the sense that it is not necessarily restricted to be used for SIP. Rather, it is thinkable to construct other versions of Babel-SIP for newly proposed protocols in order to improve transient phases for newly deployed products.

2   Related Work

Since protocols are either proprietary or standardized, using autonomous self-adapting parsers based on machine learning techniques is not as widespread as in

---

[1] http://www.cs.columbia.edu/sip/sipit/

other domains such as robotics, natural language classification, node and network utilization including estimates of future utilization, and intrusion detection.

Decision trees, and in particular the used C4.5 tree, allow to classify arbitrary entities or objects which can be used, for instance for computer vision (applied to robotics) [2] or characterization of computer resource usage [3]. In [2] decision trees were used for learning about the visual environment which was modeled in terms of simple and complex attributes and successfully implemented for improving recognition possibilities of Sony Aibo robots (e.g., the surface area or angles). Decision trees which use further linear regression have been proposed for the characterization of computer resource usage in [3]. Parameters like the CPU, I/O, and memory were used as attributes and the classification tree was finally used to successfully determine anomalies of the system's parameters. The authors claim that finding the trade-off between accurate history knowledge and time-consuming training was a major concern.

In [4] intrusion detection was introduced based on a combination of pattern matching and decision tree-based protocol analysis. This tree-based approach allows to adapt to new attack types and forms while the traditional patterns are integrated into the tree and benefit from refinement of crucial parameters. All presented decision tree based approaches are similar to our approach and are mentioned to motivate the potential for protocol analysis and message classification.

In the application area of VoIP and SIP, authors both investigate traffic behavior and failures in particular software implementations. In [5] the authors describe the need and their solution for profiling SIP-based VoIP traffic (protocol behavior) to automatically detect anomalies. They demonstrate that SIP traffic can be modeled well with their profiling and that anomalies could be detected. In [6] it is argued, that based on the SIP specification, a formal testing of an open source and a commercial SIP proxy lead to errors with the SIP registrar. Both findings are encouraging to propose a method for not only detecting incompatibilities and testing SIP proxies, but further to provide a solution for messages rejected due to slightly different interpretations of the standard or software faults.

In [7] a stateful fuzzer was used to test the SIP compatibility of User Agents and proxies by sending different (faulty) messages both in terms of syntax and in terms of protocol behavior. The idea here is only to find weaknesses in the parser implementation, without trying to adapt messages online. The work closest to our approach is presented in [8]. In this approach, incoming and outgoing SIP messages of a proxy are analyzed by an in-kernel Linux classification engine. Hereby, a rule-based approach is proposed, where the rules are pre-defined (static). Our approach extends this classification by proposing a generalizable solution capable of learning. Additionally, we propose the novel approach of autonomic adaptation and evaluate it.

3 Background: The Session Initiation Protocol

The Session Initiation Protocol (SIP) is gradually becoming a key protocol for many application areas, such as voice over IP, or general session management of

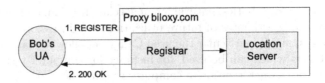

Fig. 1. Bob's UA registers Bob's location at the local registrar/proxy

```
REGISTER sip:Domain SIP/2.0
To: <sip:UserID@Domain>
From: <sip:UserID@Domain>
Call-ID: NDYzYzMwNjJhMDRjYTFj
CSeq: 1 REGISTER
```

Fig. 2. A typical SIP REGISTER message

the Internet Multimedia Subsystem (IMS) of Next Generation Networks (NGNs). Its functions target (i) user location, (ii) user availability, (iii) user capabilities, (iv) session setup, and (v) session management. The core SIP functionality is defined in RFC 3261 [1] but several other RFCs define different additional aspects of SIP, like reliability [9], interaction with DNS [10], events and notifications [11], referring [12], updating [13], call flow examples for VoIP [14], and PSTN [15], QoS and authorization [16], privacy [17], security [18], and many more.

In the context of VoIP, SIP is responsible for the whole user localization and call management. On behalf of a user, a User Agent (UA), typically a hard phone on the desk, or a soft phone running on some PC, sends REGISTER messages to a local registrar (server). The messages contain the ID of the user and the IP address of the UA. The registrar then updates the received locality information in yet another server called location server, which from this time on knows the address a certain user can be reached at (see Figure 1). RFC 3261 defines that only certain header fields are necessary for a SIP message to work properly, but of course there are many optional header fields that can be used by a VoIP phone within a SIP message as well. According to RFC 3261, a SIP REGISTER message has to contain a request line and the header fields *To, From, Call-ID* and *CSeq* (see Figure 2). Furthermore, SIP requests like INVITE messages additionally have to contain the header fields *Max-Forwards* and *Via* (see Figure 4).

Handling calls is then the task of a so-called proxy server, which also should be installed locally at each site. Calls are initiated by sending INVITE messages. A call from user Alice registered at site atlanta.com to user Bob registered at site biloxy.com is usually done by specifying a SIP URI like bob@biloxy.com. Alice's UA then sends a SIP INVITE message to her local proxy atlanta.com, which then forwards the INVITE to Bob's proxy biloxy.com, which subsequently asks the local location server where to find Bob's UA. In case Bob's UA has been registered previously, the proxy at biloxy.com forwards the INVITE to Bob's UA, which then may continue to initiate the session. Figure 3 shows this

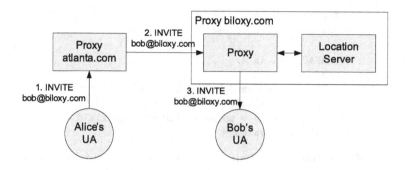

Fig. 3. Alice tries to setup a call to Bob

```
INVITE sip:CalleeUserID@CalleeDomain SIP/2.0
To: <sip:CalleeUserID@CalleeDomain>
From: <sip:CallerUserID@CallerDomain>
Via: SIP/2.0/UDP IPAdress:Port
Call-ID: NDYzYzMwNjJhMDRjYTFj
CSeq: 1 INVITE
Max-Forwards: 70
```

Fig. 4. A typical SIP INVITE message

forwarding of INVITE messages, the rest of the messages necessary to establish a call, i.e., "180 RINGING", "200 OK", and "ACK" are not shown here. Often, instead of installing physically three different servers, it suffices to integrate the functionality of registrar, location server, and proxy into one server, the local proxy, which we will assume here. In particular, we assume that there is only one single SIP parser responsible for registration and call management.

4   Autonomic SIP Adaptation

Standardization of network protocols enables interconnection, however, the principle problem with open protocols lies in the degree of freedom allowed causing different protocol dialects in practice. These small differences in the messages' header information might lead to incompatibilities between implementations of different vendors and organizations, a problem that is usually gradually solved over a time period of years.

We attack the problem of transient incompatibilities by introducing a self-learning module which can be added to arbitrary proxies. The purpose of this module is twofold: first, the module should *classify* an incoming message by analyzing its header information in order to predict a rejection by the proxy and, second, the module *suggests an adaptation* of the header information which should finally force the acceptance of the message.

```
Input:  attribute vector A
Output: attribute vector A with new values

FOREACH (Ai in A)
  Ai.value = 0
  IF (Ai.name in SIP message) THEN
    IF (SIP message field is numeric) THEN
      Ai.value = value of SIP message field
    ELSE Ai.value = 1
```

Fig. 5. Translation of SIP header into C4.5 attribute values

4.1 C4.5 Decision Trees

For classification, we use a C4.5 decision tree [19] capable of further identifying relevant header parameters causing rejections. Additionally, further properties of C4.5 trees seem to be desirable, like avoiding over-fitting of the tree and dealing with incomplete data. After a training phase, new messages can then be classified into messages that are likely to be rejected or accepted. The C4.5 decision tree implementation (J48) used is based on the Weka machine learning library [20]. All headers, header fields, and standard values (as defined by RFC 3261) are defined as attributes. For each attribute a *numerical value* is defined to describe a SIP message (274 attributes per message) as shown in the algorithm depicted in Figure 5. It must be noted that the result is a vector of dimension $d = 274$, vector components are 0 if the corresponding header/header field is not present, 1 if the header/header field is present and of type string (but 0 if the header format is incorrect), and any numeric value if the header/header field is present and of numeric type. For the current implementation, this information is stored in the format ARFF (Attribute Relation File Format).

Figure 6 shows an example tree generated by the training with SIP REGIS-TER messages. The tree actually represents a hierarchy of nested if-then rules each SIP message is tested against. The leaves of the tree represent the tree classification decision, in this case either ACCEPTED or REJECTED. For example, if the header field *Replaces* is in the SIP message (rule "Replaces > 0"), the message is classified as rejected. The rule hierarchy that was learned also shows the importance of the message's parameters for the final acceptance / rejection of the message, with important rules being at the top of the rule hierarchy. The numbers calculated for the tree leaves correspond to the number of messages which have been classified in this branch (the second number shows the number of wrong classifications in case they exist).

4.2 Babel-SIP

Babel-SIP is an automatic protocol adapter and is placed between the proxy socket that accepts the incoming messages, and the registrar's or proxy's SIP parser (see Figures 7 and 8). Babel-SIP maintains a C4.5 decision tree, and

```
Replaces <= 0
| Allow_DO <= 0
| | Content-Language <= 0
| | | Contact_methods <= 0
| | | | To_user <= 0: ACCEPTED (112.0/5.0)
| | | | To_user > 0
| | | | | Contact_q <= 0
| | | | | | Call-ID <= 0: REJECTED (2.0)
| | | | | | Call-ID > 0: ACCEPTED (12.0/1.0)
| | | | | Contact_q > 0: REJECTED (2.0)
| | | Contact_methods > 0
| | | | Accept <= 0: REJECTED (6.0/1.0)
| | | | Accept > 0: ACCEPTED (11.0/1.0)
| | Content-Language > 0
| | | Contact_flow-id <= 0: REJECTED (6.0/1.0)
| | | Contact_flow-id > 0: ACCEPTED (2.0)
| Allow_DO > 0
| | Allow-Events_talk <= 0: REJECTED (6.0)
| | Allow-Events_talk > 0: ACCEPTED (3.0/1.0)
Replaces > 0: REJECTED (11.0)
```

Fig. 6. Example C4.5 tree after training with SIP REGISTER messages

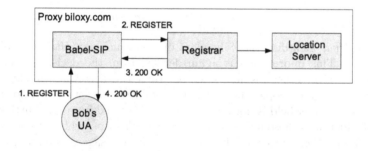

Fig. 7. Babel-SIP adapts incoming REGISTER messages and passes them on to a registrar

observes which messages are accepted by the proxy, and which are not. This information is fed into the decision tree, the tree thus learns which headers are likely to cause trouble for this particular release of the proxy software.

Once the tree has been trained, by using the same decision tree, incoming messages are then automatically classified as either probably accepted or probably rejected. Of course, at this stage, Babel-SIP does not know this for sure. However, once a message is classified to be probably rejected by the proxy parser, Babel-SIP tries to adapt SIP messages in such a way that the result turns into a probably accept.

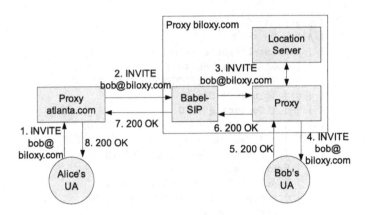

Fig. 8. Babel-SIP adapts incoming INVITE messages and passes them on to the proxy

Babel-SIP stores messages that have been accepted previously by the proxy in a local database M. Once a SIP message m_1 has been classified as probably rejected, Babel-SIP searches through its database for the message m_c being closest to m_1. For estimating the distance between two SIP messages m_1 and m_2, we use the standard Euclidean distance metric $d(m_1, m_2)$ provided by Weka (on normalized versions of the vectors). The sought for message m_c is thus given by

$$m_c = \arg \min_{m_i \in M \wedge m_i \neq m_1} d(m_1, m_i).$$

Babel-SIP then identifies those headers of m_1 which are classified as being problematic. This information is again derived from the decision tree. If the same header/header field is found in m_c then the according header/header field/values of m_c are copied into m_1, thus replacing the previous information. If the header/header field is not found in m_c, it is erased from m_1. Furthermore, Babel-SIP identifies those headers and header fields of m_c which are not used in m_1, and inserts them into m_1. The result is a new message version $\hat{m}_1$, which is then forwarded to the proxy.

At this point it must be noted that it is self-evident that such an approach must be done with care. In a real production system it is mandatory that the appropriate semantics of the different headers are also taken into account which we have not addressed so far. Rather, the aim of this work is to evaluate whether our approach based on observing and learning is able to achieve an improved rate of message acceptance or not. In our follow-up work we will thus focus on creating appropriate rules for semantics-aware header translation.

5   Experiments and Results

In our lab we installed several popular hard and soft phones and ran experiments using a commercial proxy server created by a major Austrian telecom equipment provider. At the time of our research, this commercial proxy was guaranteed to

Table 1. Hard and soft phones analyzed for our experiments

Hard Phones	Snom 300
	Polycom SoundPoint IP 330
	Linksys SPA IP Phone SPA 941
	DLink VoIP IP-Phone DPH-120S
	Thomson ST2030
	Allnet 7950 (Sipgate)
	Grandstream GXP2000 Enterprise IP Phone
	Elmeg IP 290
	Siemens
Soft Phones	X-Lite
	PortSIP
	BOL
	Express Talk
	3CX

work with only two different types of VoIP hard phones and only one type of VoIP soft phone. For all other phones the company did not guarantee that the phones would work with their SIP proxy, although mostly they did.

Our research in this work primarily focuses on the REGISTER and INVITE messages. In the initial phase we aimed at finding out how compatible our proxy is with respect to different versions of REGISTER messages. In the second phase we concentrated on probably the most important SIP message, the INVITE message. In our experiments we found a multitude of different SIP headers used by different phones, so our first step was to find out what kind of REGISTER and INVITE messages the different types of VoIP phones send. We therefore monitored REGISTER and INVITE messages from nine popular VoIP hard phones and five popular VoIP soft phones (see Table 1).

After these first experiments we found out that the SIP messages can indeed be very different. For example: one hard phone A uses less than 10 header fields in its SIP REGISTER message, another hard phone B uses 15 header fields in its SIP REGISTER message, and both phones use different header fields as well.

5.1 Initial SIP Messages

In order to obtain a substantial amount of possible REGISTER and INVITE messages for testing our proxy, we decided to artificially create different SIP messages. The newly generated messages were random combinations of the observed SIP header fields, header field values, and header field parameters from the investigated real phones, as well as others taken from RFC 3261.

For both REGISTER and INVITE messages we generated a set of the 53 most often used SIP header fields found in the observed SIP messages. For these 53 header fields we defined 145 header field values and header field parameters. In the next step we generated different SIP REGISTER and INVITE messages using these 145 header field values. The basic idea was to generate a large amount of different messages with many different parameter combinations. We therefore defined a probability for each of the 145 different header fields, the probability values were computed from the previously observed SIP messages sniffed from the real phones. Furthermore we developed a Java program that continuously sends either REGISTER or INVITE messages to the proxy, the messages being created randomly by choosing a subset of the 145 header field values according to their probabilities.

In our experiments we generated 344 different SIP REGISTER messages and 122 different SIP INVITE messages. For each SIP REGISTER message we determined whether the register process was successful, i.e., whether the client received a "200 OK" reply, or not. If it was successful we marked the message as *accepted*, otherwise we marked it as *rejected*. Out of the 344 REGISTER messages, 78 (or approximately 22.67%) were marked as rejected, as it turned out, mostly because of incomplete header information. For each SIP INVITE message we determined whether the call setup was successful and the INVITE message was successfully sent to the called party, i.e., whether the client received a "180 Ringing" reply, or not. Again, if it was successful we marked the message as accepted, otherwise we marked it as rejected. Out of the 122 INVITE messages, 69 (or approximately 56.56%) were marked as being rejected.

5.2   Rejected Messages

We ran several experiments in our lab to evaluate the effectiveness of Babel-SIP, which is measured by the improvement of acceptance of previously not accepted SIP messages. These experiments were carried out separately for REGISTER and INVITE messages.

REGISTER Messages. Initially, a C4.5 decision tree was built from the *training data set* composed of 50 messages (of which 22% are known to be rejected) randomly selected from the artificial messages generated. This initial tree classifies 90% of the training data set correctly.

Then we ran a set of experiments, consisting of 15 replicated experimental runs. In each run we sent a total of 4400 messages to Babel-SIP, chosen at random from the set of 294 test messages. Here, 22.79% of the test data messages were known to be rejected by the proxy. The partitioning of messages into a training and test set is shown in Table 2.

Since training is very resource consuming, we further decided that the decision tree is not trained after each single message. Rather, the results of a batch of 20 consecutive REGISTER messages were used to train the decision tree, which as a result gradually adapted to the acceptance behavior of the proxy.

Table 2. Initial training and test data sets

REGISTER messages			
Training data set	Accepted messages	39	78%
	Rejected messages	11	22%
	Total number	50	
Test data set	Accepted messages	227	77.21%
	Rejected messages	67	22.79%
	Total number	294	
INVITE messages			
Training data set	Accepted messages	9	45%
	Rejected messages	11	55%
	Total number	20	
Test data set	Accepted messages	44	43.14%
	Rejected messages	58	56.86%
	Total number	102	

For each message we recorded whether it was accepted or not. The 15 experiments thus resulted in 15 time series of 4400 binary observations (yes or no). For each experiment $l, 1 \leq l \leq 15$ we then calculated rejection rates over overlapping bins of size 100 messages. The first bin $B_1^l = \{m_i^l \mid 1 \leq i \leq 100\}$ includes messages 1 to 100, the rejected messages of this bin are given by $\hat{B}_1^l = \{m_i^l \in B_1^l \mid m_i^l \text{ was rejected}\}$. B_2^l and $\hat{B}_2^l$ are then computed over messages 21 to 120 from experiment l. In general, for $1 \leq k \leq 216$ we define

$$B_k^l = \{m_i^l \mid 20 \times (k-1) + 1 \leq i \leq 20 \times (k-1) + 100\}$$

and

$$\hat{B}_k^l = \{m_i^l \in B_k^l \mid m_i^l \text{ was rejected}\}.$$

Thus, an estimator $\hat{R}^l(i)$ for the rejection rate (in %) around message $m_i^l, 1 \leq i \leq 4400$ is given by

$$\hat{R}^l(i) = 100 \times |\hat{B}_{\lceil i/20 \rceil}^l| / |B_{\lceil i/20 \rceil}^l| = |\hat{B}_{\lceil i/20 \rceil}^l|.$$

Figure 9 shows a smoothened curve of the estimated rejection rate. By using

$$\bar{B}_k = \left(\sum_{l=1}^{15} |\hat{B}_k^l| \right) / 15, \ 1 \leq k \leq 216, \tag{1}$$

we define a mean estimator by

$$\bar{R}(i) = \bar{B}_{\lceil i/20 \rceil},$$

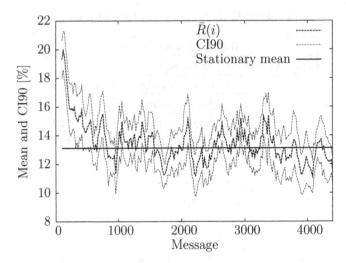

Fig. 9. Mean estimated rejection rate $\bar{R}(i)$ and 90% confidence interval (CI90) for message i. $\bar{R}(i)$ is calculated over all 15 REGISTER experiments and each bin. Stationary mean is the overall mean for messages m^l_{600} to m^l_{4400}.

i.e., the mean is calculated for each bin over all 15 experimental runs. In Figure 9 it can be seen that the time series shows a transient phase at the start, in which the rejection rate decreases. In this phase, Babel-SIP gradually learns and increases its effectiveness. The series then enters a stationary phase, in which no more gain is achieved, i.e., Babel-SIP has seen all possible messages. We have additionally computed the mean rejection rate $R^s \approx 13.12\%$ for messages in this stationary phase, taking into account only messages m^l_{600} to m^l_{4400} (Stationary mean). This rejection rate is the main result of Babel-SIP: when sending our test data to the commercial proxy, the application of Babel-SIP is able to decrease the rejection rate from 22.79% to 13.12%, i.e., the rejection rate on average is decreased by over 42%.

Table 3 shows aggregated results over all 15 experiments in more detail. Modified denotes the percentage of modified messages in relation to all messages. Successfully modified denotes those messages that were turned from a rejected into an accepted message by Babel-SIP. This statistic is given one time in relation to all messages, and one time in relation only to those messages that have been classified as rejected. This number is the number of rejected messages minus the number of false negatives, plus the number of false positives. The false positives are those that were classified as rejected, although they were not. False negatives are those messages that were classified as accepted although they were not. For these statistics the table shows the mean over all 15 runs, as well as the standard deviation between the individual runs and this mean. The standard deviations are very small, and thus on the aggregate level, all 15 experiments show almost equal results.

Table 3. Aggregated results of Babel-SIP experiments

REGISTER messages	Mean [%]	Std.dev. [%]
Modified	18.37	5.8310^{-4}
Successfully modified (from all)	9.33	0.003
Successfully modified (of those classified as rejected)	48.02	0.108
False positive	6.13	2.04110^{-4}
False negative	10.53	4.23310^{-4}
INVITE messages	Mean [%]	Std.dev. [%]
Modified	38.24	0
Successfully modified (from all)	22.39	1.210
Successfully modified (of those classified as rejected)	58.55	3.165
False positive	6.86	0
False negative	23.53	0

INVITE Messages. The experiments to validate our approach on INVITE messages were performed similarly to the REGISTER experiments. The initial C4.5 tree built from the training data set sorts all 20 training messages correctly into accepted and rejected ones. In each of the 15 experimental runs, 1000 INVITE messages were randomly selected from the test data set and sent to Babel-SIP. 56.86% of the test messages (see Table 2) are known not to be accepted by the SIP proxy. The decision tree used to predict whether an incoming message will be accepted was again updated after every 20 messages that were sent to the proxy. The rejection rates $\hat{R}^l(i)$ for two experiments are shown in Figure 10.

For the 15 INVITE experiments we again computed a mean estimator $\bar{R}(i)$ and the 90% confidence interval, as well as an estimator for the stationary rejection rate (see Figure 11). For the latter we used messages m^l_{560} to m^l_{1000}. This stationary rejection rate turned out to be 30.79%. When compared to the initial rejection rate of 56.86%, this is an improvement of 45.85%.

Details on the modified and incorrectly classified messages in all 15 experimental runs are given in Table 3. The number of messages wrongly classified as rejected (false positives) is as high as in the REGISTER experiments, whereas the number of those wrongly classified as accepted (false negatives) has strongly increased. Thus, it can be said that the decision tree classifying the INVITE headers is not as accurate in distinguishing the rejected headers from the accepted headers as the tree resulting from the REGISTER experiments.

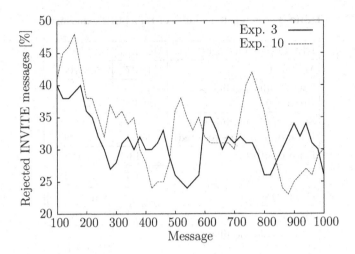

Fig. 10. Estimated rejection rates $\hat{R}^l(i)$ for two INVITE experiments

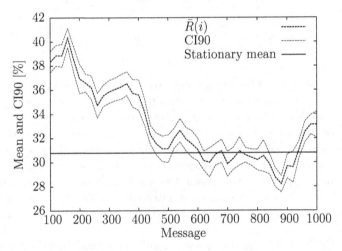

Fig. 11. Mean estimated rejection rate $\bar{R}(i)$ and 90% confidence interval (CI90) for message i. $\bar{R}(i)$ is calculated over all 15 INVITE experiments and each bin. Stationary mean is the overall mean for messages m_{560}^l to m_{1000}^l.

Another interesting observation is the observed zero standard deviation in the percentage of messages classified as rejected and, subsequently, modified over all 15 experimental runs. As a result, it seems that the trees classified all messages equally although the messages were selected in a random sequence for each run and each tree should thus learn some faulty parameters earlier and some later than trees in other runs. However, in the REGISTER experiments the observed variances for the same statistic were also quite small, and it must be noted that

Table 4. Number of necessary attempts for experiment r

# REGISTERs	1	2	3	4	≥ 5	never
$r = 1$	10					57
$r = 2$	14	8				45
$r = 3$	14	12	3			38
$r = 4$	21	5	3	1		37
$r = 5$	17	7	5	2	0	36
$r = 6$	16	13	2	0	0	36
$r = 7$	19	9	1	2	0	36
$r = 8$	16	5	7	2	1	36
$r = 9$	18	7	5	2	0	35
# INVITEs	1	2	3	≥ 4		never
$r = 1$	22					36
$r = 2$	25	3				30
$r = 3$	21	5	2			30
$r = 4$	25	1	5	1		26

in the REGISTER experiments both a much larger test message pool (294 vs. 102) and much longer experimental sequences (4400 vs. 1000) were used.

5.3 Retries

Since the basic hypothesis of Babel-SIP is that even phones which initially fail to contact the SIP proxy, after retrying a number of times, eventually may succeed because of Babel-SIP learning and transformation, we have analyzed the number of attempts that are necessary for succeeding. For this, we ran separated REGISTER and INVITE experiments with our training and test data sets (see Table 2). Each experiment was driven by a parameter r, stating the maximum number of times a phone would try to register itself or to call another phone. Babel-SIP was again trained before the experiments were started by sending the test data. In the case that the phone had not succeeded within these tries, it was counted as "never". For each of the 67 REGISTER respectively 58 INVITE messages of initially rejected test messages we recorded the number of messages necessary for registering and inviting.

Table 4 shows the number of necessary tries up to that value of r from which onwards no improvement of the number of accepted messages was achieved. The results reveal that for those phones that would need more than one try, most of them would succeed after at most four tries. Mapping this onto a realistic scenario, this means that a phone owner would have to attempt to register his phone or to initiate a call only a few times, if he would be willing to wait between the tries for some time. In addition, it was noticed that the number of accepted messages among the previously rejected ones did not increase if the phones repeatedly attempt to register more than 9 times or to start a call more than 4 times.

5.4   Rejection of Previously Accepted Messages

An important evaluation criterion is given by the question, whether Babel-SIP actually may wrongly classify a message m as probably rejected, while in reality the message would be accepted, and would change it in a way that the new version $\hat{m}$ would be actually rejected. Such a behavior is regarded as being unacceptable, since proxy providers provide a list of evaluated UAs to their customers. A translation component with such an erroneous behavior would nullify any such guarantee.

As a consequence, we ran additional experiments and added the SIP messages from 9 hard phones and 5 soft phones to the pool of our test data. The phone messages were known to be accepted by the proxy. There was not a single instant that any of these real phone messages were altered and subsequently rejected by the proxy. The same is true for all REGISTER and INVITE test messages from the accepted pool. At least our experiments with the given proxy showed that Babel-SIP indeed shows a stable behavior, and tends to change only messages which are problematic, but does not alter already accepted messages in such a way that they subsequently would be rejected.

6   Qualitative Analysis of Decision Trees

Since the C4.5 decision tree contains a summary of the SIP parser behavior, it also can be used as a hint for the proxy programmers to find bugs in their implementation. This will be demonstrated in the following sections.

6.1   REGISTER Messages

As mentioned above, after the initial training with 50 REGISTER messages the C4.5 tree is able to classify 90% of the messages correctly.

```
Event_message-summary <= 0
| Error-Info <= 0
| | Contact_transport <= 0: ACCEPTED (52.0/4.0)
| | Contact_transport > 0
| | | Via_rport <= 0: REJECTED (2.0)
| | | Via_rport > 0: ACCEPTED (8.0/1.0)
| Error-Info > 0
| | Allow-Events_presence <= 0: REJECTED (2.0)
| | Allow-Events_presence > 0: ACCEPTED (2.0)
Event_message-summary > 0: REJECTED (4.0/1.0)
```

Fig. 12. Example C4.5 tree after training with 70 REGISTER messages.

After 70 REGISTER messages, i.e., the initial training (50 messages) plus one more training (20 more messages), the resulting tree is quite small, containing only five rules which decide whether an incoming message is classified as accepted or rejected (see Figure 12). Looking at this tree, a programmer can already see important hints explaining failures of his SIP parser. The accuracy of this tree is already 91.43%.

Looking at the C4.5 decision tree derived at the end of the experiments (see Figure 13) the tree gets quite large, thus using this tree for analysis imposes more work to the programmer. On the other hand, its classification accuracy is increased to 99.32%. Thus, it can be assumed that this tree indeed sufficiently explains registration failures without knowing anything about the implementation details.

Because the final tree is quite large, for readability reasons, Figure 13 shows just the parts containing the most important rules as outcome of our experiments. As mentioned in Section 5, the developed Java client creates artificial messages, and each of the 145 header fields/values is included only according to some preset probability. Therefore it is possible that important header fields or header field values are not used, and some messages do not contain all mandatory header fields as demanded by RFC 3261. We thus investigate whether the decision tree can be used to understand why the parser rejected many of the rejected messages.

In the decision tree depicted in Figure 13, the first rule indicates that a SIP REGISTER message has to contain the header field *CSeq* (which actually is mandatory as described in RFC 3261). If an incoming message does not contain a *CSeq* header field it is very likely to be rejected, otherwise the next rule has

```
CSeq <= 0: REJECTED (104.0)
CSeq > 0
| Call-ID <= 0: REJECTED (101.0)
| Call-ID > 0
| | Replaces <= 0
| | | [...]
| | | To_IP <= 0
| | | | [...]
| | | To_IP > 0
| | | | [...]
| | | | | Via_IP <= 0
| | | | | | [...]
| | | | | Via_IP > 0
| | | | | | [...]
| | | | | | From_IP <= 0: REJECTED (2.0)
| | | | | | From_IP > 0: ACCEPTED (38.0)
| | | | | | [...]
| | | | | | Via_rport <= 0: REJECTED (11.0)
| | | | | | Via_rport > 0: ACCEPTED (30.0)
| | | | | | [...]
| | Replaces > 0: REJECTED (38.0)
```

Fig. 13. Part of a C4.5 tree (SIP REGISTER messages)

to be checked. Since the tree represents a hierarchy of rules, the tree can be traversed from top to bottom, or vice versa. When checking the C4.5 tree from top to bottom, the next rule indicates that a SIP message has to contain the header field *Call-ID*, again according to RFC 3261. We conclude that checking the decision tree from top to bottom results in precise hints about the critical header fields. Of course as the tree gets larger there are more and more branches and rules to be checked, therefore sometimes after the first quick check from top to bottom it makes sense to check the tree from bottom to top. In most cases it comes down to a final rule that indicates whether a message is likely to be accepted or rejected. Figure 13 shows that the *Via* header field parameter *rport* is such a final decision rule. This means that at a specific condition set by previous rules, the *rport* parameter of the *Via* header is mandatory for a SIP REGISTER message to work properly. Checking the decision tree from top to bottom or vice versa results in a set of rules enabling the programmer either to find bugs in a proxy's implementation or to find out why incoming SIP messages were rejected. To show the simplicity of the C4.5 decision tree we checked all 78 different faulty SIP REGISTER messages and tried to find out why they were rejected by the SIP proxy. With 51 messages (or 65.38% of all faulty messages) and with the help of the decision tree it is extremely easy to find out why the message was rejected, even for people without detailed knowledge of the RFC 3261.

6.2 INVITE Messages

Since in our experiments the INVITE messages did cause errors different from those of the REGISTER messages, the decision trees stemming from the INVITE

```
To_IP <= 0: REJ. (72.0)
To_IP > 0
| Replaces <= 0
| | [...]
| | From_IP <= 0
| | | Allow-Events_conference <= 0: REJ. (31.0)
| | | Allow-Events_conference > 0: ACC. (10.0)
| | From_IP > 0
| | | [...]
| | | Content-Type_text/html <= 0: ACC. (18.0)
| | | Content-Type_text/html > 0: REJ. (2.0)
| | | [...]
| | | Privacy_header <= 0: ACC. (58.0/2.0)
| | | Privacy_header > 0
| | | [...]
| | | Request-Line_transport <= 0: REJ. (25.0)
| | | Request-Line_transport > 0: ACC. (9.0)
| | | [...]
| Replaces > 0: REJ. (48.0)
```

Fig. 14. Part of a C4.5 tree (SIP INVITE messages)

experiments were quite different from those stemming from the REGISTER experiments. Figure 14 shows that incoming INVITE messages that do not contain the *To_IP* parameter, i.e., the *domain* in the *To* header, will probably be rejected by the SIP proxy. The *From_IP*, meaning the *domain* in the *From* header, is also an important factor if the message will be accepted or rejected.

Similar to the REGISTER case, the decision tree derived at the end of the INVITE experiments shows lots of final decision rules. Figure 14 shows that the tested SIP proxy has problems with INVITE messages either containing the "text/html" value in the *Content-Type* header, containing the *Privacy* header, or containing the "transport=udp" value in the *Request-Line*.

Figure 13 as well as Figure 14 show that both REGISTER and INVITE messages are likely to be rejected by the tested SIP proxy if the message contains the *Replaces* header. In our follow-up work we intend to test other open-source SIP proxies with the same set of SIP messages to see whether there are notable differences in this behavior.

7   Conclusion

In this paper we introduce Babel-SIP, an automatic, self-learning SIP-message translator. Its main use is in the transient phase between creating a new SIP-stack implementation or a whole new proxy, and the final release of a 100% reliable proxy version. Generally such situations occur immediately after the development of a new communication protocol which is quickly adopted and implemented by numerous vendors. Due to the immaturity of software implementations, during this phase, devices often fail to communicate, although in theory they implement the same protocol.

The task of Babel-SIP is to act as a mediator for a specific release of a SIP proxy. Babel-SIP analyzes SIP messages sent to its proxy (currently REGISTER and INVITE messages), and learns which SIP messages were accepted by this proxy, and which were not. Over time, Babel-SIP is able to accurately guess whether an incoming messages is likely to be accepted by its proxy. If not, Babel-SIP changes the message in such a way that the probability for acceptance is increased. By carrying out numerous experiments, we have demonstrated that with our approach the number of rejected messages for both SIP message types is almost halved, and that Babel-SIP gains knowledge over time and improves its effectiveness.

Additionally we have shown that the resulting decision trees indeed provide good insight into the faulty behavior of either the SIP parser or the SIP clients and phones themselves. As a consequence, the decision trees can be used by SIP programmers to remove implementation bugs.

In the near future we will focus on creating semantic rules for changing header information and test Babel-SIP with different SIP proxies. Since we regard our approach to be generic, we will also investigate the possible application of our Babel approach to other popular application protocols such as RTSP or HTTP.

Acknowledgment

The research herein is partially conducted within the competence network Softnet Austria (www.soft-net.at) and funded by the Austrian Federal Ministry of Economics (bm:wa), the province of Styria, the Steirische Wirtschaftsfoerderungsgesellschaft mbH. (SFG), and the city of Vienna in terms of the center for innovation and technology (ZIT).

References

1. Rosenberg, J., Schulzrinne, H., Camarillo, G., Johnston, A., Peterson, J., Sparks, R., Handley, M., Schooler, E.: SIP: Session Initiation Protocol. RFC 3261 (June 2002)
2. Wilking, D., Röfer, T.: Realtime Object Recognition Using Decision Tree Learning. In: RoboCup 2004: Robot World Cup VII, pp. 556–563. Springer, Heidelberg (2005)
3. Heisig, S., Moyle, S.: Using Model Trees to Characterize Computer Resource Usage. In: 1st ACM SIGSOFT Workshop on Self-Managed Systems, pp. 80–84 (2004)
4. Abbes, T., Bouhoula, A., Rusinowitch, M.: Protocol Analysis in Intrusion Detection Using Decision Trees. In: International Conference on Information Technology: Coding and Computing (ITCC 2004), pp. 404–408 (2004)
5. Kang, H., Zhang, Z., Ranjan, S., Nucci, A.: SIP-based VoIP Traffic Behavior Profiling and Its Applications. In: MineNet 2007, pp. 39–44 (2007)
6. Aichernig, B., Peischl, B., Weiglhofer, M., Wotawa, F.: Protocol Conformance Testing a SIP Registrar: an Industrial Application of Formal Methods. In: 5th IEEE Int. Conference on Software Engineering and Formal Methods, pp. 215–224 (2007)
7. Abdelnur, H., State, R., Festor, O.: KiF: A Stateful SIP Fuzzer. In: 1st Int. Conference on Principles, Systems and Applications of IP Telecommunications, iptcomm.org (2007)
8. Acharya, A., Wand, X., Wrigth, C., Banerjee, N., Sengupta, B.: Real-time Monitoring of SIP Infrastructure Using Message Classification. In: MineNet 2007, pp. 45–50 (2007)
9. Rosenberg, J., Schulzrinne, H.: Reliability of provisional responses in session initiation protocol (sip). RFC 3262 (June 2002)
10. Rosenberg, J., Schulzrinne, H.: Session initiation protocol (sip): Locating sip servers. RFC 3262 (June 2002)
11. Roach, A.B.: Session initiation protocol (sip)-specific event notification. RFC 3265 (June 2002)
12. Sparks, R.: The session initiation protocol (sip) refer method. RFC 3515 (April 2003)
13. Rosenberg, J.: The session initiation protocol (sip) update method. RFC 3311 (September 2002)
14. Johnston, A., Donovan, S., Sparks, R., Cunningham, C., Summers, K.: Session initiation protocol (sip) basic call flow examples. RFC 3665 (December 2003)
15. Johnston, A., Donovan, S., Sparks, R., Cunningham, C., Summers, K.: Session initiation protocol (sip) public switched telephone network (pstn) call flows. RFC 3666 (Decmember (2003)
16. Marshall, W.: Private session initiation protocol (sip) extensions for media authorization. RFC 3313 (January 2003)

17. Peterson, J.: A privacy mechanism for the session initiation protocol (sip). RFC 3323 (November 2002)
18. Arkko, J., Torvinen, V., Camarillo, G., Niemi, A., Haukka, T.: Security Mechanism Agreement for the Session Initiation Protocol (SIP). RFC 3329 (January 2003)
19. Mitchell, T.: Machine Learning. McGraw-Hill, New York (1997)
20. Witten, I., Frank, E.: Data Mining: Practical Machine Learning Tools and Techniques. Morgan Kaufmann, San Francisco (2005)

A Self-learning System for Detection of Anomalous SIP Messages

Konrad Rieck[1], Stefan Wahl[2], Pavel Laskov[1,3], Peter Domschitz[2],
and Klaus-Robert Müller[1,4]

[1] Fraunhofer Institute FIRST, Intelligent Data Analysis, Berlin, Germany
[2] Alcatel-Lucent, Bell Labs Germany, Stuttgart, Germany
[3] University of Tübingen, Wilhelm-Schickard-Institute, Germany
[4] Technical University of Berlin, Dept. of Computer Science, Germany

Abstract. Current Voice-over-IP infrastructures lack defenses against
unexpected network threats, such as zero-day exploits and computer
worms. The possibility of such threats originates from the ongoing convergence of telecommunication and IP network infrastructures. As a
countermeasure, we propose a self-learning system for detection of unknown and novel attacks in the Session Initiation Protocol (SIP). The
system identifies anomalous content by embedding SIP messages to a
feature space and determining deviation from a model of normality. The
system adapts to network changes by automatically retraining itself while
being hardened against targeted manipulations. Experiments conducted
with realistic SIP traffic demonstrate the high detection performance of
the proposed system at low false-positive rates.

1 Introduction

Voice-over-IP (VoIP) infrastructures provide a replacement of current circuit-
switched networks. VoIP and IP multimedia subsystem (IMS) technology reduces deployment costs and provides extensive functionality to operators and
end users. The advent of VoIP and IMS technology, however, gives rise to new
security threats originating from network-based as well as service-based vulnerabilities. For instance, IP networks connected to the Internet are plagued by
network attacks and malicious software. Unfortunately, VoIP infrastructures inherently possess properties attractive to developers of malicious software:

1. *Diversity.* Enterprise VoIP infrastructures consist of a large amount of heterogeneous network nodes covering mobile and wired end devices as well
   as gateway and registration servers of various manufacturers and brands. A
   single security breach in any of these nodes suffices to infiltrate the infrastructure, e.g, to eavesdrop communication at compromised nodes.

2. *Availability.* A second inherent property of VoIP infrastructures is availability, which is necessary for unimpeded communication between network
   nodes. Malicious software, such as a potential "VoIP worm", might exploit
   this property to rapidly propagate through the infrastructure comprising the
   vast majority of vulnerable nodes in a matter of minutes [30].

H. Schulzrinne, R. State, and S. Niccolini (Eds.): IPTComm 2008, LNCS 5310, pp. 90–106, 2008.

3. *Lack of transparency.* Terminal devices of VoIP services usually hide network and operating system details such as running processes and services from the end user. For instance, given a smartphone with VoIP capabilities it is hard to assess, whether the system has been compromised. Malicious software not disrupting functionality may control VoIP devices for a long period of time without being detected, for example to distribute unsolicited content.

It is likely from these features that current security threats will enter the realm of VoIP infrastructures in the near future. Especially the increasing commercialization of malicious software may further advance this development, e.g., as observed for the computer worm "Storm" [8].

A large body of research has focused on security defenses specific to IP telephony, such as the identification of fraudulent usage, the detection of denial-of-service attacks and the recognition of unsolicited content. Various concepts of misuse detection have been studied in the field of VoIP security, e.g., intrusion detection systems based on signatures [6, 19], rules [4, 36], protocol specifications [28, 32] and VoIP honeypots [15, 17]. Yet few research has considered the detection of *unknown and novel network attacks*, which arise with the appearance of zero-day exploits and computer worms. Systems based on misuse detection do not address this problem, as signatures or rules need to be available prior to the emerging security threats.

In this contribution, we propose a *self-learning system* for detection of unknown and novel attacks in the Session Initiation Protocol (SIP), which complements current VoIP security measures. The system enables identification of anomalous content by embedding SIP messages to a feature space and determining deviation from a model of normality. The system is "self-learning", as it is capable to automatically retrain itself in order to adapt to moderate changes in the network environment and traffic. Moreover, the retraining process is hardened against targeted manipulation. Experiments conducted on realistic SIP traffic and anomalous messages generated using a security testing tool demonstrate the high effectiveness of the proposed system at low false-positive rates – a criterion essential for practical deployment.

The rest of this paper is structured as follows: The self-learning system is introduced in Section 2 covering details on feature extraction, anomaly detection and retraining. Experiments on detection and run-time performance of the system with SIP traffic are presented in Section 3. Related work on VoIP intrusion detection is discussed in Section 4 and the paper is concluded in Section 5.

2 A Self-learning System

To protect VoIP infrastructures from unknown network attacks, we introduce a *self-learning system* for anomaly detection in the Session Initiation Protocol (SIP [26]). SIP is a widely used protocol for signaling communication and transmission of media in VoIP and IMS infrastructures. Network attacks targeting a

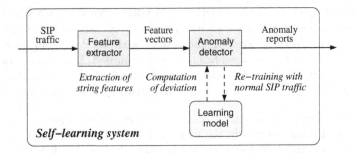

Fig. 1. Architecture of the self-learning system for SIP anomaly detection

VoIP system may occur in any element or content of incoming SIP messages; hence, our self-learning system is designed to analyze complete SIP messages as raw byte sequences – eliminating the need of preprocessing and normalization procedures. The architecture of our system is illustrated in Figure 1.

The basic processing stages of the system during operation are outlined in the following and discussed in further detail in the rest of this section.

1. *Feature extraction.* Incoming SIP messages are analyzed using a set of feature strings. Based on the occurrences of these strings, each messages is mapped to a feature vector reflecting individual characteristics of the message as captured by the feature strings. This feature extraction is covered in Section 2.1.

2. *Anomaly detection.* The feature vectors corresponding to SIP messages are compared against a model of normality. This model is either detecting global or local anomalies by computing distances in the underlying vector space. Anomalous SIP messages are flagged and reported by the system. The detection process is described in Section 2.2.

3. *Initialization & retraining.* On initial deployment of the system as well as on a periodic basis the learning model is updated using traffic flagged as normal. To prevent external manipulation of the learning process randomization, sanitization and verification of the model are performed. The initialization and retraining process is discussed in Section 2.3.

2.1 Feature Extraction

The syntax and structure of SIP messages is defined by the SIP protocol specification [26], yet such structure is not suitable for application of anomaly detection methods, as these usually operate on vectorial data. To address this issue we derive a technique for embedding SIP messages to a high-dimensional vector space, which reflects typical characteristics of the observed SIP traffic. This embedding has been successfully applied in the context of network intrusion detection [23] and its efficient implementation is detailed in [24].

A SIP message corresponds to a sequence of bytes and its content can be characterized by frequencies of contained substrings. For instance, the substrings "From", "To" and "Via" play an important role in the semantics of SIP. We define a set of *feature strings* S to model the content of SIP messages. Given a feature string $s \in S$ and a SIP message x, we determine the number of occurrences of s in x and obtain a frequency value $f(x, s)$. The frequency of s acts as a measure of its importance in x, e.g., $f(x, s) = 0$ corresponds to no importance, while $f(x, s) > 0$ reflects the contribution of s in x.

An embedding function ϕ maps all SIP messages X to an $|S|$-dimensional vector space by considering the frequencies of feature strings in S:

$$\phi : X \rightarrow \mathbb{R}^{|S|} \quad \text{with} \quad \phi(x) \mapsto (f(x, s))_{s \in S}$$

For example, if S contains the strings "foo.org" and "john", two dimensions in the resulting vector space correspond to the frequencies of these strings in SIP messages. Hence, the communication of a user "john" with a network node in the domain "foo.org" would be reflected in high frequencies of these strings in the respective SIP traffic.

However, it is impractical to define a set of feature strings S a priori, simply because not all important strings are known in advance, e.g., the user "john" might not be registered with the VoIP infrastructure when the self-learning system is deployed. To solve this problem the set of feature strings S is defined *implicitly* by introduction the notion of *tokens* and *n-grams*.

Tokens. SIP is a text-based protocol, thus, its content can be described in terms of textual tokens and words. An implicit set of feature strings in this view corresponds to all possible strings separated by specific delimiter symbols. If we denote all byte values by B and define $D \subset B$ as delimiter symbols, a set S referred to as *tokens* is given by

$$S := (B \setminus D)^*,$$

where $*$ is the Kleene closure corresponding to all possible concatenations of a set. The resulting set S has an infinite size, since strings of any length containing bytes from $(B \setminus D)$ are contained in S. A SIP message, however, comprises only a limited amount of such strings as the number of partitioned substrings in a message is bounded by its length.

The following example illustrates how a simplified SIP message is mapped to a vector space using the notion of tokens, where the set of delimiters is $D = \{\square, @, :, /\}$.

$$\phi(\ \texttt{BYE}\square\texttt{SIP:JOHN@DOE}\square\texttt{SIP/2.0}\ ) \longmapsto \begin{pmatrix} 1 \\ 2 \\ 1 \\ 1 \\ 1 \end{pmatrix} \begin{matrix} \texttt{BYE} \\ \texttt{SIP} \\ \texttt{JOHN} \\ \texttt{DOE} \\ \texttt{2.0} \end{matrix}$$

The vector at the right comprises frequency values for each token in the simplified SIP message. For instance, the two occurrences of the token "SIP" are reflected in the second column of the feature vector.

The granularity of feature extraction based on tokens can be controlled using the delimiter set D. The less delimiters are defined the more specific are the extracted tokens. For our self-learning system, we define the following delimiter symbols capturing generic SIP tokens such as header names, header values, recipients and attribute strings.

$$D = \{:,;,,,=,<,>,/,\text{SPC},\text{CR},\text{LF}\}$$

N-grams. Tokens are intuitive and expressive to the human analyst, still they may not always identify anomalous content of novel attacks, due to the definition of delimiter symbols in advance. An alternative technique for implicit definition of feature strings S are so called n-grams. Instead of partitioning a SIP message, feature strings are extracted by moving a sliding window of length n over the message content. At each position a substring of length n is considered and its occurrences are counted. Formally, the set of feature strings S referred to as *n-grams* is defined as

$$S := B^n,$$

where B^n corresponds to all possible strings of length n from the set B.

For example, if $n = 4$ we obtain 4-grams, which for the simplified SIP message considered in the previous section yields the following embedding to a feature vector space.

$$\phi(\ \texttt{BYE}\square\texttt{SIP:JOHN@DOE}\square\texttt{SIP/2.0}\ ) \longmapsto \begin{pmatrix} 1 \\ 1 \\ 2 \\ 2 \\ \vdots \end{pmatrix} \begin{matrix} \texttt{BYE}\square \\ \texttt{YE}\square\texttt{S} \\ \texttt{E}\square\texttt{SI} \\ \square\texttt{SIP} \\ \vdots \end{matrix}$$

Note, that similar to the previous example, the occurrences of the term "SIP" are reflected in the feature vector. In particular, the 4-gram "E□SI" is contained twice and its frequency is given in the third column of the feature vector. To simplify presentation further 4-grams are not shown in the example.

The vector space induced by n-grams is high-dimensional, e.g., for $n = 4$ there exist 256^4 different dimensions. Moreover, in the case of tokens the resulting space has infinite dimension as the underlying set S has infinite size. Computing and comparing vectors in such high-dimensional spaces seems infeasible at a first glance. However, for both types of features – n-grams and tokens – the number of feature strings contained in a single SIP message is linear in its length.

As a consequence, a SIP messages x of length l comprises at most l different n-grams or tokens, that is $\mathcal{O}(l)$ dimensions are non-zero in $\phi(x)$. This sparsity of the embedding $\phi(x)$ can be exploited to derive linear-time methods for extraction and comparison of feature vectors [24], which ultimately enables efficient anomaly detection over embedded SIP messages.

2.2 Anomaly Detection

An important extension to current VoIP security is the detection of unknown network attacks emerging from IP networks. Anomaly detection addresses this problem and complements signature-based analysis by modeling profiles for "normality". Although anomaly detection methods have been successfully applied in various incarnations of network intrusion detection, such as for identification of anomalous packet headers [13, 14] or payloads [23, 34], all methods share the same concept – *anomalies are deviations from a learned model of normality* – and only differ in concrete notions of normality and deviation.

The embedding of SIP messages to a vector space introduced in Section 2.1 enables expressing normality and deviation *geometrically*, which yields intuitive yet powerful learning models for anomaly detection. The basis for such geometric learning models is a distance function d, which assess the dissimilarity of two messages x and z by

$$d(x, z) = ||\phi(x) - \phi(z)||$$

and corresponds to a Euclidean distance in the vector space. Messages originating from a similar context, such as consecutive telephone calls, yield low distances and lie close to each other, while messages from different contexts, such as calls monitored at distinct locations, result in higher distances and are separated from each other. In this geometric view SIP messages are associated with points forming groups and clouds in the induced vector space depending on the underlying semantics and context.

For our self-learning system we focus on two simple realizations of geometric anomaly detection, which build on a *global* and *local* concept of normality and deviation thereof. Before introducing these concepts, we need to establish some notation. We denote the set of SIP messages used for learning by $X = \{x_1, \ldots, x_n\}$ and refer to a new incoming message as z. During the learning and anomaly detection process all messages $x_i \in X$ and z are represented as vectors $\phi(x_i)$ and $\phi(z)$ using the embedding function ϕ introduced in Section 2.1.

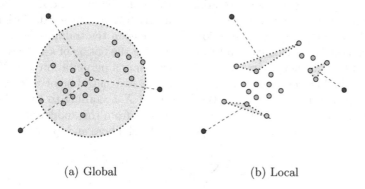

(a) Global   (b) Local

Fig. 2. Geometric anomaly detection

Global Detection. Network attacks often significantly deviate from normal traffic in terms of contained substrings. Thus, it is natural to define anomaly detection using a *global* model of normality capturing properties shared by the majority of X. A simple geometric shape reflecting this concept is a hypersphere. Normality is modeled by placing a hypersphere around the vectors of X and deviation is determined by the distance from the center μ of the hypersphere. Figure 2(a) illustrates a hypersphere enclosing a set of points, where anomalies are identified by large distances from the center.

The *smallest enclosing hypersphere* – the optimal model of normality – can be determined by solving the following optimization problem

$$\mu^* = \operatorname*{argmin}_{\mu} \max_{1 \leq i \leq n} ||\phi(x_i) - \mu||, \tag{1}$$

which returns the center μ^* of the hypersphere with the smallest radius containing all points in X. Unfortunately, unknown attacks in X may spoil this process and lead to hyperspheres with larger volume. This problem is alleviated by the technique of *regularization*, which "softens" the margin of the hypersphere, such that outliers and unknown attacks can be compensated. An introduction to this regularized learning model is provided in [12, 31], covering the respective theory as well as the efficient computation implemented in our self-learning system.

Once the center μ^* has been found, deviation δ from the model of normality is determined by computing the distance of an incoming message z from μ^*,

$$\delta(z) = ||\phi(z) - \mu^*||. \tag{2}$$

Application of the learned model in Equation (2) requires computing only a single distance value for each incoming message, as μ^* is fully determined from X during the prior learning phase.

Local Detection. If the SIP traffic monitored at a network node is inherently heterogeneous, e.g., at a large gateway, a global model of normality might not suffice for detection of unknown and novel attacks. The embedded messages are geometrically distributed in different clusters of points hindering application of a single enclosing hypersphere. To address this issue we extend our self-learning system with a *local* anomaly detection scheme, which assesses deviation of a message by considering only a fraction of messages in the training data.

A local model of normality can be derived using the notion of k-nearest neighbors. We define the neighbors of a vector $\phi(z)$ using a permutation π of X, such that the embedded message $x_{\pi[i]}$ is the i-th nearest neighbor of z in terms of distances. In other words, π sorts the vectors in X according to their distance from z in ascending order. A simple deviation δ_s from this model is calculated as the average distance of $\phi(z)$ to its k-nearest neighbors and given by

$$\delta_s(z) = \frac{1}{k} \sum_{i=1}^{k} ||\phi(z) - \phi(x_{\pi[i]})||. \tag{3}$$

Messages strongly deviating from their k-nearest neighbors yield a large average distance, while messages close to their neighbors get a low deviation score. Figure 2(b) illustrates the concept of k-nearest neighbors for $k = 3$. Anomalies deviate in Figure 2(b) from local normality in that they show a large average distance to the respective three neighboring points.

The average distance to a set of neighbors, however, is density-dependent. Points in dense regions yield low deviations, while points in sparse areas are flagged as anomalous, although they do not constitute attacks. Thus, we refine the deviation δ using the average distance between the k-nearest neighbors as normalization term

$$
\delta(z) = \frac{1}{k} \sum_{i=1}^{k} ||\phi(z) - \phi(x_{\pi[i]})||
$$
$$
- \frac{1}{k^2} \sum_{i=1}^{k} \sum_{j=1}^{k} ||\phi(x_{\pi[j]}) - \phi(x_{\pi[i]})||.
$$

(4)

The first term emphasizes points that lie far away from its neighbors, whereas the second term discounts abnormality of points in wide neighborhood regions.

In contrast to the global model in Equation (2), computing Equation (4) requires determining several distance values. In particular, for each incoming message $\mathcal{O}(|X|k^2)$ distance computations need to be performed for finding the k-nearest neighbors and calculating δ. Hence, for the local model of normality the amount of learning data X need to be constrained to achieve effective run-time performance. Experiments on the run-time as well as detection performance of the global and local anomaly detection methods are presented in Section 3.

2.3   Initialization and Retraining

Retraining enables the self-learning system to adapt itself to changes in the network environment, such as the presence of new terminal nodes or media services. To achieve this goal the learning model is trained on a periodic basis using network traffic previously flagged as normal. The interval of these retraining cycles depends on the monitored volume of SIP traffic and the estimated rate of changes in the network environment. For instance, devices processing millions of SIP messages per day might demand updates on a daily basis, while minor network nodes are sufficiently adapted in weekly or even monthly intervals.

For the initial deployment of the self-learning system, we assume that a coarse model of normality is already available, e.g., from another running system or generated using prototypical SIP traffic for the particular VoIP infrastructure. We thus restrict our scope to the retraining procedure, as initialization basicly resembles this process.

While automatic retraining provides ease of use to an operator, it introduces a new security vulnerability: attacks and anomalies in the training data may tamper learning and impede attack detection. In particular, an adversary could attempt to "poison" the learning model during retraining using specifically crafted

SIP messages, such that later attacks targeted against the system are not detected [9]. Thus, defenses against targeted manipulation of our learning system need to be provided.

Manipulation Defense. As a first defense against manipulations and unknown attacks the running self-learning system is applied to any potential training data, eliminating all attacks detectable using the present model of normality. To further harden the system against adversarial manipulation the following defense techniques are considered.

(a) *Randomization.* The traffic volume in enterprise VoIP infrastructures is huge and due to storage constraints only a limited fraction can be used for retraining. Instead of choosing a fixed partition, the self-learning system is retrained with randomly drawn samples which are collected from the monitored traffic between update cycles.

(b) *Sanitization.* The collected data is passed to a sanitization procedure filtering out irregular events, e.g., as proposed for network intrusion detection in [3]. In our self-learning system the collected SIP messages are sorted according to their deviation score and messages yielding the highest deviations are removed, e.g. a fraction of 5%-10%.

(c) *Verification.* Once a new model is trained it is applied concurrently with the previous one. As the new model originates from recent traffic, it is supposed to report similar or lower average deviation in comparison to the old. If after a fixed verification period the observed average deviation of the new model is too high, the update process fails and the model is discarded.

These defense methods particularly harden targeted manipulations against the self-learning system. On the one hand, randomization forces an attacker to constantly provide manipulated SIP messages to the system in order to resolve the random sampling. On the other hand, if the attacker sends too many manipulated messages to the system, the retrained model of normality will significantly deviate from normal traffic and, thus, a comparison with the old learning model will indicate various false anomalies. Finally, if an attacker controls the majority of traffic, he can be identified using techniques for detection of denial-of-service attacks, as proposed for instance in [21, 27, 29].

Calibration. As a last issue related to initialization and retraining of our self-learning system, we present a calibration procedure, which automatically provides a threshold for anomaly detection discriminating legitimate SIP traffic from anomalous or attack messages.

The calibration procedure builds on the concept of *cross-validation*. The preprocessed and sanitized training data is segmented into k partitions of equal size. A learning model is then trained on the SIP messages of $k - 1$ partitions and applied on the l messages of the remaining partition for computation of deviations scores $D = \{\delta_1, \ldots, \delta_l\}$. This process is repeated k times, such that for each partition i individual deviation scores D_i are determined.

A threshold t is then computed using the largest deviation scores in each partition D_i as defined by

$$t = \frac{1}{k} \sum_{i=1}^{k} \max(D_i), \quad v = \frac{1}{k} \sum_{i=1}^{k} (\max(D_i) - t)^2,$$

where t corresponds to the mean of the largest deviation scores and v to the empirical variance. The rational underlying this definition of t is that outliers and unknown attacks have been filtered from the training data and thus the largest deviation scores correspond to unusual but still legitimate traffic. The threshold is determined as the average of these scores, such that similar traffic is still accepted by the system.

The variance v acts as criterion for assessing the quality of the generated threshold. The randomization discussed in the previous section provides uniformly distributed samples from the running traffic, so that a high empirical variance of the threshold indicates irregularities in the training data. In this case the retraining process is aborted and the current calibrated learning model remains in operation.

3   Experiments

In the previous sections we have introduced the concept of a self-learning system for anomaly detection. To assess the capabilities of such a system in practice we conducted experiments on SIP traffic and artificial attacks generated using a security testing tool. In particular, we were interested to (a) evaluate the detection performance of our self-learning system on unseen attacks and (b) provide results for the run-time performance on real SIP traffic.

3.1   Evaluation Data

For our experiments we generated an evaluation data set comprising SIP request and response messages. These SIP traces contain contiguous SIP dialogs from a single SIP terminal as well as interleaved SIP dialogs recorded at a network edge ingress where multiple terminals are connected to. The messages originated mainly from several NGN test labs where multiple services and interworking tests are performed. Others are derived from research demonstrator setups where new services and functions are elaborated. The final portion of SIP traces are anonymized original signaling messages. This composition guarantees a very broad spectrum of correct SIP messages which partly contain Session Description Protocol (SDP [7]) payloads.

In contrast to Internet services, only few network attacks against SIP-based devices have been disclosed, most notably attacks identified using fuzzing techniques [1]. In the absence of a large collection of SIP attacks, we conducted our experiments using artificially generated attacks. A VoIP version of the security

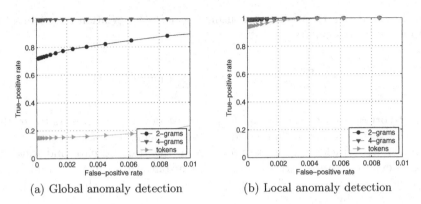

(a) Global anomaly detection   (b) Local anomaly detection

Fig. 3. Detection performance of the self-learning system for different string features

and syntax testing tool *Codenomicon Defensics*[1] was applied to produce several thousand anomalous SIP messages – covering syntactical anomalies as well as security probes for boundary condition, format string and input validation vulnerabilities. The generated anomalous SIP messages are post-processed to eliminate any remaining redundancy by permuting the sequence of the header fields and randomizing certain header and parameter values. This post-processing takes care that the original anomalous properties of each message persist, while detection via artifacts specific to the testing tool is largely prevented.

The resulting evaluation data set contains 4428 normal and 9999 anomalous SIP messages as raw byte sequences, where headers from the network and transport layer have been removed from each message. For all experiments the data set is split into *disjunct* training and testing partitions. The training data was used for learning models of normality and determining optimal model parameters, while the testing data was applied for generating results using the trained learning models.

3.2   Detection Performance

In order to evaluate the detection performance of our self-learning system, we implemented the feature extraction and anomaly detection methods presented in Section 2.1 and Section 2.2 in a prototypical system. Using this system we performed the following experimental procedure: 1,000 normal SIP messages are drawn from the training data, and models of normality are learned for different model parameters, such as the neighborhood size of the local anomaly detection method. The learning model achieving the best accuracy on the training data is then evaluated on 500 normal and 500 anomalous messages randomly drawn from the testing data. The procedure is repeated over 50 runs and the results are averaged.

Figure 3 depicts the detection performance of the self-learning system using 2-grams, 4-grams and tokens as string features. Figure 3(a) shows results for the global anomaly detection method and Figure 3(b) for the local anomaly detection

---

[1] Codenomicon DEFENSICS, http://www.codenomicon.com

method. The performance is presented as receiver operating characteristic, in short *ROC*, curves which show the false-positive rate of a methods on the x-axis and the true-positive rate on the y-axis for different thresholds. High detection accuracy is reflected in the top left of a ROC curve, while random detection corresponds to a diagonal line. Note that in Figure 3 the true-positive rate is given in the full interval 0 to 100%, while the false-positive rate shows only the range from 0 to 1%.

The local anomaly detection method yields a significantly higher detection accuracy in comparison to the global detection method. In particular, for all types of feature strings a true-positive rate over 97% is achieved *with no false-positives*. Moreover, for the 4-grams features over 99% of the attacks are detected – even though all attacks were unknown to the system during application. For the global anomaly detection method only the 4-gram features enable similar accuracy and in contrast the token features provide a very poor detection performance.

As the evaluation data used in our experiments originates from different sources, it expresses heterogeneous characteristics particularly suitable for application of a local anomaly detection method. The superior results presented in Figure 3(b) confirm this finding on real SIP traffic. Furthermore, the embedding to a vector space using 4-grams enables a very effective discrimination of normal traffic and attacks – by capturing particular substrings related to normal or anomalous messages – so that even the global method yields a high detection accuracy in the underlying vector space.

3.3   Run-Time Performance

In practice, the effectiveness of an intrusion detection system is determined by the detection rate as well as the run-time performance. In order to analyze the run-time of our self-learning system, we conducted experiments on a standard server system using AMD Opteron CPUs. The run-time, however, strongly depends on the complexity of the applied model of normality, which in turn is learned from provided training data. To model this effect, we varied the number of SIP messages used for learning from 100 to 1000 messages. For each size, we monitored the run-time performance of the system as well as the achieved detection accuracy.

In particular, we performed the following experimental procedure: 1,000 normal SIP messages are drawn from the evaluation data set and the run-time is measured for feature extraction and anomaly detection using a previously trained learning model. Based on the length of each SIP message the throughput of the system is estimated in terms of Megabits per second. The detection accuracy is determined using the setup applied in the previous experiment. The procedure is repeated 50 times and the results are averaged. As string features we focus on 4-grams, which yield the best detection in the previous experiment.

Figure 4 details the results of this experiment, where Figure 4(a) shows the run-time performance for varying size of training data and Figure 4(b) shows the corresponding detection accuracy of the self-learning system. The detection

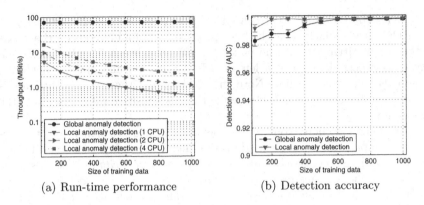

(a) Run-time performance   (b) Detection accuracy

Fig. 4. Run-time and detection performance for different sizes of training data

accuracy is given as *area under the ROC curve* (AUC), which simply integrates the true-positive rate over the false-positive rate of a ROC curve.

The run-time performance of the global anomaly detection method does not depend on the size of the training data. As discussed in Section 2.2 the training data is used to determine a single vector μ^* as learning model, and thus, the run-time is independent of the training size. The accuracy of the global anomaly detection scheme reaches an AUC value near 99% at around 600 training examples. On average a total of 70 Mbit per second in terms of SIP messages are processed using the global anomaly detection scheme.

In comparison the local anomaly detection method significantly depends on the size of the training data, as for each incoming data point a set of corresponding nearest neighbors need to be determined and evaluated. This process, however, can be easily parallelized, so that Figure 4(a) reports the run-time for a single CPU as well as SMP implementations with 2 and 4 CPUs. In this experiment, a detection accuracy at 99% is reached using a training data size of 300 instances which corresponds to a throughput between 2 and 6 Mbit per second depending on the number of CPUs.

4   Related Work

Security has been an active area of research in the domains of VoIP and IMS technology. Specifically for the SIP protocol considerable effort has been spent on identification and categorization of security threats [5, 18, 33]. Among these threats, attacks targeting the availability of VoIP play a salient role and much research has studied specific methods for detection and mitigation of denial-of-service attacks [21, 27, 29, 37].

Beside specific solutions, various concepts for generic VoIP intrusion detection have been proposed in the community. Sengar et al. [28] and Truong et al. [32]

devise specification-based detection systems using finite state machines for modeling VoIP protocols. Moreover, rule-based detection frameworks have been proposed – namely Scidive [36] and VoIP defender [4] – which provide efficient identification of VoIP attacks at different and across protocol layers.

Attack signatures as commonly used in network intrusion detection systems such as Snort [25] or Bro [20] were expanded to the SIP protocol by Niccolini et al. [19] and Apte et al. [2]. Similarly, Geneiatakis et al. [6] derived specific signatures for detection of malformed message content in the SIP protocol.

A different approach for detection of VoIP attacks using honeypots was proposed by Nassar et al. [15, 17], covering an individual "Honeyphone" as well as a network of emulated SIP devices. In both scenarios, attacks are identified when contacting the fake devices and detection rules are derived using Bayesian inference [16].

The self-learning system proposed in this contribution differs from previous research in VoIP security, as it does not require providing detection rules, signatures or protocol specifications prior to deployment. In particular, the system exploits characteristics of normal SIP traffic monitored at the network and, hence, enables identification of yet unknown attacks for which no signatures are available. In this view, it is similar to anomaly detection concepts proposed by Kruegel et al. [10, 11], Wang et al. [34, 35] and Rieck et al. [22, 23] for network intrusion detection.

5   Conclusions

Modern telecommunication in form of VoIP and IMS infrastructures requires effective defense against sudden network attacks. Current techniques for misuse detection such as signature-based intrusion detection systems fail to cope with fast emerging threats as appropriate attack signatures need to be available prior to a security incident.

We address this problem by introducing a self-learning system for detection of unknown and novel attacks in the SIP protocol. Our system proceeds by embedding SIP messages to a high-dimensional vector space defined over substrings contained in the messages. The vectorial representation induces geometric relations between SIP messages and enables the formulation of global and local anomaly detection methods. Using these methods the self-learning system generates a model of normality from given SIP traffic and identifies anomalous content in incoming SIP messages. Furthermore, the system supports retraining the model of normality automatically to adapt itself to changes in the network environment. The retraining process is hardened against manipulation and unknown attacks in the training data using randomization and sanitization techniques.

Experiments conducted on realistic SIP traffic and anomalous messages generated using a security testing tool demonstrate the high effectiveness of the proposed system. In particular, a prototypical implementation achieved a detection rate of over 99% with no false-positives in the corresponding experiments.

Depending on the applied anomaly detection method, the system is able to process SIP traffic up to 70 Megabits per second, while still providing high accuracy.

Although the realized throughput of our implementation does not yet comply with recent products for the VoIP and IMS market targeting Gigabit networks, it may provide defense in combination with filtering techniques relieving the impact of high traffic volumes. Future research will focus on techniques for pre-filtering of SIP traffic as well as development of run-time improvements.

References

[1] Abdelnur, H., Festor, O., State, R.: KiF: A stateful SIP fuzzer. In: Proc. of International Conference on Principles, Systems and Applications of IP Telecommunications (IPTCOMM), pp. 47–56 (2007)

[2] Apte, V., Wu, Y.-S., Garg, S., Singh, N.: SPACEDIVE: A distributed intrusion detection system for voice-over-ip environments. In: Abstract Paper at International Conference on Dependable Systems and Networks (DSN) (2006)

[3] Cretu, G., Stavrou, A., Locasto, M., Stolfo, S., Keromytis, A.: Casting out demons: Sanitizing training data for anomaly sensors. In: IEEESP (to appear, 2008)

[4] Fiedler, J., Kupka, T., Ehlert, S., Magedanz, T., Sisalem, D.: VoIP Defender: Highly scalable SIP-based security architecture. In: Proc. of International Conference on Principles, Systems and Applications of IP Telecommunications (IPTCOMM), pp. 11–17 (2007)

[5] Geneiatakis, D., Dagiuklas, T., Kambourakis, G., Lambrinoudakis, C., Gritzalis, S., Ehlert, S., Sisalem, D.: Survery of security vulnerabilities in session initial protocol. IEEE Communications Surverys & Tutorials 8(3), 68–81 (2006)

[6] Geneiatakis, D., Kambourakis, G., Lambrinoudakis, C., Dagiuklas, T., Gritzalis, S.: A framework for protecting a SIP-based infrastructure against malformed message attacks. Computer Networks 51(10), 2580–2593 (2007)

[7] Handley, M., Jacobson, V., Perkins, C.: SDP: Session Description Protocol. RFC 4566 (Proposed Standard) (July 2006)

[8] Holz, T., Steiner, M., Dahl, F., Biersack, E., Freiling, F.: Measurements and mitigation of peer-to-peer-based botnets: A case study on storm worm. In: First USENIX Workshop on Large-Scale Exploits and Emergent Threats (LEET) (2008)

[9] Kloft, M., Laskov, P.: A poisoning attack against online anomaly detection. In: NIPS Workshop on Machine Learning in Adversarial Environments for Computer Security (2007)

[10] Kruegel, C., Toth, T., Kirda, E.: Service specific anomaly detection for network intrusion detection. In: Proc. of ACM Symposium on Applied Computing, pp. 201–208 (2002)

[11] Kruegel, C., Vigna, G.: Anomaly detection of web-based attacks. In: Proc. of 10th ACM Conf. on Computer and Communications Security, pp. 251–261 (2003)

[12] Laskov, P., Gehl, C., Krüger, S., Müller, K.R.: Incremental support vector learning: Analysis, implementation and applications. Journal of Machine Learning Research 7, 1909–1936 (2006)

[13] Lee, W., Stolfo, S., Mok, K.: A data mining framework for building intrusion detection models. In: Proc. of IEEE Symposium on Security and Privacy, pp. 120–132 (1999)

[14] Mahoney, M.: Network traffic anomaly detection based on packet bytes. In: Proc. of ACM Symposium on Applied Computing, pp. 346–350 (2003)

[15] Nassar, M., Niccolini, S., State, R., Ewald, T.: Holistic VoIP intrusion detection and prevention system. In: Proc. of International Conference on Principles, Systems and Applications of IP Telecommunications (IPTCOMM), pp. 1–9 (2007)

[16] Nassar, M., State, R., Festor, O.: Intrusion detection mechanisms for VoIP applications. In: Proc. of VoIP Security Workshop (VSW) (2006)

[17] Nassar, M., State, R., Festor, O.: VoIP honeypot architecture. In: Proc. of IEEE Symposium on Integrated Network Management (IM), pp. 109–118 (2007)

[18] Niccolini, S.: VoIP security threats. Draft of IETF Working Group Session Peering for Multimedia Interconnect (SPEERMINT) (2006)

[19] Niccolini, S., Garroppo, R., Giordano, S., Risi, G., Ventura, S.: SIP intrusion detection and prevention: recommendations and prototype implementation. In: Proc. of IEEE Workshop on VoIP Management and Security, pp. 47–52 (2006)

[20] Paxson, V.: The bro 0.8 user manual. Lawrence Berkeley National Laboratory and ICSI Center for Internet Research (2004)

[21] Reynolds, B., Ghosal, D.: Secure IP telephony using multi-layered protection. In: Proc. of Network and Distributed System Security Symposium (NDSS) (2003)

[22] Rieck, K., Laskov, P.: Detecting unknown network attacks using language models. In: Büschkes, R., Laskov, P. (eds.) DIMVA 2006. LNCS, vol. 4064, pp. 74–90. Springer, Heidelberg (2006)

[23] Rieck, K., Laskov, P.: Language models for detection of unknown attacks in network traffic. Journal in Computer Virology 2(4), 243–256 (2007)

[24] Rieck, K., Laskov, P.: Linear-time computation of similarity measures for sequential data. Journal of Machine Learning Research 9, 23–48 (2008)

[25] Roesch, M.: Snort: Lightweight intrusion detection for networks. In: Proc. of USENIX Large Installation System Administration Conference LISA, pp. 229–238 (1999)

[26] Rosenberg, J., Schulzrinne, H., Camarillo, G., Johnston, A., Peterson, J., Sparks, R., Handley, M., Schooler, E.: SIP: Session Initiation Protocol. RFC 3261 (Proposed Standard), Updated by RFCs 3265, 3853, 4320, 4916 (June 2002)

[27] Sengar, H., Wang, H., Wijesekera, D., Jajodia, S.: Fast detection of denial of service attacks on ip telephony. In: Proc. of International Workshop on Quality of Service (IWQoS), pp. 199–208 (2006)

[28] Sengar, H., Wijesekera, D., Wang, H., Jajodia, S.: VoIP intrusion detection through interacting protocol state machines. In: Proc. of International Conference on Dependable Systems and Networks (DSN), pp. 393–402 (2004)

[29] Sisalem, D., Kuthan, J., Ehlert, S.: Denial of service attacks targeting a SIP VoIP infrastructure: Attack scenarios and prevention mechanisms. IEEE Networks Magazine 20(5) (2006)

[30] Staniford, S., Paxson, V., Weaver, N.: How to 0wn the internet in your spare time. In: Proc. of USENIX Security Symposium (2002)

[31] Tax, D., Duin, R.: Support vector domain description. Pattern Recognition Letters 20(11–13), 1191–1199 (1999)

[32] Truong, P., Nieh, D., Moh, M.: Specification-based intrusion detection for H.232-based voice over IP. In: Proc. of IEEE Symposium on Signal Processing and Information Technology (ISSPIT), pp. 387–392 (2005)

[33] VoIPSA. Voip security and privacy threat taxonomy. Report of Voice over IP Security Alliance (2005)

[34] Wang, K., Parekh, J., Stolfo, S.: Anagram: A content anomaly detector resistant to mimicry attack. In: Recent Adances in Intrusion Detection (RAID), pp. 226–248 (2006)

[35] Wang, K., Stolfo, S.: Anomalous payload-based network intrusion detection. In: Recent Adances in Intrusion Detection (RAID), pp. 203–222 (2004)

[36] Wu, Y.-S., Bagchi, S., Garg, S., Singh, N.: SCIDIVE: a stateful and cross protocol intrusion detection architecture for voice-over-ip environments. In: Proc. of International Confernce on Dependable Systems and Neteworks (DSN), pp. 433–442 (2004)

[37] Zhang, G., Ehlert, S., Magedanz, T., Sisalem, D.: Denial of service attack and prevention on SIP VoIP infrastructures using DNS flooding. In: Proc. of International Conference on Principles, Systems and Applications of IP Telecommunications (IPTCOMM) (2007)

Secure SIP: A Scalable Prevention Mechanism for DoS Attacks on SIP Based VoIP Systems

Gaston Ormazabal[1], Sarvesh Nagpal[2], Eilon Yardeni[2], and Henning Schulzrinne[2]

[1] Verizon Laboratories
gaston.s.ormazabal@verizon.com
[2] Department of Computer Science, Columbia University
{sn2259,ey2125,hgs}@cs.columbia.edu

Abstract. Traditional perimeter security solutions cannot cope with the complexity of VoIP protocols at carrier-class performance. We implemented a large-scale, rule-based SIP-aware application-layer-firewall capable of detecting and mitigating SIP-based Denial-of-Service (DoS) attacks at the signaling and media levels. The detection algorithms, implemented in a highly distributed hardware solution leveraged to obtain filtering rates in the order of hundreds of transactions per second, suggest carrier class performance. Firewall performs SIP traffic filtering against spoofing attacks; and request, response and out-of-state floods. The functionality and performance of the DoS prevention schemes were validated using a distributed test-bed and a custom-built, automated testing and analysis tool that generated high-volume signaling and media traffic, and performed fine grained measurements of filtering rates and load-induced delays of the system under test. The test-tool included SIP-based attack vectors of spoofed traffic, as-well-as floods of requests, responses and out-of-state message sequences. This paper also presents experimental results.

Keywords: SIP, DoS, DDoS, VoIP, Security, Signaling Attacks, Application Layer Firewall, Deep Packet Inspection, Distributed Computing, Scalability.

1 Introduction

Denial-of-Service (DoS) attacks are explicit attempts to disable a target thereby preventing legitimate users from making use of its services. DoS attacks continue to be the main threat facing network operators. As telephony services move to Internet Protocol (IP) networks and Voice over IP (VoIP) becomes more prevalent across the world, the Session Initiation Protocol (SIP) [1] infrastructure components, which form the core of VoIP deployments, will become targets in order to disrupt communications, gain free services, or simply to make a statement. Since DoS attacks are attempts to disable the functionality of the target, as opposed to gaining operational control, they are much more difficult to defend against than traditional invasive exploits, and are practically impossible to eliminate. We designed and demonstrated effective defenses against SIP-specific DoS attacks, with the capability to operate at carrier-class rates. We addressed all four aspects that an effective solution against DoS attacks should cover namely, definition, detection, mitigation, and validation.

H. Schulzrinne, R. State, and S. Niccolini (Eds.): IPTComm 2008, LNCS 5310, pp. 107–132, 2008.

Definition characterizes DoS attacks on the SIP infrastructure, examining the threat taxonomy to identify specific areas that require research focus. *Detection* distinguishes the attack traffic from valid traffic, whereas *mitigation* reduces the impact of DoS attacks on the target infrastructure. Detection and mitigation schemes work in tandem and aim to maintain adequate bandwidth and resources for legitimate traffic, throttle the malicious packets and streams, and perform continued analysis to enhance the detection and mitigation capabilities. *Validation* of the defense scheme for correct operation, involves modeling the system behavior, building a testing setup capable of generating VoIP DoS attacks, quantifying their impact on protected and unprotected VoIP infrastructure, and measuring the effectiveness of the defense strategies.

This paper examines the SIP threat model and DoS taxonomy in Section 2. An overview of related work is presented in Section 3. This is followed by SIP-specific DoS solutions and filter design in Section 4. The system architecture and implementation aspects are addressed in Section 5. The benchmarking methodology and the secureSIP toolkit with the experimental results are covered in Section 6. Conclusions are presented in Section 7.

2 Problem Definition: The SIP Threat Model

This section examines the SIP threat model as the basis for formulating requirements for our detection and mitigation strategies. Since SIP is used on the public Internet, the threat model assumes an environment in which attackers can potentially read any packet on the network. Furthermore, the fact that SIP runs over UDP, provides opportunities for attacks like *spoofing*[1], hijacking, and message tampering. Attackers on the network may also be able to modify packets, perhaps at some compromised intermediary node. We note that the security of SIP signaling, however, is independent from protocols used to secure transmission of media. For example, SRTP (RFC 3711) [2] may be used for end-to-end encryption of the RTP encapsulated audio stream. This section is based on the VoIP Security Alliance (VOIPSA) threat taxonomy report [3] together with definitions in RFC 3261– SIP [1].

There are three basic types of DoS attacks that may occur over a VoIP network, namely, exploitation of implementation flaws, exploitation of application level syntactic vulnerabilities, and flooding of the SIP signaling channel or the RTP media channels. These attacks may target a VoIP component, such as a SIP proxy, or supporting servers, such as a DNS, or a DHCP server. A DoS attack against a supporting server affects the VoIP service in different ways. Attacks against a domain's DNS server result in denial of VoIP calls destined to users in that domain. Attacks against an authorization service, used by a SIP proxy to store address-of-record (AOR) to User Agent (UA) mappings, can result in denial of service to the UAs registering with this proxy. This document, however, focuses exclusively on attacks against SIP-based components. The following sub-sections describes the three basic types of attacks in the SIP-specific context.

---

[1] Usually referred to as IP spoofing, where an attacker fakes or falsifies the source IP address in a SIP message header.

DoS Due to Implementation Flaws

Attack occurs when a specific flaw in the implementation of a VoIP component is exploited by a carefully crafted packet sent to cause unexpected behavior. The attacked software component, in this case, has typically not been implemented robustly enough to handle these unexpected packets, and also suffers from inadequate software assurance testing or negligent patching. The malformed packet interacts with installed software and may cause excessive memory or disk consumption, extra CPU processing, a system reboot or system crash. The targeted vulnerability may originate in different levels of the network protocol stack, such as the TCP layer or the SIP layer, or in the underlying operating system or firmware [5] and [6]. Examples of implementation flaws attacks include:

Malformed signaling: Unusually long or syntactically incorrect SIP message packets, referred to as "malformed", are sent to the UA degrading its performance, resulting in its inability to process normal setup and teardown messages for calls.

Invalid call setup messages: A number of invalid call set up messages, such as a SIP **ACK** request when none is expected, are sent to cause the endpoint to crash, reboot, or exhaust all of its resources.

DoS Due to Exploitation of Application-level Vulnerabilities

Attack occurs when a feature of the VoIP protocol syntax is manipulated to cause a DoS attack. Examples of application level attacks against SIP-based components include:

Registration hijacking: The SIP registration mechanism allows a UA to identify itself to a registrar as a device whose location is designated by an AOR. Attackers register their devices with other users' AORs, thereby directing all requests for the affected user to the attacker's device.

Call hijacking: Once a dialog has been established, subsequent requests are sent to modify the state of the dialog or session. For example, the attacker injects a **302 Moved Temporarily** message in an active session, thereby hijacking the media session.

Media sessions modification: The attacker spoofs **re-INVITE** messages, thereby modifying security attributes of a session, reducing Quality of Service (QoS), or redirecting media streams to another device for wiretapping.

Session teardown: The attacker spoofs a **BYE** message and injects it into an active session, thereby tearing down the session.

Amplification attacks: The attacker creates bogus requests containing a falsified source IP address, and a corresponding **Via** header field identifying a targeted host, as the originator of the request. Subsequently, the attacker sends this request to a large number of SIP network elements, thereby causing hapless SIP UAs or proxy servers to generate a DoS attack aimed at the target host, typically a server. Similarly, DoS can also be carried out on an individual by using falsified **Route** header field values in a request that identifies the target host, and then sending these messages to forking proxies that will amplify messages sent back to the target. **Record-Route** is used to similar effect when the attacker is certain that the SIP dialog initiated by a request will result in numerous transactions originating in the backwards direction. An attacker can also register a large number of contacts designating the same host for a given AOR, in order to use the registrar and any associated proxy servers as amplifiers in a DoS attack. Attackers may also attempt to deplete a registrar's available memory and disk resources, by registering large numbers of bindings. Multicast may be also used to transmit SIP requests, greatly increasing the potential for DoS attacks.

Note that if the volume of an application-level DoS attack is sufficient to cause resource depletion, or excessive performance degradation, the attack is reclassified as a *flooding* DoS attack.

DoS Due to Flooding

Attack occurs when a large number of packets are sent to a target IP component; hence any Internet based service is vulnerable to DoS attacks. DoS attacks on services that run on IP represent the broader perspective. The attacker floods the network link by generating more packets than the recipient can handle, or overwhelms the target making it too busy processing packets from the attack and hence unable to process legitimate packets. Flood attacks for IP components include UDP **SYN** floods, ICMP **echo** packets, where the attacker generates a large number of packets directed to the targeted sources. When this attack is done using multiple distributed sources, such as *botnets*[2], the result is a Distributed DoS (DDoS) [4]. Both the DoS and the DDoS problem for generic IP systems have received a great deal of attention over the years and several commercial products already exist that address this threat. The focus of this work, however, is on DoS, and its corresponding DDoS variety, specifically targeted to VoIP and VoIP-based components, for which currently no protection exists. Flooding DoS attacks to VoIP-based server components can be broadly classified into two categories:

Signaling floods: The most prominent of this category of attacks involves sending a large number of SIP **INVITE** or **REGISTER** messages originating from one or multiple SIP UAs to cause excessive processing at a SIP proxy server - thus delaying or dropping legitimate session establishment messages. There is a computational expense associated with processing a SIP transaction at a proxy server. This expense is greater for stateful than for stateless proxy servers as stateful servers maintain client and server transaction state machines, while stateless do not. Stateful servers are therefore more susceptible to flooding than the stateless type. Floods of messages directed at SIP proxy servers may lock up proxy server resources and prevent desirable traffic from reaching its destination.

Media floods: A range of ports known to be open for legitimate RTP streams are randomly flooded with meaningless and/or un-sequenced packets, over-claiming bandwidth and hindering the RTP QoS.

---

[2] Botnet describes a collection of software robots, or bots, running autonomously on groups of zombie computers controlled remotely. It also refers to a network of computers using distributed computing software.

3 Related Work

There has been previous effort to protect VoIP deployments from DoS threats. An early evaluation of firewalls for VoIP security was proposed in [7], but it lacked concrete architectural and implementation aspects. A mitigation strategy for flooding DoS attacks on media components using a dynamic pinhole filtering device that blocks all traffic not associated with a legitimate call was previously developed as part of an earlier phase of this research. We designed and built a scalable SIP-aware application layer firewall based on the principle of dynamic pinhole filtering for the RTP streams [8] and [9]. This was the first attempt to combine the SIP proxy with a commercial hardware based, fast packet processing application server, to achieve carrier-class performance and full SIP conformance.

Wu, Y. et al. [10] and Niccolini, S. et al. [11] have applied intrusion detection and prevention mechanisms to safeguard the SIP infrastructure, while the work described in [12] makes use of finite state machines to achieve similar goals. An interesting approach involving VoIP "honeypots" was proposed in [13]. Extensive work on detecting DoS attacks on IP telephony environments has been published in [14], [15], [16], [17] and [18]. Although promising, none of the architectures and algorithms proposed so far offer a comprehensive DoS mitigation strategy that scales up to the performance needs and complexity of carrier-class VoIP deployments, because they are based on software solutions. We are not aware of any specific performance measurements for any of these software based systems. Our solution leverages the Cloud-Shield Technologies CS-2000 distributed hardware platform [18] that combines the processing speed of a distributed network processor platform with the full functionality of a SIP proxy.

4 SIP-specific DoS Solutions and Filter Design

We propose a novel approach that builds on our earlier SIP-aware firewall design, introducing two phases of VoIP traffic filtering, a dynamic pinhole filter (Filter I) for the media traffic, followed by SIP-specific filters (Filter II) for the signaling traffic. Figure 1 gives a high-level view of a SIP security system consisting of these two levels of filtering. Filter I provides the first line of defense by allowing only the signaled media to traverse the firewall, preventing any DoS attacks on the media processing end points. Additionally, it provides standard static filtering for traditional attacks, described as "other attack traffic" in Figure 1, by only allowing traffic on the standard SIP (5060) port. The SIP signaling channel, however, can itself contain SIP-based DoS and hence the motivation forOP Filter II. Filter II, which is comprised of a series of SIP-based filters provide the second line of defense by protecting the SIP signaling port (and thereby the SIP-proxy) from DoS attacks.

This paper covers design, realization, and analysis of SIP-specific filters including a return routability filter, rate-limiting filter and state-validation filter. Together, these filters can protect the SIP infrastructure against known and currently achievable

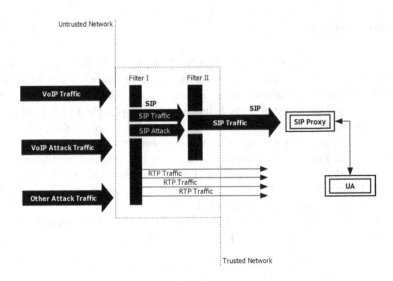

Fig. 1. Two-phase filtering (SIP and media)

spoofing attacks, flood-of-requests and flood-of-response attacks, and "out-of-state" signaling attacks. We built a scalable security system prototype based on the CS-2000 fast packet processing application server, combined with the Columbia SIP Proxy *sipd*, developed as part of the Columbia InterNet Multimedia Architecture (CINEMA) [19], enabling an effective realization of the proposed SIP security architecture for carrier-class VoIP deployments.

The filters are realized in the deep-packet processing module (DPPM) of the SIP-aware firewall system deployed at a VoIP network perimeter. The DPPM includes very high speed silicon databases that use content addressable memory (CAM) technology for table look-up and keeping state. Additionally, the DPPM is equipped with a regular expression engine used for pattern matching logic in state validation. Some of the filters require the use of a firewall control protocol (FCP) to update state tables in the DPPM, while others result from packet logic manipulation directly on the DPPM, and directly updated on the CAM tables. The filters include a return routability check, and a series of filters based on SIP method manipulation mechanisms that can be used to cause flooding.

Return Routability Filter

The return routability filter is designed to detect and block spoofed incoming requests by using the SIP Digest Authentication[3] mechanism. The SIP protocol specifies that upon receiving a request, other than **CANCEL** and **ACK**, a proxy can challenge the request initiator to provide assurance of its identity. The challenge is sent in a **Proxy-Authorization** header field of a **407 Proxy Authentication Required** response, including a

---

[3] Digest Authentication provides message authentication and replay protection only, without message integrity or confidentiality.

freshly computed *nonce*[4] value. The initiator then retries the request with the proper credentials, along with a pre-shared secret[5], in a **Proxy-Authorization** header field.

The proxy responds with the digest authentication challenge whenever it gets a new request, simultaneously instructing the firewall to create a filter rule using the FCP. This firewall filter will then block all further unauthenticated requests from the same IP address from getting to the proxy. If the request originator responds with the correct challenge response, the proxy removes the filter rule from the firewall. The filter is temporary, with a short expiration time on the order of seconds. This process can be viewed as *layer-7-controlled-layer-3-filtering*. An example call flow diagram of the return routability filter operation is shown in Figure 2. The corresponding detailed call flows are in Appendix A.

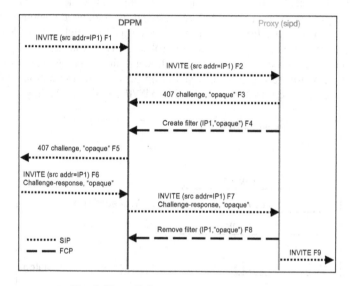

Fig. 2. The call flow for digest authentication

In the call flow described in Figure 2, the DPPM intercepted the first **INVITE** request (F1) with IP1 as the source IP address. The DPPM did not find a match in the filter table and hence forwarded the request to the proxy (F2). The proxy received the **INVITE** request and responded with a **407** message containing the challenge (F3), and also by sending an FCP message (F4) to create a temporary filter rule blocking further requests from IP1. The filter rule was based on the nonce that was part of the authentication challenge, and was expected to be included in the authentication response unchanged. This FCP message was processed by the DPPM and the filter was created. When the

---

[4] A nonce is a uniquely generated string used for one challenge only, computed using IP address, timestamp, username, password and realm, and has a lifetime of 60 seconds.

[5] SIP allows the use of "null authentication", where a proxy can authenticate an "anonymous" username with no password. The return routability filter was designed based on null authentication, which is a necessary and sufficient condition to establish return routability to the request initiator, avoiding the extra overhead inducing password management process.

new SIP request arrived, the DPPM intercepted it (F6) and tried to match the source IP address with the IP address in the filter table. If there was no match then the request was blocked. Otherwise, if the nonce values were equal, the request was forwarded to the proxy (F7) and the proxy successfully authenticated the **INVITE** request and sent an FCP message (F8) to remove the filter from DPPM. By configuring the proxy not to keep any state until the return routability was verified by the firewall, the possibility of proxy overloading with potentially spoofed request floods could be eliminated.

SIP Method-based Filters

Method-based filters were designed to mitigate attacks that exploit protocol vulnerabilities to cause flood DoS. The design focused on rate-limiting SIP requests and response floods, and also using state validation mechanisms to achieve this.

SIP is a request/response protocol. A request and its associated responses constitute a SIP transaction, which follows the same signaling path through a set of SIP servers. A SIP call, as presented in Figure 3, can be broken down to four levels of granularity. A call is composed of one or more dialogs, while a dialog contains one or more transactions. A transaction can be a client transaction or a server transaction; and each of the client/server transactions can be divided into **INVITE** and non-**INVITE** types.

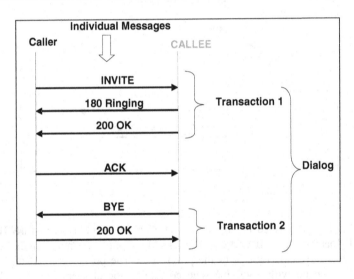

Fig. 3. Levels of granularity in a SIP session

A SIP dialog is identified by a combination of the **Call-ID**[6], **From** tag and **To** tag. A SIP transaction is identified by the **branch**[7] parameter of the **Via** header and the **Method** name in the **CSeq** field. These fields can be used to construct respective *dialog ID* and *transaction ID* identifiers. Both of these identifiers are used to maintain the corresponding state

---

[6] Call-ID is a globally unique identifier for a call, generated by the combination of a random string and the phone's host name or IP address.

[7] The branch parameter of the Via header is a unique value across space and time that is created by a UA for a particular and specific request.

information. Rate-limiting can be applied either at the dialog level or at the transaction level; however, for every SIP method except for **BYE** and **CANCEL**, the dialog level does not provide sufficiently precise parameters to perform meaningful thresholding. For example, it may be hard to distinguish a legitimate **INVITE** from a spurious one(s) if they have different transaction IDs. Hence, for every other method, transaction level is the most effective way to narrow down to more specific parameter thresholds for filtering.

Dialog based attacks include **CANCEL** and **BYE** attacks, that can only happen at the dialog level, as both are dialog terminating requests. In a **CANCEL** attack, a spurious **CANCEL** request is sent before the final response of a dialog/transaction, thereby terminating the dialog prematurely, hence causing DoS. **BYE** attacks involve *sniffing*[8] session parameters (such as Call-ID), and generating illegitimate **BYE** requests to terminate an on-going session without knowledge of any of the involved end-clients. To keep track of **BYE** messages, **record-routing** has to be enabled at the proxy. Alternatively, the firewall at the perimeter may be used to identify unsolicited **BYE** messages. In addition to **BYE** message filtering based on dialog ID, a table of all participating URIs must be maintained to verify whether **contact header** field of the **BYE** message corresponds to one of the participating URIs. The **REFER** attack, similar to a man-in-the-middle attack, involves an eavesdropper manipulating the **Referred-By** header to cause DoS. **REFER** attacks can be mitigated by deploying **S/MIME** to detect possible manipulation of the **Referred-By** header data, but are not covered in our current filter design.

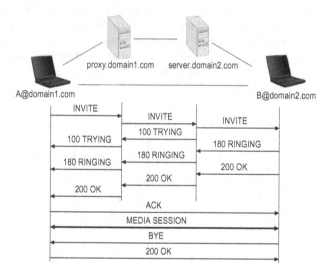

Fig. 4. SIP trapezoid

Transaction-based attacks on a proxy include floods of **INVITE** requests containing same transaction ID, thus causing processing overload. Furthermore, a re-**INVITE** attack can change on-going session parameters by issuing or resending **INVITE** or **UPDATE**

---

[8] Sniffing the Call-ID in a SIP message is easy to accomplish given the *clear-text* nature of the protocol in its basic form, i.e. non-encrypted.

requests with different parameters. Transaction-based rate-limiting filters detect and mitigate floods of **INVITE** requests with the same transaction ID, and all of their associated responses, to stop them at the perimeter.

The SIP trapezoid, as specified in RFC 3261 and shown in Figure 4, is introduced to describe the method-based rate-limiting filters in more detail. The transactions depicted in the trapezoid are shown in Figure 5 in their client/server relationships. In reference to the interaction between the User Agent Client (UAC) and an outbound proxy, the request is an **INVITE**, and the associated responses are comprised of **100 Trying, 180 Ringing** and **200 OK**. From the proxy's perspective, this is an **INVITE** server transaction, with the **200 OK** ending the transaction and taking the proxy to **Terminate** state. Accordingly, the messages at proxy are rate-limited to one **INVITE** per transaction (incoming); a finite number of **100 Trying** per transaction (outgoing); a finite number of **180 Ringing** per transaction (outgoing); and one **200 OK** per transaction (outgoing).

The finite number of allowed **100 Trying** and **180 Ringing** messages is flexible and should be decided by different network parameters depending on the complexity of the routed network. To allow for retransmissions, the threshold for **INVITE** and **200 OK** messages may also be raised from one message to a higher finite number that can be experimentally determined from the network configuration under test. Arbitrary messages that do not conform to the above sequence may leave the proxy in an unwanted state. A similar rate-limiting analysis can be applied to the transactions between the outbound proxy and inbound proxy, and User Agent Server (UAS) and inbound proxy. The number of **INVITE**s from a particular UAC is also limited to a single call at a time, or to some particular value based on the size of n-way conferences allowed. For example, if an **INVITE** message is from a particular UAC's IP address already in the CAM table, with its state label being intermediate (**in-progress**), then the new **INVITE** will be rejected. In order to avoid state exhaustion at the proxy, no state will be kept during any of these steps.

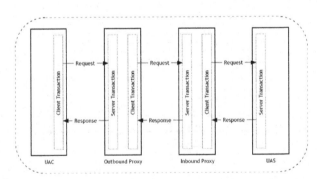

Fig. 5. SIP client-server interaction through inbound and outbound proxy

State Validation Filters

Extending the analysis in the previous section to the transactions between the UAC and outbound proxy, it is not only the rate but also the order of arrival of messages that may leave the proxy in an unexpected state. The schematics in Figures 6 and 7 describe the state machines for **INVITE** client and server transactions, respectively. A detailed description of **INVITE** and **non-INVITE** client/server transactions can be found in [1].

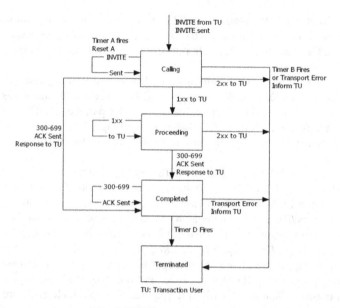

Fig. 6. INVITE client transaction

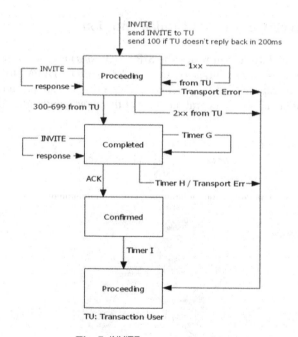

Fig. 7. INVITE server transaction

Using the SIP state machine protocol, it is possible to define the set of expected messages and hence discard the sequences considered out-of-state. The firewall filter will have state tables that point to the current state of a transaction from *(Proceeding,*

Completed, Confirmed, Terminated}, and a set of rules governing the transitions. The table structure has the format *{Transaction ID, Timestamp, State, Acceptable message codes, Next state}*. This table is applicable for both rate-limiting as well as state-validation types of method-based filters.

We have also implemented similar table-driven rate-limiting rules to filter non-standard **1xx** (except **100** and **180**), non-standard **2xx** (except **200**), and **300-699** responses to a finite number per second, depending on network parameters. This will eliminate specific handling for each of the messages in the range. The non-standard messages are logged in a table having the structure *{Transaction ID, Timestamp, Non-standard message code}*.

Rate-limiting is also performed on **INVITE** requests coming from a single source IP and identical **From** URI, in case of outbound proxy, and **INVITE** requests coming to a single destination IP, and **To URI**, in case of inbound proxy. The timestamp differences between a new **INVITE** and an identical **INVITE** in the above table should be within one second, or else the request is rejected. This is defined in the firewall filter table as *{Source/Destination IP, Timestamp, **From/To** URI}*.

Lastly, filtering at the dialog level helps the identification of spurious **BYE** messages by using the dialog ID of a message, and rejecting BYE messages that are not part of an existing Dialog. This filtering requires a simple table structure *{Dialog ID, Timestamp}*.

5   System Architecture and Implementation

We deployed an architecture in which the SIP proxy (*sipd*) uses the wire-speed packet processing and CAM capabilities of the CS-2000 server DPPM to boost overall packet-processing capacity. In this section, we describe the architecture and the implementation components as integral modules of the underlying framework.

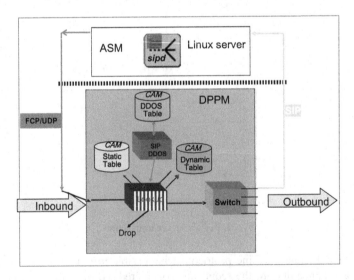

Fig. 8. Architecture components of CloudShield CS-2000

Components required for implementing the architecture shown in Figure 8 include a SIP proxy, data plane execution in the DPPM, and firewall control. The SIP proxy supports "null authentication" and a new FCP message[9] to create/remove a filter from the DPPM using {IP, nonce}. The CS-2000 data plane execution modules run filters as applications on DPPM. Filters intercept network traffic and monitor, process, and drop packets using static filtering of pre-defined ports (e.g., SIP, ssh, port 6252), dynamic filtering of legitimately opened ports (e.g., RTP) and a switch layer function performing switching between the input ports. The data plane also includes a return routability filter table, with table entries containing {IP address, string (nonce), state-label, timeout value}. Additionally, the data plane features a counter that maintains a count of requests/second for comparison with a pre-determined threshold to detect request floods. When the threshold is crossed, the DPPM starts applying the rate-limiting policy. The DPPM tries to match SIP requests with filters in the state table by matching on dialog ID and transaction ID.

The SIP proxy server runs within the CS-2000 application server module (ASM). The proxy server interacts with the DPPM using the Firewall Control Protocol (FCP) for the return routability filter. The Firewall Control Module, in the SIP proxy, talks with the DPPM, intercepts SIP call setup messages, gets nonce from the **407 Proxy Authentication Required** header, gets RTP ports from the SDP payload and maintains call state, pushes filter for SIP UA (nonce) being challenged, and pushes dynamic table updates to the data plane. FCP can be used by multiple SIP proxies that control one or more CloudShield firewalls. FCP supports the new return routability create/remove filter messages, using the same FCP message format described in [8], with the addition of a random string option to accommodate the nonce.

SIP messages are related using message lookup tables, leveraging the DPPM built-in CAM databases for very low latency lookups. Aged lookup tables are implemented to track call, dialog and transaction relationships using the {dialog ID table, transaction ID table} tuple. Messages are identified by type (request or response) and code (request method or response status code). The "error status message" rate limiter performs error message limiting within the context of a valid transaction. The error rate limiters are implemented as high-speed counters in SRAM, with granularity of one second.

Return Routability Filter

The rate at which the SIP proxy can handle incoming SIP requests is mainly bounded by CPU power. When digest authentication was enabled, this rate decreased, as for every incoming SIP request the proxy had to both process a new challenge and validate the provided authorization data. This process has been thoroughly analyzed in [20] and experimentally verified in our test-bed, as detailed in Section 6 below. An attack flood of spoofed **INVITE** messages can then overload the proxy as the authentication of each spoofed request is attempted. The CS-2000 detected the SIP request floods, and a rate-limiting policy was applied in order to reduce the load from the proxy. The type of rate-limiting policy has a direct impact on the number of false-negatives ("bad" requests that were not blocked) and/or false-positives ("good" requests that were filtered). In the rate-limiting policy suggested in this work, the

---

[9] A detailed description of the FCP protocol can be found in reference [8].

firewall established a temporary filter, based on IP address and nonce, whenever a new request needs to be authenticated. The filter was used to block any further unauthenticated request attempts coming from the same source, from getting to the proxy. When the proxy got the request, it responded with the digest authentication challenge, and simultaneously issued an FCP message to create the filter in the DPPM. If the request originator successfully responded with the correct challenge response, the proxy removed the filter from the firewall. The filter was also temporary in the sense that it expired after some short period of time on the order of seconds. The filter can be based on the **From** URI or the source IP address.

The detailed design of return routability filters involved the interception of incoming **INVITE** requests at DPPM, and extraction of source IP addresses from the requests. If no corresponding entry for the source IP address was found in the filter's CAM table, the incoming request was forwarded to the proxy. This rule ensured that the first packet from a UA always reached the proxy regardless of filters deployed. After receiving the **INVITE** request, the proxy responded back to the UA with a **407 Proxy Authentication Required** challenge, and also simultaneously sent an FCP message, containing source IP and nonce value, to the DPPM to create a filter table entry. All subsequent **INVITE** requests coming from the same UA were intercepted by DPPM, as before, but at this stage, a corresponding filter entry for this source IP was found to already exist. At that point, if the incoming request contained the same nonce value as previously stored in CAM table filter entry, the request was forwarded to the proxy, and CAM tables were updated to allow all incoming packets from this source IP (white-list), for a short interval of time. In the event of no match, however, the request was dropped right at the perimeter. White-lists are dynamic and the lifetime of each entry was automatically extended with every packet containing the correct nonce. In our experiments, we used thirty seconds for the white-list auto expiry default.

Rate-limiting Filters

Rate-limiting filters required the extraction of the dialog ID (DLGID) and transaction ID (TXNID) from every received SIP request, and their storage in different and subordinate CAM tables. Since dialog ID and transaction ID are variable length fields, a CRC-32 bit hash algorithm was applied in order to generate a fixed length index in the CAM tables, to enable state keeping. DLGID was the 32 bit integer calculated by Hash {**From IP, To IP, Call ID**} and for every DLGID entry in CAM database, there was a subordinate table for associated TXNIDs. TXNID was the 32 bit integer calculated by Hash {**Top Via: BranchID, CSeq Command Value**}. If a TXNID was not found to be duplicated, normal call processing execution continued. If TXNID was found to be duplicated, then the packet was dropped before it reached the proxy. Ideally only one SIP request message should have been allowed per TXNID, however, because of network conditions, the same request may need to be retransmitted multiple times. To allow for this, a window of finite retransmissions before packet drop was implemented and the system trained to find the optimum window length for a given network configuration. The purpose of this window was for optimization to prevent "false positives". A CAM table entry was maintained for each authenticated **INVITE**, and state was incremented for each client so that a filter was put up to accept messages corresponding to only the next allowed state, or any termination message. A timeout filter was also used to terminate a session after a predetermined interval.

Upon receiving a new subsequent status message, if the status message record is valid then the request was accepted, if bogus, the packet was dropped. Additionally, the rate of requests per transaction per second was also checked not to exceed a selected finite number (6), after which packet was dropped. The rate at which messages are received in any state from the session/UA, were limited to a predefined rate, and handled within the state a session/UA is in. Arbitrary error messages at high rates were also blocked if the rate crosses a pre-determined threshold.

SIP Transaction State Validation

This filter validated the state of each SIP transaction for each message received and complemented the other filtering mechanisms. The use of the CS-2000 regular expressions engine allowed validation of every arriving message as "in-state" or "out-of-state" in one CPU cycle, resulting in high scalability and performance. Messages that resulted in invalid states were dropped and the transaction state was always maintained in a legitimate state. The DPPM made an entry for the first transaction request, and logged all subsequent status messages in a buffer, on a per transaction basis. Each received packet was added to the status messages table for the original transaction. If the received status message fit a valid state pattern, it was accepted while if it was an invalid pattern, the message was dropped.

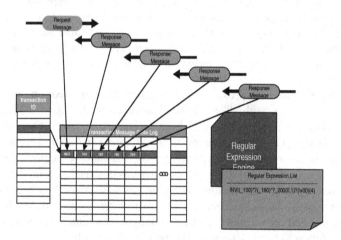

Fig. 9. Regular expressions for request-response transaction

The implementation of the rate-limiting filters, in more detail, involved extraction of the dialog ID and transaction ID from an incoming packet, and comparison with the dialog ID table and subordinate transaction ID table stored in the CAM databases. If a corresponding entry already existed, the message type was entered in a transaction message code log, as shown in Figure 9. The string formed by the sequence of messages {INVI_100_180_180_200}, in the example in Figure 9, was matched with the rules list {INVI(_100)*?(_180)*?_200{0,1}?(\x00){4}} that codify the SIP state machine pre-stored regular expression rules. The use of wild cards in regular expression syntax afforded validation of all permutations of allowed states in a single operation. If a match was found, the new arriving message was inferred to adhere to the state validation rules, and allowed to go through to the proxy; otherwise it was discarded, and also removed from the transaction message log, e.g., in the sequence {INVITE, 100, 180, 200, 180, 200}; the filters will only allow the sequence {INVITE, 100, 180, 200}, while the last {180, 200} messages are removed, as the second 180 was already out of state.

6 Benchmarking Methodology

The primary aim of the benchmarking methodology was the verification of correct filter functionality in effectively preventing DoS attacks, and their performance and scalability at carrier-class traffic rates. The security system was verified for its functional accuracy, by developing a novel benchmarking toolkit that provided an extensible and automated interface for testing and analysis based on distributed computing. The test tool generated high-volume SIP sessions, including SIP-based attack vectors of spoofed traffic, as well as floods of SIP requests, SIP responses and out-of-state message sequences. The analysis module presents the data in easy-to-read table form results.

Prior to determining the filters effectiveness, the baseline capacity of the proxy server, for our specific hardware configuration, had to be first established by launching signaling traffic to find the maximum server call handling rate, for a given set of concurrent calls. As described in [21], the call rate handling capacity is directly related to the processing power of the computer hosting the proxy server, and the number of concurrent calls is dependent on the machine's available memory. We evaluated performance of the system with 100,000 concurrent calls of legitimate traffic, as a reference number for comparing performance under different experimental call rates configurations[10].

For our experiments, two proxy setup configurations were used: one without digest authentication, and one with digest authentication enabled. Digest authentication is necessary to distinguish spoofed requests from normal traffic; hence it was also required by the filters design. Our measurements of the difference in baseline capacity of these two setups are in accordance with expected results, and validate the previously reported numbers by Salsano, S., et al. [20]. Since the filters, as designed, rely on digest authentication, we used the maximum performance from this setup as the baseline reference for comparisons against measurements carried out with filters turned on. We begin by describing our test-bed architecture, hardware configuration, attack generation tools and mechanisms, followed by an analysis of the experimental results.

Test-bed Architecture

The generation, measurements and analysis of the SIP DoS attacks were performed in a controlled VoIP test-bed, consisting of hardware and software components used to generate high-volume loads. The test-bed was comprised of an array of seventeen Sun Fire X2100 servers, equipped with an AMD Opteron 2-GHz processor and 2GB of RAM, running Ubuntu Server OS. The test-bed also included the proxy server *sipd*, resident on the application server module (ASM) of the CloudShield firewall, which consisted of a dual Pentium-III 1-GHz based CPU with 1GB of RAM, running Linux 2.6.17-10.

---

[10] The number 100,000 was arrived at from performing various experiments to be sufficient to obtain a statistically significant sample.

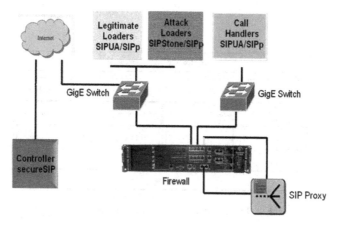

Fig. 10. Test-bed architecture

The setup was equipped with the SIPstone [22] and SIPp [23] suites of SIP traffic generation and benchmarking tools, configured in "loader" and "handler" modes[11]. SIPp is a robust, easily configurable open-source tool, with customizable XML-based scenarios for traffic generation and handling. SIPp uses multiple threads to generate higher call rates per loader-handler pair, as compared to other user agents. In the Sun Fire X2100 server cluster configuration used in these experiments, each loader/handler pair can generate a maximum of 300 calls per second (CPS). SIPstone is a Columbia-developed signaling test-suite with enhancements for null-digest authentication, and generation of spoofed requests, both capabilities required for these experiments. Each Sun fire X2100 server equipped with SIPstone can generate 1200 spoofed requests/sec in standalone mode.

The seventeen machines in the setup were loaded with both of these test tools to enable a dynamic configuration, and were connected to the CloudShield firewall using GigE switches as shown in Figure 10. One of these machines was configured to host the test-bed controller running **secureSIP**, a web-based control software described in the next section, and the remaining sixteen machines were dynamically configured as traffic generators in loader/handler mode or in individual attack generator mode (e.g., spoofers). Within this distributed setup, network traffic was also captured in real-time using **wireshark**[12] and analyzed [24].

Controller - *secureSIP*
The measurements and validation procedures are controlled by **secureSIP**, a web-based control software using distributed computing processes that provides the tester a user interface to launch, terminate, manage, measure, analyze and store the outcomes of the benchmarking tests as shown in Figure 11.

---

[11] Loaders are used to generate calls, behaving as callers, while handlers receive these calls, thus behaving as callees.
[12] A network protocol analyzer that allows packet capture from live networks, as well as reading packets from saved "capture" files.

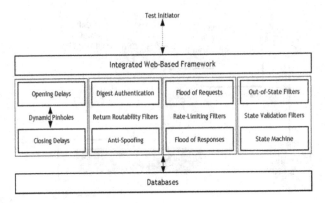

Fig. 11. Architecture of secureSIP controller

Each of the remaining sixteen machines was loaded with **secureSIP** clients, which communicated with the **secureSIP** controller on a predefined channel over UDP (port 6252), to perform the required actions. The **secureSIP** clients used a combination of SIPp, SIPstone and SIPUA (used only for registration [19]). Clients support digest authentication, and were capable of generating spoofed messages, floods of requests/responses, and out-of-state messages to verify performance of return routability, rate-limiting and state validation filters respectively. Each client updated traffic statistics in real time to a central relational database server using MySQL [25]. The data consolidation at one central server facilitated easy correlation, real-time performance analysis, exporting results to spreadsheets and drawing charts to visualize patterns from historical data.

Performance Bench-marking
The first step was the establishment of the test-bed setup baseline, without any security enhancements or attack traffic, defined as the base capacity of the proxy server. These measurements were performed first with digest authentication turned-off, and subsequently enabled. SIPp was used to generate legitimate traffic. After obtaining proxy baseline numbers with digest authentication enabled, attack traffic was introduced into the network and performance of the setup without filters was evaluated. Subsequently, filters were turned on to evaluate the portion of good and attack traffic that was filtered out. For attack traffic generation, SIPstone was used to create spoofed call attempts. Floods of requests, responses and out-of-state messages were generated using SIPp. The protocol analyzer was also used to analyze the flow of network packets to estimate the proportion of dropped calls that were part of legitimate or attack traffic respectively. The validation and measurements were all performed at two different loads; at full capacity, to determine the maximum performance of the tested configuration as a reference point, and at half capacity of the proxy to cover the typical workloads in a carrier-class VoIP service.

Base Capacity
Base capacity was determined by generating legitimate traffic through SIPp, using multiple pairs of loaders and handlers, controlled in an automated fashion by the

secureSIP controller. Base capacity was found by incrementing call rate until the proxy was unable to respond to all the incoming requests, dropping legitimate calls. As each loader/handler pair was able to generate 300 CPS, the load was incremented pair by pair until the base capacity for proxy setup without authentication was found to be 690 CPS, with three pairs. Network traffic analysis using **wireshark** also confirmed this base capacity.

Using the same methodology, the digest authentication mechanism was enabled, and the new base capacity was found. The load on proxy server was incremented pair by pair, finding the new base capacity at 480 CPS, using two pairs. The results showed the call handling capacity of the proxy dropped from about 690 CPS to 480 CPS. Considering the proxy server was operating in stateful mode, these results validate the analysis and measurements published in [20], although we present the results at an order of magnitude higher call rates. The observed call drop is attributed to the extra processing required for computation of nonce and hashing, and the extra SIP messages that are introduced into the network as previously shown in Figure 2. Since computation of hashing algorithms causes only 30% of the overhead, the main reason for the drop (70%) in performance is due to the extra messages that digest authentication introduces into the network. For all our subsequent measurements below, we assumed digest authentication to be enabled, and comparisons of call rate handling capacity for various filters are always made against this benchmark of 480 CPS.

Methodology for Filter Effectiveness Validation and Measurement

The next three sub-sections provide a detailed treatment of DoS through spoofing, method-based flooding and composite attacks. These sets of experiments measured the impact of the DoS attacks on the unprotected SIP infrastructure and evaluated the effectiveness of the firewall filters in preventing these attacks.

DoS through Spoofing

These tests verified the operation of the return routability filters. The setup was similar to the performance benchmarking section, with SIPp generating legitimate traffic, and SIPstone used to launch traffic with spoofed addresses. Incremental spoofed traffic attacks were launched under two different workloads, at full capacity (480 CPS) and half capacity representing average load conditions (240 CPS). As expected, the digest authentication mechanism was able to remove the spoofed traffic; however, the performance penalty was such that even at half capacity, the proxy was only able to process 3000 spoofed attempts per second, before collapsing. The return routability filters, however, once enabled, dropped spoofed calls right at the perimeter, thus saving the proxy server from processing the additional messages. Our measurements show that the filters removed all of the 16800 spoofed attempts per second generated by our test-bed, at its maximum workload configuration. It should be noted here that this maximum number is *the limit of our test-bed configuration* and not the limit of the firewall.

DoS through SIP Method-Based Attacks

These tests verified the operation of the rate-limiting and state-validation filters. Method-based attacks included three sub-types, consisting of floods of repetitive

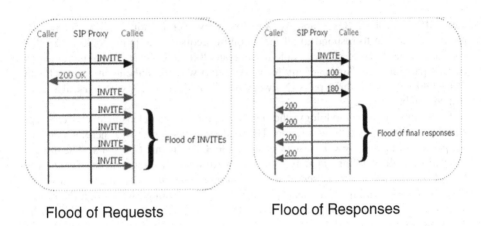

Flood of Requests   **Flood of Responses**

Fig. 12. Different types of rate-limiting attacks

requests, repetitive responses and various sequences of out-of-state messages. The proxy was subjected to these types of attacks, with and without the corresponding filters. We defined three types of attacks – request flood, response flood and out-of-state flood.

The first attack consisted of sending a flood of **INVITE** requests (exact replica of each other, with same transaction ID) after the call was setup with the initial request. The second type consisted of sending a barrage of responses (any of **1XX Provisional**, **2XX Success** or **4XX Error**). The last type consisted of flooding the proxy with requests/responses sequences in random order. For all three types of attack traffic, the flood packets that follow the first packet will have the same transaction ID, as seen in the call-flow diagrams schematic view in Figure 12. SIPp loader/handler pairs were used to generate both legitimate and attack traffic for these measurements.

DoS Filters Performance Results
Measurements from the different test scenarios, including benchmarking, return routability filters and rate-limiting filters are summarized in Table 1 below. The array of sixteen machines was used to generate the high volumes of different types of legitimate as well as attack traffic. As observed in Table 1, in general, the inbuilt software mechanisms in the SIP proxy provide negligible performance against the attack traffic in the absence of filters. In particular, the proxy server, without the benefit of filters, breaks down with fewer than 200 spoofed requests, when already at maximum, but even at half load, the proxy is only able to handle less than 3000 spoofed attempts per second. In the same setup, but with filters turned on, the performance increased considerably, to well over 17,000 spoofed attempts per second. As noted earlier, the amount of attack traffic handled in these experiments was determined by our specific test-bed hardware constraints, and not by the capacity of the filters.

The effectiveness of the rate-limiting filters can be assessed by comparing results in similar setup initially without the filters, with results with filters enabled. While setup without filters can only deal with a maximum flood of fewer than 600 calls (requests) per second, filters pushed the handling capacity to over 7,000 attacks per

Table 1. Measurements from different test scenarios

	Firewall Filters OFF			Firewall Filters ON		
	Good	Attack	CPU	Good	Attack	CPU
	CPS	CPS	Load	CPS	CPS	Load
Traffic Composition			%			%
Non-Auth Traffic	690	0	88	690	0	88
	240	0	20	240	0	40
Auth Good Traffic	480	0	81	480	0	82
Auth Good Traffic +	240	2950	84	240	16800	41
Spoof Traffic	480	195	85	480	14400	83
Auth Good Traffic +	240	3230	84	240	8400	41
Flood of Requests	480	570	86	480	7200	83
Auth Good Traffic +	240	2970	87	240	8400	41
Flood of Responses	480	330	87	480	7200	83
Auth Good Traffic +	240	2805	86	240	8400	40
Flood of Out-of-State	480	290	85	480	7200	82

second. Even at average normal load settings, at half the capacity of proxy server, the results without filters were not impressive, as the proxy could only handle up to 3,000 attacks per second. For measurements involving attack traffic comprised of floods of responses, or floods of out-of-state messages, the performance without filters was slightly worse, as the proxy collapsed around 300 attacks per second, when at maximum load. At half load, 2,800 attacks per second could be handled. The addition of filters, however, enhanced the proxy capacity to over 8,000 attacks per second, which again was the maximum attack traffic we could generate in our hardware configuration.

Furthermore, we measured zero false positives and negligible false negatives. Through protocol analysis, we could confirm that none of the legitimate traffic was dropped while the filters dropped 99% of attack traffic, leading to 1% false negatives. The filter algorithm is adaptive, and requires training, based on network conditions, before it can isolate bad traffic from good traffic. Due to this adaptive nature of filters, some amount of attack traffic manages to pass through filtering system, giving a rate of false negatives of 1%. Additionally, since the filters did not drop any packet before they were trained, rate of false positives was zero.

DoS through Composite Attacks

To test our DoS prevention mechanisms against extreme but perhaps more realistic scenarios, as attackers will attempt every attack permutation at once, all the above described attacks were launched together. Different **secureSIP** clients in the distributed network were configured to launch different types of attack traffic. For instance, the sixteen machines in the network could be configured, such that six machines generated spoofed traffic, four machines flooded the network with requests, two machines introduced out-of-state messages and the remaining four were used to generate legitimate traffic. The proxy was subjected to this composite attack, initially with no filters, and subsequently with all the filters loaded on the firewall. All the other measurement and traffic generation conditions were kept the same.

As seen in the measurement results in Table 2, a proxy conforming to the protection mechanisms specified in [1] was unable to withstand composite attacks. Without filters, even at half capacity, the proxy was only able to handle less than 1000 CPS of different types of attack traffic before it started dropping legitimate calls within a few seconds of the attack (18 seconds in this specific instantiation). At maximum capacity, the results were much worse, and showed practically no tolerance for any kind of attack traffic. Once filters were enabled, the proxy dealt efficiently with as much attack traffic as could be generated in our test-bed. Both at half load capacity, and full capacity, the proxy server showed no sign of performance lag, operating with reasonable CPU resources. Even in case of composite attacks, we observed zero false positives and almost negligible false negatives with filters turned on.

Table 2. Performance measurements of composite attacks

Filters	Traffic Rate (CPS)				Avg. CPU (%)
	Good	Spoof	Flood of Req	Out of State	
Off	240	800	800	800	85
On	240	7200	2400	2400	42
Off	480	100	100	100	87
On	480	4800	2400	2400	83

Benchmarking Summary
The CPU resource consumption increases linearly with the increased attack traffic when the firewall filters are disabled. But once enabled, the filters off-loaded the proxy of all the attack traffic, as evidenced by the non-increasing resource consumption versus attack traffic load, in all of the measurements. When all filters were enabled, they worked together to protect the system under test from a variety of attack traffic. No perceivable performance loss or overhead was observed in the SIP proxy, even at the peak of the attack traffic, clearly indicating that the hardware filters had removed the attack traffic completely.

7 Conclusions and Future Work

The solution presented in this work experimentally demonstrated various SIP vulnerabilities that may potentially result in DoS attacks. As perimeter security is becoming a factor of prime importance to VoIP service providers and carriers, this work suggests highly scalable detection and mitigation strategies against these new SIP-specific DoS attacks. This implementation leveraged a fast parallel processing packet-processing server using CAM databases for storing the huge connection state tables associated with high volumes of concurrent calls, while providing full SIP conformance. A large-scale distributed test-bed, including a high-powered SIP-specific DoS attack tool, was built to measure and verify the effectiveness and scalability of the solution. The web-based controller, also developed as a part of this framework, provides an effective tool-kit for easy use in testing laboratories. The prototype filtering handling capacity presented, with rates in the hundreds of calls per second, is indicative that these systems can be utilized in carrier class environments. In the short term, enhancements that cover a broader range of attack cases may be desirable. For example, floods of **INVITE**s (and/or responses) with *different* transaction IDs within dialogs, is a closely related, but harder, problem that needs further study. Longer term, the application of anomaly detection, pattern recognition and learning systems, will also be desirable for future systems based on the concepts developed in this work.

The methodologies described in this paper, are applicable to wireline and wireless topologies, and can be extended to secure emerging technologies such as Internet Multimedia Systems (IMS), as well as presence and unified communications infrastructures. Other efforts also continue to extend SIP to support Presence, Messaging and Unified Communications such as Web Services SIP (WSIP), leveraging the dual http and SIP stacks, to allow for reliable unified communication services. The work presented in this paper, may also help achieve secure end-to-end communication for these services.

Acknowledgements

We would like to thank Stu Elby, Vice President of Network Architecture, Chris Mayer, Vice President of Systems Integration and Testing, and Mike Daigle, Vice President of Network Planning, at Verizon Technology Organization, for the sponsorship of this work, and continued interest and support. We would also like to thank Robert Ormsby, David Dumas, James Flowers and Haidar Chamas, also at Verizon Technology Organization for their continued support and encouragement. Haidar also offered extensive commentary on the paper. David Helms from CloudShield Technologies provided excellent technical support in the implementation and fine-tuning of the filters. At Columbia University we would like to thank Jonathan Lennox, the primary architect of our SIP proxy *sipd*, and Sankaran Narayanan the primary architect of our benchmarking tool, SIPStone, for their contributions.

References

[1] Rosenberg, J., Schulzrinne, H., Camarillo, G., Johnston, A., Peterson, J., Sparks, R., Handley, M., Schooler, E.: SIP: Session Initiation Protocol, RFC 3261 (June 2002)

[2] Baugher, M., McGrew, D., Naslund, M., Carrara, E., Norrman, K.: The Secure Real-time Transport Protocol (SRTP), RFC 3711 (March 2004)

[3] VOIPSA VoIP Security and Privacy Threat Taxonomy, http://www.voipsa.org/Activities/VOIPSA_Threat_Taxonomy_0.1.pdf

[4] Worldwide, I.S.P.: Security Report, Arbor Networks (September 2005), http://www.arbor.net/downloads/Arbor_Worldwide_ISP_Security_Report.pdf

[5] CERT Advisory CA-, -06 Multiple vulnerabilities in implementations of SIP (2003), http://www.cert.org/advisories/CA-2003-06.html

[6] Wieser, C., Laakso, M., Schulzrinne, H.: Security testing of SIP implementations. Technical Report (February 20, 2005), http://www1.cs.columbia.edu/~library/TRrepository/reports/reports-2003/cucs-024-03.pdf

[7] Roedig, U., Ackermann, R., Steinmetz, R.: Evaluating and Improving Firewalls for IP-Telephony Environments. In: IP-Telephony Workshop (IPTel) (April 2000)

[8] Yardeni, E., Schulzrinne, H., Ormazabal, G.: SIP-aware Application Layer Firewall with Dynamic Pinholes for Media, Columbia Technical Report (2006), http://www.cs.columbia.edu/~hgs/papers/Yard06_Large.pdf

[9] Yardeni, E., Patnaik, S., Schulzrinne, H., Ormazabal, G., Helms, D.: SIP-aware Application Layer Firewall with Dynamic Pinholes for Media, NANOG 38 (October 2006), http://www.nanog.org/mtg-0610/mcbride.html

[10] Wu, Y., Bagchi, S., Garg, S., Singh, N., Tsai, T.K.: Scidive: A stateful and cross protocol intrusion detection architecture for VoIP environments. In: International Conference on Dependable Systems and Networks (June 2004)

[11] Niccolini, S., Garroppo, R.G., Giordano, S., Risi, G., Ventura, S.: SIP Intrusion Detection and Prevention: Recommendations and Prototype Implementation. In: IEEE Workshop on VoIP Management and Security (April 2006)

[12] Sengar, H., Wijesekera, D., Wang, H., Jajodia, S.: Intrusion Detection Through Interacting Protocol State Machines. In: International Conference on Dependable Systems and Networks (2006)

[13] Nassar, M., State, R., Festor, O.: VoIP Honeypot Architecture. In: IEEE International Symposium on Integrated Network Management (May 2007)

[14] Chen, E.Y.: Detecting DoS Attacks on SIP Systems. In: IEEE Workshop on VoIP Management and Security at NOMS (April 2006), http://www.comsoc.org/confs/noms/2006/docs/14_Chen.ppt

[15] Sengar, H., Wijesekera, D., Wang, H., Jajodia, S.: Fast Detection of Denial-of-Service Attacks on IP Telephony. In: IEEE International Workshop on Quality of Service (June 2006)

[16] Geneiatakis, D., Dagiouklas, A., Kambourakis, G., Lambrinoudakis, C., Gritzalis, S., Ehlert, S., Sisalem, D.: Survey of Security Vulnerabilities in Session Initiation Protocol. IEEE Communications Surveys and Tutorials 8(3) (2006)

[17] Sisalem, D., Kuthan, J., Ehlert, S.: Denial of Service Attacks Targeting a SIP VoIP Infrastructure- Attack Scenarios and Prevention Mechanisms. IEEE Network Special Issue on Securing VoIP 20(5) (2006)

[18] CloudShield,CS- (2000), http://www.cloudshield.com/Products/cs2000.asp

[19] Columbia InterNet Extensible Multimedia Architecture (CINEMA), http://www.cs.columbia.edu/IRT/cinema

[20] Salsano, S., Veltri, L., Papalilo, D.: SIP security issues: the SIP authentication procedure and its processing load. IEEE Network 16(6) (2002)

[21] Singh, K., Schulzrinne, H.: Failover and load sharing in SIP telephony. In: International Symposium on Performance Evaluation of Computer and Telecommunication Systems (SPECTS), Philadelphia, Pennsylvania (July 2005), http://www1.cs.columbia.edu/~kns10/publication/sipload.pdf

[22] Schulzrinne, H., Narayanan, S., Lennox, J., Doyle, M.: SIPstone - benchmarking SIP server performance. sipstone 0402.pdf (April 2002), http://www.sipstone.org/files/

[23] SIPp, http://sipp.sourceforge.net

[24] wireshark, http://www.wireshark.org/docs/man-pages/wireshark.html

[25] MySQL, Open Source SQL server, http://www.mysql.com

Appendix A

Call Flows during Digest Authentication, as seen in Figure 2

The first INVITE message received by proxy server from user agent does not contain any credentials.

F1 INVITE UA -> Proxy

```
INVITE sip:test1@cs.columbia.edu SIP/2.0
Via: SIP/2.0/UDP 127.0.0.1:7898
Max-Forwards: 70
From: sip:test5@cs.columbia.edu
To: sip:test1@cs.columbia.edu
Contact: sip:test5@127.0.0.1:7898;transport=UDP
Subject: SIPstone invite test
CSeq: 1 INVITE
Call-ID: 1736374800@lagrange.cs.columbia.edu
Content-Type: application/sdp
Content-Length: 211
v=0
o=user1 53655765 2353687637 IN IP4 128.3.4.5
s=Mbone Audio
t=3149328700 0
i=Discussion of Mbone Engineering Issues
e=mbone@somewhere.com
c=IN IP4 128.3.4.5
t=0 0
m=audio 3456 RTP/AVP 0
a=rtpmap:0 PCMU/8000
```

After receiving the first INVITE message, the proxy sends back a "407 Authentication Required" asking user for authentication. This message contains a freshly computed nonce value that must be sent back by user to prove their identity.

F3 407 Proxy Authentication Required Proxy -> UA

```
SIP/2.0 407 Proxy Authentication Required
Via: SIP/2.0/UDP 127.0.0.1:7898
From: sip:test5@cs.columbia.edu
To: sip:test1@cs.columbia.edu; tag=2cg7XX0dZQvUI1bUkFYWGA
Call-ID: 1736374800@lagrange.cs.columbia.edu
CSeq: 1 INVITE
Date: Fri, 14 Apr 2006 22:51:33 GMT
Server: Columbia-SIP-Server/1.24
Content-Length: 0
Proxy-Authenticate:Digest
realm="cs.columbia.edu",
        nonce="6ydARDP51P8Ef9H4iiHmUc7iFDE=",
        stale=FALSE,
        algorithm=MD5,
        qop="auth,auth-int"
```

User replies back to the "407 Authentication Required" challenge by providing authorization credentials, the nonce value to the proxy server:

F6 INVITE UA -> Proxy

```
INVITE sip:test1@cs.columbia.edu SIP/2.0
Via: SIP/2.0/UDP 127.0.0.1:7898
Max-Forwards: 70
From: sip:test5@cs.columbia.edu
To: sip:test1@cs.columbia.edu
Contact: sip:test5@127.0.0.1:7898;transport=UDP
Subject: SIPstone invite test
CSeq: 3 INVITE
Call-ID: 1736374800@lagrange.cs.columbia.edu
Content-Type: application/sdp
Content-Length: 211
Proxy-Authorization:Digest
username="anonymous",
realm="cs.columbia.edu",
nonce="6ydARDP51P8Ef9H4iiHmUc7iFDE=",
uri="sip:test1@cs.columbia.edu",
response="0480240000edd6c0b64befc19479924c",
opaque="", algorithm="MD5"

v=0
o=user1 53655765 2353687637 IN IP4 128.3.4.5
s=Mbone Audio
t=3149328700 0
i=Discussion of Mbone Engineering Issues
e=mbone@somewhere.com
c=IN IP4 128.3.4.5
t=0 0
m=audio 3456 RTP/AVP 0
a=rtpmap:0 PCMU/8000
```

One Server Per City: Using TCP for Very Large SIP Servers

Kumiko Ono and Henning Schulzrinne

Dept. of Computer Science
Columbia University, NY 10027, USA
{kumiko,hgs}@cs.columbia.edu

Abstract. The transport protocol for SIP can be chosen based on the requirements of services and network conditions. How does the choice of TCP affect the scalability and performance compared to UDP? We experimentally analyze the impact of using TCP as a transport protocol for a SIP server. We first investigate scalability of a TCP echo server, then compare performance of a SIP registrar server for two TCP connection lifetimes: transaction and persistent. Our results show that a Linux machine can establish 400,000+ TCP connections and maintaining connections does not affect the transaction response time. This is applicable to other servers with very large TCP connection counts. Additionally, the transaction response times using the two TCP connection lifetimes and UDP show no significant difference at 2,500 registration requests/second in our SIP server implementation. However, sustainable request rate is lower for TCP than for UDP, since using TCP requires more message processing, which causes longer delays at the thread queue for the server implementing a thread-pool model. Finally, we suggest how to reduce the impact of TCP for a scalable SIP server especially under overload control.

Keywords: SIP TCP Server Scalability Measurement.

1 Introduction

The Session Initiation Protocol (SIP) [1] is used for Internet telephony signaling, i.e., establishing and tearing down sessions. The SIP is a request-response protocol, similar to HTTP, but can work over any transport protocol such as UDP, TCP or SCTP (Stream Control Transmission Protocol) [2]. If SIP messages are sent over connection-less transport protocol, UDP, the SIP server does not have to maintain connection state, and a single socket can be shared to communicate with all the users. UDP seems a better choice to achieve a scalable SIP server in congestion-free networks.

However, TCP is preferred to UDP even in congestion-free networks, since it addresses issues, such as the SIP message size exceeding the MTU (Maximum Transfer Unit), firewall and NAT traversal. Due to its reliable nature, TCP imposes additional processing cost on the SIP server, i.e., the server has to

H. Schulzrinne, R. State, and S. Niccolini (Eds.): IPTComm 2008, LNCS 5310, pp. 133–148, 2008.

maintain a TCP socket for each connection. Typically, to facilitate inbound calls to the user phone behind a NAT or firewall, the user phone maintains a persistent TCP connection with the SIP server. It has generally been perceived as difficult for a SIP server to maintain 250,000+ active TCP connections and to keep up with the corresponding number of user registrations and call requests, in order to compete a high-capacity central office, Lucent's 5E-XC^{TM}[3], a high-capacity 5ESS.

Our goal is to measure the impact of TCP on SIP server scalability and performance, and to suggest techniques to maintain a large number of active TCP connections, such as 300,000, on a single server. The remainder of this article is organized as follows. We introduce requirements for SIP servers in Section 3. Then, we show the scalability and performance measurements of an echo server in Section 4 and those of a SIP server in Section 5. We also analyze the reason of the performance differences between TCP and UDP using component tests in Section 6. We conclude with suggestions for reducing the impact of TCP on SIP server in Section 7.

2   Related Work

Since both a SIP server and an HTTP server can use TCP, they face common problems in handling a large number of connections. Kegel [4] aggregates several tips and limits on I/O and event delivery to support more than 10,000 clients for a scalable HTTP server. Libenzi [5] developed the epoll() system call and shows that it enables an HTTP server to sustain a high throughput with active 27,000 connections. We built our SIP server on these tips to increase an upper limit of sockets and to enable the server to wait for events on a larger number of connections using the epoll() system call. However, we have to consider the differences between a SIP server and an HTTP server as explained in Section 3.

For SIP server scalability, Shemyak and Vehmanen [6] showed that a SIP server can maintain 100,000 inactive TCP connections, emphasizing the effect of using the epoll() system call. However, we need to establish the limit for the number of concurrent connections and clarify the bottleneck.

For a scalable SIP server using UDP, Singh and Schulzrinne [7] compared the performance for different software architectures: event-based, thread-pool, and process-pool. They suggested that the process-pool model has the best performance in terms of response time. Additionally, they proposed a two stage architecture, where servers at the first stage dispatch messages to multiple servers at the second stage in order to improve concurrency and reliability. For a highly concurrent server, Welsh et al. [8] proposed a staged event-driven architecture. Each stage contains a thread-pool to drive the stage execution. They showed decoupling load management from service logic increases concurrency with the measurement using 1,024 clients. We discuss the impact of the transport protocol on SIP server scalability, not the impact of the software architecture here.

3   Requirements for a SIP Server

3.1   TCP Connection Lifetime

Although SIP is similar to HTTP, it differs from HTTP in TCP connection lifetime. For example, a SIP proxy server in transaction-stateful mode needs to wait for the response from the User Agent Server (UAS). After ringing, it might take more than 30 seconds for the UAS to answer it. If the server runs in dialog-stateful mode, it needs to wait for the dialog between users to end. Thus, the TCP connection lifetime depends on human response time, and would be much longer than that for HTTP/1.0 [9], but similar to that for HTTP/1.1 [10]. While HTTP/1.0 [9] opens and closes a TCP connection to fetch each embedded object, HTTP/1.1 supports persistent connections across multiple objects by default in order to improve server performance by avoiding unnecessary TCP connection opens and closes, by reducing the impact of TCP slow-start, and by allowing pipelining requests and responses [11]. Typical HTTP clients and servers close inactive TCP connections when the session timeouts. For example, Mozilla Firefox[TM] sets the session timeout to 300 seconds by default.

However, a SIP UA behind a NAT needs to maintain even an inactive TCP connection in order to wait for incoming calls [12]. In this case, the TCP connection lifetime for SIP would be much longer even than HTTP/1.1. Therefore, the number of sustainable TCP connections and sustainable request rate are crucial factor for the scalability of an outbound SIP server.

3.2   Traffic Model

We assume a target traffic model where a single server accommodates 300,000 subscribers, which is similar scalability to that of Lucent's 5E-XC[TM], 256,000 subscribers. Each user quotes their location every 3,600 seconds as defined by default in RFC 3261 [1]. The average call duration is 180 seconds. The traffic is 0.1 erlangs. Thus, the target throughput for registrations is 300,000 BHCA (Busy Hour Call Attempt), which corresponds to 83 requests per second. The target throughput for calls is 600,000 BHCA (= 300,000 * 0.1 * (3,600 / 180)), which corresponds to 167 requests/second. If four mid-call requests, PRACK, ACK, UPDATE and BYE, are also counted as requests, the rate rises to 833 requests/second.

4   Basic TCP Measurements Using an Echo Server

Prior to the measurement for a SIP server, we measured the scalability and performance of an echo server in order to clarify the threshold and bottlenecks in terms of creating and maintaining a large number of concurrent TCP connections. We expected these basic measurements to make it easier to estimate the scalability of a SIP server using TCP.

4.1   Measurement Metrics

First, to establish the limit for the number of concurrent TCP connections on a single server, we measured the number of sustainable TCP connections, memory usage and CPU utilization by the `epoll()` system call. The echo server accepts several TCP connection requests and receives user messages depending on the order of data delivery from multiple echo clients.

Second, we measured the impact of a large number of TCP connections from two perspectives: of establishing and of maintaining active TCP connections. When echo clients send 512 byte messages to the echo server over separate TCP connections. In other words, TCP does not bundle multiple messages into a single packet when sending out.

4.2   Measurement Environment

The server under test (SUT) is an echo server using a single-process and single-thread which runs on a dedicated host with Pentium IV 3 GHz 32-bit dual-core CPU and 4 GB of memory. The SUT runs Linux 2.6.16 configured with the default virtual memory (VM) split, 1G/3G, where the kernel space is 1 GB and the user space 3 GB. We also configured the VM split to 2G/2G for the measurement of the number of sustainable connections only.

For the echo clients, we used ten hosts with Pentium IV 3 GHz 32-bit CPU and 1 GB of memory running Redhat Linux 2.6.9. These hosts communicated over a 100 Mb/s Ethernet connection at light load. The round trip time (RTT) measured by the `ping` command was roughly 0.1 ms.

We configured the SUT and clients to allow a large number of concurrent connections. The upper limit of file descriptors was increased to 1,000,000 at the SUT and to 60,000 at every client. The ephemeral local port range at the clients was expanded to 10,000-65,535, so that each client can establish approximately 55,000 (= 65535 - 1000) concurrent connections.

4.3   Results from Basic TCP Measurement

The Number of Sustainable TCP Connections. We measured the number of sustainable TCP connections at three request sending rates, 200, 2,500 and 14,800 requests/second for the echo server. The echo server accepts connection requests from echo clients, exchanges 512 byte messages over each connection, and maintain all the connections. Figure 1 indicates that the echo server can sustain the same number of connections at any request rate of them: approximately 420,000 connections with the default VM split configuration, 1G/3G, and 520,000 connections with the 2G/2G VM split configuration. Figure 1 also shows the overall memory usage and memory usage for TCP socket buffers for the echo server.

The overall memory usage increases linearly at any request rate and the amounts of memory used are approximately 1.0 GB with the 1G/3G VM split configuration, and 1.2 GB with the 2G/2G VM split configuration. However,

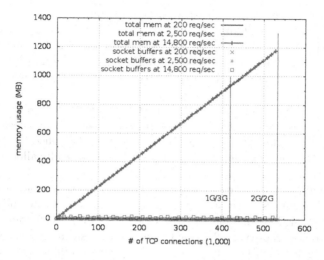

Fig. 1. Memory usage as a function of number of TCP connections at echo server

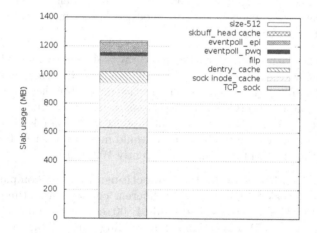

Fig. 2. Slab cache usage for 520,000 TCP connections for echo server

memory usage for TCP socket buffers is less than 20 MB at any request rate of them for both VM split configuration. We can deduce that the bottleneck is the amount of memory for TCP connections, which is allocated 2.3 KB per connection as long as the connection remains open, not the amount of socket buffer memory, which is dynamically allocated depending on the request rate.

To get a detailed picture of the memory usage for TCP connections, we monitored the usage of the slab cache, where the Linux kernel configured with a 2G/2G VM split allocates TCP socket data structures including socket buffers at 14,800 requests/second rate.

Figure 2 shows that the slab cache usage for approximately 520,000 TCP connections is 1.2 GB including the data structures for the `epoll()` system call: `eventpoll_epi` and `evenpoll_pwq`. Figure 2 also indicates that the slab cache usage dynamically allocated for the socket buffer heads, i.e., `skbuff_head_cache`, and user data, i.e., `size-512`, is only 12 MB. This result agrees with the result in Figure 1.

Therefore, we have determined that a TCP connection requires 2.3 KB of the slab cache and the bottleneck of sustainable concurrent connections is the amount of allocatable kernel memory for the slab cache, since this slab cache excluding for the socket buffer heads and user data is statically allocated as long as the TCP connection remains open.

For exchanging TCP control messages and user data, extra amount of the slab cache for socket buffers is required, depending on the request rate and the size of user data. If a target traffic model requires more than 500,000 connections, we recommend to have more than 2 GB of kernel memory, since we have experienced that the server hung without any error message when adding concurrent TCP connections because of memory exhaustion.

> In later versions of Linux, e.g., Linux 2.6.20, the system produces an error, "out of memory", when it tries to allocates kernel memory for the TCP socket data structures.

To increase kernel memory, installing more physical memory for a 32-bit kernel does not help since the kernel process can only handle 4 GB of memory including user space. The only way to increase kernel space for a 32-bit kernel is to modify the memory split to 3G/1G, where kernel space is 3 GB. Another way is to switch to a 64-bit kernel. Once kernel can support more than 4 GB of physical memory for a 64-bit kernel, the bottleneck would move to other factors, such as the number of file descriptors, which is currently 1024*1024.

The Cost of Establishing TCP Connections. Figure 3 compares the response time and peak CPU time across different connection lifetimes for TCP and to UDP at two request rates, 2,500 and 14,800 requests/second. Transaction-based TCP opens a TCP connection before sending a user data, i.e., a 512 byte message in ANSI text, and closing the TCP connection after receiving the echoed message. Persistent TCP has two scenarios: with open, where the echo server opens and maintains TCP connections, and without open, where the echo server reuses existing connections.

Comparing the results between the two persistent TCP scenarios indicates the cost of establishing a new TCP connection, which contains a RTT. This costs 0.2 ms of the response time in our local network. Since the RTT delay strongly depends on the network condition, the difference of the response times would be larger in a wide area network. Establishing a new TCP connection also costs 15 percent of CPU time only at high request rate, not at low request rate. We deduce that this difference is caused by the relationship between the required processing rate and the capacity of the CPU cycle. The SUT can process the requests at 2,500 requests/second rate, under the capacity of the CPU, but not

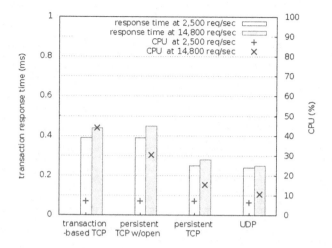

Fig. 3. Transaction response times in left axis and CPU utilization in right axis for echo server

at 14,800 requests/second rate. However, even at high request rate, these CPU cost is not so significant, since the maximum CPU time of our server running on a dual-core CPU is 200 percent.

Comparing the results between transaction-based and persistent TCP with open indicates the cost of closing a TCP connection. This costs a negligible amount of the response time and 14 percent of CPU time at high request rate.

Thus, the cost of establishing TCP connections is not significant at low request rate, 2,500 requests/second, which is significantly above the requirement. Furthermore, up to a request rate of 14,800 requests/second, the amount of kernel memory, rather than CPU cycles, limits the scalability of the echo server, as we have determined in Section 4.3.

The Cost of Maintaining TCP Connections. Figure 4 shows the response time consisting of the TCP handshake and message exchange as a function of the number of concurrent TCP connections for the echo server. The echo server establishes new TCP connections at 14,800 connections/second and leaves them. The "handshake" data points show the elapsed time for the TCP three-way handshake to establish a new connection, and the "send-recv" data points show the interval between sending and receiving an echoed message after the handshake. The "total" data points shows the sum of them.

Regardless of the number of maintaining TCP connections, the response time remains constant around at 0.3 ms for 'send-recv", which matches the results of persistent TCP in Figure 3, and at 0.4-0.5 ms for "total", of which average matches the results of persistent TCP with open. Thus, maintaining TCP connections affects neither the performance of establishing new TCP connections nor of exchanging user data.

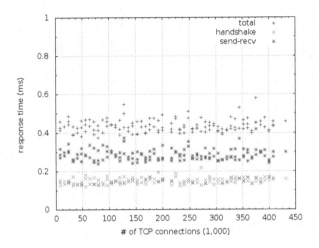

Fig. 4. Response times as a function of number of TCP connections for echo server

5   SIP Server Measurements

From the results of the basic TCP measurements, we have determined that TCP impacts mainly on kernel memory. Although each TCP connection consumes 2.3 KB of kernel memory, establishing and maintaining 300,000 TCP connections themselves does not significantly affect the performance. Compared to the echo server, a SIP server requires no additional kernel memory. Thus, the TCP impact on kernel memory is the same for a SIP server. Therefore, we can focus on measuring the performance for a SIP server.

Although RFC 3261[1] does not strictly define that a SIP server and UAs support persistent TCP connections, we can assume that a SIP server supports persistent TCP connections, but SIP UA behaviors may vary. Thus, we need to clarify how TCP connection handling affects throughput on a SIP server and data transfer latency, i.e., the sustainable request rate and the transaction response time. We measured them for two cases of TCP connection lifetime: transaction and persistent. These cases of TCP connection lifetime differ in how many SIP messages share a connection and how often TCP connections are established and closed.

Transaction-based TCP. UAs create new TCP connections for each transaction, e.g., REGISTER-200 OK, BYE-200 OK, INVITE-200 OK, ACK, BYE-200 OK, UPDATE-200 OK. For the average call or dialog, four TCP connections are established and closed. The maximum transaction duration with the default configuration in [1] is 32 seconds.

Persistent TCP. UAs and SIP servers keep TCP connections created when sending REGISTER requests, and reuse them to send INVITE requests or to update the registration. The default registration interval is 3,600 seconds.

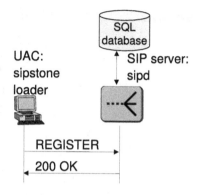

Fig. 5. Message exchanges for SIP server measurement

5.1 Measurement Environment

The SUT is our SIP server, sipd [13], running on the same host used for the echo server in Section 4.2. The sipd SIP server implements a single process and a thread-pool model, where a fixed number of threads is spawned on startup, is pooled, and handles tasks upon requests. If more tasks are requested than the number of threads, the tasks wait in a queue. The SIP server has the registrar and proxy functions. User information including registered locations is stored in a MySQL DBMS running on a different server on the same local network. For SIP UAs, we used a SIP UA emulator, part of sipstone test suite [14], running on the same hosts used for the echo clients in Section 4.2. Figure 5 shows these entities and message exchanges. We applied a scenario for a registration test, i.e., REGISTER-200 OK test, not a call test, i.e., INVITE-200 OK test, here. The registration test is similar to the basic measurement using echo server except parsing messages and SIP operation, while the call test is more complicated especially in terms of the number of SIP messages and transactions.

5.2 Registration Test Scenario: REGISTER-200 OK Test

For the registration test, 30,000 UACs send REGISTER requests at various request rate and receive the 200 OK response from the SIP server.

We measured the transaction response time of REGISTER-200 OK for two connection lifetimes: transaction in Figure 6 and persistent in Figure 7. Under persistent TCP, we measured the response time in two cases: initial registration that requires TCP connection establishment, which is corresponding to persistent TCP with open for the basic TCP measurement, and subsequent registration that reuses the existing TCP connection.

5.3 Results from REGISTER-200 OK Test

Figure 8 compares the transaction response times at various request sending rates at 100% success rate. The sustainable request rate for transaction-based

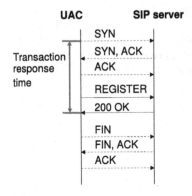

Fig. 6. Transaction-based TCP message exchanges for REGISTER-200 OK test

Fig. 7. Persistent TCP message exchanges for REGISTER-200 OK test

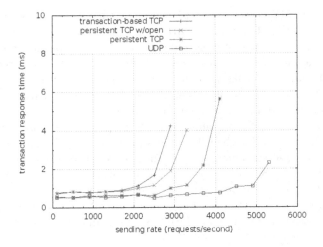

Fig. 8. Transaction response times as a function of sending rate for REGISTER-200 OK test for TCP and UDP

TCP is 2,900 requests/second, that for persistent TCP with open is 3,300 requests/second, that for persistent TCP is 4,100 requests/second, and that for UDP is 5,300 requests/second. Below 1,600 requests/second, the gaps in their response times remain constant, but above that, the gaps enlarge exponentially. This exponential increase of the response time conforms to Little's theorem. Since sipd has a M/D/c queue for handling tasks, we can deduce the increase of the response time is caused by waiting tasks' exceeding the number of pooled threads ($= c$) at these request rates.

To investigate these gaps more closely, we compare the response time and CPU utilization at 2,500 requests/second sending rate with those of the basic TCP measurements in Figure 3, as shown in Figure 9. Since the number of

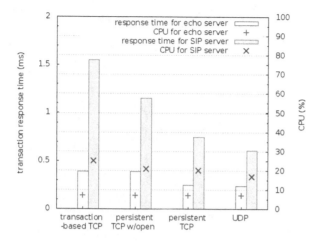

Fig. 9. Transaction response times in left axis and CPU utilization in right axis for REGISTER-200 OK test at 2,500 requests/second

messages and transactions are same, this comparison indicates the cost of handling SIP requests: message parsing and SIP operations or the difference of the software model. The cost of handling SIP requests in CPU time is 15-18 percent for all cases, and the cost in the transaction response time is 0.4-1.2 ms. These cost gaps among three TCP cases and UDP increase more in the transaction response time than those in CPU time. For example, the difference in the transaction response time between the two persistent TCP cases, indicating the cost of establishing a TCP connections, is 0.4 ms, which is 0.2 ms in the basic TCP measurement. Thus, we determined that this increased cost of establishing TCP connections were caused by the software model of the SIP server. The bottleneck of sustainable request rate is the thread queue, where the number and lifetime of threads cause queuing delay of threads in the thread-pool model. Section 6 shows the result of component tests that focus on threads in sipd to investigate this reason.

Figures 10 and 11 show that the SIP server starts to fail in handling SIP requests far before exhausting system resources for persistent TCP and UDP. Although we omit presenting the results of transaction-based TCP and persistent TCP with open, their results are similar to that for persistent TCP except the sustainable rate. For all cases, CPU utilization is still below 40 percent and usage of physical memory in RSS and virtual memory in VSZ is below 200 MB and below 800 MB, respectively. Clearly, the bottleneck is neither memory usage nor CPU utilization.

When the success rate drops, the SIP server produces warning messages saying that the overload control drops 83% of requests for persistent TCP and 10-28% of requests for UDP. Since sipd detects overload by monitoring the thread queue of waiting tasks for available threads, we have determined the bottleneck is the thread queue.

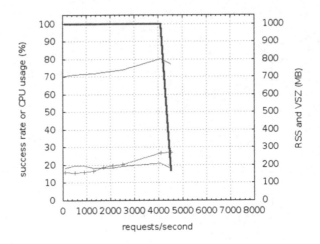

Fig. 10. Success rate, CPU utilization and memory usage for REGISTER-200 OK test: persistent TCP

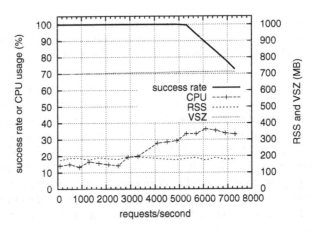

Fig. 11. Success rate, CPU utilization and memory usage for REGISTER-200 OK test: UDP

Furthermore, the success rate for persistent TCP steeply drops, while that for UDP gradually decreases. The difference between persistent TCP and UDP in droping the success rate implies that the overload control works ruthlessly for TCP, while it works gracefully for UDP. The overload control at sipd sets threshold of tasks in the thread queue and drops tasks to handle new requests excluding BYE requests, which have fewer subsequent SIP messages. To investigate the difference between TCP and UDP, Section 6 discusses the details of the overload control mechanism.

6   Component Tests

From the results of the SIP measurement, we have determined that the major cause of the difference in the sustainable request rate between TCP and UDP is message processing in a thread-pool model, rather than socket handling. Also, we have determined the overload control for the SIP server works worse for TCP than for UDP.

Since TCP is a connection-oriented protocol, the SIP server needs to handle control messages for the connections, such as TCP open and close requests. This requires more messages to be handled. Also, since TCP transfers byte-stream data, the SIP server needs to find the end of the message by parsing. This requires longer thread lifetime that causes lower throughput. Furthermore, this makes overload control harder, since it disables sorting messages by parsing the first line of the message before parsing the whole message. To confirm these analysis, we performed component tests to focus on message processing.

6.1   Message Processing Test

We performed the REGISTER-200 OK tests as a white-box test, i.e., measuring the called times and the elapsed time of the functions involved in message processing. To avoid the influence of queuing, we set the load low to 10 requests/second, and ran the test for 10 seconds.

Figure 12 compares the number of function calls and new threads required for sipd to process a REGISTER message. The base thread, not a new thread, processes sockets, e.g., calling the accept() system call to create a new connection. For TCP, a new thread reads buffer and parses a message. Transaction-based TCP requires most function calls for processing sockets, and most threads for reading

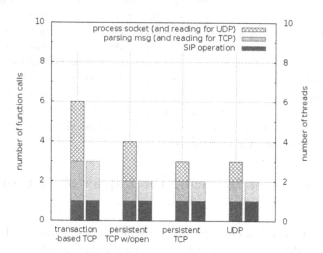

Fig. 12. Number of function calls in left axis and threads in right axis for reading and parsing a REGISTER message

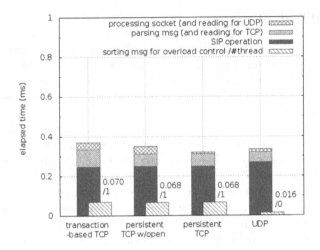

Fig. 13. Elapsed times for reading and parsing a REGISTER message

buffers, since it receives TCP-SYN and FIN. Although receiving TCP-SYN does not require to read buffer, FIN require to read a zero-sized buffer. Persistent TCP with open requires the second most function calls since it receives TCP-SYN. For UDP, on the other hand, the base thread reads buffer and parses the first line to sort messages for the overload control, then a new thread parses a message again for SIP operations. This makes the overall elapsed time for UDP slightly longer than that for persistent TCP as seen in Figure 13, although persistent TCP and UDP require the same number of function calls and threads.

However, the elapsed time for reading and sorting messages for the overload control for UDP is one forth of that for persistent TCP, since sorting message for UDP limits the number of lines to be parsed to one. Furthermore, the elapse time for parsing message by a new thread is slightly shorter for UDP than for persistent TCP, since reading buffer has already been processed by the base thread for UDP. Therefore, we can determine that these two differences cause the better sustainable rate for UDP than for persistent TCP in the registration test, although these differences in the thread lifetime is much smaller that the elapsed time of SIP operation, which dominate in the elapsed time. The cost of sorting message for the overload control makes the SIP server performance significantly worse for TCP at high loads.

7   Suggestions for Reducing the Impact of TCP on a SIP Server

Under our target traffic model, we can conclude that the impact of TCP on the scalability of a SIP server is relatively small, since it only includes the setup delay for the TCP three-way handshake and 690 MB of kernel memory for 300,000 concurrent TCP connections. However, as HTTP/1.1 defines persistent TCP to improve the HTTP server performance, persistent TCP is also recommended to avoid unnecessary the setup delay for a SIP server.

Under heavy loads, however, persistent TCP is not efficient enough to compete with the sustainable rate for UDP, since a SIP server falls to overload condition earlier than using UDP. We suggest some approaches to reduce the impact under heavy load.

7.1 Accelerating Parsing for Overload Control

We first suggest that the SIP server sort messages by parsing the first-line of a buffered message without determining the exact message boundary. As found in Section 6, the sorting message for UDP, which is by parsing the first line of the message is much lighter than that for TCP. The speeding up of sorting messages can make it easy to process the overload control for the SIP server.

Although this sorting is accurate not for all messages, it works mostly. The messages with a higher priority for the overload control, i.e., responses and BYE request, are relatively short in size. Thus, the message is unlikely to be sent partially. As a result, the size of receiving buffer to be read by user applications is usually large enough to buffer a SIP message at once. Thus, with a high possibility, the SIP server can parse the first line without determining the message size by parsing the Content-Length header. Even if the SIP server cannot determine the message type because of partial delivery or bundled delivery, the server can simply drop such a message fragment under overload.

Another suggestion is that a function required for the overload control, such as sorting messages, be processed by the base thread that does not need to wait for an additional thread. This is only applicable in a thread-pool model.

Furthermore, the software architecture should handle many concurrent requests efficiently. Rather than the thread-pool model like our SIP server, a small set of multiple processes running a single thread each is more appropriate to avoid causing large queuing delay and unnecessary context-switching.

8 Conclusion

We have shown measurement results to clarify the impact of TCP on SIP server scalability and performance. Choosing TCP requires 2.3 KB of kernel memory per TCP connection and additional CPU cycles mainly for the TCP handshake. Establishing TCP connections causes a setup delay of 0.2 ms in our environment, while maintaining TCP connections only consumes kernel memory. Thus, maintaining 300,000 TCP connections requires approximately 690 MB. These results are applicable to other TCP servers.

The impact on the response time for our SIP server is not significant under our target traffic model. However, under heavy loads, e.g., 2,900 requests/second for the registration test, the major impact is on the transaction response time and on the success rate. The response time exponentially increases around the sustainable rate in our SIP server implementation. This increase is caused by queuing delay in the thread pool model, when thread queues exceeds the maximum length. To avoid this, the software architecture should be selected to achieve a large number of concurrent requests. Above the sustainable rate, the success rate drops steeply by the overload control for our SIP server. From the results of the component tests, we suggest to speed up message parsing to ease overload control for a SIP server. By easing overload control, the SIP server could sustain a much higher request throughput beyond our target traffic model.

References

1. Rosenberg, J., Schulzrinne, H., Camarillo, G., Johnston, A., Peterson, J., Sparks, R., Handley, M., Schooler, E.: SIP: Session Initiation Protocol. RFC 3261, IETF (June 2002)
2. Stewart, R.: Stream Control Transmission Protocol. RFC 4960, IETF (September 2007)
3. Lucent-Alcatel. Lucent Technologies new high-capacity switch accelerates cost-effective migration to Internet Protocol networks (news release) (December 2002), http://www.alcatel-lucent.com/
4. Kegel, D.: The C10K problem (accessed in January 2006), http://www.kegel.com/c10k.html
5. Libenzi, D.: Improving (network) I/O performance (accessed in January 2006), http://www.xmailserver.org/linux-patches/nio-improve.html
6. Shemyak, K., Vehmanen, K.: Scalability of TCP Servers. In: Handling Persistent Connections. In: Sixth International Conference on Networking (ICN 2007) (April 2007)
7. Singh, K., Schulzrinne, H.: Failover and Load Sharing in SIP Telephony. In: International Symposium on Performance Evaluation of Computer and Telecommunication Systems (SPECTS) (July 2005)
8. Welsh, M., Culler, D., Brewer, E.: SEDA: An Architecture for Well-Conditioned, Scalable Internet Services. In: the Eighteenth Symposium on Operating Systems Principles (SOSP-18) (October 2001)
9. Berners-Lee, T., Fielding, R., Frystyk, H.: Hypertext Transfer Protocol – HTTP/1.0. RFC 1945, IETF (May 1996)
10. Fielding, R., Gettys, J., Mogul, J., Frystyk, H., Masinter, L., Leach, P., Berners-Lee, T.: Hypertext Transfer Protocol – HTTP/1.1. RFC 2616, IETF (June 1999)
11. Nielsen, H.F., Gettys, J., Baird-Smith, A., Prud'hommeaux, E., Lie, H., Lilley, C.: Network Performance Effects of HTTP/1.1, CSS1, and PNG. In: ACM SIGCOMM 1997 (September 1997)
12. Jennings, C., Mahy, R.: Managing Client Initiated Connections in the Session Initiation Protocol(SIP). Internet-draft, IETF (November 2007), http://www.ietf.org/internet-drafts/draft-ietf-sip-outbound-11.txt
13. Lennox, J., Schulzrinne, H., et al.: Cinema:sipd, http://www.cs.columbia.edu/irt/cinema/doc/sopd.html
14. Narayanan, S., Yu, A., Kapoor, T., Schulzrinne, H.: Sipstone test suite, http://www.cs.columbia.edu/IRT/cinema/sipstone

Session Initiation Protocol (SIP) Server Overload Control: Design and Evaluation

Charles Shen[1], Henning Schulzrinne[1], and Erich Nahum[2]

[1] Columbia University, New York, NY 10027, USA
{charles,hgs}@cs.columbia.edu
[2] IBM T.J. Watson Research Center, Hawthorne, NY 10532, USA
nahum@watson.ibm.com

Abstract. A Session Initiation Protocol (SIP) server may be overloaded by emergency-induced call volume, "American Idol" style flash crowd effects or denial of service attacks. The SIP server overload problem is interesting especially because the costs of serving or rejecting a SIP session can be similar. For this reason, the built-in SIP overload control mechanism based on generating rejection messages cannot prevent the server from entering congestion collapse under heavy load. The SIP overload problem calls for a pushback control solution in which the potentially overloaded receiving server may notify its upstream sending servers to have them send only the amount of load within the receiving server's processing capacity. The pushback framework can be achieved by either a rate-based feedback or a window-based feedback. The centerpiece of the feedback mechanism is the algorithm used to generate load regulation information. We propose three new window-based feedback algorithms and evaluate them together with two existing rate-based feedback algorithms. We compare the different algorithms in terms of the number of tuning parameters and performance under both steady and variable load. Furthermore, we identify two categories of fairness requirements for SIP overload control, namely, user-centric and provider-centric fairness. With the introduction of a new double-feed SIP overload control architecture, we show how the algorithms can meet those fairness criteria.

1 Introduction

The Session Initiation Protocol [1] (SIP) is a signaling protocol standardized by IETF for creating, modifying, and terminating sessions in the Internet. It has been used for many session-oriented applications, such as calls, multimedia distributions, video conferencing, presence service and instant messaging. Major standards bodies including 3GPP, ITU-I, and ETSI have all adopted SIP as the core signaling protocol for Next Generation Networks predominately based on the Internet Multimedia Subsystem (IMS) architecture.

The widespread popularity of SIP has raised attention to its readiness of handling overload [2]. A SIP server can be overloaded for many reasons, such as emergency-induced call volume, flash crowds generated by TV programs (e.g.,

H. Schulzrinne, R. State, and S. Niccolini (Eds.): IPTComm 2008, LNCS 5310, pp. 149–173, 2008.

American Idol), special events such as "free tickets to third caller", or even denial of service attacks. Although server overload is by no means a new problem for the Internet, the key observation that distinguishes the SIP overload problem from others is that the cost of rejecting a SIP session usually cannot be ignored compared to the cost of serving a session. Consequently, when a SIP server has to reject a large amount of arriving sessions, its performance collapses. This explains why using the built-in SIP overload control mechanism based on generating a rejection response messages does not solve the problem. If, as is often recommended, the rejected sessions are sent to a load-sharing SIP server, the alternative server will soon also be generating nothing but rejection responses, leading to a cascading failure. Another important aspect of overload in SIP is related to SIP's multi-hop server architecture with name-based application level routing. This aspect creates the so-called "server to server" overload problem that is generally not comparable to overload in other servers such as web server.

To avoid the overloaded server ending up at a state spending all its resources rejecting sessions, Hilt *et al.* [3] outlined a SIP overload control framework based on feedback from the receiving server to its upstream sending servers. The feedback can be in terms of a rate or a load limiting window size. However, the exact algorithms that may be applied in this framework and the potential performance implications are not obvious. In particular, to our best knowledge there has been no published work on specific window-based algorithms for SIP overload control, or comprehensive performance evaluation of rate-based feedback algorithms that also discusses dynamic load conditions and overload control fairness issues.

In this paper, we introduce a new dynamic session estimation scheme which plays an essential role in applying selected control algorithms to the SIP overload environment. We then propose three new window-based algorithms for SIP overload. We also apply two existing load adaption algorithms for rate-based overload control. We thus cover all three types of feedback control mechanisms in [3]: the absolute rate feedback, relative rate feedback and window feedback. Our simulation evaluation results show that although the algorithms differ in their tuning parameters, most of them are able to achieve theoretical maximum performance under steady state load conditions. The results under dynamic load conditions with source arrival and departure are also encouraging. Furthermore, we look at the fairness issue in the context of SIP overload and propose the notion of user-centric fairness vs. service provider-centric fairness. We show how different algorithms may achieve the desired type of fairness. In particular, we found that the user-centric fairness is difficult to achieve in the absolute rate or window-based feedback mechanisms. We solve this problem by introducing a new double-feed SIP overload control architecture.

The rest of this paper is organized as follows: Section 2 presents background on the SIP overload problem, and discusses related work. In Section 3 we propose three window-based SIP overload control algorithms and describe two existing load adaptation algorithm to be applied for rate-based SIP overload control. Then we present the simulation model and basic SIP overload results without feedback control in Section 4. The steady load performance evaluation of the control algorithms are presented in Section 5, followed by dynamic load performance with fairness consideration in Section 6. Finally Section 7 concludes the paper and discusses future work.

2 Background and Related Work

2.1 SIP Overview

SIP is a message based protocol for managing sessions. There are two basic SIP entities, SIP User Agents (UAs), and SIP servers. SIP servers can be further grouped into proxy servers for session routing and registration servers for UA registration. In this paper we focus primarily on proxy servers. In the remainder of this document, when referring to SIP servers, we mean proxy server unless explicitly mentioned otherwise. One of the most popular session types that SIP is used for is call session. This is also the type of session we will consider in this paper. In a typical SIP call session, the caller and callee have UA functionalities, and they set up the session through the help of SIP servers along the path between them. Figure 1 shows the SIP message flow establishing a SIP call session. The caller starts with sending an INVITE request message towards the SIP proxy server, which replies with a 100 Trying message and forwards the request to the next hop determined by name-based application level routing. In Figure 1 the next hop for the only SIP server is the callee, but in reality it could well be another SIP server along the path. Once the INVITE request finally arrives at the callee, the callee replies with a 180 Ringing message indicating receipt of the call request by the callee UA, and sends a 200 OK message when the callee picks up the phone. The 200 OK message makes its way back to the caller, who will send an ACK message to the callee to conclude the call setup. Afterwards, media may flow between the caller and callee without the intervention of the SIP server. When one party wants to tear down the call, the corresponding UA

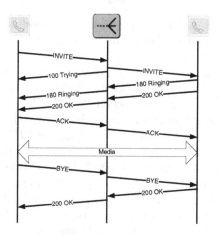

Fig. 1. SIP call session message flow

sends a BYE message to the other party, who will reply with a 200 OK message to confirm the call hang-up. Therefore, a typical SIP call session entails processing of five incoming messages for call setup and two incoming messages for call teardown, a total of seven messages for the whole session.

SIP is an application level protocol on top of the transport layer. It can run over any common transport layer protocol, such as UDP and TCP. A particular aspect of SIP related to the overload problem is its timer mechanism. SIP defines a large number of retransmission timers to cope with message loss, especially when the unreliable UDP transport is used. As examples, we illustrate three of the timers which are commonly seen causing problems under overload. The first is timer A that causes an INVITE retransmission upon each of its expirations. With an initial value of $T_1 = 500\ ms$, timer A increases exponentially until its total timeout period exceeds 32 s. The second timer of interest is the timer that controls the retransmission of 200 OK message as a response to an INVITE request. The timer for 200 OK also starts with T_1, and its value doubles until it reaches $T_2 = 4\ s$. At that time the timer value remains at T_2 until the total timeout period exceeds 32 s. The third timer of interest is timer E, which controls the BYE request retransmission. Timer E follows a timeout pattern similar to the 200 OK timer. Note that the receipt of corresponding messages triggered by each of the original messages will quench the retransmission timer. They are the 100 Trying for INVITE, ACK for 200 OK, and 200 OK for BYE. From this description, we know that for example, if an INVITE message for some reason is dropped or stays in the server queue longer than 500 ms without generating the 100 Trying, the upstream SIP entity will retransmit the original INVITE. Similarly, if the round trip time of the system is longer than 500 ms, then the 200 OK timer and the BYE timer will fire, causing retransmission of these messages. Under ideal network conditions without link delay and loss, retransmissions are purely wasted messages that should be avoided.

2.2   Types of SIP Server Overload

There are many causes to SIP overload, but the resulting SIP overload cases can usually be grouped into either of the two types: server to server overload or client to server overload.

A typical server to server overload topology is illustrated in Figure 2. In this figure the overloaded server (the Receiving Entity or RE) is connected with a relatively small number of upstream servers (the Sending Entities or SEs). One example of server to server overload is a special event such as "free tickets to the third caller", also referred to as flash crowds. Suppose RE is the Service Provider (SP) for a hotline N. SE_1, SE_2 and SE_3 are three SPs that reach the hotline through RE. When the hotline is activated, RE is expected to receive a large call volume to the hotline from SE_1, SE_2 and SE_3 that far exceeds its usual call volume, potentially putting RE into a severe overload. The second type of overload, known as client-to-server overload is when a number of clients overload the next hop server directly. An example is avalanche restart, which happens when power is restored after a mass power failure in a large metropolitan area.

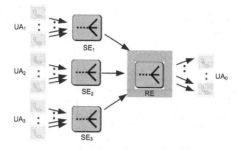

Fig. 2. Server to server overload

At the time the power is restored, a very large number of SIP devices boot up and send out SIP registration requests almost simultaneously, which could easily overload the corresponding SIP registration server. This paper only discusses the server-to-server overload problem. The client-to-server overload problem may require different solutions and is out of scope of this paper.

2.3 Existing SIP Overload Control Mechanisms

Without overload control, messages that cannot be processed by the server are simply dropped. Simple drop causes the corresponding SIP timers to fire, and further amplifies the overload situation.

SIP has a 503 Service Unavailable response message used to reject a session request and cancel any related outstanding retransmission timers. However, because of the relatively high cost of generating this rejection, this message cannot solve the overload problem.

SIP also defines an optional parameter called "Retry-after" in the 503 Service Unavailable message. The "Retry-after" value specifies the amount of time that the receiving SE of the message should cease sending any requests to the RE. The 503 Service Unavailable with "Retry-after" represents basically an on/off overload control approach, which is known to be unable to fully prevent congestion collapse [2]. Another related technique is to allow the SE to fail over the rejected requests to an alternative load-sharing server. However, in many situations the load-sharing server could ultimately be overloaded as well, leading to cascading failure.

2.4 Feedback-Based Overload Control

The key to solving the SIP server overload problem is to make sure the upstream SEs only send the amount of traffic that the RE is able to handle at all times. In this ideal situation, there will be no message retransmission due to timeout and no extra processing cost due to rejection. The server CPU power can be fully utilized to deliver its maximum session service capacity.

A feedback loop is a natural approach to achieve the ideal overload control goal. Through the loop, RE notifies SEs the amount of load that is acceptable.

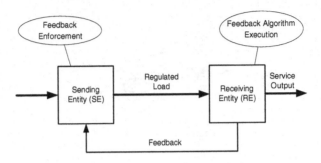

Fig. 3. Generalized feedback architecture

To some extent the existing SIP 503 Service Unavailable mechanism with the "Retry-after" header is a basic form of the feedback mechanism. Unfortunately, its on/off control nature has proven to be problematic. Therefore, the IETF community has started looking at more sophisticated pushback mechanisms including both rate-based and window-based feedback. A generalized model of the feedback-based control model is shown in Figure 3. There are three main components in the model: feedback algorithm execution at RE, feedback communication from RE to SE, and feedback enforcement at the SE.

Feedback Algorithm Execution. Absolute rate, relative rate and window feedback are three main SIP feedback control mechanisms. Each mechanism executes specific control algorithms to generate and adapt the feedback value.

In absolute rate-based feedback, the feedback generation entity RE needs to estimate its acceptable load and allocate it among the SEs. The feedback information is an absolute load value for the particular SE. The key element in absolute rate feedback is an algorithm for dynamic acceptable load estimation.

In relative rate-based feedback, the feedback generation entity RE computes an incoming load throttle percentage based on a target resource metric (e.g., CPU utilization). The feedback information is a dynamic percentage value indicating how much proportion of the load should be accepted or rejected relative to the original incoming load. The key element in relative rate feedback is the dynamic relative rate adjustment algorithm and the choosing of the target metric.

In window-based feedback, the feedback generation entity RE estimates a dynamic window size for each SE which specifies the number of acceptable sessions from that particular SE. The feedback information is the current window size. The key element in window-based feedback is a dynamic window adjustment algorithm.

The feedback generation could be either time-driven or event-driven. In time-driven mechanisms, the control is usually exercised every pre-scheduled control interval, while in event-driven mechanisms, the control is executed upon the occurrence of some event, such as a session service completion. We will examine both time-driven and event-driven algorithms in this paper.

Feedback Enforcement Mechanisms. The *SEs* may choose among many well-known traffic regulation mechanisms to enforce feedback control, such as percentage throttle, leaky bucket and token bucket, automatic call gapping, and window throttle. Since our focus is on the feedback algorithms, throughout this paper we will use percentage throttle for rate-based feedback and window-throttle for window-based feedback mechanisms. In our percentage throttle implementation we probabilistically block a given percentage of the load arrival to make sure the actual output load conforms to the regulated load value. For window throttle implementation, we only forward a specific session arrival when there is window slot available.

Feedback Communication. The feedback information for SIP signaling overload control can be communicated via an in-band or out-of-band channel. In this paper, we have chosen to use the in-band feedback communication approach. Specifically, any feedback information available is sent in the next immediate message that goes to the particular target *SE*. This approach has an advantage in server to server overload because there is generally no problem finding existing messages to carry feedback information under overload and it incurs minimal overhead.

2.5   Related Work

Signaling overload itself is a well studied topic. Many of the previous work on call signaling overload in general communication networks is believed to be usable by the SIP overload study. For instance, Hosein [4] presented an adaptive rate control algorithm based on estimation of message queuing delay; Cyr *et al.* [5] described the Occupancy Algorithm (OCC) for load balancing and overload control mechanism in distributed processing telecommunications systems based on server CPU occupancy; Kasera *et al.* [6] proposed an improved OCC algorithm call Acceptance-Rate Occupancy (ARO) by taking into consideration the call acceptance ratio, and a Signaling RED algorithm which is a RED variant for signaling overload control.

Specifically on SIP, Ohta [7] showed through simulation the congestion collapse of SIP server under heavy load and explored the approach of using a priority queuing and Bang-Bang type of overload control. Nahum *et al.* [8] reported empirical performance results of SIP server showing the congestion collapse behavior.

In addition, Whitehead [9] described a unified overload control framework called GOCAP for next generation networks, which is supposed to cover SIP as well. But there has been no performance results yet and it is not clear at this time how the GOCAP framework may relate to the IETF SIP overload framework.

In the most closely related work to this paper, Noel and Johnson [10] presented initial results comparing a SIP network without overload control, with the built-in SIP overload control and with a rate-based overload control scheme. However, their paper does not discuss window-based control, or present performance results under dynamic load, and it does not address the overload fairness problem.

3   Feedback Algorithms for SIP Server Overload Control

The previous section has introduced the main components of SIP overload feedback control framework. In this section we investigate its key component - the feedback algorithm. We propose three window-based SIP overload control methods, namely *win-disc*, *win-cont*, and *win-auto*. We also apply two existing adaptive load control algorithms for rate-based control. Before discussing algorithm details, we first introduce a dynamic SIP session estimation method which plays an important role in applying selected rate-based or window-based algorithms to SIP overload control.

3.1   Dynamic SIP Session Estimation

Design of SIP overload control algorithm starts with determining the control granularity, i.e., the basic control unit. Although SIP is a message-based protocol, different types of SIP messages carry very different weights from admission control perspective. For instance, in a typical call session, admitting a new IN-VITE message starts a new call and implicitly accepts six additional messages for the rest of the session signaling. Therefore, it is more convenient to use a SIP session as the basic control unit.

A session oriented overload control algorithm frequently requires session related metrics as inputs such as the session service rate. In order to obtain session related metrics a straightforward approach is to do a *full session check*, i.e., to track the start and end message of all SIP signaling sessions. For example, the server may count how many sessions have been started and then completed within a measurement interval. In the case of a call signaling, the session is initiated by an INVITE request and terminated with a BYE request. The INVITE and BYE are usually separated by a random session holding time. However, SIP allows the BYE request to traverse a different server from the one for the original INVITE. In that case, some SIP server may only see the INVITE request while other servers only see the BYE request of a signaling session. There could also be other types of SIP signaling sessions traversing the SIP server.These factors make the applicability of the *full session check* approach complicated, if not impossible.

We use an alternative *start session check* approach to estimate SIP session service rate . The basic idea behind is that under normal working conditions, the actual session acceptance rate is roughly equal to the session service rate. Therefore, we can estimate the session service rate based only on the session start messages. Specifically, the server counts the number of INVITE messages that it accepts per measurement interval T_m. The value of the session service rate is estimated to be $\mu = N_{inv}^{accepted}/T_m$. Standard smoothing functions can be applied to the periodically measured μ.

One other critical session parameter often needed in SIP overload control algorithms is the number of sessions remaining in the server system, assuming the server processor is preceded by a queue where jobs are waiting for service. It is very important to recognize that the number of remaining sessions is NOT equal to the number of INVITE messages in the queue, because the queue is shared by all types of messages, including those non-INVITE messages which represent sessions that had previously been accepted into the system. All messages should be counted for the current system backlog. Hence we propose to estimate the current number of sessions in the queue using Eq. 1:

$$N_{sess} = N_{inv} + \frac{N_{noninv}}{L_{sess} - 1} \tag{1}$$

where N_{inv} and N_{noninv} are current number of INVITE and non-INVITE messages in the queue, respectively. The parameter L_{sess} represents the average number of messages per-session. N_{inv} indicates the number of calls arrived at the server but yet to be processed; $N_{noninv}/(L_{sess} - 1)$ is roughly the number of calls already in process by the server.

Eq. 1 holds for both the *full session check* and the simplified *start session check* estimation approaches. The difference is how the L_{sess} parameter is obtained. When the *full session check* approach is used, the length of each individual session will be counted by checking the start and end of each individual SIP sessions. With our simplified *start session check* approach, the session length can be obtained by counting the actual number of messages N_{msg}^{proc}, processed during the same period the session acceptance rate is observed. The session length is then estimated to be $L_{sess} = N_{msg}^{proc}/N_{inv}^{accepted}$.

3.2 Active Source Estimation

In some of the overload control mechanisms, the RE may wish to explicitly allocate its total capacity among multiple SEs. A simple approach is to get the number of current active SEs and divide the capacity equally. We do this by directly tracking the sources of incoming load and maintaining a table entry for each current active SE. Each entry has an expiration timer set to one second.

3.3 The *win-disc* Window Control Algorithm

A window feedback algorithm executed at the RE dynamically computes a feedback window value for the SE. SE will forward the load to RE only if window slots are currently available. Our first window based algorithm is *win-disc*, the short name for *window-discrete*. The main idea is that at the end of each discrete control interval of period T_c, RE re-evaluate the number of new session requests it can accept for the next control interval, making sure the delays for processing sessions already in the server and upcoming sessions are bounded. Assuming the RE advertised window to SE_i at the kth control interval T_c^k is w_i^k, and the total window size for all SEs at the end of the kth control interval is w^{k+1}, the *win-disc* algorithm is described below:

$w_i^0 := W_0$ where $W_0 > 0$
$w_i^k := w_i^k - 1$ for INVITE received from SE_i
$w^{k+1} := \mu^k T_c + \mu^k D_B - N_{sess}^k$ at the end of T_c^k
$w_i^{k+1} := round(w^{k+1}/N_{SE}^k)$

where μ^k is the current estimated session service rate. D_B is a parameter that reflects the allowed budget message queuing delay. N_{sess}^k is the estimated current number of sessions in the system at the end of T_c^k. $\mu^k T_c$ gives the estimated number of sessions the server is able to process in the T_c^{k+1} interval. $\mu^k D_B$ gives the average number of sessions that can remain in the server queue given the budget delay. This number has to exclude the number of sessions already backlogged in the server queue, which is N_{sess}^k. Therefore, w^{k+1} gives the estimated total number of sessions that the server is able to accept in the next T_c control interval giving delay budget D_B. Both μ^k and N_{sess}^k are obtained with our dynamic session estimation algorithm in Section 3.1. N_{SE}^k is the current number of active sources discussed in Section 3.2. Note that the initial value W_0 is not important as long as $W_0 > 0$. An example value could be $W_0 = \mu_{eng} T_c$ where μ_{eng} is the server's engineered session service rate.

3.4   The *win-cont* Window Control Algorithm

Our second window feedback algorithm is *win-cont*, the short name for *window-continuous*. Unlike the time-driven *win-disc* algorithm, *win-cont* is an event driven algorithm that continuously adjusts advertised window size when the server has room to accept new sessions. The main idea of this algorithm is to bound the number of sessions in the server at any time. The maximum number of sessions allowed in the server is obtained by $N_{sess}^{max} = \mu^t D_B$, where D_B is again the allowed message queuing delay budget and μ^t is the current service rate. At any time, the difference between the maximum allowed number of sessions in the server N_{sess}^{max} and the current number of sessions N_{sess} is the available window to be sent as feedback. Depending on the responsiveness requirements and computation ability, there are different design choices. First is how frequently N_{sess} should be checked. It could be after any message processing, or after an INVITE message processing, or other possibilities. The second is the threshold number of session slots to update the feedback. There are two such thresholds, the overall number of available slots W_{ovth}, and the per-SE individual number of available slots W_{indvth}. To make the algorithm simple, we choose per-message processing N_{sess} update and fix both W_{ovth} and W_{indvth} to 1. A general description of the *win-cont* algorithm is summarized as below:

$$w_i^0 := W_0 \text{ where } W_0 > 0$$
$$w_i^t := w_i^t - 1 \text{ for INVITE received from } SE_i$$
$$w_{left}^t := N_{sess}^{max} - N_{sess} \text{ upon msg processing}$$
$$if(w_{left}^t \geq 1)$$
$$w_{share}^t = w_{left}^t / N_{SE}^t$$
$$w_{i'}^t := w_{i'}^t + w_{share}^t$$
$$if(w_{i'}^t \geq 1)$$
$$w_i^t := (int) w_{i'}^t$$
$$w_{i'}^t := (frac) w_{i'}^t$$

Note that since w_i^t may contain a decimal part, to improve the feedback window accuracy when w_i^t is small, we feedback the integer part of the current w_i^t and add its decimal part to the next feedback by using a temporary parameter $w_{i'}^t$. In the algorithm description, μ^t, N_{sess} and N_{SE} are obtained as discussed in Section 3.1 and Section 3.2. The initial value W_0 is not important and a reference value is $W_0 = \mu_{eng}T_c$ where μ_{eng} is the server's engineered session service rate.

3.5   The *win-auto* Window Control Algorithm

Our third window feedback algorithm, *win-auto* stands for *window-autonomous*. Like *win-cont*, *win-auto* is also an event driven algorithm. But as the term indicates, the *win-auto* algorithm is able to make window adjustment autonomously. The key design principal in the *win-auto* algorithm is to automatically keep the pace of window increase below the pace of window decrease, which makes sure the session arrival rate does not exceed the session service rate. The algorithm details are as follows:

$w_i^0 := W_0$ where $W_0 > 0$
$w_i^t := w_i^t - 1$ for INVITE received from SE_i
$w_i^t := w_i^t + 1$ after processing a *new* INVITE

The beauty of this algorithm is its extreme simplicity. The algorithm takes advantage of the fact that retransmission starts to occur as the network gets congested. Then the server automatically freezes its advertised window to allow processing of backlogged sessions until situation improves. The only check the server does is whether an INVITE message is a retransmitted one or a new one, which is just a piece of normal SIP parsing done by any existing SIP server. There could be many variations along the same line of thinking as this algorithm, but the one as described here appears to be one of the most natural options.

3.6   The *rate-abs* Rate Control Algorithm

We implemented an absolute rate feedback control by applying the adaptive load algorithm of Hosein [4], which is also used by Noel [10]. The main idea is to ensure the message queuing delay does not exceed the allowed budget value. The algorithm details are as follows.

During every control interval T_c, the *RE* notifies the *SE* of the new target load, which is expressed by Eq. 2.

$$\lambda^{k+1} = \mu^k(1 - \frac{(d_q^k - D_B)}{C}) \tag{2}$$

where μ^k is the current estimated service rate and d_q^k is the estimated server queuing delay at the end of the last measurement interval. It is obtained by $d_q^k = N_{sess}/\mu^k$, where N_{sess} is the number of sessions in the server. We use our dynamic session estimation in Section 3.1 to obtain N_{sess}, and we refer to this absolute rate control implementation as *rate-abs* in the rest of this document.

3.7   The *rate-occ* Rate Control Algorithm

Our candidates of existing algorithms for relative rate based feedback control are Occupancy Algorithm (OCC) [5], Acceptance-Rate Occupancy (ARO), and Signaling RED (SRED) [6]. We decided to implement the basic OCC algorithm because this mechanism already illustrates inherent properties with any occupancy based approach. On the other hand, tuning of RED based algorithm is known to be relatively complicated.

The OCC algorithm is based on a target processor occupancy, defined as the percentage of time the processor is busy processing messages within a measurement interval. So the target processor occupancy is the main parameter to be specified. The processor occupancy is measured every measurement interval T_m. Every control interval T_c the measured processor occupancy is compared with the target occupancy. If the measured value is larger than the target value, the incoming load should be reduced. Otherwise, the incoming load should be increased. The adjustment is reflected in a parameter f which indicates the acceptance ratio of the current incoming load. f is therefore the relative rate feedback information and is expressed by the Eq. 3:

$$f^{k+1} = \begin{cases} f_{min}, & \text{if } \phi^k f^k < f_{min} \\ 1, & \text{if } \phi^k f^k > 1 \\ \phi^k f^k, & \text{otherwise} \end{cases} \tag{3}$$

where f_k is the current acceptance ratio and f_{k+1} is the estimated value for the next control interval. $\phi^k = min(\rho_B/\rho_t^k, \phi_{max})$. f_{min} exists to give none-zero minimal acceptance ratio, thus prevents the server from completely shutting off the SE. ϕ_{max} defines the maximum multiplicative increase factor of f in two consecutive control intervals. In this paper we choose the two OCC parameters ϕ and f_{min} to be 5 and 0.02, respectively in all our tests.

We will refer to this algorithm as *rate-occ* in the rest of this paper.

4   Simulation Model

4.1   Simulation Platform

We have built a SIP simulator on the popular OPNET modeler simulation platform [11]. Our SIP simulator captures both the INVITE and non-INVITE state machines as defined in RFC3261. It is also one of the independent implementations in the IETF SIP server overload design team, and has been calibrated in the team under common simulation scenarios.

Our general SIP server model consists of a FIFO queue followed by a SIP processor. Depending on the control mechanisms, specific overload related pre-queue or post-queue processing may be inserted, such as window increase and decrease mechanisms. The feedback information is included in a new *overload* header of each SIP messages, and are processed along with normal SIP message parsing. Processing of each SIP messages creates or updates transaction states as defined by RFC3261. The transport layer is UDP, and therefore all the various SIP timers are in effect.

Our UA model mimics an infinite number of users. Each UA may generate calls at any rate according to a specified distribution and may receive calls at any rate. The processing capacity of a UA is assumed to be infinite since we are interested in the server performance.

4.2   Simulation Topology and Configuration

We use the topology in Figure 2 for current evaluations. There are three UAs on the left, each of which represents an infinite number of callers. Each UA is connected to an SE. The three SEs all connect to the RE which is the potentially overloaded server. The queue size is 500 messages. The core RE connects to UA_0 which represents an infinite number of callees. Calls are generated with exponential interarrival times from the callers at the left to the callees on the right. Each call signaling contains seven messages as illustrated in Figure 1. The call holding time is assumed to be exponentially distributed with average of 30 seconds. The normal message processing rate and the processing rate for rejecting a call at the RE are 500 messages per second (mps) and 3000 mps, respectively.

Note that the server processor configuration, together with the call signaling pattern, results in a nominal system service capacity of 72 cps. All our load and goodput related values presented below are normalized to this system capacity. Our main result metric is goodput, which counts the number of calls with successful delivery of all five call setup messages from INVITE to ACK below 10 s.

For the purpose of this simulation, we also made the following assumptions. First, we do not consider any link transmission delay or loss. However, this does not mean feedback is instantaneous, because we assume the piggyback feedback mechanism. The feedback will only be sent upon the next available message to the particular next hop. Second, all the edge proxies are assumed to have infinite processing capacity. By removing the processing limit of the edge server, we avoid the conservative load pattern when the edge proxy server can itself be overloaded.

These simple yet classical network configuration and assumptions allow us to focus primarily on the algorithms themselves without being distracted by less important factors, which may be further explored in future work.

4.3   SIP Overload without Feedback Control

For comparison, we first look at SIP overload performance without any feedback control. Figure 4 shows the simulation results for two basic scenarios. In the "Simple Drop" scenario, any message arrived after the queue is full is simply dropped. In the "Threshold Rejection" scenario, the server compares its queue length with a high and a low threshold value. If the queue length reaches the high threshold, new INVITE requests are rejected but other messages are still processed. The processing of new INVITE requests will not be restored until the

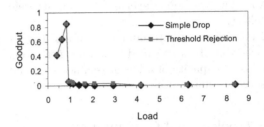

Fig. 4. SIP overload with no feedback control

queue length falls below the low threshold. As we can see, the two result goodput curves almost overlap. Both cases display similar precipitous drops when the offered load approximates the server capacity, a clear sign of congestion collapse. However, the reasons for the steep collapse of the goodput are quite different in the two scenarios. In the "Simple Drop" case, there are still around one third of the INVITE messages arriving at the callee, but all the 180 RINGING messages are dropped, and most of the 200 OK messages are also dropped due to queue overflow. In the "Threshold Rejection" case, none of the INVITE messages reaches the callee, and the RE is only sending rejection messages.

5   Steady Load Performance

We summarize in Table 1 the parameters for all the rate-based and window-based overload control algorithms we discussed in Section 3. In essence, most of the algorithms have a *binding* parameter, three of them use the budget queuing delay D_B, and one uses the budget CPU occupancy ρ_B. All three discrete time control algorithms have a control interval parameter T_c.

There is also a server metric measurement interval T_m used by four of the five algorithms. T_m and T_c need to be separate only when T_c is relatively large compared to T_m. The choice of the T_m value depends on how volatile the target server metric is over time. For example, if the target metric is the server service rate, which is relatively stable, a value of 100 ms is usually more than sufficient. If on the other hand, the target metric is the current queue length, then smaller or larger T_m makes clear differences. In our study, when the specific algorithm requires to measure the server service rate and CPU occupancy, we apply T_m; when the algorithm requires information on the current number of packets in the queue, we always obtain the instant value. Our results show that $T_m = min(100\ ms, T_c)$ is a reasonable assumption, by which we basically reduce the two interval parameters into one.

We looked at the sensitivity of D_B and T_c for each applicable algorithms. Figure 5 and Figure 6 show the results for *win-disc*. All the load and goodput values have been normalized upon the theoretical maximum capacity of the server.

We started with a T_c value of 200 ms and found that the server achieves the unit goodput when D_B is set to 200 ms. Other $0 < D_B < 200\ ms$ values

Table 1. Parameter sets for overload algorithms

Algorithm	Binding	Control Interval	Measure Interval	Additional
rate-abs	D_B	T_c	T_m	
rate-occ	ρ_B	T_c	T_m	f_{min} and ϕ
win-disc	D_B	T_c	T_m	
win-cont	$D_B{}^*$	N/A	T_m	
win-auto	N/A†	N/A	N/A	

D_B: budget queuing delay
ρ_B: CPU occupancy
T_c: discrete time feedback control interval
T_m: discrete time measurement interval for selected server metrics; $T_m \leq T_c$
    where applicable
f_{min}: minimal acceptance fraction
ϕ: multiplicative factor
* D_B recommended for robustness, although a fixed binding window size can
    also be used
† Optionally D_B may be applied for corner cases

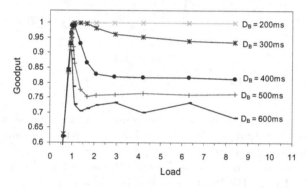

Fig. 5. *win-disc* goodput under different queuing delay budget

also showed similar results. This is not surprising given that both the SIP caller
INVITE and callee 200 OK timer starts at $T_1 = 500$ ms. If the queuing delay is
smaller than $1/2$ T_1 or 250 ms, then there should be no timeout either on the
caller or callee side. A larger value of D_B triggers retransmission timeouts which
reduce the server goodput. For example, Figure 5 shows that at $D_B = 500$ ms,
the goodput has already degraded by 25%.

Letting $D = 200$ ms, we then looked at the influence of T_c. As expected, the
smaller the value of T_c the more accurate the control would be. In our scenario,
we found that a T_c value smaller than 200 ms is sufficient to give the theatrical
maximum goodput. A larger T_c quickly deteriorates the results as seen from
Figure 6.

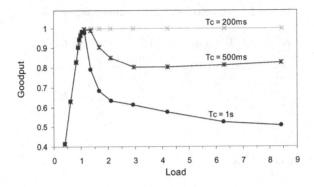

Fig. 6. *win-disc* goodput under different control interval T_c

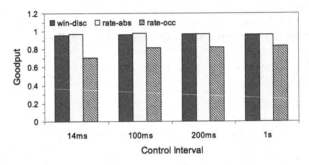

Fig. 7. Goodput vs. T_c at load 1

The effect of D_B for *win-cont* and *rate-abs* show largely the similar shape, with slightly different sensitivity. Generally speaking, a positive D_B value centered at around 200 ms provides a good outcome for all cases.

Figure 7 and Figure 8 compare the T_c parameter for *win-disc*, *rate-abs* and *rate-occ* with $D_B = 200ms$. For the *rate-occ* binding parameter ρ_B, we used 85% for the tests in Figure 7 and Figure 8. We will explain why this value is chosen shortly. It can be seen that the performance of *win-disc* and *rate-abs* are very close to maximum theoretical value in all cases except for when $T_c = 1s$ in the heavy load case. This shows *win-disc* is more sensitive to control interval than *rate-abs*, which could also be caused by the more busty nature of the traffic resulted from window throttle. It is clear that for both *win-disc* and *rate-abs* a shorter T_c improves the results, and a value below 200 ms is sufficient. Overall, *rate-occ* performs not as good as the other two. But what is interesting about *rate-occ* is that from 14 ms to 100 ms control interval, the goodput increases in light overload and decreases in heavy overload. This could be a result of rate adjustment parameters which may have cut the rate too much at the light overload.

To further understand the binding parameter ρ_B of *rate-occ*, we illustrate in Figure 9 the relationship between the goodput and the value of ρ_B under different load conditions. A ρ_B value higher than 95% easily degrades the performance

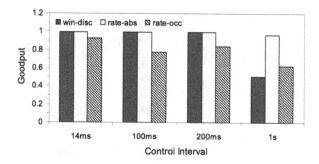

Fig. 8. Goodput vs. T_c at load 8.4

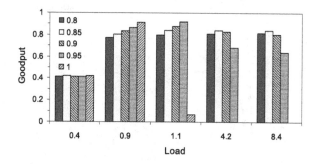

Fig. 9. Goodput vs. ρ_B at different loads

under heavy overload, because the instantaneous server occupancy could still exceeds the healthy region and causes longer delays which result in SIP timer expiration and message retransmissions. A tradeoff ρ_B value with the highest and most stable performance across all load conditions in the given scenario is 85%, which is the reason we used it in Figure 7 and Figure 8.

Finally, for the *win-auto* algorithm, we have found in most cases with a reasonable initial window size in the order of 10, the output matches perfectly the theoretical maximum line. We also see some cases where the system could experience periods of suboptimal yet still stable performance. The most common case happens when the server is started with a large initial window and the offered load is a steep jump to a heavily loaded region. Our investigation reveals that, this suboptimal performance is caused by the difference in the stabilized queuing delay. In most of the normal cases, when the system reaches steady state, the queuing delay is smaller than half of the SIP timer T_1 value or 250 ms. In the suboptimal case, the system may become stable at a point where the queuing delay can exceed 250 ms. The round-trip delay then exceeds 500 ms, which triggers the 200 OK timer and the BYE timer, each of which uses 500 ms. The two timer expirations introduce three additional messages to the system, a retransmitted 200 OK, the ACK to the retransmitted 200 OK, and a retransmitted BYE. This change increases the session length from seven to ten and reduces the

Table 2. Parameters used for comparison

	$D_B(ms)$	$T_c(ms)$	$T_m(ms)$
rate-abs	200	200	100
rate-occ1[‡]	N/A	200	100
rate-occ2[‡]	N/A	14	14
win-disc	200	200	100
win-cont	200	N/A	100
win-auto	N/A	N/A	N/A

[‡] in addition: $\rho_B = 0.85, \phi = 5, f_{min} = 0.02$

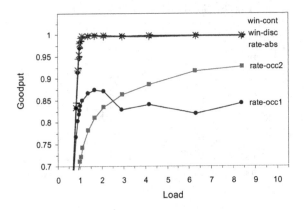

Fig. 10. Goodputperformance for different algorithms

maximum server goodput by 28%. A cure to this situation is to introduce an extra queuing delay parameter to the window adjustment algorithm. Specifically, before the server increases the window size, it checks the current queuing delay. If the queuing delay value already exceeds the desired threshold, the window is not increased. However, we found that determining the optimal value of the queuing delay threshold parameter is not very straightforward and makes the algorithm much more complex. The small chance of the occurrence of the suboptimal performance in realistic situations may not justify the additional delay binding check.

Having looked at various parameters for all different algorithms, we now summarize the best goodput achieved by each algorithm in Figure 10. The specific parameters used for each algorithm is listed in Table 2.

It is clear from Figure 10 that all algorithms except for *rate-occ* are able to reach the theoretical maximum goodput. The corresponding CPU occupancy also confirms the goodput behavior. What is important to understand is that the reason *rate-occ* does not operate at the maximum theoretical goodput like the others is not simply because of the artificial limit of setting the occupancy to 85%. This point can be confirmed by the earlier Figure 9. The inherent issue with an occupancy based heuristic is the fact that occupancy is not as direct a metric as queue length or queuing delay in solving the overload problem. Figure 10 shows one factor that really helps improve the *rate-occ* performance at heavy load seem to be using extremely small T_c. But updating the current CPU occupancy every 14 ms is not straightforward in all systems. Furthermore, when this short T_c is used, the actual server occupancy rose to 93%, which goes contrary to the original intention of setting the 85% budget server occupancy. Yet another issue with setting the extremely short T_c is its much poorer performance than other algorithms under light overload, which should be linked to the tuning of OCC's heuristic increase and decrease parameters.

The merits of all the algorithms achieving maximum theoretical goodput is that they ensure no retransmission ever happens, and thus the server is always busy processing messages, with each single message being part of a successful session.

Another metric of interest for comparison is the session setup delay, which we define as from the time the INVITE is sent until the ACK to 200 OK message is received. We found that the *rate-occ* algorithm has the lowest delay but this is not significant considering it operates at the suboptimal region in terms of goodput. *win-cont* comes next with a delay of around 3 ms. The *rate-abs* offers a delay close to that of *win-cont* at about 3.5 ms. The remaining two *win-disc* and *win-auto* have a delay of 5 ms and 6 ms respectively. In fact all these values are sufficiently small and are not likely making any difference.

From the steady state load analysis so far, we conclude that the occupancy based approach is less favorable than others because of its relatively more number of tuning parameters and not being able to adapt to the most efficient processing condition for the maximum goodput. *win-disc* and *abs-rate* are by definition quite similar and they also have the same number of parameters. Their performance is also very close, although *rate-rate* has shown a slight edge, possibly because of the smoother arrival pattern resulting from the percentage throttle. *win-cont* has less tuning parameter than *win-disc* and *abs-rate*, and offers equal or slightly better performance Finally, *win-auto* is an extremely simple algorithm yet achieves nearly perfect results in most situations.

6 Dynamic Load Performance and Fairness for Overload Control

Although steady load performance is a good starting point for evaluating the overload control algorithms, most of the regular overload scenarios are not persistent steady overload. Otherwise, The issue would become a poor capacity planning problem. The realistic server to server overload situations are more likely short periods of bulk loads, possibly accompanied by new sender arrivals or departures. Therefore, in this section we extend our evaluation to the dynamic behavior of overload control algorithms under load variations. Furthermore, we investigate the fairness property of each of the algorithms.

6.1 Fairness for SIP Overload Control

Defining Fairness. Under overload, the server may allocate its available capacity among all the upstream senders using criteria considered fair. Theoretically,

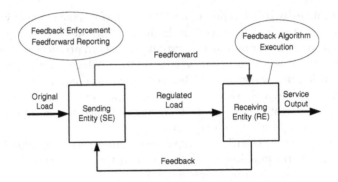

Fig. 11. The double feed architecture

fairness can be coupled with many other factors and could have an unlimited number of definitions. However, we see two basic types of fairness criteria which may be applicable in most scenarios: service provider-centric and end user-centric.

If we consider the upstream servers representing service providers, a service-provider centric fairness means giving all the upstream servers the same aggregate success rate.

The user-centric fairness criteria aim to give each individual user who are using the overloaded server the same chance of call success, regardless of where the call originated from. Indeed, this end user-centric fairness may be preferred in regular overload situation. For example, in the TV hotline "free tickets to the third caller" case, user-centric fairness ensures that all users have equal winning probability to call in. Otherwise, a user with a service provider who happens to have a large call volume would have a clear disadvantage.

Achieving Fairness. Technically, achieving the basic service provider-centric fairness is easy if the number of active sources are known, because the overloaded server simply needs to split its processing capacity equally in the feedback generated for all the active senders.

Achieving user-centric fairness means the overloaded server should split is capacity proportionally among the senders based on the senders original incoming load. For the various feedback mechanisms we have discussed, technically the receiver in both the absolute rate-based and window-based feedback mechanisms does not have the necessary information to do proportional capacity allocation when the feedback loop is activated. The receiver in the relative rate-based mechanism does have the ability to deduce the proportion of the original load among the senders.

To achieve user-centric fairness in absolute rate and window-based mechanisms, we introduce a new feedforward loop in the existing feedback architecture. The resulting double-feed architecture is shown in Figure 11. The feedforward information contains the sender measured value of the current incoming load. Like the feedback, all the feedforward information is naturally piggybacked in existing SIP messages since SIP messages by themselves travel in both directions. This way the feedforward introduces minimal overhead as in the feedback case. The feedforward information from all the active senders gives the receiver global knowledge about the original sending load. It is worth noting that, this global knowledge equips the receiver with great flexibility that also allows it to execute any kind of more advanced user-centric or service provider-centric fairness criteria. Special fairness criteria may be required, for example, when the server is experiencing denial of service attack instead of regular overload.

6.2   Dynamic Load Performance

Figure 12 depicts the arrival pattern for our dynamic load test. We used the step function load pattern because if the algorithm works in this extreme case, it should work in less harsh situations. The three UAs each starts and ends at different time, creating an environment of dynamic source arrival and departure. Each source also has a different peak load value, thus allowing us to observe proportional fairness mechanisms when necessary.

For dynamic behavior, our simulation shows that all algorithms except *win-auto* adapts well to the offered dynamic load, showing little transition difference during new source arrival and existing source departure as well as at load change boundaries. As far as fairness is concerned, the *rate-occ* by default can provide user-centric fairness; the basic *rate-abs*, *win-disc* and *win-cont* algorithms are capable of basic service provider centric fairness by allocating equal amount of capacity to each *SE*. After implementing our double-feed architecture with

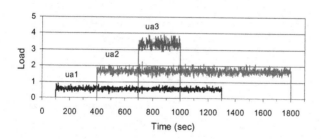

Fig. 12. Dynamic load arrival

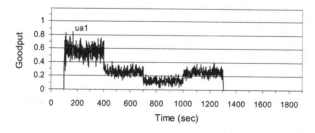

Fig. 13. *win-cont* UA1 goodput with dynamic load

sources reporting the original load to the RE, we are able to achieve user-centric fairness in all *rate-abs*, *win-disc* and *win-cont* algorithms through a proportional allocation of total RE capacity according to SEs' original incoming load. In addition, having knowledge of the incoming load proportion from each SE could also help us refine the algorithms when necessary. For example, in the *win-cont* case, we can improve the window allocation accuracy by using "weighted fair processing", i.e., available processing resources are probabilistically assigned to the SEs based on their proportional share of total incoming load. The improved algorithm is illustrated below:

$$w_i^0 := W_0 \text{ where } W_0 > 0$$
$$w_{left'}^0 := 0$$
$$w_i^t := w_i^t - 1 \text{ for INVITE received from } SE_i$$
$$w_{left}^t := N_{sess}^{max} - N_{sess} \text{ upon msg processing}$$
$$w_{left}^t := w_{left}^t + w_{left'}^t$$
$$if(w_{left}^t \geq 1)$$
$$\quad w_{left'}^t = (frac)(w_{left}^t)$$
$$\quad w_{share}^t = (int)(w_{left}^t)$$
$$\quad \text{assuming the proportion of original load from } SE_i \text{ is } P\%$$
$$\quad w_i^t := w_{share}^t \text{ with probability } P/100$$

Results of the *win-cont* algorithm with user-centric fairness are shown in Figure 13 through Figure 15. As can be seen, UA1 starts at the 100th second with load 0.57 and gets a goodput of the same value. At the 400th second, UA2 is

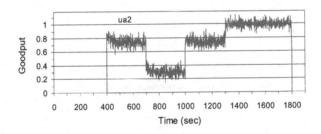

Fig. 14. *win-cont* UA2 goodput with dynamic load

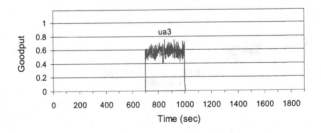

Fig. 15. *win-cont* UA3 goodput with dynamic load

started with load 1.68, three times of UA1's load. UA1's goodput quickly declines and reaches a state where it shares the capacity with UA2 at a one to three proportion. At the 700th second, UA3 is added with a load of 3.36. The combination of the three active sources therefore has a load of 5.6. We see that the goodputs of both UA1 and UA2 immediately decrease. The three sources settle at a stable situation with roughly 0.1, 0.3, and 0.6 goodput, matching the original individual load. At the 1000th second, the bulk arrival of UA3 ends and UA3 left the system. The allocation split between UA1 and UA2 restores to the similar situation before UA3's arrival at the 700th second. Finally, at the 1300th second, UA1 departs the system, leaving UA2 with load 1.68 alone. Since the load is still over the server capacity, UA2 gets exactly the full capacity of the system with a goodput of 1.

The graph for service-provider centric fairness is similar, with the total allocation equally shared by the current number of active sources during each load interval.

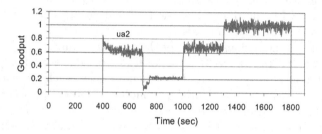

Fig. 16. *win-auto* UA2 goodput with dynamic load

We also evaluated the dynamic performance of the simplest *win-auto* algorithm. We found that with source arrival and departure, the system still always reaches the maximum goodput as long as the current load is larger than the server capacity. A difference from the other algorithms is that it could take a noticeably longer adaptation time to reach the steady state under certain load surge. For example, we show in Figure 16 the goodput for UA2. At the 700th second when the load increases suddenly from 2.25 to 5.6, it took over 60 s to completely stabilize. However, the good thing is once steady state is reached, the total goodput of all three UAs adds up to one. Moreover, performance under source departure is good. At the 1300th second, when UA2 becomes the only UA in the system, its goodput quickly adapts to 1. There is, however, one specific drawback of the *win-auto* mechanism. Since there is basically no processing intervention in this algorithm, we found it hard to enforce an explicit share of the capacity. The outcome of the capacity split seem to be determined by the point when the system reaches the steady state which is not easy to predict. Therefore, *win-auto* may not be a good candidate when explicit fairness is required. But because of its extreme simplicity, as well as near perfect steady state aggregate performance, *win-auto* may still be a good choice in some situations.

7 Conclusions and Future Work

The SIP server overload problem is interesting for a number of reasons: first, the cost of rejecting a request is not negligible compared to the cost of serving a request; Second, the various SIP timers lead to many retransmissions in overload and amplify the situation; Third, SIP has a server to server application level routing architecture. The server to server architecture helps the deployment of a pushback SIP overload control solution. The solution can be based on feedback of absolute rate, relative rate, or window size.

We proposed three window adjustment algorithms *win-disc*, *win-cont* and *win-auto* for window-based feedback and resorted to two existing rate adjustment algorithms for absolute rate-based feedback *rate-abs* and relative rate-based feedback *rate-occ*. Among these five algorithms, *win-auto* is the most SIP specific, and *rate-occ* is the least SIP specific. The remaining three *win-disc*, *win-cont*, and *rate-abs* are generic mechanisms, and need to be linked to SIP when being applied to the SIP environment. The common piece that linked them to SIP is the dynamic session estimation algorithm we introduced. It is not difficult to imagine that with the dynamic session estimation algorithm, other generic algorithms can also be applied to SIP.

Now we summarize various aspects of the five algorithms.

The design of most of the feedback algorithms contains a binding parameter. Algorithms binding on queue length or queuing delay such as *win-disc*, *win-cont* and *rate-abs* outperform algorithms binding on processor occupancy such as *rate-occ*. Indeed, all of *win-disc*, *win-cont* and *rate-abs* are able to achieve theoretical maximum performance, meaning the CPU is fully utilized and every message processed contributes to a successful session, with no wasted message in the system at all. On the other hand, occupancy based heuristic is a much coarser control approach. The sensitivity of control also depends on the extra multiplicative increase and decrease parameter tuning. Therefore, from steady load performance and parameter tuning perspective, we favor algorithms other than *rate-occ*.

The adjustment performed by each algorithm can be discrete time driven such as in *win-disc* and *rate-abs*, *rate-occ* or continuous event driven such as in *win-cont* and *win-auto*. Normally the event-driven algorithm could have smaller number of tuning parameters and also be more accurate. But with a sufficiently short discrete time control interval the difference between discrete and continuous adjustments would become small.

We found that all the algorithms except *win-auto* adapt well to traffic source variations as well as bulk arrival overload. When we further look at the fairness property, especially the user-centric fairness which may be preferable in many practical situations, we found the *rate-occ* algorithm realizes it by default. All other algorithms except *win-auto* can also achieve it with our introduction of the double-feed SIP overload control architecture.

Finally, *win-auto* frequently needs to be singled out because it is indeed special. With an extremely simple implementation and virtually zero parameters, it archives a remarkable steady load aggregate output in most cases. The tradeoff to this simplicity is a noticeable load adaptation period upon certain load surge, and the difficulty of enforcing explicit fairness models.

Our possible work items for the next step may include adding delay and loss property to the link, and applying other arrival patterns as well as node failure models to make the scenario more realistic. It would be interesting to see whether and how the currently closely matched results of each algorithm may differ in those situations. Another work item is that although we currently assumed percentage-throttle for rate-based and window-throttle for window-based control only, it may be helpful to look at more types of feedback enforcement methods at the SE and see how different the feedback algorithms will behave.

Acknowledgments

This project receives funding from NTT. The OPNET simulation software is donated by OPNET Technologies under its university program. Part of the research was performed when Charles Shen was an intern at IBM T.J. Watson Research Center. The authors would also like to thank Arata Koike and the IETF SIP overload design team members for helpful discussions.

References

1. Rosenberg, J., Schulzrinne, H., Camarillo, G., Johnston, A., Peterson, J., Sparks, R., Handley, M., Schooler, E.: SIP: Session Initiation Protocol. RFC 3261 (Proposed Standard) RFCs 3265, 3853, 4320 (June 2002)
2. Rosenberg, J.: Requirements for Management of Overload in the Session Initiation Protocol. Internet draft work in progress (January 2008)
3. Hilt, V., Widjaja, I., Malas, D., Schulzrinne, H.: Session Initiation Protocol (SIP) Overload Control. Internet draft work in progress (February 2008)
4. Hosein, P.: Adaptive rate control based on estimation of message queueing delay. United States Patent US 6,442,139 B1 (2002)
5. Cyr, B.L., Kaufman, J.S., Lee, P.T.: Load balancing and overload control in a distributed processing telecommunication systems. United States Patent US 4,974,256 (1990)
6. Kasera, S., Pinheiro, J., Loader, C., Karaul, M., Hari, A., LaPorta, T.: Fast and robust signaling overload control. In: Ninth International Conference on Network Protocols, pp. 323–331 (2001)
7. Ohta, M.: Overload Protection in a SIP Signaling Network. In: International Conference on Internet Surveillance and Protection (ICISP 2006) (2006)
8. Nahum, E., Tracey, J., Wright, C.: Evaluating SIP server performance. ACM SIGMETRICS Performance Evaluation Review 35, 349–350 (2007)
9. Whitehead, M.: GOCAP - one standardised overload control for next generation networks. BT Technology Journal 23(1), 144–153 (2005)
10. Noel, E., Johnson, C.: Initial simulation results that analyze SIP based VoIP networks under overload. In: Mason, L.G., Drwiega, T., Yan, J. (eds.) ITC 2007. LNCS, vol. 4516, pp. 54–64. Springer, Heidelberg (2007)
11. OPNET, http://www.opnet.com

Improving the Scalability of an IMS-Compliant Conferencing Framework Part II: Involving Mixing and Floor Control

A. Amirante, T. Castaldi, L. Miniero, and S.P. Romano

University of Napoli "Federico II"
Via Claudio 21, 80125 Napoli, Italy
{alessandro.amirante,tobia.castaldi,lorenzo.miniero,spromano}@unina.it

Abstract. At *IPTComm*2007 we presented a paper in which we analyzed the performance of a distributed conferencing framework we have recently designed and implemented. The paper focused on the scalability of the overall framework and demonstrated that the switch from a centralized to a distributed approach can significantly improve the achievable performance. Though, in the cited work, we mainly addressed the signalling aspects of the framework. We did not make any attempt at assessing the performance of our architecture (neither in the centralized, nor in the distributed case) in the presence of mixed media streams. This left us, and perhaps the readers, with a fine sensation of unfinished and motivated us to keep on working on the measurements, this time focusing on the two main aspects that come into play when a real conference is activated in a moderated environment like the one we propose: (i) mixing of the real-time streams generated by the users; (ii) floor control.

Keywords: Distributed conferencing, scalability, protocol dispatching, moderation.

1 Introduction

In this article we present the results of a scalability analysis conducted on a real-world implementation of an open-source distributed conferencing framework capable to provide users with enhanced functionality like mixing of the media flows and moderation. The considered architecture has been the main subject of our efforts during the last years and it definitely represents for us, and for the interested researchers in the international community as well, a sort of playground where to experiment with the protocols and applications which characterize the emerging IMS (*IP Multimedia Subsystem*) scenario.

The present work does not come alone: it actually represents an extension to our previous work on the same topic. Indeed, in [1] we presented the first results of the above mentioned analysis, which mainly focused the attention on the complex aspects related to the signaling plane. We showed that performance figures highly benefit from the adoption of a paradigm envisaging at the outset the presence of two fundamental features like separation of concerns and distribution of components.

H. Schulzrinne, R. State, and S. Niccolini (Eds.): IPTComm 2008, LNCS 5310, pp. 174–195, 2008.

With this work, we aim to provide a new contribution, by quantitatively estimating both the overhead introduced by an advanced function like moderation (which inevitably calls for the adoption of floor control mechanisms and protocols) and the attainable performance improvement, this time at the level of the media plane, associated with a switch from a centralized to a distributed paradigm.

We will address both the aforementioned issues, by also highlighting the critical aspects that come into play when solutions originally conceived for a centralized scenario have to be transparently brought to a distributed environment. This is the case, for example, of the *Binary Floor Control Protocol* (BFCP) [2], which currently represents the only standard solution for moderating access to shared resources and which has been conceived at the outset as a centralized protocol. With respect to the second objective of our work, we will follow for our analysis the same approach as the one we adopted in our previous work. Hence, we will concentrate on a comparison between the centralized and the distributed architectures in real-world scenarios involving both audio mixing and floor control. CPU utilization will represent the key performance indicator we will look at.

The paper is organized as follows. In section 2 we will briefly recall the main characteristics of both the centralized and the distributed conferencing architectures we have realized. Then, in section 3 we will better clarify how the two functions which are the subject of our study, namely media mixing and floor control, have been implemented in our architecture. Section 4 contains the core of our contribution, since it first presents and then discusses the experimental campaign we conducted. This will also include some interesting considerations about the implementation insights we were able to gain thanks to the trials we performed. Section 5 concludes the paper by summarizing the main achievements while also presenting the main directions of our future work.

2   A Brief Reminder

In the framework of our latest research activities, we have designed and implemented two conferencing solutions which embrace, respectively, a centralized and a distributed paradigm. In the following subsections we will briefly describe both of them, with the sake of helping the readers appropriately position our previous work and consequently appreciate the contribution of the present article.

2.1   CONFIANCE: A Centralized Conferencing Architecture

We recently presented an open source conferencing framework, which we called *CONFIANCE (CONFerencing IMS-enabled Architecture for Next-generation Communication Experience)*. Such framework is compliant with the IMS specification and takes into account ongoing standardization efforts inside the various active international bodies (IETF, 3GPP, OMA, etc). Compatibility with the

IMS architecture was achieved through a mapping between the logical IMS entities and several real-world components. To offer advanced conferencing capabilities, we developed an actual implementation of the centralized conferencing framework [3] as proposed by the IETF working group XCON. We worked both on the server side (*Focus*) and on the client side (*Participant* and *Administrator*), as well as on the communication protocols between them, namely the *Conference Control Protocol* (CCP) and the aforementioned BFCP. CCP takes care of session management, whereas BFCP looks after moderation aspects of the framework, so to allow coordinated access to the set of resources it offers. Such protocols complement the functionality already provided within a conferencing context by signaling protocols, which in our implementation was represented by the *Session Initiation Protocol* (SIP) [4].

We are not providing herein the details of the implementation of the CONFIANCE architecture. We invite those who might be interested in such information to have a look at the work presented in [5].

2.2 DCON: Extending CONFIANCE through Components Distribution

After completing the design and implementation of CONFIANCE, we started working on an enhancement specifically conceived with the aim of improving its scalability properties. We then defined a distributed conferencing architecture which was to be both reliable and scalable. Such architecture has been called *DCON* [6], standing for *Distributed Conferencing*, but at the same time explicitly recalling the already mentioned XCON model which CONFIANCE was built upon.

DCON is based on the idea that a distributed conference can be setup by appropriately orchestrating the operation of a set of XCON focus elements, each in charge of managing a certain number of participants distributed across a geographical network. Interaction between each participant and the corresponding conference focus is based on the standard XCON framework, whereas inter-focus interaction has been completely defined and specified by us. More precisely, in order to build distributed conferencing on top of the already available centralized conferencing framework, we basically introduced four additional functions: (i) a coordination level among conference focus entities; (ii) a way to effectively distribute conference state information; (iii) a strategy to let centralized protocols work in a distributed environment; (iv) a mechanism to distribute the media mixing process. To achieve these functions, our prototype has been realized by extending the functionality offered by the *eXtensible Messaging and Presence Protocol* (XMPP) [7], specifically for what concerns its server-to-server (s2s) communication mechanism.

Once again, for the sake of conciseness we will not delve into the details of the above mentioned functions. The interested reader can find such information in [8].

3   Monitored Functionality: Mixing and Floor Control

3.1   Mixing

The work we presented in [1] did not involve, on purpose, any detail about how media mixing works in our architecture. The reason for this can be found in the nature of the paper itself, which was much more focused on the signaling facet of the distribution issue, rather than on the provided media. The present paper, on the contrary, explicitly debates relevant mixing-related matters, and so a few words upon our design choices are worth being spent. Our architecture currently envisages distributed mixing for both audio and video media streams. However, considering only audio will be taken into account in the performance evaluation herein presented, our architectural design concerning distributed video mixing is left to future work.

For what concerns the mixing in the centralized scenario (XCON), the design was quite straightforward. Indeed, CONFIANCE is based on Asterisk, which natively provides a module, called *MeetMe*, implementing basic audio conferencing functionality. This module, acting as a conference bridge, easily provided us with the needed audio mixing capability in centralized conferences. However, the introduction of conference distribution (DCON) confronted us with the need to also deal with some kind of distributed mixing. In fact, while simply relaying all the media streams coming from remote participants to the focus hosting the conference would do the job, we considered such an approach to be explicitly out of discussion for many obvious reasons, like the lack of scalability and the unfair share of responsibilities among the involved foci. To achieve such functionality we decided to introduce a cascaded-like approach to implement the needed distributed mixing. A cascaded approach means that each remote conference focus is seen as a single participant by the main conference bridge it is attached to. To better clarify this, mixing can be seen as if taking place at two levels of granularity: (i) each remote focus takes care of mixing the participants it is responsible for, and of relaying its global mix to the main focus; (ii) the main focus, instead, besides taking care of its local participants, also mixes all the remote foci it is aware of, each of them being seen as a single participant providing a single, already mixed, stream. Of course, each remote focus also includes the mix coming from the main focus, which contains the contributions of all other remote foci. This approach allows us to enable all participants, whatever focus they are attached to, to actively participate in a conference, by also distributing mixing in a fair and scalable way.

This functionality, however, did not come free of issues. In fact, having each focus mix its own share of participants also meant it should be made aware of the policies, like floor control, related to the users it was responsible for. This issue will be explained in detail in the next section, where distributed floor control is introduced and explained.

3.2   Floor Control

General description. Before dealing with distributed floor control it is worth spending some words on floor control itself, and on the way it can currently be achieved. As the name already suggests, floor control is a way to handle moderation of resources in a conference. In fact, a floor can be seen, from a logical point of view, as the right to access and/or manipulate a specific set of resources that might be available to end-users. Introducing means to have participants request such a right is what is called floor control. A typical example is a lecture mode conference, in which interested participants might need to ask the lecturer for the right to talk in order to ask a question.

The IETF recently standardized, within the context of the XCON WG, a dedicated protocol to deal with floor control, the Binary Floor Control Protocol (BFCP). This protocol envisages the above mentioned floor as a token that can be associated with one or more resources. Queues and policies associated with such floors are handled by a Floor Control Server (FCS), which acts as a centralized node for all requests coming from Floor Control Participants (FCP). Decisions upon incoming requests (e.g. accepting or denying requests for a floor) can be either taken on the basis of automated policies by the FCS itself, or relayed to a Floor Control Chair (FCC), in case one has been assigned to the related floor. These decisions affect the state of the queues associated with the related floors, and consequently the state of the resources themselves. To go back to the lecture mode scenario example presented before, a participant who has been granted the floor (i.e. the right to ask a question to the lecturer) would be added to the conference mix, whereas participants without the floor (or with pending requests) would be excluded from the same mix, thus being muted in the conference.

BFCP in XCON-CONFIANCE. The first available implementation of BFCP was realized by our research group (in collaboration with Ericsson's Nomadic Lab) as a library [1], and is currently an integral part of CONFIANCE. This means that CONFIANCE takes the role of the FCS, whereas the participants take the role of FCPs and, if designated, FCCs. The negotiation of a BFCP connection between the FCS and a FCP has been implemented as well, as specified in [9]. Of course, the addition of floor control affected the way CONFIANCE had to mix incoming streams: in fact, we had to make sure that participants who had not been granted the floor would not be included in the conference mix. The enforcement of the policies envisaged by floor control (e.g. muting and un-muting participants according to the state of floors) has been accomplished by integrating floor-related events in the conferencing module itself.

Nevertheless, as explained in the previous paragraph, BFCP is a natively centralized protocol. This means that, while it worked like a charm when limited to centralized conferences as envisaged in XCON and in the CONFIANCE platform, it represented an issue when we moved towards a distributed approach. This was even more true when we involved a cascaded-based mixing, as it will be discussed in the next section.

BFCP in DCON. According to [10] a DCON compliant architecture must provide users with the capability to transparently join a conference which is hosted

---

[1] http://sourceforge.net/projects/libbfcp

by a focus entity belonging to a foreign centralized island. Furthermore, it must forward any centralized protocol message to its related peer in the distributed overlay whenever the message is directed to a receiver who does not belong to the local centralized system. Our implementation of the DCON system fully complies with the mentioned requirements. In fact, in order to join a remote conference the participant only needs to interact with its corresponding focus in exactly the same way as he did in the centralized case. Upon reception of the participant's request, the local focus forwards join information to the focus entity belonging to the island in which the conference in question was created. Due to the large number of peer entities each focus could be in touch with, in a distributed scenario a mechanism to prevent collisions in the assignment of centralized protocols identifiers is needed. We achieved this goal by means of the label swapping process explained with the following example.

To make the whole thing clearer, we deal with the case where a user (Client (A)) belonging to XCON cloud (A) wants to remotely participate in a distributed conference hosted by XCON cloud (B). Fig. 1 shows how this kind of join requests is handled by the local focus in order to both dispatch them and create a sort of *virtual labels path* needed to correctly manage future messages addressed to the same user in the same conference.

1. Once the client has locally joined the distributed conference by placing a SIP call to the focus it belongs to (XCON (A)), the focus chooses a new label for Client (A) which will be used to appropriately dispatch all messages related to it;
2. XCON (A) at this point forwards the join request to its related DCON focus entity (DCON (A)); in this example this is done by sending, through the *XCON-DCON Synchronization Protocol (XDSP)* [11], a message called *AddUser*, containing the newly assigned client's label A;
3. DCON (A) receives the join request; since it regards a new client, the DCON focus entity chooses a new label (e.g. XYZ) and associates it with the just received label A; depending on the distributed conference the client wants to join, it associates the label (XYZ) with the DCON focus entity managing the XCON focus physically hosting the conference (DCON (B)) and forwards the join request to it;
4. DCON (B) receives the forwarded message through a *server-to-server* (s2s) channel based on the XMPP protocol; since it regards a new client, DCON (B) chooses a new label (e.g. B) and associates it with the just received label XYZ; since the conference the remote Client (A) wants to join is physically hosted by XCON (B), the join request is forwarded there using the XDSP protocol, with an *AddUser* message containing the newly assigned label B which identifies the remote client;
5. XCON (B) receives the request, and thus associates the received label B with the remote Client (A); all the operations needed to add the new user to the conference are performed, and the new information is sent back to the client through the same path. All the involved labels (B, XYZ, A) will be properly swapped to route all XCON protocols messages between the two entities.

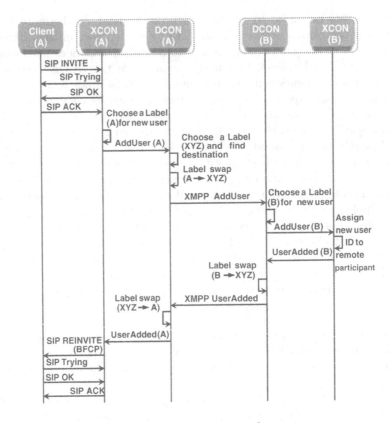

Fig. 1. Joining a remote conference

Once XCON (A) receives the confirmation that the user has been successfully added to the remote conference, together with the related information, the Client (A) is updated through a *SIP re-INVITE* containing the BFCP information needed to communicate with the Floor Control Server.

From this moment on and for the entire life cycle of its participation in the remote conference the local focus takes care of the user acting as a gateway for all what concerns natively centralized protocols.

In order to make the reader as aware as possible of the mechanisms involved in the experimental campaign presented in the following sections, Fig. 2 illustrates how BFCP is dispatched across the distributed environment.

Continuing from the previous example, since XCON (B) is physically hosting the conference, floor control will be entirely managed by its Floor Control Server. All BFCP messages sent by the clients to the Floor Control Server are intercepted by the local focus (specifically by its *Gateway* component), and then forwarded to the Floor Control Server of XCON (B). We have already seen how labels are assigned and swapped: the same labels will be used for dispatching.

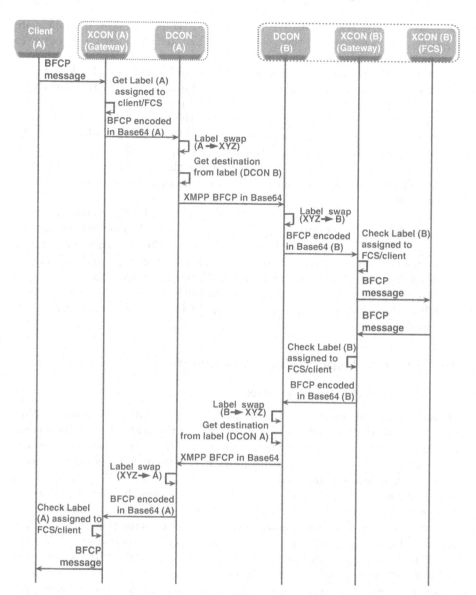

Fig. 2. BFCP dispatching

The flow of a typical message exchange can be seen as follows:

1. Client (A) sends a BFCP message to the Floor Control Server; the message is intercepted by XCON (A)'s gateway; the label assigned to client (A) is retrieved, and used to forward the BFCP message to the Dispatcher in DCON (A); of course, since BFCP messages are binary, a proper Base64 encoding is performed to encapsulate the message in our text-based XDSP protocol data unit;

2. Once DCON (A) receives the encapsulated BFCP message, the labels are once again swapped (in this case, A → XYZ) and the message is routed to the right destination (DCON (B));

3. DCON (B) will receive the message and swap labels again (XYZ → B); at this point, the encapsulated message will be forwarded to the underlying XCON (B) Gateway to be further processed there;

4. The Gateway in XCON (B) will receive the encapsulated (and Base64-encoded) BFCP message; after decoding it, the Gateway will analyze the label marked in the message (B, in this case), and will understand it is a message sent by a remote user (Client (A)) to the local Floor Control Server. It will forward the (now 'natively' binary) message there, where it will be processed;

5. In case FCS (B) needs to send a message to Client (A), exactly the same operations will be performed, and the same path will be followed through the needed label swaps among the involved peers. FCS (A), while not actually managing the floors related to the remote conference in which Client (A) is participating, will however be notified upon each floor status change, so to appropriately update the local media mixes when needed (e.g. to mute Client (A), thus excluding her/him from XCON (A)'s local mix if FCS (B) has decided so).

4   The New Experimental Campaign

4.1   Preliminary Considerations

We have already demonstrated in [1] how the migration from a centralized platform to a distributed environment can improve the scalability of the overall architecture. The objective of this section is to demonstrate that such an improvement is still achievable when taking into account both mixing of media flows and floor control. Both such functions automatically come into play when envisaging moderated conferencing scenarios, i.e. when the BFCP protocol is employed. As in the old test campaign conducted, the performance tests carried out focused on the CPU load and hardware resource consumption given a certain amount of users in the system, and in order to perform them we exploited the SIPp[2] tool, an open source performance testing tool for the SIP protocol that can generate both signaling and multimedia traffic.

By using SIPp, we were hence capable to stress both the centralized and the distributed platform. Though, in order to involve all the components of the architecture in our analysis (including the media mixer and the Floor Control Server), we also had to implement a "stresser" for the BFCP protocol. Such a tool is capable to send *FloorRequest* and *FloorRelease* BFCP messages to the FCS, thus enabling or disabling the mixing operation for each call instance. We briefly describe our implementation of the *BFCP stresser* in the next subsection (4.1). Fig. 3 summarizes the performance analysis as previously conducted in [1], i.e. with no moderation features, in the case of GSM-encoded RTP audio flows.

---

[2] http://sipp.sourceforge.net

Number of islands	Number of local users	Number of remote users	Main focus CPU load	Remote focus 1 CPU load	Remote focus 2 CPU load
1	240	-	99.4%	-	-
2	120	120	30.04%	20.19%	-
3	80	160 (80/80)	20%	18%	18%
3	120	120 (60/60)	31.05%	12%	12%

Fig. 3. A comparative table summarizing performance figures without BFCP

In the following, instead, we present the results obtained when we let BFCP come into play, thus involving in our tests the media mixer (subsection 4.2) and the FCS (subsection 4.3), once again in the presence of GSM-encoded audio flows.

The BFCP stresser. We provide in the following some information about the *BFCP stresser* we implemented. As already mentioned, we wanted to involve in our measurement campaign both the media mixer and the Floor Control Server, so the need arose for a tool capable to send BFCP messages on behalf of the participants of a conference. We remind that in order to build a BFCP message, we need the transport address of the FCS, together with the related identifiers. Such information is encapsulated in the SDP body of the re-invite message the focus sends back when a user joins a conference, as specified in [9]. In spite of this, we decided to statically provide our tool with these data by means of a configuration file, since we did not want to force the *BFCP stresser* to be co-located with the *SIPp stresser* (which is in charge of signaling tasks). Furthermore, in order to build a BFCP message, the *BFCP stresser* has to be aware of user-specific parameters (i.e. UserID and ConferenceID). In our implementation, these parameters are extracted from an asynchronous event raised by the Asterisk server whenever a new user joins a conference. So, we let our tool connect to Asterisk through the *Asterisk Manager Interface*, making it capable to catch any suitable event and act consequently. We remark that the software developed also maintains information about each user's state, saving the related floor status (granted/not granted). This is useful since we envisaged the possibility of setting two parameters, p_{req} and p_{rel}, related to the probability per second with which the tool generates, respectively, *FloorRequest* and *FloorRelease* messages on behalf of each user, according to her/his status. For example, if we set $p_{req} = 0.15$ and $p_{rel} = 0.05$, every second the stresser checks each user's status and: (i) if she/he has not been granted the floor, the tool performs a *FloorRequest* with a 15% probability; (ii) if she/he has already been granted the floor, a *FloorRelease* is performed with a 5% probability. The desired values of these probabilities are to be specified through the already mentioned configuration file.

4.2 Involving the Media Mixer

Centralized scenario. Fig. 4 illustrates the testbed configuration in the case of the centralized conferencing scenario. The *SIPp console* is used to remotely

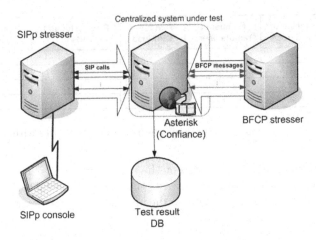

Fig. 4. Testbed configuration: centralized scenario

control and coordinate a single test, by issuing commands to the call originating server (*SIPp stresser* in the picture). Such server in turn creates and sends call requests to the Confiance server in accordance with the SIPp console indications, thus emulating a real-world calls profile. The *BFCP stresser*, instead, hosts the tool we developed in order to generate BFCP messages and consequently allow/deny the mixing of the media flows related to each call. During a test's lifetime, the logging database is continuously updated with information about the Confiance server status. We then exploit the gathered information in order to perform off-line analysis of the collected data and evaluate the results.

For the sake of completeness, we observe that all the machines used for the testbed (except the SIPp console, which might be any host equipped with a network interface) are hosting a Linux Debian 4.0 "Etch" operating system equipped with a $2.6.18 - 5 - 686$ kernel. They have a $3.2GHz$ Intel XEON cpu and $2GB$ RAM. Bandwidth was not a limiting factor for the performance evaluation, since we used a dedicated gigabit ethernet network for the campaign.

The experimental campaign we conducted is based on the realization of a great number of tests for a single scenario. This is done in order to avoid basing our analysis on a potentially biased set of data. For each scenario, we herein present a single result which is representative of the average case for that scenario.

As already stated, we assessed that the bottleneck is definitely represented by the CPU utilization level, rather than other relevant hardware parameters like, for example, available RAM memory. In the following, and in the next subsections as well, we will hence focus just on CPU as the key performance indicator.

Fig. 5 shows the CPU utilization level in the presence of only one active conference and considering all the participants to have been granted the audio floor. This behavior was obtained by appropriately instructing the *BFCP stresser* to send a *BFCP FloorRequest* on behalf of each user who joined the conference.

We explicitly remark that in such a way we added the media mixer to the elements of our platform under test. It can be seen that when the number of participants approaches 180 the CPU load of the focus managing the conference is close to 100%. This first result, when compared with the corresponding one in Fig. 3, gives us an idea of how mixing is a cpu-intensive operation.

The result of 180 users as the peak value for the centralized scenario in the presence of BFCP functionality will be used as a benchmarking parameter in the following subsection, which discusses the achievable performance improvement in the distributed case.

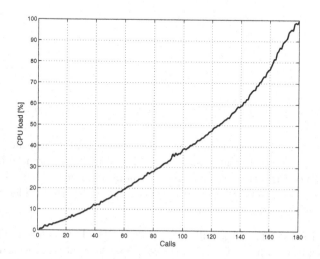

Fig. 5. CPU utilization in the centralized scenario (GSM codec) with moderation

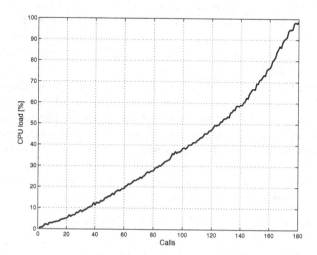

Fig. 6. CPU utilization in the centralized scenario (GSM codec) with moderation, in the presence of 10 active conferences

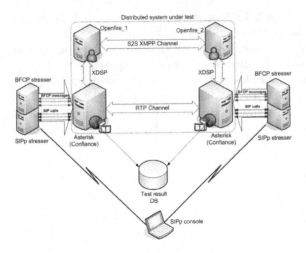

Fig. 7. Testbed configuration: distributed scenario with just two XCON islands

It is worth noting that the results presented above, and in the following as well, do not strictly depend on the assumption that all users participate in the same conference. To confirm this, we considered a more realistic scenario characterized by 10 active conferences with 18 participants each. This situation led to identical performance figures as shown in Fig. 6.

Distributed scenario. Fig. 7 illustrates the testbed configuration in the case of the distributed conferencing scenario with just two interconnected islands.

With respect to the centralized case, we now find the *Openfire* component, which is specifically dedicated to information spreading and protocol dispatching. We also notice that the *SIPp console* is now used to manage both of the available *SIPp_stresser* entities. As to the *BFCP stresser*, it generates BFCP messages against both foci. In the following of this subsection we will present results obtained in the distributed scenario, envisaging the presence of either two or three interconnected clouds, respectively.

As already said, we wanted to study how the CPU performance improved when moving from a centralized to a distributed environment. More specifically, our goal was to evaluate if the improvement obtained without involving moderation (and, consequently, mixing operations) is still achievable when computational cycles are spent both to mix the media flows coming from the participants and to perform floor control operations. With this objective in mind, we performed several testing experiments, assuming, as in the centralized case, the presence of just one active conference with 180 participants. Specifically:

1. we first considered a two-islands topology with 90 local users and 90 remote users;
2. we then moved to a three-islands scenario with:
   (a) 60 local users and 120 remote users, equally split between the two available remote foci;

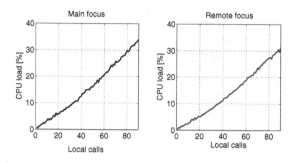

Fig. 8. CPU utilization in the distributed scenario envisaging the presence of two XCON islands

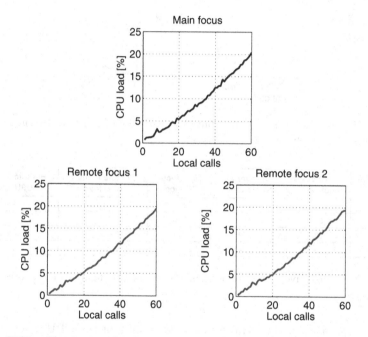

Fig. 9. CPU utilization in the distributed scenario envisaging the presence of three XCON islands: case 2a

(b) 90 local and 90 remote users, equally split between the two available remote foci.

In the first scenario, the CPU load of the main focus was about 34%, while the remote focus was about 30%, as shown in Fig. 8.

In case 2a, instead, the main focus CPU level was about 21% and the remote foci were both loaded around 19%. This is shown in Fig. 9.

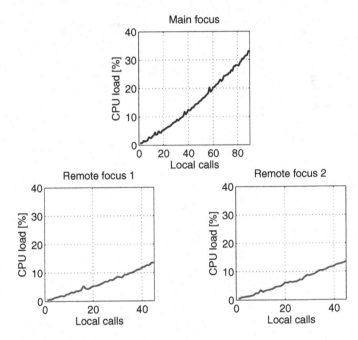

Fig. 10. CPU utilization in the distributed scenario envisaging the presence of three XCON islands: case 2b

Number of islands	Number of local users	Number of remote users	Main focus CPU load	Remote focus 1 CPU load	Remote focus 2 CPU load
1	180	-	100%	-	-
2	90	90	34%	30%	-
3	60	120 (60/60)	21%	20%	20%
3	90	90 (45/45)	32%	13%	13%

Fig. 11. A comparative table summarizing performance figures in the presence of BFCP

Finally, in case 2b, the main focus took up 32% of the CPU, while the remote foci were almost unloaded (CPU utilization level at around 13%). This is witnessed by Fig. 10.

Comparative analysis. In this subsection, we analyze the results presented above, showing (see Fig. 11) that, even when involving the media mixer, distribution brings us to an improvement degree similar to the one obtained when all the RTP packets received from the users were dropped.

In fact, having a look at the two tables in Fig. 3 and Fig. 11, it comes out that the huge improvement in terms of CPU performance obtained without moderation is still attained when envisaging BFCP functionality. In fact, in the centralized scenario examined, the CPU load was near 100% while it reduced to about 34% in the two-islands case and to 21% in the three-islands scenario.

Finally, as shown by the experiments presented in case 1 and case 2b, we note how the distribution of the remote users behind different remote foci keeps on causing a small decrease in the performance of the main focus. This is reasonable since we know that the main focus has in such cases to spread conference events to all active foci across the server-to-server channels. Furthermore, it is also in charge of all floor control tasks.

4.3   Involving the Floor Control Server

In this subsection, we present the results obtained when the system under stress also included the Floor Control Server. To do this, we had to modify the previous test configuration scenario where a *FloorRequest* message was sent every time a new user joined a conference. During this campaign, instead, we configured the *BFCP stresser* with two parameters, p_{req} and p_{rel}, representing, respectively, the desired probability per second with which the stresser generates *FloorRequest* and *FloorRelease* messages on behalf of each participant. In the following, hence, we analyze the behavior of the system by assuming different values for those probabilities. We also point out the additional load due to moderation operations.

Centralized scenario. Starting from the centralized environment, we show the CPU utilization level obtained when fixing two different values for the probability parameters previously introduced. Specifically, we first assumed $p_{req} = 0.15$ and then $p_{req} = 0.30$, while in both cases the probability (per second) with which each participant performed a *FloorRelease* was set to 0.05. Such values just reflect the actual behavior inferred from empirical experiments previously arranged, and consequently represented a reasonable choice for our tests.

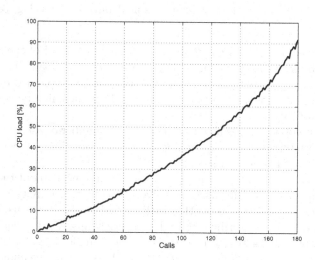

Fig. 12. CPU utilization in a centralized scenario characterized by $p_{req} = 0.15$ and $p_{rel} = 0.05$

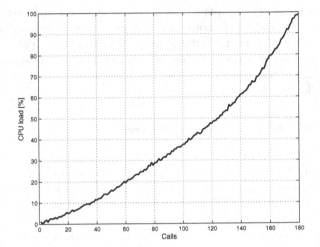

Fig. 13. CPU utilization in a centralized scenario characterized by $p_{req} = 0.30$ and $p_{rel} = 0.05$

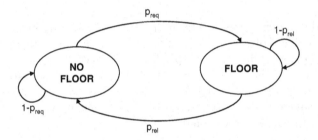

Fig. 14. A Markov chain which describes moderated conferencing scenarios

As to the first scenario, Fig. 12 shows that the CPU load of the focus when managing 180 users was about 92%. This reduction in the load when compared with the case of all participants owning the floor, can be explained by observing that in this case the focus did not have to mix all the incoming media flows, but just a subset of them.

Fig. 13, instead, witnesses how the same overall number of users in the second scenario (characterized by a higher floor request probability) almost overloads the cpu (whose utilization level reaches 99%).

The figures just presented bring us to some consideration about the consumption of resources specifically and exclusively due to the activity of the Floor Control Server, regardless of any other task carried out by the focus. In fact, the scenarios above can be described through the very simple Markov chain depicted in Fig. 14, representing the state transitions of a single participant. From the analysis of that Markov chain, it follows that each user owns the audio floor with

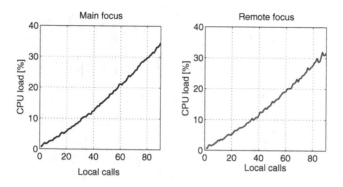

Fig. 15. CPU utilization in a two-islands scenario characterized by $p_{req} = 0.15$ and $p_{rel} = 0.05$

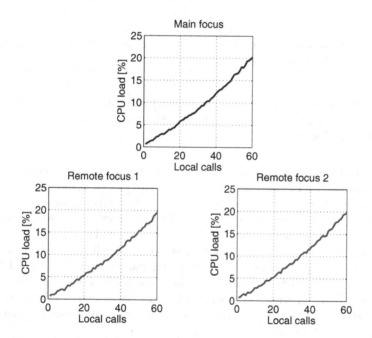

Fig. 16. CPU utilization in a three-islands scenario characterized by $p_{req} = 0.15$ and $p_{rel} = 0.05$

a probability of $P_{floor} = p_{req}/(p_{req} + p_{rel})$. Consequently, in the first scenario considered there are on average 135 audio flows to be mixed (which are related to participants owning the floor) in spite of the overall 180 users. Then, since subsection 4.2 showed us that 135 users owning the floor take up about 56% of the CPU and as long as 45 users without the floor require a further 8% (cf. [1]), it is straightforward that the resource consumption specifically due to moderation operations is about 24%.

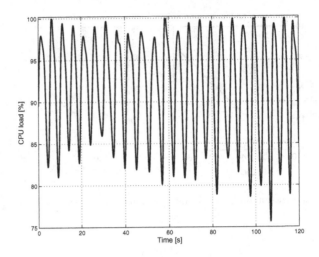

Fig. 17. Time evolution of the CPU level in a centralized scenario characterized by $p_{req} = 0.15$ and $p_{rel} = 0.05$, when there are 180 users

This value is indeed quite high and clearly indicates to us that one of the directions for our future work follows the path of improving the performance of the floor control server.

Distributed scenario. Coming to the distributed case, for the sake of brevity we just focused on the scenario characterized by $p_{req} = 0.15$ and $p_{rel} = 0.05$. Fig. 15 shows that in the case of two interconnected islands and supposing the users to be equally split between them, the CPU level of the main focus was about 33% while the remote focus was loaded at around 32%.

Keeping on considering the participants equally split among the available domains, the three-islands case was characterized, instead, by 21% CPU consumption at the main focus and 20% at both remote foci (see Fig. 16).

In this subsection we do not deal with a comparative analysis between the centralized and the distributed environment, since the same considerations as in subsection 4.2 totally apply here.

Rather, we want to highlight how in the considered configuration of tests, working with average values becomes really crucial. In fact, when a scenario is characterized by a number of participants owning the floor that varies in time, the CPU occupancy given a certain amount of users varies too. This statement is confirmed by Fig. 17, showing the variation in time of the CPU level given a fixed number of participants, in a single-island case with $p_{req} = 0.15$ and $p_{rel} = 0.05$. Such a variable CPU level depends on the actual number of audio flows that have to be mixed, since the less are the users able to talk, the less is the load of the focus and vice versa.

4.4   Considerations and Implementation Nits

The work carried out in the last months and presented in this paper, was mainly focused on a scalability assessment of the DCON framework in the presence of audio mixing operations and floor control. The results obtained have been discussed in the previous sections and show that our efforts in defining and implementing a distributed framework, with the corresponding issues about both distributed mixing and distribution of the floor control protocol, were well directed.

Though, the stressing operations conducted during this test campaign were conceived with an additional target in mind, that is finding any bug that may be hidden in the code and consequently affect the expected behavior of the platform. The BFCP library in particular was subject to a critical evaluation, considering it constituted the fundamental node of the entire server-side policy management.

Besides several small, relatively unimportant code bugs that were found during the tests, and promptly solved, the most interesting issue we found in the library was related to the management of networking activities. In fact the simultaneous presence of many simulated users, each implementing a behavior characterized by several protocols of interaction, caused each of the involved foci to handle a large number of file descriptors. This gave us the opportunity of experiencing an unexpected behavior in the select() system call, which was used throughout several components of the architecture as the method to check for incoming connections and data from active participants. The problem in select() is that it relies on special data structures called *file descriptor sets*, which in turn are manipulated by means of dedicated macros. These macros are constructed in terms of a properly defined variable called FD_SETSIZE, which in almost all UNIX kernel installations is statically assigned a default 1024 value. This means that, out of the box, select() only works fine as long as the file descriptors to check are not greater than that default value, i.e. 1024. In case this limitation is not obeyed, the involved *file descriptor sets* get corrupted, thus completely affecting the expected behavior. This is exactly what we experimented, with the floor control server and other services as well which stopped responding to incoming network inputs whenever the number of connections trespassed a specific threshold.

Of course this was all but desired behavior. A solution might have been redefining the FD_SETSIZE in the kernel headers, but such an approach would mean recompile the kernel on every box the framework would be installed on. To avoid such a nuisance, we further investigated the issue and managed to solve it by just moving from the use of select() to the poll() system call. This system call achieves exactly the same purpose as select(), though not suffering from the same limitation. The use of the poll() call is actually often fostered when network functionality is to be provided in large scale environments, which is exactly the potential case of the architecture we conceived.

5   Conclusions and Future Work

In this paper we presented the latest results related to a scalability analysis conducted on a real-world implementation of a distributed conferencing framework providing advanced functionality like controlled access to media resources. Based on our previous achievements, which mainly dealt with the analysis of the signaling plane, in the present work we rather focused on the data plane, by letting the media mixer come into play. Besides this, we quantitatively assessed the overhead imposed by the presence of an element, the so-called *Floor Control Server*, which is in charge of managing users' policies related to the right of accessing a specified floor (i.e. a specified resource) in the conference.

From the experimentations we can draw some interesting considerations.

First, with respect to floor control, the performance figures we derived, when compared to the analysis conducted in the absence of such functionality, confirm the intuitive expectation that nothing comes for free. Moderation has to be paid for, since it does represent an expensive task, especially on the server side, where state information has to be kept and updated with reference to each and every user who is participating in a conference. Though, we already highlighted in the paper that our implementation can definitely be tuned in order to better tackle this issue. The current implementation of the floor control server can be improved and this represents one of the main objectives of the refinement work we are undertaking in the next few months.

Second, as regards the performance figures, we still lack detailed information about the behavior of our system when video is also taken into account. Up to now, we just focused on audio mixing since our architecture is currently undergoing a refinement phase for what concerns video support (with special regard to layout management and mixing strategies). This is a further direction for our future investigations.

The mentioned point is also strictly related to the third and final direction of future work, which deals with a further exploitation of the principle of separation of concerns. Indeed, we are currently actively contributing to the standardization efforts that the IETF is devoting to the definition of an effective framework for the remote control of a Media Server (MS) from an Application Server (AS). Such framework, which is the subject of the work inside the MEDIACTRL Working Group, is aimed at clearly separating the business logic (which has to be implemented in the AS) from the actual management of the data exchanging phase (involving, in the case of a conference, all users through intervention of the media server which provides them with the appropriate information mix). It looks clear that the separation between the AS and the MS goes into the direction of further improving the scalability of any framework envisaging the presence of both functions. We are currently working on these aspects by embracing, as usual, an engineering approach. We already have a running prototype of the overall MEDIACTRL framework[3] and we have plans to involve it in our DCON architecture in order to push its scalability properties one step further.

---

[3] See http://mediactrl.sourceforge.net for the details.

Acknowledgments

This work has been carried out with the financial support of the European projects NetQoS and Content. Such projects are partially funded by the EU as part of the IST Programme, within the Sixth Framework Programme.

References

1. Amirante, A., Castaldi, T., Miniero, L., Romano, S.P.: Improving the scalability of an IMS-compliant conferencing framework through presence and event notification. In: Proceedings of the 1st International Conference on Principles, Systems and Applications of IP Telecommunications (IPTComm), New York City (2007)
2. Camarillo, G., Ott, J., Drage, K.: The Binary Floor Control Protocol (BFCP). RFC4582 (November 2006)
3. Barnes, M., Boulton, C., Levin, O.: A Framework for Centralized Conferencing. draft-ietf-xcon-framework-10.txt (November 2007)
4. Rosenberg, J., Schulzrinne, H., Camarillo, G.: et al. SIP: Session Initiation Protocol. RFC3261 (June 2002)
5. Buono, A., Castaldi, T., Miniero, L., Romano, S.P.: Design and Implementation of an Open Source IMS Enabled Conferencing Architecture. In: Koucheryavy, Y., Harju, J., Sayenko, A. (eds.) NEW2AN 2007. LNCS, vol. 4712, pp. 468–479. Springer, Heidelberg (2007)
6. Romano, S.P., Amirante, A., Castaldi, T., Miniero, L., Buono, A.: A Framework for Distributed Conferencing. draft-romano-dcon-framework-02.txt (January 2008)
7. Saint-Andre, P.: Extensible Messaging and Presence Protocol (XMPP): Core. RFC3920 (October 2004)
8. Buono, A., Loreto, S., Miniero, L., Romano, S.P.: A Distributed IMS Enabled Conferencing Architecture on Top of a Standard Centralized Conferencing Framework. IEEE Communications Magazine 45(3) (March 2007)
9. Camarillo, G.: Session Description Protocol (SDP) Format for Binary Floor Control Protocol (BFCP) Streams. RFC4583 (November 2006)
10. Romano, S.P., Amirante, A., Castaldi, T., Miniero, L., Buono, A.: Requirements for Distributed Conferencing. draft-romano-dcon-requirements-02.txt (January 2008)
11. Romano, S.P., Amirante, A., Castaldi, T., Miniero, L., Buono, A.: Requirements for the XCON-DCON Synchronization Protocol. draft-romano-dcon-xdsp-reqs-02.txt (January 2008)

On Mechanisms for Deadlock Avoidance in SIP Servlet Containers

Y. Huang, L.K. Dillon, and R.E.K. Stirewalt

Department of Computer Science and Engineering
Michigan State University
East Lansing, MI 48824, USA
{huangyi7,ldillon,stire}@cse.msu.edu

Abstract. Increasingly, VoIP applications are being deployed to multi-threaded SIP servlet containers. Unfortunately, the standard specification for these containers is silent with regard to synchronization issues, and the lack of direction has led different vendors to adopt a variety of different and incompatible policies for preventing data races among concurrent threads. In addition to the obvious portability problems, some policies make servlet code prone to deadlock under common scenarios of use. This paper documents this problem with concrete examples and proposes modifications to the standard to allow programmers to implement the protocols needed to avoid these common deadlocks. These extensions will open the way for automatic generation of the synchronization logic needed to implement these avoidance protocols, thereby increasing the safety and reliability of applications deployed in this environment.

Keywords: Concurrency, converged container, deadlock prevention, negotiation, servlet, SIP, synchronization contract.

1 Introduction

A typical Voice-over-IP (VoIP) application comprises multiple, dynamically configurable services (i.e., features), such as *call waiting*, *call forwarding*, and *call merge* [8]. Such services are usually implemented atop a signaling protocol, called the session initiation protocol (SIP) [20], for setting up and tearing down media sessions. To simplify their implementation and composition, these services may be implemented as *SIP servlets* and deployed to *SIP application servers* that reside in nodes across the Internet. The JSR 116 standard defines the API for programming SIP servlets [15]. A key concept in this standard[1] is a middleware abstraction called a *container*, which automates the handling of various concerns, thereby separating them from the "business logic" of a service. This paper explores one of these concerns—thread synchronization—which, to date, has proved difficult to relegate to the container.

---

[1] And also in application-server architectures, e.g., Apache Tomcat [26], WLSS [1], and Sailfin [23].

H. Schulzrinne, R. State, and S. Niccolini (Eds.): IPTComm 2008, LNCS 5310, pp. 196–216, 2008.

To demonstrate the difficulties, we show how the policies adopted by one popular container are prone to deadlock, and discuss problems of using vendor-specific APIs to implement common deadlock avoidance techniques. This demonstration provides motivation for prescribing extensions to the SIP Servlet API that enable separation of concurrency concerns and automated deadlock prevention. We then outline a method by which such extensions can be achieved. For brevity, this paper discusses only deadlock avoidance, although the general approach also provides for avoidance of critical races. In a nutshell, the idea is to encapsulate a deadlock avoidance protocol within *negotiators*, which are specialized *concurrency controllers* [6] for SIP threads. We further advocate that negotiators should be generated automatically from high-level *synchronization contracts* [4,25].

The need to synchronize threads executing within a container arises because, upon receiving a message, the container dispatches a dedicated thread to process the message. As a result, multiple threads processing different messages may attempt to concurrently access the same session data. Additionally, a thread may create and use data that persists in the server beyond the thread's lifetime and, consequently, that may be accessed by multiple threads. For instance, various kinds of *session* objects are used to maintain the evolving state of a call [2]. To prevent data corruption, containers employ some policies for concurrency control, typically locking these shared objects prior to processing the message.

Unfortunately, these *container-level synchronization policies* are rarely documented, and current standards documents (e.g., [15] and [27]) are silent on the issue. Container operations implicitly lock some resources but leave the application to explicitly lock others. Without knowing precisely what locks the container acquires and when it acquires them, application developers are ill equipped to judge whether the container will guarantee a given set of synchronization requirements or whether and how to develop custom synchronization logic to guarantee these requirements. In fact, results of experiments suggest that different vendors have adopted different container-level synchronization policies. This situation leads to synchronization-related failures, typically corruption of session data or deadlocks. Moreover, the synchronization policies adopted by some vendors make it impossible to avoid deadlocks in some situations for which a servlet could be designed to avoid deadlocks if the container did not implicitly acquire any locks on session data.

The remainder of the paper explores these issues in the context of a specific container—the container in a BEA WebLogic SIP Server (WLSS) [2]. We first present background on the context in which the problems arise and background relating to our proposed approach for addressing these problems (Section 2). We then provide concrete examples to illustrate how the container's synchronization policy leads to deadlock under two scenarios of use that occur in practice (Section 3). The key contributor to these deadlocks is that some resources are implicitly acquired and held whereas other resources must be explicitly acquired during the processing of a message. In one of these scenarios (Section 4.1), deadlock can be avoided by using non-standard operations in the

WLSS API. But this deadlock avoidance method does not scale, limits reuse, and is prone to error. In the other scenario (Section 4.2), deadlock cannot be prevented in a WLSS container. However, a mechanism proposed for the new standard, JSR 289 [27], which is currently under public review, can be used to implement a common, albeit somewhat crude, deadlock avoidance heuristic. We discuss problems and limitations of this mechanism for avoiding deadlock. The issues raised by these "work-arounds" motivate extending the SIP Servlet[2] API with facilities for avoiding deadlocks by a technique that separates concerns involving deadlock avoidance from the servlet's "business logic" (Section 5). Finally, we summarize and identify directions for future research (Section 6).

2 Background

For concreteness of exposition, we consider the synchronization policy and implementation adopted by one vendor—BEA WebLogic SIP Server (WLSS) [1]. Thus, by way of background, we briefly describe the synchronization policy implemented in a WLSS (Section 2.1). The motivation for a container-supplied synchronization policy is to simplify the programming of applications and make them less prone to synchronization-related errors. This goal is achievable only to the extent that (1) the synchronization logic can be cleanly separated from the "business logic" of an application and (2) the synchronization code can be automatically generated. We thus briefly overview the related work on separation and automatic programming of synchronization concerns (Section 2.2). Finally, we provide some background on synchronization contracts, which the approach suggested in Section 5 builds on (Section 2.3). Synchronization contracts are designed for separation and automated enforcement of synchronization concerns in a special class of systems, which includes telecommunications systems.

2.1 The BEA WLSS

The WLSS policy mandates that the thread handling a message must have exclusive access to the *call state* associated with the message. Intuitively, call state comprises the persistent data pertaining to a call, which might be consulted or modified by the thread processing the message. Unfortunately, we could not find a precise definition of call state in the WLSS documentation. This situation is problematic, as application developers need to know precisely what constitutes a call state in order to create applications that do not exhibit data races, deadlock, or other synchronization errors. In fact, the WLSS policy leads to deadlock in some contexts, as we demonstrate in subsequent examples.

Lacking a clear definition of call state, we take it to mean at least the *SIP application session* associated with the message. A SIP application session (hereafter *SAS* for brevity) is an instance of the SIP Servlet API class SipApplicationSession and is used to encapsulate and provide uniform access to the persistent

---

[2] Follow the convention in [2], "SIP Servlet" (uppercase "S") refers to the standard API, while "SIP servlet" refers to a program that uses the API.

data for an instance of an application. We know that the WLSS policy guarantees the thread handling a message will have exclusive access to the SAS associated with that message. Thus, when illustrating problems that derive from this policy, we use examples whose synchronization requirements are limited to the sharing of SASs rather than the data that these SASs encapsulate.

WLSS is a *SIP and HTTP converged container*, which means that it provides for processing of both SIP messages and HTTP messages. It contains a single *message handler*, which hosts a dedicated thread, and zero or more SIP and/or HTTP threads. The message handler listens to the network for incoming messages. When a message arrives, it dispatches the message to a thread and then returns to listening. It dispatches SIP messages to SIP threads and HTTP messages to HTTP threads. Based on information in the dispatched message, a SIP thread selects an appropriate *SIP servlet* and invokes the `service` operation on this servlet, passing the message as an argument. When the invocation of `service` returns, the thread terminates. For HTTP messages, WLSS performs the same steps, except that it selects an HTTP servlet instead of a SIP servlet. A SIP application comprises at least one SIP servlet, zero or more HTTP servlets, and supporting resources (e.g., JSP pages and images).

A key difference between how a SIP thread processes a message and how an HTTP thread processes a message is that a SIP thread (implicitly) performs synchronization operations, whereas an HTTP thread does not. A SIP thread acquires a lock on the SAS associated with the message prior to invoking the `service` method and releases the lock once the invocation returns. Consequently, any operation invoked during an activation of a SIP servlet's `service` operation may freely access the SAS associated with the message without concern for data races or consistency of transactions. For brevity in the sequel, we refer to the SAS associated with the message a thread is processing as the *thread's SAS*.

The SIP Servlet API provides operations using which a SIP thread may access and modify sessions, including SASs associated with messages that might be being processed by other SIP threads. In WLSS, the implementations of some of these API operations contain synchronization logic over and above the implicit SAS locking functionality provided by the container when servicing an incoming message. More precisely, an API operation that accesses a SAS embeds code to lock the SAS at the start and to release the lock on the SAS just before returning, unless the SAS is already locked by the thread that invokes the API operation (as is the case for the thread's SAS).

2.2 Approaches to Separation and Automatic Programming of Synchronization Concerns

The separation and automatic programming of synchronization concerns serves as the motivation for many concurrent programming frameworks, including D [16], concurrency controllers [6], SyncGen [10], Szumo [3,25], and Java transactions [13,14]. Separating the synchronization logic from the "business logic" is intended to simplify programming both concerns by virtue of not needing to "mix" the two. However, separated or not, synchronization protocols can be difficult to implement correctly. Thus, automatic programming of the synchronization logic is preferred to leaving this responsibility to the application programmer. Of particular concern in this paper are synchronization protocols that provide mutually exclusive access to sets of shared resources and the deadlock problems that easily arise when these protocols are not correctly implemented.

Concurrency controller is a design pattern that generally supports the separation and automatic generation of complex synchronization protocols. The name of the pattern was first suggested by [6], whose system of the same name uses the pattern. In the sequel, we use the term to refer to the general style of concern separation embodied in the pattern as opposed to the particular framework in [6]. A concurrency controller can be thought of as a generalization of a *monitor* that can be made to apply to multiple resources. Application code invokes an operation to lock a set of resources, understanding that the call will block if the controller cannot successfully acquire the whole set. When the call returns, the application assumes exclusive access to these resources. The API to a controller is very simple, with operations designed to resemble event notifications or actions. However, the operations might implement complex collaborations with other controllers to acquire a set of resources while avoiding deadlock. Approaches that employ this pattern include SyncGen, which generates them from declarative *region invariants* [10], the system of Betin-Can and Bultan, which generates them from action-language specifications [6], and our own Szumo system, which generates them from declarative *synchronization contracts* [5,25].

Unlike WLSS, where the container serves as a gatekeeper to the SASs, a concurrency controller does not monitor when each thread attempts to access which resources. Instead, it provides a public controller interface, which publishes available actions that a thread could perform on the shared resources under its control as well as acceptable patterns of use—i.e., usage obligations and exclusion guarantees. In multi-threaded systems that are designed according to the pattern, a thread consults the controller before it performs actions on any of the shared resources under the controller's control. A key feature of this approach is that the application programmer is responsible for invoking operations on the controller to obtain permission to access shared resources.

Finally, we should mention that concurrency frameworks that support *transactional memory* sidestep the deadlock problem by avoiding the use of locks altogether [13]. Rather than locking shared resources, a thread performs operations on copies of the shared resources and then attempts to reconcile conflicting updates when the transaction commits. While an elegant abstraction, especially in the context of data-oriented enterprise applications, transactions must be able to be aborted (and the changes rolled back or discarded). This assumption is not reasonable in the communications domain because operations cannot in general be rolled back (if, for instance, an operation involved the issuing of a message over the network) and because application sessions might be much too large to clone. To some degree, the need to clone large shared objects can be ameliorated using *transaction synchronizers*, which permit multiple transactions to operate on the same objects [17]. Still, the resulting transactions must be abortable, which again, is not generally feasible in this domain.

2.3 Synchronization Contracts

Our ideas for deadlock-avoiding SIP servlets build on a model of synchronization for object-oriented (OO) programs, called Szumo [3], which leverages synchronization contracts to support component-based development of a limited class of multi-threaded OO applications. Termed *strictly exclusive systems*, this class comprises applications in which threads compete for exclusive access to dynamically changing sets of shared resources. In addition to telecommunication applications, examples include extensible web servers and interactive applications with graphical user interfaces. This narrowing of focus was motivated by the observation that many applications fit well in this category and that, in such cases, we can exploit a clean, compositional model of synchronization.

Szumo adopts the principles of Meyer's design-by-contract approach to reliable software [18]. It associates each thread with a synchronization contract, which describes client and supplier rights and responsibilities when performing operations that use shared resources. The contracts themselves are formed by instantiating and conjoining module-level *synchronization constraints*, which a programmer declares in the modules' interfaces. For example, a synchronization constraint for a servlet that implements a call-merge service might declare that, when processing a request to merge two calls, a SIP thread needs exclusive access to the SASs associated with the calls. The application developer is responsible for verifying that a SIP thread accesses these SASs only under conditions covered by a synchronization constraint. The developer then writes the servlet code assuming exclusive access to the SASs under these conditions; i.e., she does not write explicit synchronization logic to acquire and release the SASs. In this way, synchronization contracts provide a useful separation of concerns.

In lieu of synchronization logic, synchronization contracts are automatically enforced and negotiated at run-time. Contract models, such as SCOOP [18] and Szumo [3,4,25], assign much of the responsibility for contract negotiation to a run-time system or a middleware, which schedules processes based on deadlock- and starvation-avoidance heuristics. We previously integrated Szumo into an extension of the Eiffel language [3,25] and, more recently, implemented it in C++ as a framework [11]. A case study in evolving and maintaining a multi-threaded web server demonstrates how the use of synchronization contracts supports maintenance activities [5]. The work described in the current paper shows how synchronization contracts can be used to make container-level synchronization policies more flexible with regard to how, when, and how many objects are locked during the servicing of a message. Containers that employ these more flexible policies are able to avoid a large class of deadlocks, some of which cannot currently be avoidable in containers that employ more rigid policies.

---

[3] For the SynchroniZation Units Model; an early version of this model was called the "universe model" [4].

3   Example Deadlocks

To illustrate how deadlock can arise in a SIP container, we present two scenarios that arise in practice. The first involves a Call-Merge service, which is a SIP service used in conferencing applications (Section 3.1). The second involves a Click-To-Dial service, which is a SIP and HTTP converged service (Section 3.2). We then briefly reflect on the fundamental problem illustrated by these examples (Section 3.3).

3.1   Deadlock in a Call-Merge Service

A Call-Merge (CMG) service merges two calls for use in implementing a conference call. A *CMG request message* designates two calls: a *source call*, involving the user agent requesting the merge, and a *target call* that is to be merged. If the source and target calls belong to different application sessions, the thread that processes the request message must lock multiple SASs, and deadlock could arise if two or more concurrent threads each attempts to lock these SASs in a different order. Such a situation arises in practice, e.g., when two user agents, each involved in a call, both try to merge the call involving the other agent at nearly the same time.

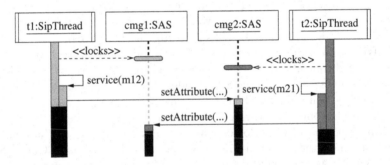

Fig. 1. Sequence diagram illustrating a deadlock in the CMG scenario

Figure 1 depicts a deadlocking call-merge scenario using extensions to UML 2.0 sequence diagrams to visualize key aspects of thread and synchronization state. A filled activation bar[4] on the lifeline of a thread represents an activation of that thread's run method. Shading distinguishes activations that are executed by different threads (different shades) and activations that are blocked (filled black). To indicate the acquisition of a lock on a shared object, we use a dashed arrow, labeled by the stereotype <<locks>>, that emanates from an activation and ends in a shaded bubble that is centered on the shared object's lifeline. Moreover, we shade the lifeline of a shared object that has been locked according to the

---

[4] Called an *execution specification* in UML 2.0 [22].

shading of the activation that locked it. Finally, we depict operation invocation and return in the usual manner with one exception: When a thread invokes an operation on a servlet, we depict that activation as a nested activation of the thread object. Thus, in Figure 1, activations of the servlet's `service` operation abut the activations of the run operation of the two threads, $t1$ and $t2$, that invoke `service`. Without this convention, our diagrams would need to explicitly depict the servlet object, which would then need to host multiple, concurrent, activations of `service` operations by different threads.

Prior to this scenario (and thus not depicted in the figure) the container received two CMG request messages—$m12$ requesting to merge source call $c1$ with target call $c2$, and $m21$ requesting to merge source call $c2$ with target call $c1$. Suppose call $c1$ belongs to SAS $cmg1$ and $c2$ belongs to SAS $cmg2$. Upon receiving $m12$ and $m21$, the container dispatched two threads, $t1$ and $t2$, to handle them. In the scenario, each thread first locks its own SAS, as required by the WLSS synchronization policy, and then invokes the `service` operation on the CMG servlet. Each thread then proceeds to process its message, during which it must access the SAS for its target call. In this scenario, $t1$ invokes the API operation `setAttribute` on $cmg2$. Because $t1$ does not hold the lock on $cmg2$, the `setAttribute` operation under WLSS tries to acquire this lock. This attempt causes $t1$ to block because the lock is already held by $t2$. Likewise, $t2$ blocks when it invokes `setAttribute` on $cmg1$. At this point, deadlock ensues.

3.2   Deadlock in a Click-To-Dial Service

A Click-To-Dial (CTD) service allows a subscriber to initiate a call from a web browser by selecting or entering a party to call, hereafter the *callee*, and then clicking on a "dial" button. Clicking this button triggers the browser to send a *CTD request message*, an HTTP message designating the subscriber and the callee, to a CTD service. When the container receives this message, it dispatches the request to an HTTP thread, which then attempts to establish two SIP calls— one between the CTD service and the subscriber and the other between the CTD service and the callee. The HTTP thread attempts to establish these calls by creating and sending out two SIP invitation messages and by creating a new SAS that will encapsulate any relevant call state associated with these messages and with the SIP calls that are ultimately established.

The HTTP thread also creates an instance of a class called `callManager`, which is designed to allow the subscriber to monitor and affect the state of a call from her web browser. The call manager is used, for instance, to perform management tasks such as pausing the SIP calls if the subscriber's balance drops to zero and then prompting her to deposit new funds via a web interface. To properly reflect the state of a call, the call manager must be notified once the SIP calls are established. To enable this notification, the HTTP thread registers the call manager as a *listener* of the SAS associated with the call. A SIP thread processing a message associated with this SAS may then notify the manager to signal changes in the state of the call. Because the call manager may need to

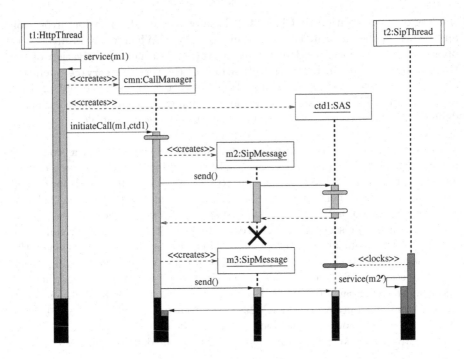

Fig. 2. Sequence diagram illustrating a deadlock in the CTD scenario

be accessed by multiple threads, including both HTTP and SIP threads, class callManager is implemented as a monitor.[5]

Figure 2 illustrates a deadlock that may arise when using the CTD service. Prior to the start of this scenario, the container dispatches the HTTP thread $t1$ to process the CTD request message, $m1$. In processing $m1$, the HTTP thread first creates a call manager object, cmn, and a new SAS, $ctd1$. It then invokes an operation on cmn to initiate the call requested by $m1$. As part of initiating the call, the call manager registers itself with $ctd1$ (not shown) and then creates and sends the two SIP invitation messages $m2$ and $m3$. When sending a message, the container locks the SAS associated with the message. Thus, calls to send will proceed only if the lock on the SAS can be acquired. To reduce clutter, when an operation on an object locks or unlocks the object itself, we omit showing dashed arrows and stereotypes. A shaded bubble on the activation signifies that the lock is acquired and a clear bubble signifies that the lock is released. Thus, in this scenario, the activation of send on $m2$ succeeds in acquiring the lock, and so $m2$ is sent. However, the activation of send on $m3$ blocks because the concurrent thread $t2$, which is dispatched with the response $m2'$ to the invitation message $m2$, acquires the lock on $ctd1$ before cmn invokes the send operation on $m3$. Subsequently, when $t2$ attempts to notify cmn (which is registered with $ctd1$ to

---

[5] By means of the idioms in Java, its methods are declared to be **synchronized**.

be notified of responses), it also blocks because $t1$ is still executing within cmn (a monitor).

3.3   Deadlock Prevention

Because JSR 116 is silent on issues of synchronization, container vendors are free to provide their own policies and primitives. Unfortunately, the WLSS policy of determining and then implicitly locking an application session based on the message to be serviced is prone to deadlock in common use cases, as illustrated by the CMG and CTD deadlock scenarios. Clearly, some means for deadlock prevention are needed. Deadlock-prevention strategies are generally well known and fall into one of two categories—*avoidance* and *recovery* [19]. In Szumo, we used a combination of these strategies to prevent a large class of deadlocks. Such strategies are key to the approach we describe in Section 5 and suffice to avoid the deadlocks illustrated by the CTD and CMG scenarios. However, before describing our approach, we now briefly describe how programmers can use existing (vendor-specific) APIs to implement common deadlock avoidance heuristics and discuss limitations of doing so. Recovery heuristics are not really possible under the WLSS policy, as there are no means for one SIP thread to force another to release its lock on a SAS.

4   Known Work-Arounds

Deadlock avoidance strategies use information about the resources that might be requested to develop a protocol for making requests. If every client requests its resources in the order prescribed by this protocol, then deadlock can be avoided. The CTD deadlock can be avoided in this manner by designing the HTTP thread to access the $ctd1$ application session indirectly through a *transaction proxy*, which allows a programmer some control over when an application session is locked and for how long. Currently, transaction proxies must be implemented using proprietary extensions to JSR 116 (Section 4.1). Not all deadlocks are avoidable using transaction proxies. In fact, the CMG deadlock scenario cannot be avoided by such means. However, the JSR 289 draft specification provides a feature called *session key based targeting* [27, § 15.11.2], which allows the programmer more control in selecting the application session to implicitly lock when a message is received (Section 4.2). Servlet programmers could use this feature to avoid the CMG deadlock; however, the feature was not designed for this purpose, and its use in this context is brittle, inflexible, and ultimately error prone. We now briefly delve into these workarounds to better illustrate the approaches and to motivate why we believe deadlock prevention should be automated whenever possible.

4.1   Extensions to Support Transactions

To implement a deadlock-avoiding request protocol, programmers must be able to control when a lock on an application session should be acquired.

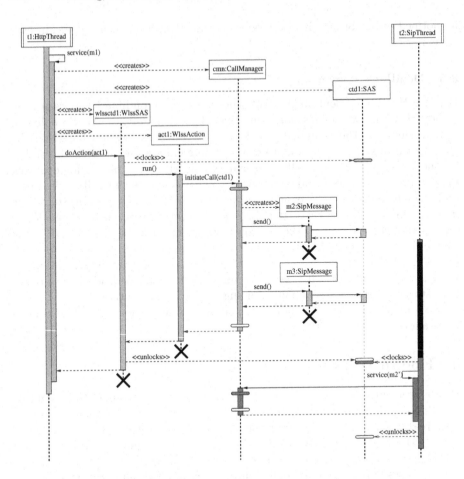

Fig. 3. Using WLSS proprietary API's to avoid the CTD deadlock scenario

Unfortunately, such control is quite limited in the current WLSS implementation of JSR 116. When a SIP message arrives, the container determines the application session associated with this message and locks this session before ceding control to the servlet. If a servlet needs to access some other application session, the lock on this other session is acquired and released on demand, as the servlet invokes methods on that session. Those locks are necessarily acquired after the servlet has been made to hold the lock on the SAS associated with the message it is serving. Consequently, if a servlet requires access to multiple application sessions, these are necessarily locked and accessed one after another; they cannot be locked atomically[6] before being accessed.

To cope with this problem, WLSS provides proprietary extensions to program what we call transaction proxies, which are implemented using a combination of

---

[6] In the sense that either the servlet locks all of them without blocking or it blocks without holding any of them until such time as it is able to lock them all.

two design patterns—*proxy* and *command* [12]. A transaction proxy is a proxy that acts as a surrogate application session. It provides all of the operations of an application session but implements them by delegating to some other instance of class `SipApplicationSession`, i.e., the "real" application session. In addition, a transaction proxy provides a method called `doAction`, which is parameterized by an *activity*, i.e., a sequence of operations encapsulated into an object via the command pattern. When `doAction` is invoked with an activity, the transaction proxy locks the real SAS and then executes the `run` method of the activity. Because the proxy holds the lock on the real SAS while executing the activity, the sequence of operations within the `run` method execute as a single transaction on this SAS.

Transaction proxies allow the servlet programmer to affect the order in which some of the resources needed to execute a transaction are acquired. Figure 3 depicts how the CTD deadlock can be avoided by encapsulating the `initiateCall` operation into an activity (instance of interface `WlssAction`) which is supplied to the `doAction` method of a transaction proxy (instance of class `WlssSipApplicationSession`) to *ctd1*. Notice that both *t1* and *t2* now request *cmn* and *ctd1* in exactly the same order, thereby avoiding deadlock.

Transaction proxies provide one way for programmers to implement deadlock-avoidance protocols in their servlet code. The approach works for the CTD scenario because of an inherent asymmetry in the problem: Because the container does not implicitly lock resources on behalf of the HTTP thread, that thread can use a transaction proxy to mimic the acquisition protocol of any SIP threads that might respond to the generated messages. Without this asymmetry, deadlock cannot be avoided using transaction proxies. In addition, because a transaction proxy locks only a single application session, if a servlet requires access to more than two application sessions, it will need to use nested transaction proxies. As nesting grows deeper, designs become more brittle and more difficult to extend. Thus, when viewed as a mechanism for implementing deadlock-avoidance protocols, transaction proxies are limited in power and suffer problems of scalability.

Moreover, regardless of implementation mechanism, we contend that it would be poor policy to make servlet programmers responsible for developing and adhering to deadlock-avoidance protocols. Deadlocks are avoided only if every servlet deployed to a container respects the protocols that apply to the resources it needs. If a service that requested resources in violation of some protocol were ever deployed, it could cause deadlock in services that were designed correctly. Given the explosive growth and dynamic nature of VoIP services, developing, documenting, maintaining, and enforcing correct usage of these protocols would be a daunting task. For all of these reasons, we believe deadlock avoidance should be automated—either completely relegated to the container or automatically generated from higher-level specifications—but not programmed explicitly by application programmers.

4.2   Controlling Target of Implicit Locking

While neither JSR 116 nor the WLSS extensions can be used to avoid the CMG deadlock, JSR 289 introduces a mechanism that could be used to avoid it. Recall that the WLSS container implicitly locks the application session associated with

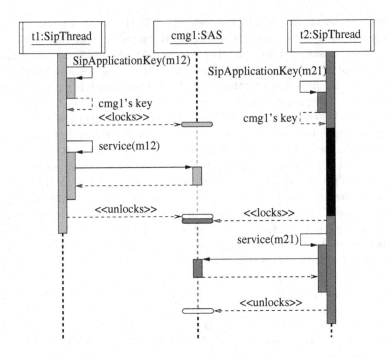

Fig. 4. Using JSR 289's session key based targeting mechanism to avoid the CMG deadlock scenario

a message before any servlet code is executed. This implicit locking policy makes it impossible to implement deadlock-avoidance protocols, save for protocols in which the application session associated with the message is the first to be requested. In sharp contrast to the conventions of JSR 116, which specifies that an initial request message always results in creation of a new application session, the session key based targeting mechanism allows the programmer to select which application session should be associated with an initial request message. Using this mechanism, servlet programmers can implement deadlock-avoidance protocols involving arbitrary sequences of resource requests.

A programmer uses the targeting mechanism to associate a request message with a specific SAS using a static servlet-class method. This method is specially annotated in order that the container can differentiate it from other methods. The method so annotated takes a request message (i.e., a `SipServletRequest` object) as its argument and returns a *key* (string). Before dispatching an initial request message to a thread, the container checks whether the servlet it is routed to has such a static method. If so, it passes the message to this method and associates the message with the SAS whose identifier matches the returned key. If this method does not exist or if the returned key does not match that of any existing SAS the container creates one and associates it with the message.

To avoid the CMG deadlock, a programmer could use the targeting mechanism to associate both $m1$ and $m2$ with the same application session. Figure 4 illustrates how this mechanism works [7]. Assuming without loss of generality that the targeting mechanism associates both messages with $cmg1$, both $t1$ and $t2$ start by requesting the same application session. One of them (here, $t2$) blocks, allowing the other ($t1$) to acquire the other application session and proceed.

While the targeting mechanism supports the implementation of protocols that avoid CMG-like deadlocks, the solution is inelegant and inflexible. To compute which application-session identifier to return, the targeting method may need to query one or more application sessions. These queries would need to be thread-safe, which means one or more application sessions may need to be locked in order to compute which other application session(s) should be locked. In addition, the use of the targeting mechanism to synchronize request processing may impose unnecessary synchronization requirements on response processing. This occurs because, according to the SIP protocol, the application session associated with a request must also be associated with all responses to that request. Consider two request messages, $m1$ and $m2$, which under normal circumstances would be associated with application sessions $a1$ and $a2$. Suppose further that, to avoid deadlock, the targeting mechanism is used to associate both messages with $a1$. The corresponding response messages, $m1'$ and $m2'$, will then necessarily be associated with $a1$, even though $m2'$ may only need to modify application session $a2$. That is, the container will artificially synchronize execution of threads that process response messages even if the resource needs of these responses do not overlap. Moreover, if processing response messages requires additional synchronization over and above that needed to process the initial request, the solution cannot be safely used.

5   Proposed Extension

Clearly, the SIP Servlet API should be extended with facilities for avoiding the kinds of deadlocks mentioned previously. At a minimum, it might require a mode that performs no implicit locking so that servlet programmers can choose to use an approach such as we describe here. However, to foster the development of sound and maintainable servlets, facilities that separate concerns involving deadlock avoidance from the servlet's "functional logic" would be preferable. As mentioned previously (Section 2.2) the concurrency controller design pattern affords such separation by encapsulating complex synchronization protocols behind a simple API, which client code can invoke prior to entering a critical region. We now propose a modest extension to the SIP Servlet API to support the development of servlets that are designed according to this pattern (Section 5.1), and we illustrate how servlets so designed could avoid the afore-mentioned deadlocks (Sections 5.2-5.3). The complex synchronization logic used in this approach could be generated from abstract models of a servlet's synchronization states and transitions and a collection of declarative synchronization contracts (Section 5.4).

---

[7] Here, we assume the static method is named `SipApplicationKey`.

5.1   Proposed Extensions

In our proposed extension, when the container allocates a thread to service a message, the container would create a *negotiator* object and pass that object along with the message to the `service` method. The negotiator object plays the role of a concurrency controller, where the thread executing the `service` method is the client program that uses the negotiator to guard entry into critical regions. We use the term *synchronization state* to refer to an abstract state of execution within which a servlet needs exclusive access to some set of resources. While servicing a message, a thread might cycle through several distinct synchronization states. Thus, before entering a new synchronization state, a thread would need to notify its negotiator of this intention. The negotiator, being a concurrency controller, would then negotiate for exclusive access to the resources denoted by the target synchronization state, blocking until such time as these resources can be acquired.

For this approach to work, a thread's negotiator must have been designed with knowledge of its owner's synchronization states. Moreover, because each synchronization state might denote multiple resources, each transition is a potential source of deadlock, which means the negotiator must implement an appropriate deadlock-avoidance protocol. To this end, the negotiator could potentially implement any of a number of different strategies; however, the negotiators for different servlets would need to agree on the strategy. For sake of generality, negotiators will likely need to implement sophisticated avoidance protocols, possibly involving some combination of simple resource numbering with age-based heuristics, e.g., wound–wait [21]. Fortunately, the details of these sophisticated protocols will be encapsulated within the negotiator and should not impact the design of the servlet code.

To accommodate this proposal, the SIP Servlet API would need to be extended to define a new abstract base class `Negotiator`, which a servlet programmer would extend to implement a negotiation protocol according to the synchronization states of the servlet being developed. Moreover, when the container creates a thread to service an incoming SIP message, it would need to analyze the message to choose an appropriate subclass of `Negotiator`.[8] The container would then instantiate this class and pass the object along with the incoming SIP message to the servlet's `service` method. The servlet is then responsible for initializing this negotiator object and notifying it of synchronization state transitions when appropriate. In sharp contrast to the WLSS policy, the container does not acquire any locks implicitly before invoking `service`.

In order to separate out the details of synchronization from the servlet, the negotiator must know the synchronization states that are meaningful to the servlet, and it must know the resources needed in each state. Knowledge about the states and the names of the resources denoted by each state must be programmed into the negotiator. However, dynamic information, such as the actual resources that should be bound to these names, must be supplied at run time.

---

[8] Here, we assume the mapping of message type to Negotiator subclass could be specified in a deployment descriptor.

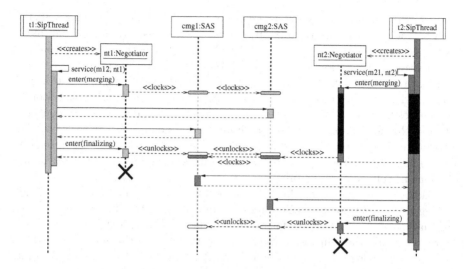

Fig. 5. Sequence diagram illustrating how negotiator use avoids the deadlock in the CMG scenario

For instance, suppose as in the CMG example, the CMG message encodes information about the source and destination calls. To access this information, the servlet will need to access the SIP application sessions (SASs) associated with each call. The negotiator will have been programmed using names that must be bound to these resources. The message should, therefore, be passed as a parameter to the constructor of the particular negotiator so that these SASs can be extracted from the message and bound to the names. Moreover, if the running servlet redirects a name to a new resource, it will need to communicate this change to the negotiator.

This proposal has the advantage of separating the logic of resource negotiation from the functional logic of a servlet; however, it requires that a servlet invokes a negotiator prior to entering a new synchronization state. This need to keep the servlet and its negotiator in sync suggests that negotiators (and the servlet-based notification code) should be generated automatically. Fortunately, negotiators can be automatically generated from high-level specifications, such as action languages [6], region invariants [10], and synchronization contracts [4,25]. Synchronization contracts have the added advantage of being able to ensure freedom from certain kinds of data races [25]. We will therefore say more about generation from synchronization contracts in Section 5.4.

5.2   CMG Scenario Using Negotiators

Figure 5 illustrates how a servlet designed using our proposed approach can avoid deadlock in the CMG example. As in the deadlocking scenario, the container dispatches two CMG request messages to two SIP threads. However, rather than locking application sessions *cmg*1 and *cmg*2 prior to invoking service, each thread creates a negotiator object and passes this object as a parameter to the service operation. Here, the code for service notifies its negotiator of its intention to transition to a new synchronization state. In this example, both threads attempt to enter a synchronization state called *merging*, which (for both threads) denotes the resource set {*cmg*1, *cmg*2}. In this case, the negotiator for *t*1 acquires both of these resources and returns, thereby allowing *t*1 to continue; whereas the negotiator for *t*2 cannot immediately acquire either resource. The latter thread therefore blocks until such time as it can acquire both resources. During negotiation, the negotiators use a deadlock-avoidance strategy, the details of which are elided here for brevity.

Deadlock is avoided using this solution because the container made no implicit locking decisions prior to calling service and because the designer(s) of these negotiator objects were able to formulate a request protocol that avoids deadlock. Moreover, unlike the solutions presented in Section 4, all of the details of deadlock avoidance are relegated to the negotiators. A servlet merely needs to notify its negotiator when it transitions to a new synchronization state.

5.3   CTD Scenario Using Negotiators

Figure 6 illustrates how our proposed approach avoids deadlock in the CTD example. As in the deadlocking scenario, the container dispatches an HTTP thread to service the incoming message. As before, the first actions of the service method are to create *cmn* and *ctd*1. However, before invoking initiateCall on *cmn*, the servlet notifies the negotiator of its intention to enter a synchronization state called *initiating*, which denotes the resource set {*cmn*,*ctd*1}. Having been notified, the negotiator proceeds to acquire these resources while avoiding deadlock.

In this scenario, *t*1 continues to hold the lock on *ctd*1 for the duration of its transaction. Thus, when *t*2 is dispatched to service *m*2′ and attempts to enter its *accepting* state, which denotes {*ctd*1, *cmn*}, *t*2's negotiator cannot acquire the lock on either resource. At this point, *t*2 blocks. Eventually *t*1 transitions to a synchronization state called *finalizing*, which denotes the empty set of resources. At this point, *nt*1 releases its locks on *cmn* and *ctd*1, after which *t*2 is awakened, acquires these resources, and continues. Deadlock is therefore avoided.

5.4   Automated Generation of Negotiators

The effectiveness of our approach in practice relies on the following:

- the negotiator must be designed with knowledge about the synchronization states of the corresponding servlet,
- the servlet must notify the negotiator of state changes and communicate other information, such as the run-time identity of resources to bind to names, and
- negotiators must agree on the protocol used to acquire resources.

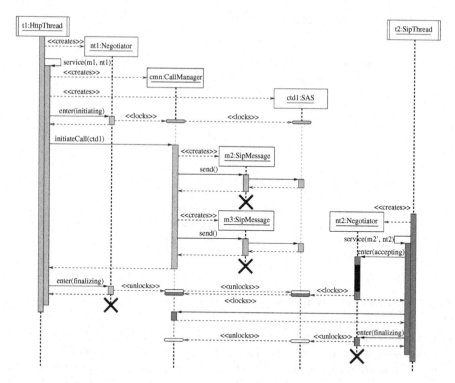

Fig. 6. Sequence diagram illustrating how negotiator use avoids the deadlock in the CTD scenario

If these tasks were left to the programmer, negotiator development would be highly error prone.

Fortunately, our prior experience integrating synchronization contracts into object-oriented languages leads us to believe that both negotiators and also the logic needed to instrument a servlet to notify/update a negotiator can be generated automatically [25,5,11]. Two inputs would be required:

- a suitably precise model of a thread's synchronization states and transitions, and
- a collection of *synchronization contracts*, each of which maps a synchronization state to a collection of *resource names*.

A resource name is an identifier or a navigation expression, such as might be expressed using Blaha's object-navigation notation [7], which refers to a resource. Resource names can be viewed as program variables or expressions that show how to traverse a sequence of links starting from some named program variable. In the CMG example, the resource names source and target refer to SIP sessions, which maintain call state needed for the servlet to communicate with the endpoints of the call. By contrast, the resource names source.SAS,

```
public machine CallMergeFSM {
  <*
    FeatureBox box;
    SipPort source, target;
    BoxPort boxPort;
  *>

  initial state IDLE sync-constraint { }

  state MERGING sync-constraint { source.SAS, target.SAS }

  state FINALIZING sync-constraint { }

  transition IDLE - boxPort ? Invite / {
    source = message.getAttribute("source");
    target = message.getAttribute("target");
  } -> MERGING;
  ...
```

Fig. 7. ECharts representation of the elided CMG machine, extended with contracts

and `target.SAS` are navigation expressions that specify how to retrieve the application sessions associated with these SIP sessions. Resource names must be *bound* to resources at run time. By virtue of name binding, each contract can be interpreted as mapping a synchronization state to its denotation, i.e., the set of resources that a thread needs when in that state.

The ECharts notation [9] holds promise as a means for specifying a SIP servlet's synchronization states and transitions. An ECharts machine is essentially a state-machine representation of a program unit. Smith *et al.* [24] show how to simplify the development of SIP servlets using ECharts by creating an adaptation layer between ECharts and the SIP Servlet API. By augmenting the notation to associate sets of resource names with states, we should be able to generate the negotiator object that a given EChart machine would use. Moreover, we could generate code within the EChart machine so that it will notify the generated negotiator of a change in synchronization state.

Figure 7 depicts an elided example of an EChart machine specification, extended with optional `sync-constraint` clauses that specify the resource needs associated with a given state. The specification declares three states, IDLE, MERGING, and FINALIZING, all of which declare synchronization constraints. The declaration associated with MERGING specifies that when the machine is in this state, it requires exclusive access to the resources bound to the resource names `source` and `target`. By contrast, when the machine is in either of the states IDLE or FINALIZING, it does not require exclusive access to any resources. The resource names `source` and `target` are bound to values in the action on the transition from synchronization state IDLE to state MERGING. These values are encoded as part of the invite message, which is passed as a parameter to the constructor (not shown in the figure) of this ECharts machine.

6   Conclusions and Future Work

With respect to synchronization concerns, current container architectures are lacking, both in terms of precisely documenting the policies used to synchronize threads and in the configurability of the policies themselves. Using examples from the telephony domain, we illustrated how these deficiencies manifest in servers that are prone to deadlock in use cases that occur in practice. Interestingly, these deadlocks are avoidable in principle, but not under the implicit-locking policy adopted by some vendors in the absence of precise guidance by the JSR 116 standard. The examples are symptomatic of the problems that arise when a standard is silent on an important non-functional concern and vendors are left to fill in the gaps.

To address these deficiencies, the research community must investigate means to precisely specify and document existing policies and to develop new, more configurable policies that account for more fine-grain needs of a given service. Clearly, the next version of the SIP Servlet API should provide some means for explicit synchronization with deadlock avoidance. Our proposal, inspired by the concurrency controller pattern involves a minimum of new mechanism at the API level, while allowing the generation of powerful synchronization protocols from highly declarative specifications.

Acknowledgements. Partial support was provided for this research by NSF grant CCF 0702667, LogicBlox Inc., and AT&T Research Laboratory. The authors also thank G. Bond, E. Cheung, H. Purdy, T. Smith, V. Subramonian, and P. Zave for indispensable explanations, feedback and guidance.

References

1. BEA white paper: BEA WebLogic Server 10—the rock-solid foundation for SOA (2007)
2. BEA WebLogic SIP Server - developing applications with WebLogic SIP Server (December 2006)
3. Behrends, R.: Designing and Implementing a Model of Synchronization Contracts in Object-Oriented Languages. PhD thesis, Michigan State University, East Lansing, Michigan USA (December 2003)
4. Behrends, R., Stirewalt, R.E.K.: The Universe Model: An approach for improving the modularity and reliability of concurrent programs. In: Proc. of FSE 2000 (2000)
5. Behrends, R., Stirewalt, R.E.K., Dillon, L.K.: A self-organizing component model for the design of safe multi-threaded applications. In: Heineman, G.T., Crnković, I., Schmidt, H.W., Stafford, J.A., Szyperski, C.A., Wallnau, K. (eds.) CBSE 2005. LNCS, vol. 3489. Springer, Heidelberg (2005)
6. Betin-Can, A., Bultan, T.: Verifiable concurrent programming using concurrency controllers. In: Proc. of the IEEE International Conference on Automated Software Engineering (2004)
7. Blaha, M.R., Premerlani, W.J.: Object-Oriented Modeling and Design for Database Applications. Prentice-Hall, Englewood Cliffs (1998)

8. Bond, G., et al.: Experience with component-based development of a telecommunication service. In: Heineman, G.T., Crnković, I., Schmidt, H.W., Stafford, J.A., Szyperski, C.A., Wallnau, K. (eds.) CBSE 2005. LNCS, vol. 3489. Springer, Heidelberg (2005)

9. Bond, G.W., Goguen, H.: ECharts: Balancing design and implementation. In: Proceedings of the 6th IASTED International Conference on Software Engineering and Applications, pp. 149–155. ACTA Press (2002)

10. Deng, X., et al.: Invariant-based specification, synthesis, and verification of synchronization in concurrent programs. In: Proc. of the IEEE International Conference on Software Engineering (ICSE 2002) (2002)

11. Fleming, S.D., et al.: Separating synchronization concerns with frameworks and generative programming. Technical Report MSU-CSE-06-34, Michigan State University, East Lansing, Michigan (2006)

12. Gamma, E., Helm, R., Johnson, R., Vlissides, J.: Design Patterns: Elements of Reusable Object-Oriented Software. Addison–Wesley Publishing Company, Reading (1995)

13. Harris, T., Fraser, K.: Language support for lightweight transactions. In: Proc. of the ACM SIGPLAN Conference on Object-Oriented Systems, Languages, and Applications (OOPSLA 2003) (2003)

14. Herlihy, M., et al.: Software transactional memory for dynamic-sized data structures. In: Proc. of the twenty-second annual symposium on Principles of distributed computing, pp. 92–101 (2003)

15. Kristensen, A.: JSR 110: SIP Servlet API version 1.0 (February 2003)

16. Lopes, C.: D: A language framework for distributed programming. PhD thesis, Northeastern University (1997)

17. Luchangco, V., Marathe, V.J.: Transaction synchronizers. In: 2005 Workshop on Synchronization and Concurrency in Object Oriented Languages (SCOOL 2005) held at OOPSLA 2005 (October 2005)

18. Meyer, B.: Object-Oriented Software Construction. Prentice-Hall, Englewood Cliffs (1997)

19. Peterson, J.L., Silberschatz, A.: Operating System Concepts, 2nd edn. Addison–Wesley, Reading (1985)

20. Rosenberg, J., et al.: SIP: Session Initiation Protocol, RFC 3261 (2002)

21. Rosenkrantz, D.J., Stearns, R.E., Philip, I., Lewis, M.: System level concurrency control for distributed database system. ACM Transactions on Database Systems 3(2), 178–198 (1978)

22. Rumbaugh, J., Jacobson, I., Booch, G.: The Unified Modeling Language Reference Manual, 2nd edn. Addison–Wesley, Reading (2004)

23. Sailfin, `https://sailfin.dev.java.net`

24. Smith, T.M., Bond, G.W.: ECharts for SIP servlets: a state-machine programming environment for VoIP applications. In: IPTComm 2007: Proceedings of the 1st international conference on Principles, systems and applications of IP telecommunications, pp. 89–98. ACM, New York (2007)

25. Stirewalt, R.E.K., Behrends, R., Dillon, L.K.: Safe and reliable use of concurrency in multi-threaded shared memory sytems. In: Proc. of the 29th Annual IEEE/NASA Software Engineering Workshop (2005)

26. Apache Tomcat, `http://tomcat.apache.org`

27. Wilkiewicz, J., Kulkarni, M.: JSR 289 PR: SIP Servlet Specification v1.1

Lawful Interception in P2P-Based VoIP Systems

Jan Seedorf

NEC Laboratories Europe
Kurfuerstenanlage 36
69115 Heidelberg, Germany
jan.seedorf@nw.neclab.eu

Abstract. Lawful Interception of Voice-over-IP communications is technically more challenging than Lawful Interception in the PSTN. Currently, Lawful Interception for Voice-over-IP traffic is being standardised with respect to VoIP service architectures where central entities are on the signalling path, as this is the way VoIP is being deployed today. However, future types of VoIP service architectures may be characterised by a higher degree of decentralisation. In the extreme case, there is no central entity in the network through which signalling will pass.

As an example for such a highly decentralised VoIP system, several proposals have suggested to use a P2P-network for VoIP signalling in conjunction with the Session Initiation Protocol (SIP), commonly referred to as P2PSIP. This paradigm change to P2P-based signalling has significant implications for authorised interception of communications. In this paper, we analyse the problem of applying Lawful Interception to P2P-based Voice-over-IP systems technically, highlighting the characteristic properties of such an approach and the corresponding implications that complicate Lawful Interception. Further, we inspect potential solutions for implementing Lawful Interception in a P2PSIP system in general and discuss advantages and drawbacks of such solutions.

1 Introduction

Lawful Interception (LI) is the process of legally authorised wiretapping of communications carried out by law enforcement organisations. It is conducted without the intercepted parties being aware of it. Lawful Interception is of great importance since it can provide very important information for criminal and security investigations. It may be used to collect information that can be used as evidence in court afterward as well as to gather information regarding criminal or terrorist activities in order to even prevent crimes or attacks.

Lawful Interception of *Voice-over-IP (VoIP)* is technically more challenging than in the *Public Switched Telephone Network (PSTN)*. One reason for this is the mobility of users, as enabled by the *Session Initiation Protocol (SIP)* [14]. In practise, user mobility implies that the current location of an identity can not always be determined prior to a call. Currently, Lawful Interception is being standardised for VoIP and IP networks in general in ETSI [8] and other standards organisations [1] [6] [22].

H. Schulzrinne, R. State, and S. Niccolini (Eds.): IPTComm 2008, LNCS 5310, pp. 217–235, 2008.

In general, the more central components are on the signalling path, the more manageable LI becomes. In current approaches VoIP service architectures are considered where central entities are on the signalling path (as this is the way VoIP is being deployed today). However, future types of VoIP service architectures may be characterised by a higher degree of decentralisation. For instance, if a P2P-network is used for VoIP signalling there is no central entity in the network through which signalling will pass. As an example for such a system, P2PSIP is currently being standardised by the IETF [10]. In principle, this means that not only the users, but also signalling and location servers are mobile and highly dynamic, rendering LI even more challenging.

There is a lot of controversy surrounding the topic of Lawful Interception in VoIP networks regarding social, political, and economic issues [4]. However, in this paper we analyse the problem of applying Lawful Interception to P2P-based Voice-over-IP systems solely technically, highlighting the characteristic properties of such an approach and the corresponding implications that complicate Lawful Interception. Further, we inspect potential solutions for implementing Lawful Interception in a P2PSIP system in general and discuss advantages and drawbacks of such solutions.

The rest of this paper is organised as follows: Section 2 describes Lawful Interception in IP-based networks and how it is currently applied to client-server based types of VoIP service architectures. Section 3 explains how VoIP signalling can be accomplished with a P2P network instead of servers. In section 4 the unique properties of P2P systems that make Lawful Interception for P2PSIP challenging are analysed in detail and the implications for LI are outlined. In section 5 potential solutions are discussed. Section 6 concludes the paper with a summary.

2   Lawful Interception of Voice-over-IP Communications

This section provides some background on Lawful Interception and an overview on how it is generally implemented in IP networks. Further, some examples of applying LI to Voice-over-IP communications will be presented.

2.1   Lawful Interception Terminology and Reference Model for IP Networks

A Lawful Interception activity gets triggered by a *Law Enforcement Agency (LEA)* which authorises a Network Operator, Access Provider, or Service Provider to intercept traffic for a target identity. Generally, two different types of interception data can be distinguished:

- *Intercept Related Information (IRI)* denotes the signalling data identifying the communication. This data may comprise the source identity, the destination identity, call duration, and other signalling information.

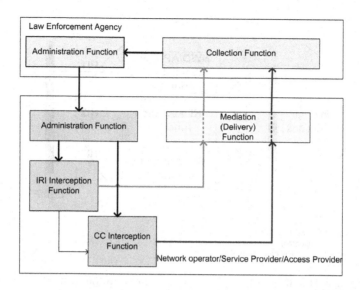

Fig. 1. Generic Model for Lawful Interception in IP Networks

- The *Content of Communication (CC)* denotes the actual payload being transmitted. For VoIP, this refers to the audio content of the call, i.e., the RTP-packets transferred from/to the subject which is the target of the LI operation.

In general, when analysing various standards for Lawful Interception in IP networks (e.g., [1] [6] [8] [22]), one can extract the generic model depicted in figure 1 [12]. This model shows the core functions necessary for Lawful Interception. An administration function serves for the operator to securely receive Lawful Interception requests authenticated by the LEA. This information is used by the operator to trigger the interception function for the IRI and the CC, respectively. The data collected by these interception functions is mediated and then collected by the LEA for analysis.

Figure 2 shows the reference model for Lawful Interception in IP networks as standardised by ETSI [8]. Three handover interfaces are defined (and standardised by ETSI) between the operator that carries out the LI and the LEA that authorises the LI for a specific target: an interface for the administration function *(HI1)*, an interface for the IRI mediation function *(HI2)*, and an interface for the CC mediation function *(HI3)*.

2.2 Lawful Interception of Voice-over-IP in Server-Based Systems

LI has been carried out in the PSTN and GSM networks successfully for quite some time. With voice communications transmitted over IP networks, some fundamental differences in signalling and media transport make VoIP challenging in such systems.

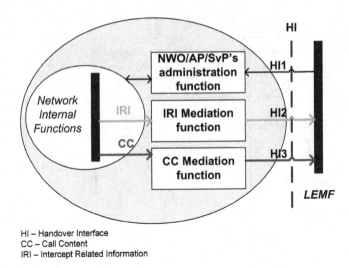

HI – Handover Interface
CC – Call Content
IRI – Intercept Related Information

Fig. 2. ETSI Reference Model for Lawful Interception in IP Networks

Signalling for VoIP is usually facilitated with the *Session Initiation Protocol (SIP)* [14]. SIP enables user mobility with a *Unified Resource Identifier (SIP-URI)*. Users can register their current location (e.g., IP-address and port) at a SIP registrar server. In this way, a SIP user can receive SIP messages for the same SIP-URI at different locations[1]. For Lawful Interception of VoIP communications in SIP networks, the SIP-URI is the target identity of a LI operation.

Some of the characteristics of SIP-signalling complicate LI. First, signalling and media traffic take different routes in the network. Second, the network provider can be different from the VoIP service provider (e.g., the SIP provider). Third, because SIP offers mobility to users, the network provider used by a specific target identity can change frequently. Thus, the following fundamental problem arises for LI: How to enable interception of the CC *in real-time* if the network providers of the call participants are not known prior to the call?

Figure 3 shows how Lawful Interception can technically be implemented in a setting were the network provider is also the VoIP service provider. In this case, the IP-address of the target identity can be extracted from the SIP signalling messages intercepted at a SIP server of the target identity. This data is then used to trigger the interception of the CC (the media) at the corresponding aggregation router.

Figure 4 displays a different setting where the target identity is located in a different access network than the VoIP service provider. However, in this setting a so-called *Session Border Controller (SBC)* is used to force signalling and media (i.e., the IRI and CC data) to traverse a single central entity. As depicted in

---

[1] We assume that the reader is familiar with SIP signalling as specified in RFC 3261 [14]. Here we just highlight the most important characteristics of SIP that affect Lawful Interception in contrast to the PSTN.

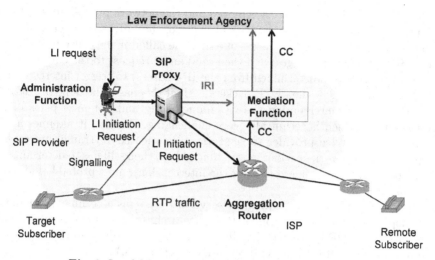

Fig. 3. Lawful Interception of VoIP Communications

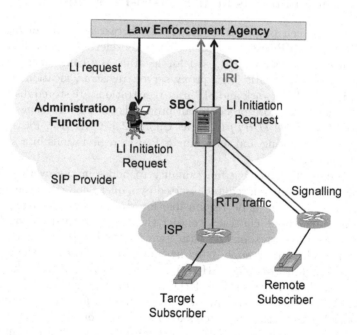

Fig. 4. Lawful Interception of VoIP Communications with a Session Border Controller

the figure, in such a setting the SBC becomes the central element to carry out LI requests received by the VoIP Service Provider and essentially Lawful Interception of VoIP communications is not much different from the PSTN-case in this scenario.

In a setting where no SBC is deployed and the network provider of the target identity is different from the network provider of the VoIP service provider, it is necessary to extract the IP-address of either the caller or the callee from the IRI (i.e., SIP signalling messages) and then send an LI request to the corresponding network provider (as determined from the IP-address) to trigger interception of the corresponding CC (i.e., RTP packets). All of this has to be done in *real-time* in order to start intercepting the CC immediately and not miss parts of the conversation, which is technically very challenging. Further, it assumes a way for the VoIP service provider to send an authenticated IP-traffic interception request to the network provider in *real-time* (which then still has to determine the corresponding aggregation router for the interception), most probably indirectly via the LEA.

Thus, Lawful Interception in client-server SIP systems is technically challenging, depending on the type of VoIP service architecture and setting. We will now introduce P2P-based SIP signalling (chapter 3) in order to analyse how this approach complicates LI for VoIP even more (chapter 4).

3   VoIP Signalling Using a Peer-to-Peer Network

Recently, it has been proposed to use a P2P network instead of SIP-servers for establishing a VoIP session [5] [20], commonly referred to as *P2PSIP*. With P2PSIP, all central components used for locating the callee in a session establishment attempt in SIP (e.g., proxy server, registrar, location server) are replaced with a P2P network and SIP user registrations are stored distributedly in this P2P network. More precisely, all proposals for P2PSIP suggest using a *Distributed Hash Table (DHT)* (such as Chord [23], CAN [13], Pastry [15], or Tapestry [24]) for storing and retrieving SIP user registrations in a structured P2P overlay network.

A DHT offers the following functionality to nodes in the overlay network: Given a key-ID (as a search request inserted by a query node into the network), the network returns the node responsible for storing data belonging to that key-ID. The query node can then contact the node returned by the DHT in order to receive the corresponding data item for the key-ID. Most DHTs map participating nodes onto a node-ID by hashing the IP-address of the node with a specified hash function (e.g., SHA-1) and keys get mapped to key-IDs by using the same hash function. The DHT protocol then defines which node-ID is responsible for which key-ID and a routing function for queries to reach the node responsible for storing data items for a key (therefore the name *Distributed Hash Table*). Each node in the DHT has a routing table with a small number of links to other DHT nodes in order to enable routing to a node that stores a particular key-ID.

3.1   General Architecture

To use a DHT for locating SIP identities, users register their location (i.e., the IP-address through which they are reachable and intend to receive calls) not at

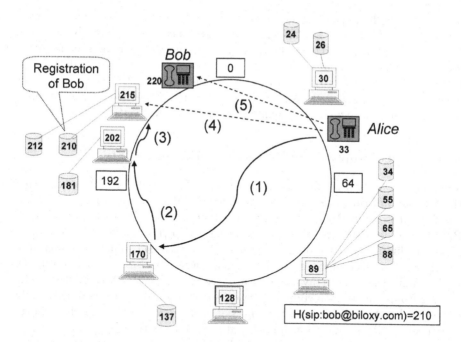

Fig. 5. Locating the Callee of a VoIP Session with P2PSIP

a central server which can be derived from their SIP-URI. Instead, the location for a SIP-URI is stored distributedly in a Distributed Hash Table. Thus, the SIP-URI is the key and any node can compute the key-ID for a particular SIP-URI by computing the hash-value for the SIP-URI and start a lookup query for that particular key-ID to obtain the corresponding location (i.e., IP-address and port) stored in the DHT for this key-ID.

Figure 5 shows an example of a P2P-SIP network using a DHT for locating the callee of a multimedia communication. In the example a Chord [23] network is displayed[2]. Chord uses a virtual ring as the DHT structure and nodes are responsible for storing data items belonging to key-IDs with a value between their node-ID and the predecessor in the ring. In the simplified example network 8 nodes are in the network, including two users *Alice* (with node-ID 33) and *Bob* with node-ID 220). Further, some nodes store data items for keys they are responsible for (e.g., node 170 stores data for key-ID 137). In the example, Bob has stored his SIP user registration (i.e., the binding between his current IP-address and his SIP-URI) in the network. Assuming the hash of Bob's SIP-URI is 210, node 215 is responsible for the key-ID of Bob's SIP-URI and stores the corresponding location.

When Alice tries to call Bob, she sends a lookup request for key-ID 210 to the closest node to the key-ID she has in her local routing table, node 170 (1). This

---

[2] Other DHT algorithms provide similar functions and the same properties with respect to Lawful Interception.

node forwards the request in the same manner[3] (2). Finally, the request reaches the node responsible for key-ID 210, node 215, and it gets routed back to the query node (not displayed in the figure). At this point, the query node can contact node 215 directly, without using the overlay network (depicted with a dotted line in the figure), in order to receive the corresponding content, i.e., Bob's current location (4). Subsequentially, Alice contacts Bob directly peer-to-peer to establish a SIP session with regular SIP signalling as specified in [14] (5).

3.2 Current Proposals and Standardisation of P2PSIP

Some early prototype implementations for P2PSIP exist [2] [21], demonstrating the feasibility of this novel approach to VoIP signalling. Additionally, the IETF has formed a P2PSIP working group. Currently, many different proposals for P2PSIP are discussed in this IETF working group [11]. There are many open issues (including the overall architecture, NAT traversal, routing details, and the choice of a DHT protocol) and not many design decisions have been made. Additionally, there are many different use-cases for actual P2PSIP deployments, ranging from small early responder networks in the case of disasters to extremely large world-wide end-user telephone networks. Therefore, it is difficult to judge how future P2PSIP systems will evolve at this point in time.

Despite many open questions, the IETF P2PSIP working group seems to have consensus that for security reasons (i.e., to protect against attacks on DHTs) any system must have a central authority as an enrollment server. Such an enrollment server could authenticate participants of the system and provide secure node-ID assignment to nodes[4]. However, it is important to realise that such a central entity (as envisioned in the IETF) would only provide *enrollment* in the system. In particular, it would not be on every signalling path and it would not be involved in call establishment attempts among nodes at all.

4 Challenges for Lawful Interception in P2PSIP Systems

Using a P2P-network implies a significant paradigm shift for VoIP signalling. First, there are no centralised components on the signalling path. Second, the network is dynamic and there are no static routing paths between entities. From a Lawful Interception perspective, these characteristics have serious implications, rendering current Lawful Interception practices used in client-server VoIP systems unfeasible. In the following subsections we analyse the specific properties of P2PSIP that make Lawful Interception a challenge in such systems and highlight what the implications of these characteristics are for LI.

---

[3] This example uses so-called *recursive* routing [23] where a lookup request gets forwarded until it reaches the node responsible for the key-ID.

[4] This can prevent attacks on node-ID assignment where attackers generate a large amount of virtual node-IDs or try to enter the DHT at a specific location in order to attack specific nodes [18].

P2PSIP inherits (from client-server SIP with respect to LI) the problem that signalling and media not only take different routes in the network but also that the media path cannot be determined prior to a call. We therefore focus on the signalling differences in P2PSIP (compared to client-server SIP) and the consequences for Lawful Interception in our analysis. Additionally, any P2PSIP LI solution still has to solve the problems of deriving the corresponding point for interception of media in the network (e.g., the aggregation router of a network provider) and intercepting the corresponding CC in real-time, just as LI solutions for VoIP systems today.

4.1   Lack of a Central Entity for Interception

The most fundamental problem for Lawful Interception in a P2PSIP system is the lack of a central entity on the signalling path. This has two important implications: First, there is technically no single point in the network to intercept all outgoing call establishment attempts for a specific target identity. Second, there is legally no body with whom a Law Enforcement Agency can have a trustworthy and legally binding relationship for sending authorised interception requests to.

No server involved in call-setup. Since there is no server involved in call-setup, for a specific target identity it cannot be determined prior to a call which nodes will be on the signalling path for outgoing calls. In contrary, for client-server SIP the first signalling hop for outgoing calls can be determined prior to a call based on the domain of the target's SIP-URI. Thus, for Lawful Interception the problem arises where to intercept signalling traffic for a target identity *at all* in the network.

No VoIP Service Provider to receive interception requests from LEA. Lawful Interception as specified within the ETSI reference model [8] assumes an operator (e.g., the Network Operator, Access Provider, or Application Service Provider such as a VoIP Service Provider) in order for the LEA to be able to trigger a Lawful Interception for a specific target identity through the administration function provided by such an operator (compare figure 2). Further, it is assumed that there will be legal agreements or requirements forcing the provider to co-operate with Law Enforcement Agencies. With P2PSIP, the role of an operator can only vaguely be estimated and depends to a large extent on the use case and actual deployment of P2PSIP. As envisioned by the IETF P2PSIP working group [11], it may be the case that an operator merely fulfills the role of secure node-ID assignment, i.e., enrollment in the system. In this case, the LEA has no legal agreement with nodes involved in routing signalling messages through the network.

4.2   P2P-Routing

Routing in P2PSIP differs from routing in client-server SIP drastically. Essentially, for every call there is a unique routing path for signalling messages.

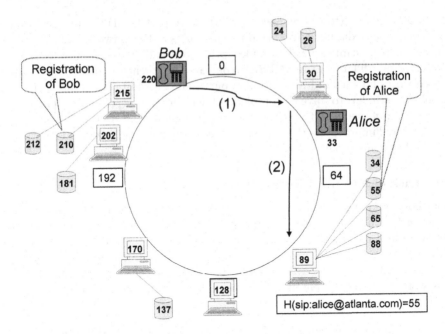

Fig. 6. Incoming Signalling Messages take a different Routing Path

Inbound and outbound signalling messages take different paths. In contrary to client-server SIP, with P2PSIP the last signalling hop of an incoming call is usually different than the first signalling hop of an outgoing call for a specific target identity. As an example, figure 6 shows the example-DHT from the previous figure. However, this time Bob tries to call Alice, assuming that Alice's key-ID (i.e., the hash of her SIP-URI) is 55 and that she has stored the corresponding location previously in the network. It can be observed that in this case routing traverses a completely disjoint set of nodes than when Alice called Bob (compare to figure 5). Note that the value of Alice's key-ID determines the signalling routing when Bob tries to call her, not the location of her node (i.e., her node-ID as the hash of her current IP-address). For LI this implies that in order to intercept outgoing and incoming calls there needs to be more than one interception point for signalling messages for *each* target identity.

Different outgoing signalling node for different callee. With client-server SIP, there is a static relationship between a target identity and the first signalling hop for outgoing calls. With P2PSIP, the SIP-URI of the callee determines the first signalling hop. For instance, in the example displayed in figure 5 if Alice would call a different callee, say Carol whose key-ID is 88, there would be a single routing hop to node 89 which stores the current location for key-ID 88. Thus, there is potentially a different first signalling hop for every callee. For LI this means that even for outgoing messages there is no single point in the network where all signalling messages for a target identity can be intercepted.

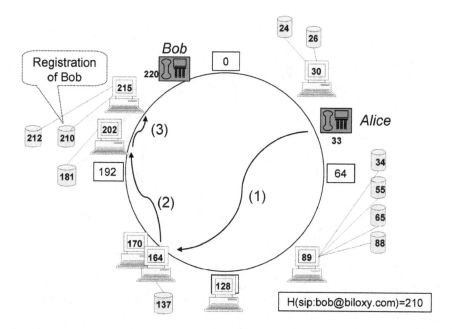

Fig. 7. Node Join in a P2PSIP Network

These radical differences in routing compared to client-server SIP (where a single SIP server can be used for intercepting many target identities of a single domain) demand a *per target identity* solution and possibly a *per callee* solution for LI in P2PSIP.

4.3 Dynamic Nature of P2P Systems

Because P2P systems are highly dynamic, network membership and routing paths change as the network state (i.e., the nodes in the network, the routing links between them, and data items stored in the network) changes. Overall, this characteristic makes the previously analysed properties even worse for LI because the network state can change at any time, resulting in different routing paths and key-ID responsibility.

Joining and leaving of nodes. In a P2P network, participating nodes join and leave the network frequently. As a consequence, the signalling routing path between a specific caller and a specific callee cannot be determined prior to call-setup time because it changes frequently over time. Thus, any LI attempt must derive the first signalling hop for an outgoing call attempt of a target identity in real-time.

Figure 7 displays again the example network from figure 5. However, in this example a node with node-ID **164** has joined the network. As a consequence, if Alice calls Bob again her first lookup message would be sent to the newly joined

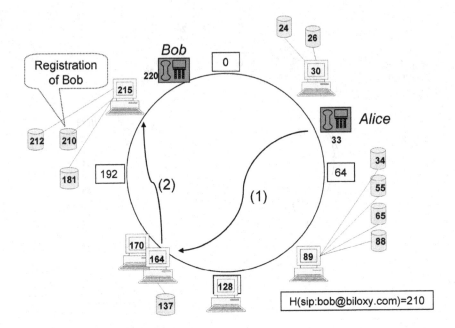

Fig. 8. Node Leave in a P2PSIP Network

node 164. Also, node 170 which was previously on the routing path between Alice and Bob does not receive routing messages anymore if Alice calls Bob.

Figure 8 shows the same DHT as in figure 7 after node 202 has left the network (e.g., because its user went offline). Note that in this case node 215 takes over the responsibility for key-ID 181 from node 202. Also, routing changes and node 164 directly routes to node 215 (2).

Responsibility for user registrations changes frequently. The node storing the location binding for a particular SIP-URI changes frequently (if a new node is responsible for a particular SIP-URI the location/identifier-binding is transferred to this node). For instance, in figure 7 and 8 it can be observed that by joining the network, node 164 has also taken over the responsibility for storing the SIP-registration for key-ID 137. Additionally, when node 202 left the network, data responsibility for key-ID 181 was taken over by node 215[5].

Hence, joining and leaving of nodes affects the signalling routing path between a caller and a callee dynamically as the network state changes as well as the responsibility among nodes for certain key-IDs and corresponding data items. For LI this implies that even if there would be a relationship (or legal agreement) between the LEA and the node storing the registration data in the DHT this would

---

[5] DHTs normally store redundant data items at nodes close in the DHT structure to cope with the case when a node fails or leaves the network without transferring data items.

be of very limited value because at any time the registration responsibility may get transferred to another node because of nodes joining and leaving the network.

4.4 P2P Nodes Are Not Trustworthy

In general, it cannot be guaranteed that P2P nodes follow the DHT operations properly. In any large network with regular hosts or even VoIP terminals it must be considered that some nodes have been compromised or act maliciously. This complicates LI because with P2PSIP such potentially compromised nodes are part of signalling routing and store location-to-URI bindings in the DHT.

User registrations are stored at peers/terminals. With P2PSIP, location bindings of users (i.e., SIP-registrations that bind the current location of a user to a SIP-URI) are distributedly stored at all participating nodes in the network, potentially at users' terminals. However, P2P nodes cannot be considered trustworthy. Also, it is possible that attackers launch a *chosen-location attack* in the DHT, trying to place a node under their control at a specific location in the virtual DHT routing structure (e.g., the Chord routing ring). Because user registrations are stored at potentially compromised and generally non-trustworthy nodes or terminals, the integrity of user registrations stored in the network cannot be guaranteed [17]. Consider the example in figure 5: Bob has no means of preventing node 215 to forge the location stored for his SIP-URI.

Difficult to authenticate user registrations. Besides not being trustworthy, a node storing registrations for some SIP-URI has no means of authenticating the corresponding data item due ot the lack of a shared secret or trust relationship with the owner of a SIP-URI. Consider again the example in figure 5: node 215 has no means of authenticating a store-message for Bob's SIP-URI in order to detect attacks by intermediate nodes that route the store-message and replace Bob's location with a forged one.

Thus, unless cryptographic add-ons are used (e.g., a public key infrastructure [16] or self-certifying SIP-URIs [17]), user registrations stored in a P2PSIP network can be forged, possibly misleading Lawful Interception operations.

5 Potential Solutions

As highlighted in the previous section, the paradigm of P2P computing imposes significant challenges for Lawful Interception of VoIP signalling and media that seem almost unachievable technically. Nevertheless, there are some approaches to incorporate LI even in highly decentralised systems like P2PSIP. In this section, we discuss these potential solutions on a general level, highlighted the advantages and disadvantages of each potential solution for Lawful Interception in a P2P-based SIP system.

The primary problem for Lawful Interception in P2PSIP systems is the lack of a centralised entity in the network through which all signalling traffic traverses. Thus, to still render Lawful Interception feasible, any solution needs to solve the problem of where to intercept communications in a highly dynamic system. Considering the dynamic network structure and routing in P2P systems described previously, it seems an option to move the interception point in the network for Lawful Interception from the network core towards the edge. In the discussion of possible P2PSIP LI solutions, we will therefore inspect solutions at the network edge first and then look at solutions that intercept closer to the network core.

5.1 Footprint in Devices

One solution that has been suggested for Lawful Interception of IP-traffic and VoIP communication in server-based systems is to implant a footprint in devices. Such a footprint could intercept all outgoing traffic at the source and would also have access to all incoming traffic for the target identity. Currently, many countries are considering this option. For instance, in Germany there is a discussion about trojan horses developed by government agencies to be secretly installed on hosts of target identities [9]. Of course, such footprints can also be installed prior to deployment of devices.

Since signalling and media are correlated in terminals, one key advantage of a footprint in devices would be that there is no need to trigger the interception of media traffic (at another location in the network) from the intercepted signalling, hence coping with user-mobility. For P2PSIP, this solution could also handle the constantly changing structure of a DHT. In general, having a footprint in the device of the target identity would solve the problem where to intercept in the network and also mitigate the problem of a dynamic network structure and routing.

The core problem with this approach is forcing terminals to incorporate such a footprint in their code. With hardphones, it might be feasible to enforce this legally prior to deployment. Still, hackers might find solutions to break firmware and thus circumvent LI. But even worse, with softphones and open standards like SIP (or potentially P2PSIP once it is standardised by the IETF) almost anyone can change the behaviour of terminals or even write a new P2PSIP application. Thus, it seems impossible to enforce a mandatory LI footprint in open systems with open standards. Future work in this direction might explore trusted computing and smartcards as hardened platforms that could protect the integrity of P2PSIP applications including a pre-installed footprint (still not preventing self-written applications).

5.2 Intercepting at IP-Layer

Because P2PSIP essentially replaces SIP servers with a highly dynamic and unpredictable interconnection of P2P-nodes, a possible solution for LI could be to intercept all traffic of the target identity at the IP-layer. This would assume stateful packet inspection on the IP-layer, filtering SIP messages, and then extracting signalling information in order to trigger interception of the CC. Further, it would assume that the LEA knows the network operator of the target in order to authorise LI through the administration handover interface.

In a setting where the target identity always uses the same network operator this may be a feasible approach. In such a setting, the target identity might get assigned a different IP-address frequently (as is common for home users connected via an ISP) which would result in a new DHT position on the signalling layer (remember that most DHTs compute a node-ID by hashing the node's current IP-address). Since the network operator usually authenticates the target identity on the IP-layer, it seems more practical to intercept at the IP-layer in this setting as described above.

However, in a scenario where the target of a Lawful Interception operation changes its network operator frequently (due to mobility on the IP-layer as specifically offered by SIP), this approach becomes very challenging. First, in order to intercept on the IP-layer in this case the LEA would need to inform *virtually all* network operators in its legislative domain and provide them with the target identity (i.e., the SIP-URI of the target). Second, all network providers must have the technical ability to correlate CC interception with SIP signalling extracted from filtered SIP messages.

Overall, it seems that this approach is hard to deploy in practise. If users change the IP access provider (e.g., by using wireless networking hotspots) frequently, this approach demands for a completely correlated surveillance of users on the IP-layer among network operators. Such a comprehensive Lawful Interception system would be very expensive, possibly imposing large costs to network/access providers.

5.3   Infiltrating the Peer-to-Peer Network

In order to make LI feasible not at edge nodes but in the network core, the only option seems to infiltrate the network with nodes under control of the LEA. Note that this would imply an important paradigm shift to LI carried out today where the LEA does not actively conduct LI but rather sends authorised LI requests to operators which are legally bound to carry them out.

It is well known that this approach is pursued by the music industry in order to track illegal uploading of music in P2P file-sharing networks. However, there is an important difference to Lawful Interception: the goal of the music industry is to find *some* illegal file-sharing activity, whereas the goal of Lawful Interception is to intercept *all* traffic for a *specific* target identity. Since even the control of a very large amount of nodes cannot guarantee being on every possible signalling path, effectively the LEA would need to place itself at specific locations (depending on the DHT structure and properties of the particular P2PSIP network) in relation to the target identity's node-ID and key-ID in the network. Essentially this meant that the LEA becomes a kind of attacker carrying out *chosen-location attacks* for the target identity.

Intercepting incoming signalling messages by guarding the key-ID. For instance, with an unidirectional DHT such as Chord [23], the LEA could control all access to a specific key-ID by controlling a node[6] with a node-ID marginally smaller

---

[6] E.g., by joining the network with such a node-ID.

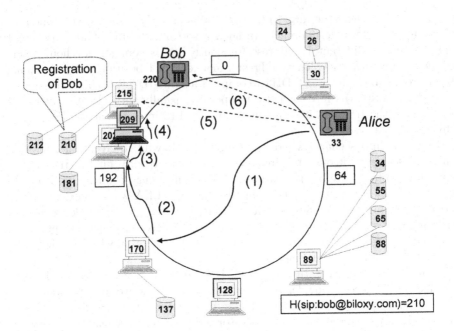

Fig. 9. A node under the control of a Law Enforcement Agency joining a DHT in order to intercept all incoming signalling messages for a target identity

then the key-ID (i.e., very close in the unidirectional DHT routing structure). For other DHT protocols (e.g., CAN [13] or Pastry [15]), the DHT structure determines *closeness* to a key, respectively. As an example, figure 9 shows the DHT from the previous figures after a new node (assumed to be under the control of the LEA) has joined with node-ID 209. By becoming the direct predecessor of the node responsible for storing data for key-ID 210, due to routing properties specific to Chord (i.e., uniderctional greedy routing) [18] the LEA can control all queries for key-ID 210 (i.e., all incoming signalling messages for Bob's SIP-URI). This would enable the LEA to intercept incoming signalling messages for a specific target identity.

Intercepting outgoing signalling messages by infiltrating routing tables. To intercept all outgoing messages from a target identity on the signalling layer, the LEA would need to infiltrate all DHT routing table entries of the target identity's node in the DHT. Since the target identity gets assigned a new node-ID whenever the target obtains a new IP-address, this seems unjustifiable effort. Additionally, for some DHTs such *routing table poisoning attacks* [7] are hard to conduct due to *constrained routing tables* [19]. Hence, due to the rapidly changing network structure in P2P-systems, it is almost impossible for a LEA to infiltrate all routing table entries of a target identity's DHT-node.

Using an enrollment server of the operator. If an enrollment server is operated by an operator which has a legal agreement with a LEA, joining the network at some specific location and infiltrating routing table entries of a target identity may become feasible for the LEA. An enrollment server could take out the effects of network dynamics by assigning the same node-ID to a target identity even in the case of mobility on the IP-layer (in [3] an approach for this is presented), assuming participants authenticate themselves at the enrollment server. Potentially, this could enable a LEA to intercept all outgoing calls for an identity even in a highly dynamic network because a particular target identity would have the same node-ID in the DHT even if it changed its IP-address. Therefore, using an enrollment server could mitigate some of the problems in infiltrating a P2P network mentioned previously. This opens an opportunity for *bootstrapping* Lawful Interception with specific nodes that infiltrate the network at specific locations as demanded by the LEA (with respect to the target identity).

6 Conclusion

This paper provided a technical analysis of Lawful Interception in P2P-based VoIP systems. The key properties of P2P systems that impose challenges for Lawful Interception have been inspected in detail: The lack of a central entity, changing participants and varying data responsibility, P2P-routing characteristics, and the non-trustworthiness of nodes. Further, potential solutions to these problems have been presented and examined, including a Lawful Interception footprint in devices, intercepting all communication on the IP-layer, and actively infiltrating the P2P network.

None of the presented solutions seems to be a very promising and satisfactory approach for implementing Lawful Interception in P2PSIP networks at large, each having its own drawbacks as well as practical issues. Therefore, at the current state, providing a general solution for Lawful Interception in P2P-based VoIP systems must be regarded as technically highly challenging and it is an open research problem how to circumvent the problems inspected in this paper.

The preferable approach for Lawful Interception in a P2PSIP network largely depends on the exact properties and use case of the system. It remains to be seen which type of service architecture will prevail for P2PSIP and to what extent a potential operator will be involved in signalling at all. If a P2PSIP network is *operated* by a provider which is in charge of enrollment and node-ID assignment, there is an opportunity for Law Enforcement Agencies to bootstrap Lawful Interception from this procedure. Further research needs to be done in order to investigate precise requirements for such an approach and its feasibility.

Acknowledgments

The author would like to thank Frank Fransen and Ilona Rappu for valuable discussions on Lawful Interception in the context of Voice-over-IP systems that helped writing this paper. Additionally, the author would like to thank the anonymous reviewers for their helpful comments and Nico d'Heureuse for his help in revising the paper.

References

1. American National Standards Institute: Lawfully Authorized Electronic Surveillance (LAES) for Voice over Packet Technologies in Wireline Telecommunications networks, ATIS-1000678.200X (ANS T1.678), Version 2. Draft (proposed)
2. Baset, S.: P2PP prototype implementation, http://www1.cs.columbia.edu/~salman/peer/
3. Baumgart, I.: P2PNS: A Secure Distributed Name Service for P2PSIP. In: Proceedings of the 5th IEEE International Workshop on Mobile Peer-to-Peer Computing (MP2P 2008) in conjunction with IEEE PerCom 2008, Hong Kong, China, pp. 480–485 (March 2008)
4. Bellovin, S., Blaze, M., Brickell, E., Brooks, C., Cerf, V., Diffie, W., Landau, S., Peterson, J., Treichler, J.: Security Implications of Applying the Communications Assistance to Law Enforcement Act to Voice over IP, http://www.itaa.org/news/docs/CALEAVOIPreport.pdf
5. Bryan, D.A., Lowekamp, B.B., Jennings, C.: SOSIMPLE: A Serverless, Standards-based, P2P SIP Communication System. In: Proceedings of the International Workshop on Advanced Architectures and Algorithms for Internet Delivery and Applications, Orlando, USA (June 2005)
6. CABLE TELEVISION LABORATORIES: PacketCable Electronic Surveillance Specification, PKT-SP-ESP-I04-040723 (July 2004)
7. Castro, M., Druschel, P., Ganesh, A., Rowstron, A., Wallach, D.S.: Secure routing for structured peer-to-peer overlay networks. In: Proc. of the 5th Symposium on Operating Systems Design and Implementation, Boston, MA. ACM Press, New York (December 2002)
8. ETSI: ETSI Lawful Interception Architecture, ETSI TS 102 528 v1.1.1 Lawful Interception (LI), Interception domain Architecture for IP networks, technical specification (November 2006)
9. International Herald Tribune Europe: German minister defends 'Trojan horse' spy tactic as needed to fight terror, http://www.iht.com/articles/ap/2007/08/31/europe/EU-GEN-Germany-Trojan-Horses.php
10. Jennings, C., Lowekamp, B., Rescorla, E., Rosenberg, J., Baset, S., Schulzrinne, H.: REsource LOcation And Discovery (RELOAD), internet draft (draft-bryan-p2psip-reload-03) (work in progress) (February 2008)
11. P2PSIP Status Pages:Peer-to-Peer Session Initiation Protocol (Active WG), http://tools.ietf.org/wg/p2psip/
12. Rappu, I.: Lawful Interception of VoIP in SIP-based Networks, Project Work, Technical-University Hamburg-Harburg (TUHH) (May 2007)
13. Ratnasamy, S., Francis, P., Handley, M., Karp, R., Shenker, S.: A Scalable Content-Addressable Network. In: Proc. of SIGCOMM 2001, San Diego, USA, August 27-31 (2001)
14. Rosenberg, J., Schulzrinne, H., Camarillo, G., Johnston, A., Peterson, J., Sparks, R., Handley, M., Schooler, E.: SIP: Session Initiation Protocol, RFC 3261 (June 2002), http://www.ietf.org/rfc/rfc3261.txt
15. Rowstron, A., Druschel, P.: Pastry: Scalable, decentralized object location and routing for large-scale peer-to-peer systems. In: Guerraoui, R. (ed.) Middleware 2001. LNCS, vol. 2218, pp. 329–350. Springer, Heidelberg (2001)
16. Seedorf, J.: Security Challenges for P2P-SIP. IEEE Network Special Issue on Securing Voice over IP 20(5), 38–45 (2006)

17. Seedorf, J.: Using Cryptographically Generated SIP-URIs to Protect the Integrity of Content in P2P-SIP. In: 3rd Annual VoIP Security Workshop, Berlin, Germany (June 2006)
18. Seedorf, J., Muus, C.: Availability for DHT-based Overlay Networks with Unidirectional Routing. In: Onieva, J.A., Sauveron, D., Chaumette, S., Gollmann, D., Markantonakis, K. (eds.) WISTP 2008. LNCS, vol. 5019. Springer, Heidelberg (2008)
19. Singh, A., Castro, M., Druschel, P., Rowstron, A.: Defending against eclipse attacks on overlay networks. In: Proc. of the ACM SIGOPS European Workshop (September 2004)
20. Singh, K., Schulzrinne, H.: Peer-to-Peer Internet Telephony using SIP. In: Proc. of the international workshop on Network and operating systems support for digital audio and video, Stevenson, Washington, USA, pp. 63–68 (2005)
21. SIPDHT, http://sipdht.sourceforge.net
22. Sharp, C., Baker, F., Foster, B.: Cisco Architecture for Lawful Intercept in IP Networks, RFC 3924 (October 2004)
23. Stoica, I., Morris, R., Liben-Nowell, D., Karger, D.R., Kaashoek, M.F., Dabek, F., Balakrishnan, H.: Chord: A Scalable Peer-to-Peer Lookup Protocol for Internet Applications. IEEE/ACM Transactions on Networking 11(1) (February 2003)
24. Zhao, B.Y., Huang, L., Stribling, J., Rhea, S.C., Joseph, A.D., Kubiatowicz, J.: Tapestry: A Resilient Global-Scale Overlay for Service Deployment. IEEE Journal on Selected Areas in Communications 22(1) (January 2004)

Security Analysis of an IP Phone: Cisco 7960G

Italo Dacosta, Neel Mehta, Evan Metrock, and Jonathon Giffin

School of Computer Science, Georgia Institute of Technology
{idacosta,giffin}@cc.gatech.edu
{nmehta,evan.metrock}@gatech.edu

Abstract. IP phones are an essential component of any VoIP infrastructure. The hardware constraints and newness of these devices, as compared to mature desktop or server systems, lead to software development focused primarily on features and functionality rather than security and dependability. While several automated tools exist to test the security of IP phones, these tools have limitations and can not provide a strong guarantee that a particular IP phone is secure.

Our work evaluates the attack resilience of a widely deployed IP phone, the Cisco 7960G, employing techniques such as: vulnerability scans, fuzz tests, and static binary analysis. While the first two techniques found no vulnerabilities, the static analysis of the firmware image revealed critical vulnerabilities and fundamental software design flaws. We conclude that security designs proven useful in desktop and server software architectures should similarly appear as part of the software design for devices such as IP phones.

Keywords: VoIP security, IP phone, static binary analysis, embedded system security.

1 Introduction

Voice over IP (VoIP) is changing the nature of physical telephones. For more than a century [1], a telephone endpoint consisted of a transmitter and receiver connected to the public switched telephone network (PSTN) via twisted pair wiring. In contrast, VoIP handsets, or *hard phones*, are connected to data networks via broadband Ethernet cables and configured with an IP address. They execute operating systems and application software on general purpose device-class computer hardware. Their architecture is closer in design to desktop computer systems than to PSTN-connected telephones, and as a result, they introduce the security weaknesses of the computing world into telephony. Telephones can now be targets of attack and entry points into an enterprise's internal network, concepts unfamiliar in the telephone network of the past.

Security is one of the main challenges of VoIP systems, and the security of the IP phones is a part of this challenge. The widespread deployment of these devices in organizations and the possible persons that could be using them—company executives, congressmen and -women, and so on—make IP phones an

H. Schulzrinne, R. State, and S. Niccolini (Eds.): IPTComm 2008, LNCS 5310, pp. 236–255, 2008.

Fig. 1. Cisco IP Phone 7960G

interesting target for attackers. The implications of a compromised IP phone could be enormous (e.g. the Greek Watergate case [2]): from simple denial of service attacks to eavesdropping of confidential information, unauthorized use of the device, and financial losses (e.g. unauthorized international calls).

In this paper, we analyze the security of the software executing on a widely deployed IP phone: the Cisco 7960G (Figure 1), part of the Cisco Unified IP Phone series. Prior to our research, the IP phone had a good security record of only several non-critical software flaws. Our analysis included a mix of runtime execution analysis using off-the-shelf fuzz testing software for implementations of the session initiation protocol (SIP), as well as static analysis of the binary firmware image stored in the read-only memory (ROM) of the IP phone. Fuzz testing revealed no flaws in Cisco's software, which we hypothesize indicates that Cisco has included similar fuzz testing as part of their software development and quality assurance procedures. Our static code analysis, however, yielded a troubling conclusion: the software contained buffer overflows and other implementation errors that would allow a remote attacker to gain full control of the IP phone. Of greater concern is architectural design weaknesses in the operating system, which provides no memory protection among applications or between applications and the kernel.

IP phone software development seems poised to repeat the security errors that occurred during past desktop and server software development. By our analysis, the buffer overflow vulnerabilities existed in the Cisco phone because the firmware image contained calls to functions similar to known flawed functions, like `strcpy`, used in desktop and server systems. The software architecture appears to be evolving in a manner similar to desktop operating system development over the past 30 years. The maturity of the IP phone's current operating system resembles that of real-mode operating systems, such as DOS. Unfortunately, this new software evolution is occurring in a networked environment much different than that present during the development of desktop systems, and IP phone developers should recognize the risks of today's networks while architecting these network-connected systems. Although this paper focuses specifically on the Cisco 7960G firmware, we have performed preliminary studies into the security quality of other devices, including a Siemens IP phone and a Windows Mobile installation on a mobile handheld. Our conclusions drawn from the Cisco firmware analysis indeed appear representative of security weaknesses in these other systems.

Our threat model includes an attacker that gained access to a corporate network where the 7960G has been deployed, and the expectation that the attacker is able to reach IP phones through this network. The ability to send input to the IP phone could be available to an attacker in the Internet at large, although some network configurations may limit this to attackers on the internal LAN. The hardware needed for a typical attacker to write and test exploit code is inexpensive and readily available. The access to an IP phone would likely be as simple as purchasing one from Cisco, a reseller, or an auction site. We assumed that the IP phones are configured with basic SIP functionality and that the IP phone administrator has taken basic steps to limit trivial historical attacks such as supplying compromised firmware using a TFTP server [3]. Cisco today distributes signed firmware images that limit the efficacy of these legacy attacks.

The Cisco 7960G uses an embedded ARM processor which makes the analysis of the firmware image challenging. Previous researchers have used static binary analysis to understand the execution of x86 or SPARC executables, but unique properties of ARM processors, such as the support of multiple instruction sets, introduce complications to the static analysis of IP phone firmware. However, a knowledgeable attacker or analyst should be able to work through the difficulties to learn security properties of the IP phone. We present the static binary analysis techniques that we used to uncover security vulnerabilities in the firmware with the expectation that the techniques may prove instructive to other security analysts intending to improve an IP phone's security.

Our study produced the following contributions and results:

- **Limitations of automated security testing.** Our first set of tests used automated vulnerability scanning and fuzz testing tools in an attempt to trigger faults in the IP phone, but found no flaws (Section 4). In addition, published security advisories regarding this device described vulnerabilities discovered using automated tools but none of the vulnerabilities found by our in-depth static analysis. These facts show that the IP phone likely has been previously analyzed with automated tools but that critical vulnerabilities still exist.
- **Vulnerability discovery.** Using static binary analysis, we discovered fundamental architectural weaknesses in the design of the firmware, three stack buffer overflow vulnerabilities, and one heap overflow vulnerability (Section 5). The most critical vulnerability could be exploited by a remote attacker with a single network packet and would result in full device access.
- **Suggested architectural changes and other recommendations to improve security.** We examined security measures that were present or

absent on this embedded device and compared this feature set to modern non-embedded systems. Combined with our security assessment, we were then able to suggest patches for vulnerabilities and other improvements that could make the platform more secure. These included architectural changes, changes to compilers, changes to APIs, and further security review by the embedded device vendor.

This paper contains descriptions of the vulnerabilities found by our security analysis, but we have deliberately delayed publication of this paper so that the details would no longer be relevant to the current firmware deployed on Cisco IP phones. We performed our analysis during spring months of 2007 and reported to Cisco the vulnerabilities discovered by our research in the summer of 2007. In February 2008, Cisco publicly disclosed the existence of our critical vulnerabilities and released patched firmware for the affected IP phones in the Unified IP Phone series [4].

The next section provides background information on IP phones and previous commentary regarding their security. Section 3 describes the experimental testbed used for our runtime tests. Section 4 presents those automated tests performed against the IP phone and the test results. Section 5 describes the methodology and challenges faced during the disassembly of the binary firmware image and the results of the static binary analysis, including examples of the vulnerabilities found and our recommendations. Finally, Section 6 contains related research work in the area of VoIP vulnerability analysis and embedded system security, and in Section 7 we present our conclusions.

2 Background

This section provides background information on IP phones that knowledgeable readers may choose to omit.

IP phones can be classified in two types: hard phones and soft phones. Hard phones are typically embedded devices with a real time operating system (firmware), applications, and physical appearance similar to traditional telephone handsets. In comparison, soft phones are software applications that run on general-purpose desktop computers and handle voice traffic using the standard computer speakers and microphone (or any other specialized equipment connected to the computer). IP hard phones from companies such as Cisco, Siemens, and Avaya are widely deployed in many business organizations, and soft phone applications such as Skype and Google Talk are very popular on desktop computers in business and home environments. By 2005, Cisco sold more than 6 million IP hard phones [5] belonging to same product family of the device studied in this paper, the Cisco 7960G.

In general, soft phones are considered less secure than hard phones because soft phones inherit the vulnerabilities of the operating system where they run. For example, any malicious software, such as a virus, worm, trojan horse, or bot, that affects a vulnerable computer can also affect the soft phone applications running on that computer. Due to such attack potential, NIST's *Security Considerations for Voice over IP systems* [6] recommends that soft phones should not be used where security or privacy are a concern.

On the other hand, hard phones (henceforth referred to as IP phones) are considered more secure because they run a smaller and simpler operating system with few applications and services: they are embedded devices with limited hardware resources. For example, a common metric used to measure the security quality of code is the number of bugs per thousand lines of code (KLOC). This varies from system to system, but public estimates document bug densities in the range of 5 to 50 bugs per KLOC [7]. While today's desktop operating systems consist of millions of lines of code, embedded operating systems consist of only thousands of lines. Microsoft Windows Vista requires 15 GB of available space for installation while the firmware for the IP phone used in this paper requires around 1 MB of space. Given this comparison, it is easy to assume that IP phones and embedded devices in general have fewer vulnerabilities.

However, the resource constraints of the IP phones can also have a negative impact on their security. In most cases, the user of an embedded system does not have the ability to add security applications (i.e. antivirus, firewalls, etc.) that were not included by the manufacturer, and it can be difficult to apply security patches or firmware upgrades. Moreover, Raghunathan et al. [8] and Kocher et al. [9] described how the unique characteristics of embedded systems such as IP phones made it difficult to implement effective security in their software.

The 7960G has a good security history with only five reported vulnerabilities [10] between 2003 and the time of our analysis in spring 2007: four denial of service (DoS) vulnerabilities and one security bypass vulnerability due to a design flaw in its TFTP-based firmware distribution method. Arkin [3] pointed out flaws related to the deployment and supporting environment of the Cisco IP phones, particularly in the use of TFTP to configure the devices. Today, firmware files are digitally signed by Cisco to protect their integrity and the files are authenticated against a certificate trust list to limit an attacker's ability to tamper with the files in transit on the network. It is still up to the user to properly configure certificate trust lists and sign configuration files before they are distributed across a network. In particular, without a full Cisco Call Manager deployment, it can be very challenging to implement this hardening feature. There are no publicly documented numbers that state the percentage of Cisco IP phone real-world deployments using these security features.

Several automated security tools such as vulnerability scanners and fuzzers have been developed to test for VoIP vulnerabilities in the different elements of a VoIP system, including IP phones. A comprehensive list of such tools is maintained by the Voice over IP Security Alliance (VOIPSA) [11]. These tools have helped academic and industry security researchers find several critical vulnerabilities in IP phones, resulting in security advisories, new firmware versions, and security patches. For example, the Madynes research team at INRIA Lorraine reported several vulnerabilities in IP phones using their stateful SIP fuzzer [12].

However, the use of these tools is limited because they can not find or test for all the possible vulnerabilities in a given device. Therefore, one must be careful with the results obtained by running these automated tools. In this paper we show how static binary analysis techniques similar to those used for desktop operating systems and applications can be used to find critical vulnerabilities that have not been identified by the automated tools.

3   Experimental Design

In our tests, we used a Cisco IP phone 7960G (Figure 1), one of the most popular models of the Cisco Unified IP Phones Series 7900. This is a flexible device that supports three VoIP protocols according to the firmware image loaded: skinny client control protocol (SCCP), media gateway control protocol (MGCP), and session initiation protocol (SIP). The 7960G also supports several network protocols (DHCP, NTP, TFTP, and LDAP3), audio compression codecs (G.711 and G.729a), compatibility with H.323 and Microsoft NetMeeting, and XML services support.

We analyzed version 8.2 of the free SIP firmware image available from Cisco's website. The firmware is distributed as a compressed ZIP archive containing 5 files, described in Table 1. As mentioned in Section 2, the comparison of the size of the firmware files with the size of today's general purpose operating systems (kilobytes vs. gigabytes) provides an idea of the complexity of the software applications running in the IP phone and the probability of finding bugs in the firmware image.

Table 1. SIP Flash Image for 7940/7960 IP Phone v8.2 (0)—Non CallManager

File Name	Size	Description
OS79XX.TXT	14 bytes	Contains the universal application loader image name
P0S3-08-2-00.loads	461 bytes	Contains the universal application loader and application image names
P003-08-2-00.bin	129,240 bytes	Non-secure universal application loader for upgrades from pre-5.x images
P003-08-2-00.sbn	129,644 bytes	Secure (digitally signed) universal application loader for upgrades from pre-5.x.images
P0S3-08-2-00.sb2	785,338 bytes	Application firmware image

To transfer the SIP firmware image to the IP phone, we set up a TFTP server with the files described in Table 1. We included an additional configuration file, SIPDefault.cnf, which configured most of the IP phone's parameters, such as network information, SIP configuration, and security parameters. For more details about the IP phone initialization and configuration options, see the Cisco SIP IP Administrator Guide version 8.0 [13].

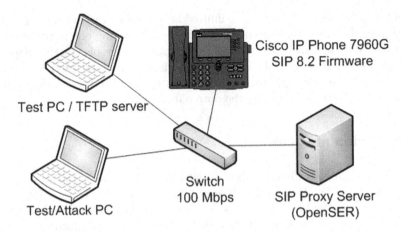

Fig. 2. Experimental Testbed

After loading the SIP firmware in the IP phone, we configured a SIP proxy server (OpenSER v1.1.1) to provide a basic SIP environment for the IP phone. A SIP proxy server helps route requests to the user's current location, authenticate and authorize users for services, implement provider call-routing policies, and provide features to users [14]. We configured and tested the IP phone functionality establishing VoIP calls between the IP phone and a SIP softphone (3CX IP Phone) installed in a test PC. The resulting infrastructure is depicted in Figure 2.

4   Runtime Analysis

To test the IP phone's runtime behavior, we performed both vulnerability scans and fuzz tests of the device. For our vulnerability scans, we connected to the IP phone from our test machines, established a variety of malformed connections, and observed the IP phone's responses. We used the Nmap network scanner to detect listening network ports on the IP phone. Nmap only detected two open ports: 123/UDP (NTP) and 5060/UDP (SIP). The scanner was also able to identify that we were scanning a Cisco device. After the network scan, we ran a vulnerability scan against the IP phone using the Nessus vulnerability scanner with all attack plugins activated (12,239 plugins). The vulnerability scan did not reveal any security-relevant results, and the IP phone continued operating normally during and after the scan. However, we expected this result because vulnerability scanners can only detect previously discovered vulnerabilities via the use of attack signatures (Nessus' plugins).

Fuzz tests send random and malformed input to software to quickly assess its security quality [15]. We used open-source SIP and RTP protocol aware fuzzers to test the IP phone for commonly made coding mistakes that may reveal vulnerabilities. Specifically, we were looking for signs of instability, such as device resets or high CPU utilization, when exposed to unexpected input. Any sign of instability in the IP phone would have implications for device availability, and could lead us to significant vulnerabilities in the software application. We chose four fuzzing tools based on the VoIP Security Alliance (VoIPSA) VoIP Security Tool List [11] (Table 2).

Table 2. Scanning and fuzzing tools used

Name	Type	Comment
Nmap	Network Scanner	65,535 TCP/UDP ports scanned
Nessus	Vulnerability scanner	12,239 vulnerability plugins tested
PROTOS	SIP Fuzzing tool	4,527 SIP INVITE test messages
ASTEROID	SIP Fuzzing tool	Approximately 36,000 SIP test messages
SIP Forum Test Framework	SIP Fuzzing tool	Approximately 70 SIP tests
Ohrwurm	RTP Fuzzing tool	RTP payload is fuzzed with a constant bit error ratio (BER)

PROTOS is a framework for testing implementations of protocols using a black-box approach. It has several test suites for testing different protocols, including HTTP, DNS, and LDAP. For our tests, we used the SIP test-suite (c07-sip), which consists of 4,527 maliciously modified SIP INVITE messages. Test messages are grouped by the type of vulnerability that they try to exploit: buffer overflows, format string attacks, malformed sequences, and others. However, PROTOS is stateless and therefore can only test for attacks that required just one message to be sent to the targeted device. A further disadvantage is that it only tests INVITE messages, therefore, possible vulnerabilities associated with other SIP messages will not be found. While it is possible to add more test cases, there is no automated way to do so.

Asteroid is a more rudimentary fuzzing tool. It has around 36,000 crafted messages and it can test several types of SIP messages, such as INVITE, REGISTER, BYE, CANCEL, OPTION, SUBSCRIBE, and NOTIFY. However, the test messages are prepared less carefully (i.e. random data), and it also stateless and does not track the status of the SIP sessions.

SIP Forum Test Framework (SFTF) is a testing framework to test different SIP elements for common errors in protocol implementations. This tool uses more knowledge about the semantics of the SIP sessions, and it can test more advanced scenarios, including the use of registration and DNS. The number of test cases included in the distribution package is small (around 70 tests) when compared with the previous tools. As with other tools, SFTF has a flexible design that supports the addition of new test cases, although there is no automated way to generate tests.

Ohrwurm is a small and simple real time protocol (RTP) fuzzer. To use it, an existing media session must exist between two IP phones, and a man-in-the-middle attack is necessary to access the RTP streams between the end-points if a switched LAN is used for the test. The tool reads the sequence numbers of the RTP streams and injects noise with a constant bit error ratio (BER).

We ran each tool multiple times against the IP phone and monitored the phone's behavior in response to the specially crafted malicious input streams generated by the fuzzing tools. We did not notice any abnormal behavior on the IP phone during our testing. In an unexpected result, the soft phone used to establish an RTP session with the IP phone while using Ohrwurm repeatedly stopped responding.

The results of the runtime tests were unsurprising because previous studies exposed the IP phone to a wide variety of vulnerability scanners and fuzzing tools. Many of the previous publicly-announced security issues with this device were indeed found through fuzz testing. For example, the latest reported vulnerability against this IP phone model was a denial of service vulnerability found by the Madynes VoIP fuzzer [16]. One might assume that because fuzz testing did not reveal any security vulnerabilities, we could conclude that the Cisco 7960G IP phone is very secure. However, the additional perspective gained from in-depth static binary analysis provided us with a better understanding of the platform and a different conclusion.

5   Static Analysis

We statically analyzed the binary firmware of the Cisco 7960G to identify coding flaws that could lead to security exploits against the IP phone. This analysis occurred in three steps. First, we disassembled the binary image to obtain the ARM assembly code of the firmware. Second, we manually analyzed the control flow and data flow of the code to understand how the software executes. Finally, we applied security analyses to identify fundamental design flaws and four coding vulnerabilities that weaken the IP phone.

5.1   Firmware Disassembly

The first step in disassembling the device was to determine the underlying processor architecture for the operating system and applications running on the IP phone. This allowed us to infer other attributes about the code we were examining, such as the split between code and data and the absolute virtual addresses where portions of the file would be mapped.

As stated in Section 3, the firmware contains several files within a compressed archive (Table 1). Each application on the device is denoted by an 8-byte identifier easily located within the file header. It is possible to have multiple applications within one discrete file. Much of the code that was security-relevant and operated on externally-supplied data was located in the file ending with the extension .sb2. The .sb2 file can be subdivided into two distinct applications, one of which, "PAS3ARM1", contained the basic components of a real-time operating system responsible for maintaining operation of the IP phone and processing any network I/O.

We identified "PAS3ARM1" as interesting for security analysis. In the firmware version examined in our research, the digital signature comprised the first 404 bytes of the file. After this has been manually removed, the beginning of the application data was found. A quick disassembly with IDA Pro, a common commercial disassembler, revealed that the application contains ARM processor code. We could locate distinct functions with correct function prologues and epilogues. The identification and confirmation of the processor architecture was the first step towards creating an accurate disassembly for this application, which then would enable a human or static analysis tool to perform a security analysis of the code.

However, the ARM processor introduced a challenge: modern ARM processors support two related instruction sets. The ARM instruction set is a RISC-based set which contains 32-bit fixed-width instructions. An additional 16-bit fixed-width instruction set, called THUMB, is also supported. An application has the ability to link together both ARM and THUMB code and indicate to the processor which instruction set to execute. The division between THUMB and ARM instructions must be inferred by following control flow or by manual verification of code at a particular address.

An initial attempt was made to locate the absolute virtual address of the application segment located at the beginning of the firmware image. The virtual address for this segment was determined by locating constructs similar to C-language switch statements in compiled code. When switch case values are sequential and dense, the values are often converted into an index into a jump table that contains data values specifying the absolute virtual addresses of all the valid switch cases. This table allows the person disassembling the code to infer the absolute virtual address of a piece of nearby code.

For example, the code and data in Figure 3 was found within an initial disassembly of the firmware. In this case, the compiler has a switch construct with valid cases from 0 to 19. A test for invalid switch cases is performed at 0x12C64, with the BHI instruction at 0x12C66 branching to the default case. Following this, the switch case value is multiplied by 4 (via a left shift by two bits) and is used as an index into an array of 32-bit values that specify addresses for all valid known switch cases. In this example, it was possible to infer that the default case would be located at the virtual address 0x412D2E in memory. Since this code was at a file offset of 0x12D2E, we were able to infer that the code at the beginning of the file was mapped at 0x400000 in memory.

Upon making this assumption, we quickly noticed that several relative linked branches (an ARM equivalent to function calls) from within this executable segment referenced invalid locations at lower addresses. After navigating further into the firmware, we found that linked branches referenced invalid addresses at higher addresses, rather than lower addresses as was previously true for other portions of the code. By locating the split in the application where invalid linked branches stopped referencing lower addresses and began referencing higher addresses, we were able to locate a split in the memory mapping of the file. This allowed us to divide the file up into two distinct memory segments. We then examined code beyond the split and looked for C switch statement constructs as was done before. With this information, we were able to create a file that had

```
ROM:12C64              CMP    R2, #19
ROM:12C66              BHI    loc_12D2E
ROM:12C68              LSL    R2, R2, #2           Bounds check and dispatch
ROM:12C6A              ADR    R3, dword_12C70      operation
ROM:12C6C              LDR    R2, [R3,R2]
ROM:12C6E              MOV    PC, R2
-------------------------------------------------

ROM:12C70 dword_12C70  DCD 0x412D24
ROM:12C74              DCD 0x412D1E
    ...                    ...                     List of switch case targets
ROM:12CB4              DCD 0x412D2E                (dispatch table)
ROM:12CB8              DCD 0x412D2E
ROM:12CBC              DCD 0x412CC0
-------------------------------------------------

ROM:12CC0              BL     sub_1435C
ROM:12CC4              POP    PC
-------------------------------------------------

    ...                    ...                     Case statement implemen-
ROM:12D24              BL     sub_13BC4            tations (dispatch targets)
ROM:12D28              POP    PC
-------------------------------------------------

ROM:12D2A              BL     sub_13684
ROM:12D2E              POP    PC
```

Fig. 3. Switch code with absolute addressing given in the dispatch table. An attacker or analyst can use these addresses to identify the memory address at which the code would be loaded.

the correct data mapped at the correct virtual addresses, and at this point the disassembly began to become coherent.

The overall process to obtain a valid and accurate disassembly was long and tedious. However, there likely will not be a necessity to replicate this work for any future security analysis done on this platform because knowledge gained in this process could be automated and applied widely in the future. While the initial difficulty of creating a disassembly was a challenging hurdle to overcome, we do not believe this process is beyond the scope of what can be feasibly attained by security researchers or skilled attackers. As such, using an unknown but generally unobfuscated firmware format is not of real security benefit and does not deter security analysis of an embedded platform.

5.2   Binary Analysis

As with any binary security analysis of a large application or operating system, we focused our efforts on portions of the IP phone's firmware that were likely to contain serious security vulnerabilities. This was done by using several commonly used manual auditing methodologies. As of the time of research and publication, we were not aware of any publicly available tools that would help perform an automatic security analysis of a compiled and linked ARM binary, so we worked manually in IDA Pro.

Although the Cisco IP phone runs an embedded operating system, the applications within this framework are developed in what appears to be the C programming language, and the developers have re-implemented the functionality present in most standard C runtime libraries. A primitive methodology used in our binary analysis was to identify functions within the disassembly that mapped to known C-runtime library functions. These could be identified by calling conventions, examination of function arguments, and the application's use of return values. Identifying string manipulation and dynamic memory allocation functions such as `strcpy`, `strcat`, `sprintf`, `strncpy`, `malloc`, `realloc`, and similar functions gave us a starting point for security analysis.

After these functions were identified, it was possible to follow their use within an application in order to look for potential misuse. A challenge with this approach is that the person performing manual binary review must have an idea of the data flow leading up to the potentially dangerous API call in order to properly assess the actual presence or severity of a potential vulnerability. Several potential vulnerabilities were identified through this methodology, however their true risk would not be fully known without a better understanding of the control and data flow through the applications on the IP phone. As such, a more formal analysis was undertaken to understand this aspect of the IP phone.

In order to understand more about the IP phone, we performed a functionality assessment to identify entry points for untrusted and attacker-supplied data. Our assessment of the IP phone was aided by the presence of debugging functionality in the firmware for the IP phone. By enabling a telnet server on the device, it was possible to obtain debugging output for many of the features of the IP phone. In many cases, this debugging output could be matched to the input that the IP phone received from an external source.

In addition to debugging output available on the console, there was a significant presence of debugging output within the firmware disassembly. Many of the critical functions within the firmware contained string references which indicated their likely original name within the source code or their intended functionality and purpose. The presence of function names within strings in the binary helped tremendously in the enumeration of likely input points for untrusted data.

After input points for untrusted data were identified, it was possible to enumerate possible sources of untrusted input and then begin a more in-depth security analysis. Some of the sources of untrusted input identified in our analysis were: Cisco Discover Protocol (CDP), Ethernet (802.3), IPv4, TCP, UDP, NTP, SIP requests, SIP responses, RTP, DNS responses, DHCP responses, TFTP responses, TFTP file downloads, SDP, media codec frames (g711ulaw, g729a), and telnet.

Our security analysis followed control and data flow from known untrusted input sources, looking for security vulnerabilities. We paid careful attention to common mistakes such as unbounded memory copy operations, loop constructs, integer issues, information leakage, and many other classes of vulnerabilities.

5.3   Results and Recommendations

The security quality of Cisco IP phone's SIP firmware initially appeared to be strong. Fuzz testing with publicly available testing suites for SIP did not lead to any instability in the device. However, manual security analysis revealed a more accurate assessment of the security quality of the code. Through manual analysis, it was possible to detect security flaws that would be very difficult to anticipate or test for through fuzz testing. Although there is evidence that the code has been reviewed for security, there were still serious vulnerabilities that were uncovered by manual security review.

In contrast to the runtime analyses of Section 4, our manual security analysis revealed weaknesses in the security of the IP phone's software. We identified both general architectural mistakes in the design of the software as well as implementation errors that can directly lead to successful exploits. Taken alone, the design flaws may not be security weaknesses. However, when combined with the other software vulnerabilities, they can cause simple attacks to rapidly escalate into full device compromise.

The fundamental design weaknesses center on the lack of memory protection among processes and the operating system itself. Most ARM processors allow for the separation of user-mode virtual memory from the supervisor-addressable memory that is typically reserved for the operating system kernel. The Cisco 7960G IP phone appeared to have *no separation of privilege levels associated with its memory management model*. As such, a compromise in any portion of the IP phone can lead to full compromise of the device. Artificial security constraints, such as an unprivileged `telnet_level` mode, have very little meaning. An unprivileged telnet user who can cause memory corruption in any portion of the application can escalate her privileges to those of a fully privileged user.

Another potential security weakness became evident when examining debugging output from the "show stacks" command on the telnet terminal (Figure 4). After rebooting the IP phone several times, it was apparent that the stack addresses for each task on the IP phone were fixed. The predictable memory layout makes it extremely easy for an attacker to predict the exact location where data she has supplied might reside on the stack, increasing the reliability of memory corruption exploitation against these devices.

It is also evident that the stacks for different tasks are immediately adjacent to each other without any unmapped page or guard page in between. As such, memory corruption from one task's stack can directly influence the operation or control flow of another task. In a similar way, any recursive call patterns within the firmware code can lead to unintended corruption of the stack of an adjacent task. The stack grows down on all ARM processors we have experience working with. On this architecture, it appears that recursive control flow, a relatively common coding practice, can lead to compromise of the device.

Implementation flaws can provide the entry point for an attacker to leverage the architectural weaknesses. Our binary analysis uncovered four coding errors: *one heap-based buffer overflow* and *three stack-based overflows*. In this public document, we will present only a high-level overview of the vulnerabilities.

```
SIP Phone> show stacks
Task: SOC  (27)  stkhi=0041b6ac  stklo=0041beab  Size=2048   Unused=1328
Task: RTP  (26)  stkhi=0041beac  stklo=0041c6ab  Size=2048   Unused=1916
Task: DSP  (25)  stkhi=0041c6ac  stklo=0041ceab  Size=2048   Unused=1732
Task: PHN  (24)  stkhi=0041ceac  stklo=0041deab  Size=4096   Unused=2108
Task: GSM  (23)  stkhi=0041deac  stklo=0041f6ab  Size=6144   Unused=5972
Task: SIP  (22)  stkhi=0041f6ac  stklo=00421eab  Size=10240  Unused=7476
Task: GUI  (21)  stkhi=00421eac  stklo=00422eab  Size=4096   Unused=1012
Task: NET  (19)  stkhi=00422eac  stklo=004236ab  Size=2048   Unused=624
Task: CFG  (18)  stkhi=004236ac  stklo=00423eab  Size=2048   Unused=1052
Task: TTY  (17)  stkhi=00423eac  stklo=00424eab  Size=4096   Unused=3280
Task: AUD  (16)  stkhi=00424eac  stklo=004256ab  Size=2048   Unused=1688
Task: PTMR (29)  stkhi=004256ac  stklo=00425eab  Size=2048   Unused=1924
Task: TMR  (28)  stkhi=00425eac  stklo=004266ab  Size=2048   Unused=1148
```

Fig. 4. Output of the show stacks telnet command

First, we analyzed the heap overflow. In non-embedded systems, heap overflows are often exploited by corruption of heap control structures that are stored in-band with application data, or by direct manipulation of application-specific data on the heap. Generally speaking, heap implementations that store heap control structures out-of-band of application data are less susceptible to exploitation than those that store critical information in a place easily corrupted by application vulnerabilities.

We performed a cursory examination of the Cisco IP phone's heap implementation to assess the severity of heap corruption on the platform. Although there are heap control structures in-band on the heap, there appears to be sanity checking of at least certain portions of the heap structure, including the field specifying the heap chunk size. Corruption of application data prior to freeing of the corrupt block seems to be a viable vector for exploitation. There is a good possibility that heap corruption can lead to reliable remote code execution, although it might be less straightforward than on many non-embedded systems.

Figure 5 shows the assembly code of this vulnerability. We have redacted the full assembly code addresses to prevent straightforward discovery of the vulnerable code by unskilled attackers. The attack can occur if when a specially-crafted message is sent to the phone in response to a SIP request sent by the phone to its proxy. When the IP phone receives the malicious message, register R5 points to a pre-parsed list of authentication parameters from the message, such as realm, URI, and nonce. The IP phone allocates a statically-size heap buffer of 0x400 (1024) bytes at ROM:XXXXXX40. The software then performs an unbounded sprintf function call into this heap buffer at ROM:XXXXXX8E. If the sum of the string lengths and count of characters present in the format string is greater than 1024, then a heap overflow occurs. While this vulnerability is easy to exploit, it requires special preparation on the part of the attacker, making it difficult to test automatically. The attacker must first set up a man-in-the-middle attack and then wait for the IP phone to send a request to its proxy.

```
ROM:XXXXXX36      MOV R6,#0
ROM:XXXXXX38      CMP R5,R6
ROM:XXXXXX3A      BEQ loc_XXX4A
ROM:XXXXXX3C      MOVL R0,0x400
ROM:XXXXXX40      BL malloc
ROM:XXXXXX44      ADD R4,R0,#0
ROM:XXXXXX46      CMP R4,R6
ROM:XXXXXX48      BNE loc_XXX4E
   . . .
ROM:XXXXXX4E      LDR R0,[R5,#4]
ROM:XXXXXX50      CMP R0,#2
ROM:XXXXXX52      BEQ loc_XXX62
   . . .
ROM:XXXXXX62      LDR R0,[#0x10]
ROM:XXXXXX64      STR R0,[SP,#0x38+var_38]
ROM:XXXXXX66      ADR R0,aRealm ; realm
ROM:XXXXXX68      STR R0,[SP,#0x38+var_34]
ROM:XXXXXX6A      LDR R0,[R5,#0xC]
ROM:XXXXXX6C      STR R0,[SP,#0x38+var_30]
ROM:XXXXXX6E      ADR R0,aUri_0 ; uri
   . . .
ROM:XXXXXX8A      ADR R2, aDigest ; Digest
ROM:XXXXXX8C      ADR R3, aUsername ; username
ROM:XXXXXX8E      BL sprintf_0
```

Fig. 5. Assembly code showing the SIP authentication request vulnerability in the Cisco 7960G

The remaining three vulnerabilities discovered in this security review were stack corruption issues. We found two of the stack corruption vulnerabilities in portions of the code that could not be easily tested by fuzz testing with random input. In one case, a stack corruption vulnerability required authentication and was therefore limited to only a privilege escalation issue.

In another case, a stack corruption vulnerability was remotely exploitable by sending a crafted SIP authentication request message to the IP phone. To exploit this vulnerability, an attacker waits for the IP phone to send a SIP request (i.e., INVITE) to its proxy and then, using a man-in-the-middle attack, the attacker sends back to the IP phone a malicious *407 Proxy Authorization Required* message. A stack overflow is produced by the malicious message when the IP phone tries to parse it to compute the response to the authentication request.

A final stack corruption issue uncovered by our analysis has no known mitigating factors preventing exploitation, and is likely exploitable in virtually every functioning configuration of the device. An attacker can exploit this vulnerability with a single network packet (a SIP INVITE message). This final error is likely the most serious of the issues discovered in this security review, and the only viable solution for this flaw in many organizations will be to deploy intelligent network filtering or to upgrade the firmware for all IP phones to a patched version. This can be challenging for large enterprises to deploy efficiently, and patches will likely have to be created for many different IP phone protocol firmware versions.

In order to better understand the security consequences of stack corruption on this platform, we examined the firmware for additional security measures that might make exploitation more difficult. Surprisingly, there were no security features present to detect or limit the impact of stack corruption. Although some of the most effective stack protection technologies might not be feasible on an embedded platform due to processing and resource constraints, there are some simple protection features that are widely used and have minimal memory and computational footprints. For example, compile-time additions such as Stack Guard [17] can detect many instances of stack corruption at runtime via intelligent stack frame reordering and the placement of a randomly-seeded canary value adjacent to critical register values stored on the stack. The addition of this type of feature to a Cisco IP phone would likely require little additional effort on the part of developers and would help prevent exploitation of basic stack corruption vulnerabilities. At the moment, there is nothing to prevent an attacker who is able to corrupt the stack from redirecting execution to an arbitrary location in memory and executing arbitrary code on a Cisco IP phone.

Exploiting memory corruption vulnerabilities on an ARM architecture can be challenging because the processor uses split data and instruction caches. The data cache operates in a write-back mode in which writes from cache to physical memory are delayed until the dirty cache line is evicted. This lack of coherency between the data and instruction caches is a challenge for exploits of memory corruption vulnerabilities. In a typical memory corruption exploit, an attacker will supply shellcode as part of the attack. This shellcode is comprised of assembly instructions that will eventually be executed by the vulnerable application if the attack is successful. This code is written to memory by the application or as a result of network I/O prior to it being executed.

However, in the case of an ARM processor, the writing of shellcode to memory is delayed by the data cache until it is drained and the changes are flushed out of cache back into main memory. If this does not occur prior to the attacker redirecting control to the location where the code is supposed to reside, then the instruction cache will fetch instructions from main memory prior to them being flushed out of the write buffer or data cache. As such, the instructions that will end up being executed are not those supplied by the attacker and the attack will generally fail. It is possible to drain write buffers and flush data cache by making use of the coprocessor register 15 (cp15) in a specific manner on most modern ARM processors. It is also possible to cause the cache to get flushed by inducing certain memory accesses. This might be possible by causing a Read After Write (RAW) in some cases, and this type of cache manipulation has been proven successful in publicly documented vulnerability research projects [18].

Further investigation will likely yield the most efficient way to achieve this on a Cisco IP phone.

6 Related Work

In the area of VoIP vulnerability analysis, Abdelnur et al. [19] proposed a network information model able to represent the information required to perform VoIP assessment and a framework based on attack tree modeling in order to represent and write VoIP attacks. In other work, Abdelnur et al. [12] designed and implemented a stateful protocol fuzzer for SIP capable of tracking the state of the targeted application and device. This tool was used to test a Cisco IP Phone 7940, part of the same family and firmware as the 7960G, and was able to find vulnerabilities different from those we found using static binary analysis. McGann and Sicker [20] presented a study of the known VoIP-related vulnerabilities and the results of testing several of the more popular open source and commercial VoIP security tools. Their results showed that many of these security tools do not cover the extend of the known vulnerabilities. We reached a similar conclusion from our study.

Binary analysis techniques have also been applied to other embedded devices. Fogie [18], San [21], Hurman [22], and Mulliner [23] demonstrated the feasibility of reverse engineering, memory corruption attacks, and shellcode development to exploit vulnerabilities in mobile devices running Windows CE operating system on ARM processors. Similar work has been done in the area of networked embedded systems, where FX [24, 25] and Lynn [26] described several vulnerabilities and exploits against Cisco network devices. Barnaby [27] showed how to reverse firmware using a JTAG debugging interface. Finally, Grand [28] and O'Connor [29] presented several techniques to compromise other embedded systems such as mobile phones, printers, scanners, and similar devices.

Security mechanisms to protect embedded systems have been also published by several academic and industry researchers. Verma [30] described a Texas Instruments technology, named *Static Packet Filter* (SPF), which consisted of a programmable engine that can be configured into an IP phone to protect it against many different types of DoS attacks. Shao et al. [31] developed a protection and checking mechanism to protect embedded systems against buffer overflow attacks and efficiently check if a component has been protected, even without the presence of source code. Arora et al. [32] described a mechanism for secure program execution in embedded systems based on a hardware monitor that can be connected to any embedded processor to observe its dynamic execution trace as it executes the program, check whether the trace conforms to the definition of permissible behavior, and flag violations by triggering appropriate response mechanisms.

7 Conclusions

The evolution from traditional telephony to VoIP systems is adding more intelligence, functionality, and complexity to the end points. This increasing complexity is making the end points vulnerable to many of the security problems that affect today's desktop computer systems. In the same way, security analysis techniques commonly used in desktop computer systems, such as binary analysis, can also be used to find vulnerabilities in embedded devices like IP phones, as we showed in this paper.

Even though the IP phone was resilient to all the vulnerability scans and fuzzing attacks that we attempted, the disassembly and static analysis was able to uncover serious flaws: a design weakness and four memory corruption vulnerabilities that pose significant risks to organizations deploying the IP phone. We can conclude from this experience that while automated tools can help to detect security problems more efficiently, it can be risky to rely only on that kind of tool to assess the security of these devices. Automated security tools have to continue improving their techniques to detect new vulnerabilities in embedded systems such as IP phones, and new tools have to be developed to automate techniques such as static binary analysis in embedded platforms.

While we specifically selected the Cisco IP phone due to its relevance and the lack of comprehensive security research on the subject, there are broader implications that can be drawn from this research. It is safe to assume that similar vulnerabilities exist for a great deal of other IP phones in particular and embedded devices in general, and their increased deployment in a variety of uses poses a significant security risk. The historical pattern of coding errors from major software developers indicates that security vulnerabilities will not disappear without significant effort on the part of the development and security communities. Until better secure development practices and sufficient security testing are performed before embedded devices such as Cisco IP phones are released into the marketplace, there is no reason to assume that these vulnerabilities will be eradicated.

Acknowledgments. This work was sponsored in part by AT&T and IBM Internet Security Systems.

We thank the anonymous reviewers and the VoIP research group at Georgia Tech for their helpful feedback that improved the quality of this paper. We thank IBM ISS for generously providing test equipment used in this study.

References

1. Bell, A.G.: Improvement in telegraphy. United States Patent #174,465 (March 1876)
2. Prevelakis, V., Spinellis, D.: The Athens affair. IEEE Spectrum 44(7) (July 2007)
3. Arkin, O.: The trivial Cisco IP phones compromise. Whitepaper, The Sys-Security Group (September 2002)
4. Cisco Security Advisory: Cisco unified IP phone overflow and denial of service vulnerabilities (2008),
   http://www.cisco.com/warp/public/707/cisco-sa-20080213-phone.shtml
5. Cisco Press Release: Cisco sells its 6 millionth IP phone as worldwide demand soars for IP communications (September 2005)

6. Kuhn, D., Walsh, T., Fries, S.: Security Considerations for Voice Over IP Systems. US Dept. of Commerce, National Institute of Standards and Technology (2005)

7. Hoglund, G., McGraw, G.: Exploiting Software: How to Break Code. Addison-Wesley, Reading (2004)

8. Raghunathan, A., Ravi, S., Hattangady, S., Quisquater, J.-J.: Securing mobile appliances: new challenges for the system designer. In: Design, Automation and Test in Europe, Munich, Germany (March 2003)

9. Kocher, P., Lee, R., McGraw, G., Raghunathan, A., Ravi, S.: Security as a new dimension in embedded system design. In: Design Automation Conference, San Diego, CA (June 2004)

10. Secunia: Cisco IP phone 7960—vulnerability report (2007), http://secunia.com/product/287/?task=advisories

11. VoIPSA: Voip security tool list (2007), http://www.voipsa.org/Resources/tools.php

12. Abdelnur, H., State, R., Festor, O.: KiF: A stateful SIP fuzzer. In: 1st International Conference on Principles, Systems and Applications of IP Telecommunications (IPTComm), New York (July 2007)

13. Cisco SIP IP Administrator Guide, Version 8.0 (2007), http://www.cisco.com/en/US/docs/voice_ip_comm/cuipph/7960g_7940g/sip/8_0/english/administration/guide/8_0.html

14. Rosenberg, J., Schulzrinne, H., Camarillo, G., Johnston, A., Peterson, J., Sparks, R., Handley, M., Schooler, E.: RFC3261: SIP: Session initiation protocol (2002)

15. Miller, B.P., Fredriksen, L., So, B.: An empirical study of the reliability of UNIX utilities. Communications of the ACM 33(12) (December 1990)

16. State, R.: Cisco phone 7940 remote DOS. CVE-2007-5583 (2007)

17. Cowan, C., Pu, C., Maier, D., Hinton, H., Walpole, J., Bakke, P., Beattie, S., Grier, A., Wagle, P., Zhang, Q.: StackGuard: automatic adaptive detection and prevention of buffer-overflow attacks. In: USENIX Security Symposium, San Antonio, TX (January 1998)

18. Fogie, S.: Embedded reverse engineering: Cracking mobile binaries. In: Defcon 11, Las Vegas, NV (2003)

19. Abdelnur, H., State, R., Chrisment, I., Popi, C.: Assessing the security of VoIP services. In: 10th IFIP/IEEE International Symposium on Integrated Network Management, Munich, Germany (May 2007)

20. McGann, S., Sicker, D.C.: An analysis of security threats and tools in SIP-based VoIP systems. In: 2nd Workshop on Securing Voice over IP, Cyber Security Alliance, Washington, DC (June 2005)

21. San.: Hacking Windows CE. In: Defcon 13, Las Vegas, NV (2005)

22. Hurman, T.: Exploring Windows CE shellcode. Whitepaper, Pentest Limited (June 2005)

23. Mulliner, C.: Advanced attacks against PocketPC phones. In: Defcon 14, Las Vegas, NV (2006)

24. FX.: Attacking networked embedded systems. In: Black Hat Windows Security, Seattle, WA (February 2003)

25. FX.: More embedded systems. In: Black Hat USA, Las Vegas, NV (July 2003)

26. Lynn, M.: The holy grail: Cisco IOS shellcode and exploitation techniques. In: Black Hat USA, Las Vegas, NV (July 2005)

27. Barnaby, J.: Exploiting embedded systems. In: Black Hat Europe, Amsterdam, Netherlands, February/March (2006)

28. Grand, J.: Introduction to embedded security. In: Black Hat USA, Las Vegas, NV (July 2004)

29. O'Connor, B.: Vulnerabilities in not-so embedded systems. In: Black Hat USA, Las Vegas, NV, July/August (2006)
30. Verma, A.: IP phone security: Packet filtering protection against attacks. Texas Instruments White Paper (2006)
31. Shao, Z., Xue, C., Zhuge, Q., Qiu, M., Xiao, B., Sha, E.H.M.: Security protection and checking for embedded system integration against buffer overflow attacks via hardware/software. IEEE Transactions on Computers 55(4) (April 2006)
32. Arora, D., Ravi, S., Raghunathan, A., Jha, N.K.: Hardware-assisted run-time monitoring for secure program execution on embedded processors. IEEE Transactions on Very Large Scale Integration (VLSI) Systems 14(12) (December 2006)

Understanding SIP through Model-Checking

Pamela Zave

AT&T Laboratories—Research, Florham Park, New Jersey, USA
pamela@research.att.com

Abstract. In recent years, SIP has become an important and widely-used protocol for IP-based multimedia services. Despite voluminous documentation, there is only scattered and informal material explaining the states of the protocol and the events that can occur in each state. To fill this gap, this paper presents a Promela model of invite dialogs in SIP. The model has been verified and validated with the Spin model-checker. The paper discusses the practical value of this model, explains some problems in SIP revealed by it, makes recommendations for solutions, and presents some directions for future work.

1 Introduction

In recent years, SIP has become an important and widely-used protocol for IP-based multimedia services. The SIP standard is documented in many IETF "Request for Comments" (RFC) documents, most notably [9]. Although this documentation is voluminous, its style emphasizes some points of view over others. One of the least-emphasized viewpoints is the state-oriented viewpoint, from which a user agent always has a dynamic protocol state, and in each protocol state some events can happen and some cannot.

To give an example of what a state-oriented viewpoint contains, the RFC on reliable provisional responses [8] says, "The UAS MUST NOT send a second reliable provisional response until the first is acknowledged." In other words, this state-oriented constraint says that in the UAS state of having sent a first provisional response, and not having received an acknowledgment of it, the UAS cannot send a provisional response.

As this example shows, state-oriented information is often present, but it is informal, scattered, and incremental. As an inevitable consequence of being informal, scattered, and incremental, it is incomplete.

The purpose of this paper is to improve the documentation of SIP by working toward state-oriented documentation that is formal, centralized, and complete. A necessary part of producing such documentation is to find the places where the standards documents are incomplete or erroneous, and to fix these problems. This paper reports on five such problems, and recommends changes that will eliminate them.

The documentation is primarily intended for people who build applications using SIP. A good state-oriented formal model of SIP would have many other uses in addition to that of user documentation, however. For example, the model could also serve as:

H. Schulzrinne, R. State, and S. Niccolini (Eds.): IPTComm 2008, LNCS 5310, pp. 256–279, 2008.
© Springer-Verlag Berlin Heidelberg 2008

- a new technical viewpoint that might suggest improvements and best practices;
- a basis for checking proposed new extensions to SIP, to prevent inconsistencies and other problems;
- a basis for modeling network elements, such as proxies and back-to-back user agents;
- an aid to conformance and interoperability checking of SIP implementations.

To serve these purposes well, a model should be written in a language that is not only formal, but subject to automated analysis. Promela is a language for finite-state modeling of concurrent processes. It is well-suited to this modeling task for two reasons. First, the scope of the study is limited to aspects of SIP that can be expressed conveniently in Promela. Second, Promela models can be validated and verified using the model-checker Spin [3]. As subsequent sections will show, Spin provides "push button" verification of a large number of relevant properties of the model.

In related work, Bishop et al. provided a more complete and formal specification of TCP and UDP than was available in RFCs [1]. They were interested in *all* aspects of the behavior of these protocols, which necessitated the use of a wider-spectrum language, namely higher-order logic (HOL). HOL's automated support is a theorem prover, which is a powerful tool but unfortunately requires a great deal of time and skill to wield productively.

This paper reports on a first attempt to construct a state-oriented formal model of SIP. As such, it is inevitably limited in scope. Section 2 delimits what is and is not included.

Section 3 summarizes the formal methods used in this work. It gives a brief overview of model-checking, then explains the specification, verification, and validation techniques used on the model.

Section 4 presents the full SIP model, up to the scope given in Section 2. Section 5 presents two alternate models with slightly different properties. The paper concludes with recommendations and plans for future work.

2   Scope of the Modeling

In this paper, all the models contain a SIP user agent on the client side (UAC) and a SIP user agent on the server side (UAS), modeled as concurrent processes. These processes communicate with each other only by sending and receiving messages.

As stated in Section 1, the primary purpose of the models is to assist builders of applications. For this reason, the chosen level of abstraction is that of the "transaction user" as defined in Section 17 of [9], and many phenomena that occur at lower levels of the SIP stack are not included. These phenomena include transaction timeouts, retransmissions, absorption of some messages, and *100(Trying)* messages. As a consequence, in the view of the models, transactions are reliable.

The models document SIP for a transaction user by representing everything that a transaction user can do while complying with the standards, and nothing that would violate the standards. Because no behavior of the models is erroneous, the models do not contain any handling of errors introduced by transaction users.

The primary focus of modeling is the control of media sessions. Thus the models include the offer/answer negotiation of media sessions, but are limited to covering only dialogs created by *invite* requests. *Subscribe* and *refer* requests can also create dialogs, but these requests are not considered. As a result, the dialogs in these models cannot be extended by embedded *subscribe* and *refer* dialogs, a phenomenon that is described in [10].

For purposes of simplicity and efficiency, most requests that are not concerned with media sessions are omitted. These requests are *subscribe* and *refer*, as noted above, and also *register, options, notify,* and *message*. The exception is the *info* request, which is not involved in media session negotiation, but is included because of its value for providing extensible signaling. For example, *info* requests and responses are used to control media servers [4].

For purposes of simplicity, a message carries at most one session description (SDP field). To evaluate the significance of this restriction, there is an example in [2] of a message with two session descriptions, one an offer and one an answer. The offer refers to an early media session, while the answer refers to an ordinary media session.

Finally, the models are coarse-grained in the sense that they usually do not distinguish between different messages of the same type. Thus most aspects of SIP that depend on message fields are not represented. This is the main reason why this study presents a narrower view of SIP than [1] does of TCP and UDP.

3   Semantics and Analysis

3.1   A Brief Overview of Model-Checking

A Promela model has concurrent processes that communicate by sending and receiving messages. Messages in transit are stored in bounded, FIFO queues.

A model is intended to represent a range of possible behaviors. For this reason, execution of a model is highly nondeterministic. Within each process, in any state, several different steps may be executable. If there are executable steps in several different processes, then there is also a nondeterministic choice of which process to execute. A *trace* is the sequence of steps in one particular execution, so it is the result of many nondeterministic choices among possible next steps. A trace can be finite or infinite, because nonterminating models are valid and correct for some applications.

Model-checking is a form of analysis that attempts to explore all possible traces of a model, whether finite or infinite. It creates a finite state-transition graph in which each state is a state of the entire model (all processes and queues), and each transition is a possible execution step. Thus the entire graph represents all possible interleavings of executable steps.

A Promela model has a single initial state. A terminal state is one in which there are no possible execution steps, and thus no outgoing state transitions. A trace is a path through the state-transition graph, starting at the initial state.

If the trace is finite, the path eventually ends at a terminal state. If the trace is infinite, the path loops through the graph forever, without entering a terminal state.

Often a model checker cannot construct a complete state-transition graph, because the graph is too large. Because the Spin model-checker is a well-engineered tool, it offers many ways in which a user can optimize the checking for better results. When the state-transition graph can be completed, the number of transitions in it is a measure of the overall complexity of the model.

3.2   Model Semantics

The purpose of our models is to describe all possible user-agent behaviors and how they can affect the other user agent in a dialog. In each state, the model should indicate which messages can be sent and which messages might be received.

These concepts will be illustrated with a very simple model that is a small fraction of the size of the real SIP models. To make it simple, the only message types are *invite, invSucc* (any 2xx response to an invite), *invFail* (any 3xx-6xx response to an invite), *ack, bye,* and *byeRsp* (any 200 OK response to a *bye* message). Furthermore, there are no re-invites. For this simple model, the UAC and UAS processes are defined as follows.

```
proctype UAC() {
bool endedc = false;
            reqc!invite;
inviting:   do
            :: irps?invFail -> goto preEnd
            :: irps?invSucc -> sakc!ack; goto confirmed
            :: reqs?bye -> brpc!byeRsp; goto preEnd
            :: brps?byeRsp -> assert(false)
            od;
confirmed:  do
            :: irps?invFail -> assert(false)
            :: irps?invSucc -> assert(false)
            :: reqs?bye -> brpc!byeRsp; goto preEnd
            :: brps?byeRsp -> assert(false)
            :: reqc!bye -> goto byeing
            od;
byeing:     do
            :: irps?invFail -> assert(false)
            :: irps?invSucc -> assert(false)
            :: reqs?bye -> brpc!byeRsp
            :: brps?byeRsp -> goto preEnd
            od;
preEnd:     endedc = true;
end:        do
            :: irps?invFail -> assert(false)
```

```
            ::  irps?invSucc -> assert(true)
            ::  reqs?bye -> brpc!byeRsp
            ::  brps?byeRsp -> assert(false)
            od
}

proctype UAS() {
bool acked = true;
bool endeds = false;
            reqc?invite;
invited:    do
            ::  ackc?ack -> assert(false)
            ::  reqc?bye -> assert(false)
            ::  brpc?byeRsp -> assert(false)
            ::  irps!invFail -> goto preEnd
            ::  irps!invSucc -> acked = false; goto confirmed
            od;
confirmed:  do
            ::  ackc?ack -> assert(!acked); acked = true
            ::  reqc?bye -> brps!byeRsp; goto preEnd
            ::  brpc?byeRsp -> assert(false)
            ::  reqs!bye -> goto byeing
            od;
byeing:     do
            ::  ackc?ack -> assert(!acked); acked = true
            ::  reqc?bye -> brps!byeRsp
            ::  brpc?byeRsp -> goto preEnd
            od;
preEnd:     endeds = true;
end:        do
            ::  ackc?ack -> assert(!acked); acked = true
            ::  reqc?bye -> brps!byeRsp
            ::  brpc?byeRsp -> assert(false)
            od
}
```

The expression *reqc!invite* sends an invite to the queue *reqc*, which contains all requests sent by the UAC. (The other queues and their purposes are discussed in the next section.) A send expression such as *reqc!invite* is always executable unless the queue is full.

The expression *reqc?invite* receives an invite from the queue *reqc*; it is executable if and only if the queue is nonempty and the message at its head is an invite.

In each labeled state, the semantics of a *do* loop is to choose nondeterministically from among the executable guarded commands (executability is based only on the executability of the guard), execute the entire command, and repeat forever. Thus only a *goto* causes a change to another labeled state.

For a formal model, both *validity* and *correctness* are important. A *valid* model is faithful to the needs and assumptions of its human readers. A *correct* model conforms to some separate formal specification of its intended properties. Because correctness is a relation between two formal objects, it can be verified formally, using model-checking or other techniques.

The models in this paper are intended to describe SIP rather than achieve a particular user goal, so their external specifications are weak. For the simple model, the only external specification is that every dialog should end, and both user agents should agree that it has ended.

To formalize this property, in the desired end state of a dialog, the two Boolean variables *endedc* and *endeds* are true. The variables are used in a linear-time temporal logic formula:

$$\Diamond\Box(endedc = true \land endeds = true)$$

This formula is called a *stability property*, because it says that in any trace, there is eventually ($\Diamond$) a point where the variable assertion becomes invariantly true ($\Box$) for the rest of the trace. Spin verifies that the simple model satisfies this property specification.

There is a much more useful form of specification for this study, however. Assertions on state variables can be interspersed with the executable code in the model. Each such assertion is a specification that, at the control point where the assertion is written, the assertion's predicate must always be true.

For example, the simple model of the UAS sets the Boolean variable *acked* to false when it sends an *invSucc* message. Wherever in the UAS code an *ack* message is received, an assertion states that *acked* is false, and an assignment sets it to true again. The assertions specify formally our expectations about when acks should and should not arrive. Spin reports any assertion violation as an error, so complete model-checking without any such errors is a verification that all of the assertions are satisfied. The real SIP models contain a large number of assertions.

3.3 Validity of SIP Models

For our purposes, validity is as important as correctness. The most important aspect of validity is whether a model agrees with the RFCs, and this can only be decided by consensus.

Although validity is ultimately an informal property, validity in this context has formal aspects that model-checking can help us with. A valid model should include no illegal or impossible behavior, and should represent all legal and possible behaviors in a clear and obvious way. This raises subtle issues, because send events cause receive events, send and receive events create new dialog states, and new dialog states create the need to describe the events that can occur during them. In this formal sense, a valid model is a "fixed point" that contains all the consequences of its own behavior.

This section presents four formal properties that contribute to model validity and can be checked, sometimes with the help of Spin. All the models in this study were checked for these properties, which are:

- The behavior of message queues matches what is possible in implementations.
- Send events are always immediately enabled when execution control gets to them.
- A message can be received as soon as it arrives.
- The model has no unreachable code.

Each of these characteristics will be discussed in turn.

It is obvious that the behavior of message queues in the model should match what is possible in implementations. All SIP user agents must implement both UDP and TCP for signal transport ([9], Section 18). UDP makes no ordering guarantees, so messages need not arrive in the order they were sent. Promela queues, on the other hand, are FIFO. To make their behavior as unconstrained as UDP, it is necessary to have a separate queue for each message type in each direction. It is not necessary to worry about the ordering of different instances of the same message type, because the models cannot distinguish between instances.

For example, in this simple model two of the message types are *ack* and *byeRsp*, and each type has its own queue. The queues are *ackc* (for acks from UAC), *brpc* (for bye responses from UAC), and *brps* (for bye responses from UAS). The model is too simple to need acks from the UAS.

There can be exceptions to this basic rule when there is specific information to justify them. For example, the SIP standard requires that requests have sequence numbers so that they are received and processed in the same order that they were sent. Because of this, all the requests in each direction of the dialog can share a FIFO queue. The queue *reqc* carries requests from the UAC to the UAS, while *reqs* carries requests from the UAS to the UAC.

As another example of an exception, there can only be one final response in transit in each direction at a time, so *invSucc* and *invFail* events can share the queue *irps* (invite response) from UAS to UAC. In this simple model there are no final responses from the UAC to invites. This accounts for all the message queues in the simple model.

The next important validity property is that send events are always immediately executable when execution control gets to them. For example, in the *confirmed* state of UAC, as soon as *reqs?bye*, is executed, *brpc!byeRsp* should be executable. Also, between execution of any two guarded commands in the *confirmed* state, the send event *reqc!bye* should always be executable. This characteristic is important for validity because this is what a reader of the model would normally expect and assume.

The only reason that a send might not be executable is that its queue is already full. It is awkward to check for blocked sends directly, but there is an easy indirect way. First, do an exhaustive check of a model with proposed queue sizes. Then increase the sizes of all the queues and check again. If the number of state transitions in the second check is the same as in the first, then the additional space in the queues has not added any new behavior to the model. This proves that the proposed queue sizes are adequate to prevent blocking of send events. Because the example model is so simple, all its queue sizes are 1.

The third validity property is that a message can be received as soon as it arrives. For example, in the *confirmed* state of UAS the following receive events are specified: *ackc?ack, reqc?bye,* and *brpc?byeRsp*. It should not be possible for there to be some other message waiting in one of the UAS queues to be received. If there were, the model would not be giving the reader a clear and complete description of the possible next steps.

This property can be achieved simply by constructing the model so that in every user-agent state, there is a receive event for every message type in every queue directed to that agent. The model above is constructed in this way, with the single exception of *invite* messages. Each dialog begins with a unique, single invite, so it is easy to determine by inspection that no invite can ever be received later.

Finally, the model should have no unreachable or useless code. Unreachable code deceives the reader into seeing more behavioral possibilities than there really are.

In a guarded command, each guard is always technically reachable because Spin checks to see if it is executable. However, if the guard is never executable, the entire guarded command is useless. To determine whether a guard is ever executable in any trace, it is necessary to put a statement after it in the body of the command. If the guard is never executable, then the body of the command is not reachable, which will be reported by Spin. In the example model, every guarded command has a body.

For those receive events that we believe are never executable in any trace, it is convenient to use *assert(false)* as a body. If that body is ever reached, Spin reports an error. For example, neither user agent can receive a *byeRsp* message in an *inviting* or *invited* state. After a model has been checked completely, it can be cleaned up for readability by removing all the guarded commands with *assert(false)* as their body.

For those receive events that should be executable sometimes but require no further action, it is convenient to use *assert(true)* as a body, because it has no effect on execution. For example, the UAC can receive *invSucc* in its *end* state, when the order of *bye* and *invSucc* from UAS has been reversed in transit, but the message comes too late to matter. After a model has been checked completely and all such bodies are known to be reachable, they can be removed for readability.

4   Basic Model of Invite Dialogs

The basic model of *invite* dialogs in SIP is too large to print in this paper (441 lines without comments or whitespace). It can be viewed at http://www.research.att.com/ ~pamela/ sip.html. This section presents its structure and interesting characteristics.

In addition to the six message types introduced in Section 3.2, this model uses nine new ones. There are new request types *prack, update, cancel,* and *info.* Provisional responses are partitioned into unreliable ones *unProv* and reliable ones *relProv.* The *200(OK)* responses to *prack* and *update* are named *prackRsp* and *updSucc,* respectively. Finally, the failure response to an update (a 491) is named *updFail.*

The channel partition is similar to that explained in Section 3.3. There is one channel in each direction for requests; *invSucc* and *invFail* share a channel, as do *updSucc* and *updFail,* for the same reason. All other message types have their own channels.

4.1 Omissions

A few SIP phenomena are omitted from the model, for the reasons presented here.

First, responses to *cancel* requests are not included, because they are required for transport reliability only, and make no difference to the transaction user. This omission may seem a bit strange, because cancels can succeed or fail. However, a cancel fails only when the dialog it is meant to destroy is already gone (for some other reason). When the canceling UAC receives notice of failure of the cancel, it has nothing to do.

It is much more important that a *cancel* request can succeed without having the desired effect ([9], Section 9). This scenario is illustrated by Figure 1. As the figure shows, in the *canceling* state the UAC responds to invSucc with bye, because that is the only way to end the dialog. The *200(OK)* response to the cancel is irrelevant to the UAC at the application level.

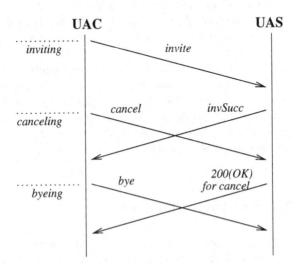

Fig. 1. A scenario in which canceling has no effect. Labels on the left are UAC states in the model.

Second, a UAS never sends a subsequent relProv until it has a received a prack for the previous one. This is recommended by the standard [8], and the model follows this recommendation.

Third, a user agent does not send *update* requests within confirmed dialogs, using re-invites instead. This is recommended by the standard [6], and the model follows this recommendation.

Fourth, unreliable provisional responses do not have SDP fields. It seems clear that reliability is required for offer/answer exchange, and that reliability is now available in the form of reliable provisional responses [8].

4.2   State Variables

In addition to having almost the same labeled dialog states as the simple model in Section 3.2, this model has a large number of state variables.

Most important of all, the model records each UA's current media state in a variable *media*. The four possible values of this variable are *noFlow* (there has been no offer/answer exchange), *offering* (this UA has made an offer but has not yet received an answer), *offered* (this UA has received an offer but has not yet answered), and *flow* (the most recent offer/answer exchange is completed). Each message whose type can ever contain an SDP field contains a value *offer*, *answer*, or *none*. This value indicates whether the message is carrying an offer, an answer, or neither, respectively.

In the UAS, the variable *media* is initialized to *noFlow*. The UAS receives the initial *invite* message with the following code:

```
reqc?invite,sdp;
if
:: sdp != none -> assert(sdp == offer); media = offered
:: sdp == none; assert(true)
fi;
```

When the invite is received, the local variable *sdp* receives the value of the SDP field in the message. An *if* statement in Promela executes exactly one of its guarded commands (and blocks if no guard is executable).[1] In this case the *if* statement is a case statement on whether the received value of *sdp* is *none* or not. If it is not *none*, then it is an offer, and *media* is updated to *offered*; if it is *none*, *media* continues to have the value *noFlow*.

As we shall see, the *media* variable is critical for understanding the state of a UA, and indispensable for interpreting received messages, because a UA cannot tell from syntax alone whether an incoming SDP field is an offer or an answer. This means that any correct implementation of a SIP user agent must have a similar state variable.

In the UAC, there are state variables whose value is important when the UAC is in the labeled state *inviting*, after sending the initial invite and before receiving

---

[1] In Promela syntax, the arrow separating guard from command can also be written as a semicolon. The actual models use semicolons.

a final response to it. One of these variables is the Boolean *dialog*, which starts false and becomes true when the dialog is established. The other *inviting* state variables are explained in Sections 4.4 and 4.5.

In the UAS, there are state variables whose value is important when the UAS is in the labeled state *invited*, after receiving the initial invite and before sending a final response to it. These variables include *dialog* (as in the UAC) and the Boolean *relOut*. As mentioned in Section 4.1, reliable provisional responses are sent sequentially. The variable *relOut* is true when there is a relProv outstanding, so when it is true a relProv cannot be sent. The other *invited* state variable is explained in Section 4.4.

Both UAC and UAS have the same variables that are important in the labeled *confirmed* state, when the dialog has been confirmed and not yet torn down. These variables include the Booleans *reInviting* and *reInvited*, which indicate whether the user agent has an uncompleted outgoing or incoming re-invite transaction, respectively.

When a user agent in a confirmed dialog receives a re-invite, its *reInvited* variable becomes true. In the large *do* loop that defines a *confirmed* state in the UAS, this is one of the guarded commands:

```
:: reInvited -> reInvited = false; ackDiff++;
   if
   :: media == flow -> irps!invSucc,offer; media = offering
   :: media == offered -> irps!invSucc,answer; media = flow
   :: else -> assert(false)
   fi
```

Whenever *reInvited* is true, the user agent can choose to make a final response to the re-invite. The variable can remain true, and the re-invite can remain pending, for as long as the user agent chooses. This models the fact that a user agent is not required to make an immediate response to a re-invite.

There are two other *confirmed* state variables, which are explained in Section 4.5.

In both user agents, there are variables that keep track of expected acknowledgments or responses, as *acked* does in the simple model. For a request type that cannot be sent until the last request of that type has been acknowledged, namely *update*, the corresponding variable *updRsped* is Boolean. For request types that can have multiple responses outstanding, such as prack, an integer such as *prackRspDiff* holds the number of requests sent minus the number of responses (prackRsps) received.

Finally, because *info* requests and unreliable provisional responses (*unProv* messages) are almost completely unconstrained, a full model might loop forever sending these messages, thereby overflowing the message queues and blocking sends unexpectedly. To prevent this, there are Boolean variables *infoSent* and *unProvSent* to limit each user agent to sending at most one message of each type. This small number is sufficient because receiving these messages has no effect on user-agent state; the only purpose of modeling them is to document when they can be sent and received.

4.3   Assertions

Writing and checking assertions is the heart of the modeling and verification process. Assertions find errors, deepen understanding, and provide reassurance.

In this model, the intention of the assertions is to elucidate the value of every relevant state variable at every important point in execution. This can be seen in the (rather large) guarded command in the UAC that receives a final *invSucc* response to the original invite:

```
:: irps?invSucc,sdp; assert(!relProvBuffered); dialog = true;
   if
   :: media == noFlow; assert(!initOffering && sdp == offer);
      ackc!ack,answer; media = flow
   :: media == flow; assert(!initOffering && sdp == none);
      ackc!ack,none
   :: media == offering && sdp == none; assert(!initOffering);
      ackc!ack,none
   :: media == offering && sdp != none;
      assert(initOffering && sdp == answer);
      ackc!ack,none; media = flow
   :: media == offered; assert(false)
   fi;
   goto confirmed
```

If this command is executable, then the UAC is in the *inviting* state, and the relevant state variables are *media, dialog, sdp, initOffering* (the meaning of which is explained in Section 4.4), and *relProvBuffered* (the meaning of which is explained in Section 4.5).

If this command is executable, then *relProvBuffered* should be false. The initial assertion guarantees this.

If this command is executable, the dialog may or may not have been established. If it is not established, receiving invSucc establishes it, which we see in the assignment *dialog = true*.

If this command is executable, *media* should not have the value *offered*, which would mean that the UAS had sent an offer to the UAC in an *update* or *relProv* message, and the UAC had not yet responded to it with an answer. The *assert(false)* guarantees that the media state is not *offered*, and that our understanding is correct.

The embedded *if* statement is a case statement on the value of *media* (and sometimes whether *sdp* is *none* or not). For each of the reachable cases, there is an assertion about what the current values of *sdp* and *initOffering* must be. In summary, for each path through this command, we know by inspection the final value of each relevant state variable.

It is easy to deduce that, when the UAC enters the *confirmed* state, *media* must be *offering* or *flow*. If you become curious about how its value might be *offering*, it is fairly easy to discover from the model that there are two scenarios

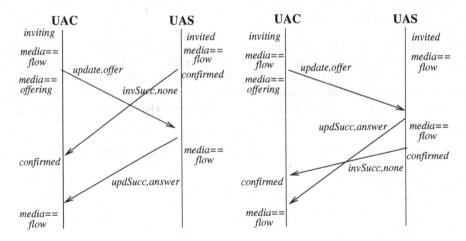

Fig. 2. Scenarios in which the UAC enters the *confirmed* state with *media == offering*

in which an update or updSucc is received by a user agent in the *confirmed* state. These scenarios are shown in Figure 2.

In the UAS code that produces the scenarios above, receiving a successful update and sending its response are in the same guarded command. They cannot be separated by the execution of any other guarded command. This reflects the fact that a user agent is required to respond to an update immediately, and contrasts with the modeling of re-invites as presented in the previous section.

There is a possible scenario very similar to that on the right side of Figure 2, in which the offer is carried in a prack and the answer is carried in a prackRsp.

4.4   Reliable Provisional Responses

Reliable provisional responses can be quite complex to use. To help clarify them, Figure 3 is a finite-state machine showing all the ways they can be used to carry SDP fields.

In each oval state of the figure, the top label is the current media state of the UAC, while the bottom label is the current media state of the UAS. In the final state, the dialog has been confirmed.

It is important to recognize the limitations of this figure. It is a synchronous model, in which sending and receiving a message are one atomic event. All messages from the UAS are shown as sent on the channel *uas*, while all messages from the UAC are sent on the channel *uac*. In reality, there are many other behaviors in which these send and receive events are interleaved with other events.

Note that in some states of this machine, the UAS cannot send *invSucc* to confirm the dialog, even though it has received an initial *invite* request and has not yet made a final response. The reason is that there is an offer/answer negotiation in progress that must be completed first. When the Promela model is in these states, the UAS's state variable *relOut* is true, and its state variable

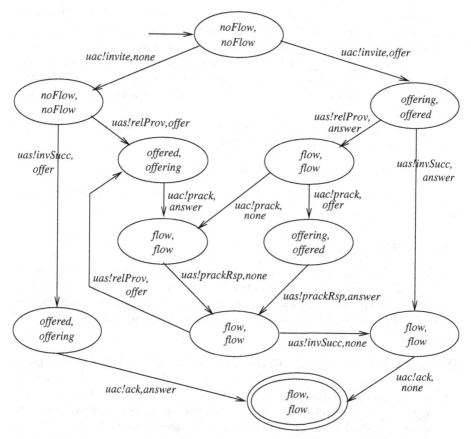

Fig. 3. A synchronous model of reliable provisional responses with SDP

canSucc is false. After the UAS receives a prack and sends a prackRsp, its *relOut* is false and its *canSucc* is true.

Another limitation of the figure is that it does not include *relProv* messages without SDP, which can be sent by the UAS whenever *relOut* is false. The subsequent *prack* and *prackRsp* messages cannot have SDP, either. Sending a *relProv* message without SDP sets *relOut* to true (until it is acknowledged) but does not set *canSucc* to false.

In the model, neither user agent can send an *update* message unless its media state is *flow*. In the RFC on updates [6], the same constraint is stated in 31 lines of dense text. This text is attempting to enumerate all the ways that offers and answers can be interleaved when carried in initial invites, relProvs, pracks, prack responses, updates, and update responses. Its purpose is to say that there must have been an initial offer/answer exchange, and that there are no offer/answer exchanges in progress, which is the exact meaning of *media == flow*.

It is easy to see from Figure 3 that SDP in a relProv is an answer if and only if there is an unanswered offer from the initial invite. Because (with fully interleaved behavior) the UAC cannot infer this from any of its other state variables, it has a Boolean state variable *initOffering* for exactly the purpose of determining whether SDP in a relProv is an offer or answer.

A reader might wonder about the following statement in [8], Section 4: "The UAC MAY acknowledge reliable provisional responses received after the final response or MAY discard them." What if the relProv is important? What if it contains SDP?

Assertions in the model can reassure the nervous reader. In the *confirmed* state of the UAC model, we see the statement:

```
:: rlps?relProv,sdp -> assert(sdp == none)
```

Thus model-checking has verified that the late relProv cannot carry SDP, and can be safely ignored.

4.5 SIP Problems

Model checking uncovers some apparent problems with the standards documents. The model incorporates work-arounds for all the problems found. This is necessary because the problems show up as errors in model-checking. Without the work-arounds, known errors prevent full model exploration and the discovery of further errors.

Dialog Establishment and Confirmation. An *invite* dialog is established by the first provisional or final success response to the invite ([9], Section 12.1). There is an implicit assumption that if a message is part of a dialog, and the message does not establish the dialog, then the message is received after the dialog is established in the agent where the message is received.

In contradiction to this implicit assumption, *info* messages from the UAS to the UAC can arrive at the UAC before the dialog they belong to is established. This can occur because *info* messages from the UAS are requests, the dialog is established by responses traveling in the same direction, and requests are unordered with respect to responses traveling in the same direction. In the model, this is simply noted, and the requests are handled as if the dialog were established.

It is obvious that an invite dialog becomes *confirmed* in a UAC when the UAC receives a final response to the initial invite. It is not so easy, however, to find in [9] whether a dialog becomes confirmed in a UAS when the UAS sends a final response or when it receives an ack to it.

This is quite important. For example, Section 14.1 of [9] applies the terms *completed, confirmed,* and *terminated* to invite transactions, and uses them to specify how overlapping re-invite transactions should be avoided.

These terms are formally defined in Figures 5 and 7 of Section 17 of [9]. According to these figures, on the UAS side, a failing invite transaction becomes *completed* when the final response is sent, and *confirmed* when the ack is received. According to these figures, a successful invite transaction is never in a *completed* or *confirmed* state, going directly from *proceeding* to *terminated*. The common-sense interpretation is that these figures are wrong with respect to the definition

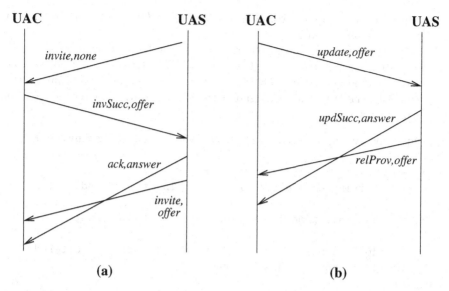

Fig. 4. (a) A scenario with a late acknowledgment to a re-invite. (b) A scenario with a late acknowledgment to an update.

of these terms, and that *completed* and *confirmed* have the same meanings for both successful and failing transactions.

To avoid confusion, the UAS model has been described as having a labeled state *confirmed*. In actuality it has a labeled state *completed* and a Boolean variable *confirmed* to represent the state of the initial invite transaction and therefore the dialog as a whole.

Re-invites. Figure 4(a) shows a scenario in which the UAS issues two re-invites. The first re-invite does not contain an offer, so the invSucc response contains an offer and the ack contains an answer.

This scenario is not covered in the RFCs, and it violates the clear intentions that offer/answer exchanges are sequential, and that a successful re-invite can be processed as soon as it is received. The second re-invite cannot be processed in the normal manner because it arrives at the UAC during an unfinished offer/answer exchange. The second re-invite cannot fail, because the cause of the invFail will not be understood by the UAS.

As in the previous section, the cause of the problem is that there is no enforced ordering on the *ack* message and the second *invite* request.[2] The two were sent in a proper order, but arrived in the wrong order.

The work-around used in the model is to buffer the second re-invite until the ack arrives and is processed, then handle the re-invite. This causes no additional problems because a user agent is not required to respond immediately to the

---

[2] Although the *ack* is technically a request, like the *invSucc* it bears the sequence number of its invite.

re-invite. The Boolean state variable *reInviteBuffered* is true when a re-invite is buffered in the user agent.

The problem is in fact more general, because the late acknowledgment could just as easily be a *prackRsp*, *updSucc*, or *updFail*. However, not all late acknowledgments are expected to carry answers, so not all of them require delay. Consequently, the UAC model diagnoses the condition by the media state when the re-invite arrives:

```
:: reqs?invite,sdp -> assert(!reInviteBuffered && !reInvited);
   if
   :: reInviting -> irpc!invFail,none
   :: !reInviting && media != flow -> reInviteBuffered = true;
                                      bufsdp = sdp
   :: !reInviting && media == flow -> reInvited = true;
      if
      :: sdp != none -> assert(sdp == offer); media = offered
      :: sdp == none -> assert(true)
      fi
   fi
```

If the UAC is not re-inviting when the re-invite arrives, and the media state is anything but *flow*, then a late acknowledgment carrying an answer is expected. After the *ack, prackRsp, updSucc,* or *updFail* arrives, if the media state is *flow*, then the re-invite is unbuffered and processed.

The same can happen within a UAS, but the only possible type of late acknowledgment is *ack*.

In the model with its work-around, if a user agent is expecting an *ack* message without SDP, the user agent does not wait for it. When it arrives, it has no effect on the model state except to enable the user agent to sent its own re-invites. Thus, in theory, there could be any number of *ack* messages with $sdp == none$ in transit between the user agents.

To prevent state explosion in the model checking, the size of channels for *ack* messages is limited arbitrarily to 2. This means that a send of an *ack* message can actually block. As the blockage is an artifact of model checking, however, and never causes deadlock, it seems safe enough.

Because there can be two *ack* messages in transit, the model tracks *ackDiff*, the difference between the number of *invSucc* messages sent and acks received. All of the observations in these last three paragraphs are equally true of *prackRsp* messages in the model.

More Late Acknowledgments. Figure 4(b) shows a scenario very like Figure 4(a). In Figure 4(b) the dialog is not yet confirmed, and the late acknowledgment is to an update. The offer could also have been sent in a prack, in which case the late answer would have been sent in a prackRsp.

As with the previous problem, the relProv cannot be processed normally because its offer arrives during an unfinished offer/answer exchange. As with the previous problem, the RFCs do not mention this possibility.

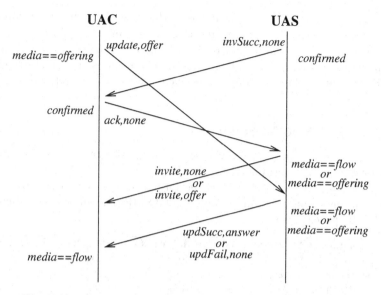

Fig. 5. A scenario with a race between an update and a re-invite

For both update and prack cases the work-around is the same, which is to buffer the *relProv* message. The Boolean state variable *relProvBuffered* is true when a relProv is buffered.

This is arguably a more serious problem than the previous one, because buffering a relProv is less desirable than buffering a re-invite. A user agent is supposed to respond to a *relProv* message immediately, while it is allowed to delay its response to a re-invite.

A Race Condition. Figure 5 illustrates a race condition between an update and a re-invite. There are actually two scenarios represented, one in which the re-invite carries SDP, and one in which it does not. All the top parts of "or" labels go together in one scenario, while all the bottom parts of "or" labels go together in another scenario.

There is no standardized resolution to this race condition. Yet the UAC cannot process the re-invite until it receives a response to its update, which will return its media state to *flow* whether the update has succeeded or failed.

The model resolves the race condition with the same work-around used for late acknowledgments to re-invites, which is to buffer the unprocessable re-invite until it can be processed.

Another Race Condition. In an unconfirmed dialog, there can be a race condition between a *relProv* message with an offer from the UAS, and an *update* message from the UAC. The resolution of this race condition is not standardized.

There is a usual way of resolving race conditions in SIP. In both re-invite/re-invite races and update/update races, both sides receive an invFail (4xx) response, then are allowed to retry with differing timing constraints. This usual approach does not seem to be available in the case of a relProv/update race, because a relProv is not a request, and there is no failure response it.

In the model, the work-around is that the *relProv* message always wins the race. In the UAS, the update fails and an *updFail* response is sent. In the UAC, the relProv is buffered until *updFail* is received, after which the relProv is handled normally.

4.6   Results of Model-Checking

The Promela model can cycle forever, so unlike the simple model in Section 3.2, it was not checked for termination.

The table (left column) shows the performance of exhaustive search of the state-transition graph on a Sun Solaris M9000 SMP machine with dual-core 2.4 GHz SPARC processors.

Performance Measure	Basic Model	FIFO Model	Pruned Model
lines of reachable code	404	300	266
state vector (bytes)	200	88	88
depth reached	6,165	1,068	464
state transitions	780,538,240	9,043,855	3,429,348
memory usage (Mbytes)	20,904	308	105
elapsed time (seconds)	4,200	38	13

"Lines of reachable code" refers to the size of the Promela code (without comments or whitespace) after unreachable code (see Section 3.3) has been removed for readability. The more-readable version of the basic model is also available at http:// www.research.att.com/ ~pamela/ sip.html.

"State vector" is the amount of memory required to represent each state of the model. "Depth reached" is the number of steps in the longest path through the graph that does not repeat a state. "State transitions" is the number of edges in the graph, and is the best measure of model complexity. The memory usage was improved by compression, and would have been 88,896 Mbytes without it.

The elapsed time varies from run to run, so it is less reliable than the other numbers. The value of compression in minimizing memory usage seems to outweigh its time penalty.

5   Alternate Models

This section presents two alternate versions of the basic model. All the models, in both model-checked and readable versions, are available at http:// www.research.att.com/ ~pamela/ sip.html. For comparison, the table reports their sizes and performance numbers.

5.1   The FIFO Model

The first four of the five problems with the basic model all have the same underlying cause: the fact that SIP messages traveling from one user agent to the other need not arrive in FIFO order. This is obvious for the first three problems.

It is less obvious for the fourth problem, which presents itself as a race between messages traveling in opposite directions, but is nevertheless true. As we can see in Figure 5, the update and ack from the UAC arrive out of order. If they could not arrive out of order, then the UAS would receive the update before it sent the re-invite (which is enabled by receiving ack), so there would be no race.

The FIFO model removes all these problems by using only a single Promela channel for all the messages traveling in one direction.

The FIFO model is smaller than the basic model in every measure, for two main reasons. First, the work-arounds required for SIP Problems 1-4 have been removed. Second, FIFO ordering constrains the behavior much more. For example, in most states the FIFO model can receive fewer different message types.

According to the most important measure, which is the number of state transitions, the complexity of the FIFO model is 1.2% of the complexity of the basic model. Its analysis requires 1.5% of the memory to analyze the basic model, and 0.9% of the time to analyze the basic model.

The FIFO model is a faithful representation of an *invite* dialog in which each user agent uses a single TCP connection, or a sequence of TCP connections, to send messages to the other user agent. It does not matter whether messages traveling in opposite directions use the same TCP connection or not. In either case, TCP ensures that the messages in one direction are received in FIFO order.

A signaling implementation based on UDP, or on a pool of TCP connections, cannot be guaranteed FIFO. This will be discussed further in Section 6.2.

5.2   The Pruned Model

Reliable provisional responses [8] were added to SIP before *update* requests [6]. Reliable provisional responses are sent by the UAS only. So that the UAC would have some capacity to modify media sessions before receiving a final response, the RFC on reliable provisional responses gives the *prack* request the ability to carry an offer, as shown in Figure 3.

Update requests allow a UAC to modify media sessions in an unconfirmed dialog, without waiting to receive a reliable provisional response to which it can respond with a prack (provided that the media state has advanced beyond *noFlow*). Thus the presence of updates makes offers in pracks redundant and their extra complexity unnecessary. In the "pruned" model, this redundant capability has been removed.

Similarly, any media modification that a UAS might attempt with an *update* request could just as easily be performed by sending a reliable provisional response (unconfirmed dialog) or a re-invite (confirmed dialog). Thus the use of updates by UASs is redundant and its extra complexity unnecessary. In the "pruned" model, this redundant capability has also been removed.

The "pruned" model is the same as the FIFO model, except for these removals. Based on the number of state transitions, the complexity of the pruned model is 38% of the complexity of the FIFO model. Its analysis requires 34% of the memory to analyze the FIFO model, and 34% of the time to analyze the FIFO model. Based on the number of state transitions, the complexity of the pruned model is 0.4% of the complexity of the basic model.

The significant reduction in complexity caused by the relatively minor change from the FIFO model to the pruned model is an excellent demonstration that the size of the state-transition graph grows exponentially.

6   Recommendations

6.1   Why Complexity Matters

It seems abundantly clear that modeling and model-checking SIP is a worthwhile thing to do. The investment is small compared to the thousands of person-hours that have been spent on the SIP RFCs. Yet it reveals previously undiscovered problems, and provides a useful kind of documentation that is not otherwise available.

It seems almost as clear that the complexity of the resulting model is significant. Every line of Promela code represents some case that an application developer must be aware of and must take into account. Every state and transition in the state-transition graph represents behavior that can occur "in the field" and interact with other layers of network and software. Finally, if a model becomes too complex it can no longer be model-checked, given practical limitations on time and memory.

So far all the SIP models are easy to check on a powerful machine. However, it is important to remember that the models represent only a small subset of SIP and its interesting component configurations, and that growth of complexity is exponential.

This argument can be quantified by relying on an analogy. Another research project [12] entailed modeling and model-checking a new protocol that is similar to SIP in its purpose and functions.

In that study, the models fall into two categories. There are models containing only two user endpoints, which means that they have the same configuration as the models in this paper. There are also models containing two user endpoints with a third process between them. This third process is analogous to a back-to-back user agent in SIP.

It is interesting to compare a pair of models in [12], one from each of the two categories above, with all other factors in the pair held constant. The jump from checking endpoints alone to checking endpoints with a back-to-back user agent causes the number of state transitions, the memory, and the time to grow by factors of 800, 300, and 1000, respectively. These are round numbers obtained by averaging many comparisons.

If we apply these numbers to the models here, we predict that the basic model, extended with a back-to-back user agent between the UAC and UAS, would have 620 billion state transitions. Model-checking it would require 6 terabytes of RAM and 1200 hours, or the equivalent with virtual memory used and swapping time added.

This is only an analogy. The protocols and models in the two studies are different (although balanced in the sense that each has sources of complexity that the other does not have). Nevertheless, if the analogy holds at all, model-checking the basic model with a back-to-back user agent is not practical.

6.2   What to Do about It

The overall complexity of SIP can be reduced considerably, and the five problems reported in Section 4.5 eliminated, by standardizing the pruned model as the definition of *invite* dialogs. This proposal does not reduce the functionality of SIP in any way.

The most important issue is that of FIFO signaling. Even if we assume that TCP is used for signal transport, there are many open questions concerning the number of TCP connections within a dialog, which messages are sent in each, and whether they are overlapped or sequential in time. This appears to be a complex issue, with many ramifications for performance and security [5].

A common interpretation of the recommendations in [9], Section 18, is that an invite dialog should have at most two TCP connections at any one time, one for the transactions initiated by the UAC, and one for the transactions initiated by the UAS. Unfortunately this recommendation does not produce FIFO signaling; two messages traveling in the same direction can still arrive out of order. For example, a request from the UAS and a response from the UAS both travel from the UAS to the UAC, but they travel in different connections because the response belongs to a transaction initiated by the UAC. Categorized by message types, Section 4.5 describes 7 non-FIFO scenarios, of which this recommendation eliminates 5, leaving 2 still possible.

To repeat the conclusions of Section 5.1, FIFO signaling is guaranteed if all of the *messages* (not transactions) from one user agent to the other use the same TCP connection, or a sequence of them (with no overlapping in time). It would be highly advantageous to the SIP community to settle on some way of doing this that meets reasonable performance and security requirements.

The other issues are more straightforward. Current recommendations that should be strengthened into requirements, from Section 4.1, are:

- A UAS does not send SDP in unreliable provisional responses [8].
- A UAS does not send a new reliable provisional response until it has received a prack from the last one sent [8].
- A user agent does not send *update* requests within confirmed dialogs [6].

The pruned model relies on the following further changes:

- A *prack* message does not contain an offer.
- A UAS does not send *update* messages.

Finally, all the models require a resolution to Problem 5, which can be summarized as: if there is a race between a *relProv* message with an offer from the UAS, and an *update* message from the UAC, then the update always fails.

7   Conclusion

This paper has presented three formal, state-oriented models of *invite* dialogs in SIP. It has discussed five places where the SIP standards are incomplete or erroneous, and proposed solutions to all the problems they cause.

As a final observation on the standards, it has already been noted that the update RFC [6] recommends using re-invites instead of updates in confirmed dialogs. The recommendation is explained as follows: "This is because an UPDATE needs to be answered immediately, ruling out the possibility of user approval. Such approval will frequently be needed, and is possible with a re-INVITE."

In fact, there is an additional way that re-invites are more powerful than updates: a re-invite can be sent with no offer, which requires its recipient to send an offer in the successful response, if there is one. There are numerous examples to show that this capability is an important ingredient in third-party call control [7,11].

Most of the scope restrictions in Section 2 do not seem to compromise the validity and usefulness of the models presented here. In each case, it is fairly easy to see how broadening the scope would extend the models or necessitate a complementary model.

The exception is the carrying of multiple session descriptions in a single message, as in [2], which completely invalidates this modeling. The RFCs cited in this paper contain a large number of constraints concerning when offers can be sent, when answers can be sent, and which messages they can be sent in (all of which are reflected in the Promela models). It is not at all clear how the presence of multiple session descriptions in a message would interact with these constraints.

No argument or proposal from a single viewpoint can be conclusive. Many factors, with many stakeholders and at many levels of abstraction, affect the current SIP and its possible futures. Nevertheless, formal modeling of SIP has proved its value as a source of relevant information. It should be pursued as a way of shedding light on other aspects of SIP.

There are many ways that the models could be improved and exploited in their role as documentation. For example, the model could be cross-indexed to RFCs, there could be tools that construct—from a user's query—a particular trace allowed by a model, and so forth.

Of all the possible uses for a formal model, the one worst served by the current technology is checking the conformance of implementations. There are two problems. First, there must be a suitable formal representation of the implementation that can be compared to the specification model. Second, even with such a representation, the scale of the verification could be beyond current feasibility (even though hardware implementations are now routinely verified).

Bishop et al. dealt with these problems, in their work on TCP and UDP, by building a special-purpose checker for captured real-world traces from implementations [1]. Capturing a trace is a lightweight way to get a formal representation of an implementation's behavior. The checker performs symbolic evaluation to determine whether a trace satisfies the specification. Although the results are limited by the quality of test coverage, this is a big advance in conformance technology, and one that might be applicable to SIP.

Acknowledgments

Most of what I know about SIP I learned from my colleagues Greg Bond, Eric Cheung, Hal Purdy, and Tom Smith. They are not responsible, however, for my remaining misconceptions.

References

1. Bishop, S., Fairbairn, M., Norrish, M., Sewell, P., Smith, M., Wansbrough, K.: Rigorous specification and conformance testing techniques for network protocols, as applied to TCP, UDP and sockets. In: Proceedings of SIGCOMM 2005. ACM, New York (2005)
2. Camarillo, G.: The early session disposition type for the Session Initiation Protocol (SIP). IETF Network Working Group Request for Comments 3959 (2004)
3. Holzmann, G.J.: The Spin Model Checker: Primer and Reference Manual. Addison-Wesley, Reading (2004)
4. JSR 309: Java media server control. Java Community Process, http://jcp.org/aboutJava/communityprocess/edr/jsr309
5. Mahy, R., Gurbani, V., Tate, B.: Connection reuse in the Session Initiation Protocol (SIP). Internet Draft draft-ietf-sip-connect-reuse-09 (2008)
6. Rosenberg, J.: The Session Initiation Protocol (SIP) UPDATE method. IETF Network Working Group Request for Comments 3311 (2002)
7. Rosenberg, J., Peterson, J., Schulzrinne, H., Camarillo, G.: Best current practices for third party call control in the Session Initiation Protocol (SIP). IETF Network Working Group Request for Comments 3725 (2004)
8. Rosenberg, J., Schulzrinne, H.: Reliability of provisional responses in Session Initiation Protocol (SIP). IETF Network Working Group Request for Comments 3262 (2002)
9. Rosenberg, J., Schulzrinne, H., Camarillo, G., Johnston, A., Peterson, J., Sparks, R., Handley, M., Schooler, E.: SIP: Session Initiation Protocol. IETF Network Working Group Request for Comments 3261 (2002)
10. Sparks, R.: Multiple dialog usages in the Session Initiation Protocol. IETF Network Working Group Request for Comments 5057 (2007)
11. Zave, P.: Audio feature interactions in voice-over-IP. In: Proceedings of the First International Conference on Principles, Systems and Applicatons of IP Telecommunications, ACM SIGCOMM, pp. 67–78 (2007)
12. Zave, P., Cheung, E.: Compositional control of IP media, IEEE Transactions on Software Engineering (to appear, 2008)

Detecting VoIP Traffic Based on Human Conversation Patterns[*]

Chen-Chi Wu[1], Kuan-Ta Chen[2], Yu-Chun Chang[1], and Chin-Laung Lei[1]

[1] Department of Electrical Engineering, National Taiwan University
[2] Institute of Information Science, Academia Sinica
{bipa,congo}@fractal.ee.ntu.edu.tw, ktchen@iis.sinica.edu.tw,
lei@cc.ee.ntu.edu.tw

Abstract. Owing to the enormous growth of VoIP applications, an effective means of identifying VoIP is now essential for managing a number of network traffic issues, such as reserving bandwidth for VoIP traffic, assigning high priority for VoIP flows, or blocking VoIP calls to certain destinations. Because the protocols, port numbers, and codecs used by VoIP services are shifting toward proprietary, encrypted, and dynamic methods, traditional VoIP identification approaches, including port- and payload-based schemes, are now less effective. Developing a traffic identification scheme that can work for general VoIP flows is therefore of paramount importance.

In this paper, we propose *a VoIP flow identification scheme based on the unique interaction pattern of human conversations*. Our scheme is particularly useful for two reasons: 1) flow detection relies on human conversations rather than packet timing; thus, it is resistant to network variability; and 2) detection is based on a short sequence of voice activities rather than the whole packet stream. Hence, the scheme can operate as a traffic management module to provide QoS guarantees or block VoIP calls in real time. The performance evaluation, which is based on extensive real-life traffic traces, shows that the proposed method achieves an identification accuracy of 95% in the first 4 seconds of the detection period and 97% in 11 seconds.

Keywords: Human Speech, Internet Measurement, Markov Model, Skype, Traffic Classification, Voice Activity Detection.

1 Introduction

VoIP is becoming increasingly popular because it provides low call costs and the voice quality is comparable to that of traditional toll telephones. The trend is exemplified by the fact that one of the most widely used VoIP applications, Skype, has 246 million registrars and 100-million online users[1]. Because of the

---

[*] This work was supported in part by Taiwan Information Security Center (TWISC), National Science Council of the Republic of China under the grants NSC 96-2219-E-001-001, NSC 96-2219-E-011-008, and NSC 96-2628-E-001-027-MY3.

[1] http://seekingalpha.com/article/50328-ebay-watch-59-earnings-growth-skype-reaches-10-million-concurrent-users.

H. Schulzrinne, R. State, and S. Niccolini (Eds.): IPTComm 2008, LNCS 5310, pp. 280–295, 2008.

steady growth of VoIP usage, providing reliable service and satisfactory voice quality is now a high-priority for Internet and VoIP service providers.

In order to provide a dependable means of voice transmission over the Internet, it is essential that network gateways have the ability to differentiate VoIP flows from flows generated by other applications. By identifying VoIP flows, network gateways can provide QoS features, such as allocating more bandwidth or assigning a high priority to identified voice flows. Traffic management is another important application of flow classification. Enterprises often have to manage VoIP traffic in line with institutional policies, such as restricting calls to certain destinations, or blocking calls at certain times. Given these emerging needs, developing an efficient and accurate identification algorithm for VoIP flows is now of paramount importance.

To accurately identify VoIP flows in real time, we may face the following challenges:

1. **Non-standard protocols and ports.** Different VoIP applications may use different signaling protocols, such as SIP [1], H.323 [2], and several other proprietary P2P protocols [3,4]. Additionally, many VoIP applications are peer-to-peer based and may use random port numbers rather than a fixed port number. Thus, it is difficult to detect VoIP flows by analyzing their signaling protocols.

2. **Non-standard codecs.** Modern VoIP applications may use different audio codecs to adapt to different network environments, e.g., using a wideband codec when a broadband medium is used and a narrowband codec if a wireless connection is detected. Given the numerous audio codecs available, detecting VoIP traffic by the signatures of audio codecs is not practical.

3. **Payload encryption.** VoIP applications now tend to encrypt their packet payloads to protect privacy. Even if a VoIP application does not encrypt its packets, the packet payload may still be inaccessible because trying to obtain such information would be a violation of privacy. Thus, payload-based identification is ineffective.

4. **Silence suppression.** A large number of traffic classification methods rely on traffic patterns, e.g., the mean and variation of packet interarrival times. However, the pattern of VoIP traffic can vary a great deal over time because many audio encoders support silence suppression. In other words, they suppress a packet stream when speech is absent and resume data delivery when speech is detected. Therefore, schemes based on traffic patterns are not very effective for identifying silence-suppression-enabled VoIP flows.

In this paper, we propose *a VoIP flow identification scheme based on human conversation patterns*. We consider that the conversation pattern of VoIP traffic is *unique* compared to that of other applications. For example, a file transfer session comprises a group of unidirectional traffic flows that are very different from VoIP traffic, which normally comprises highly interactive speech bursts. Because the presence of speech is decided solely by the speakers and the interaction context, the conversation pattern remains constant regardless of the network dynamics. Therefore, a VoIP flow identification scheme based on human conversation patterns would be robust to *silence suppression* and *traffic dynamics* due to congestion control and packet retransmissions.

When two parties, A and B, are talking to each other, we can model their interaction by a process of four states: A talking, B talking, double-talking, and mutual silence. By so doing, we show that *the process can be well modeled by a 4-state Markov chain*, which is our basis for identifying whether a conversation is *human-like*. Our VoIP flow identification scheme comprises two phases: a training phase and an identification phase. In the training phase, a set of human conversation patterns are used to derive the transition probabilities of a Markov model and train the classifier that will be used in the next phase. Then, in the identification phase, we use the trained Markov chain to compute the likelihood value and derive the pattern features of an unknown interaction process, which indicate the *humanness* of the conversation, and apply a supervised classifier to determine whether a flow is VoIP.

One advantage of our scheme is that the detection process can be implemented in the *early stages* of a network flow; thus, it is particularly useful in traffic management and QoS provisioning. In terms of performance in detecting VoIP flows, the scheme achieves 95% identification accuracy in the first 4 seconds of the detection time and 97% within 11 seconds.

In this paper, our contribution is two-fold. 1) We propose a real-time VoIP flow identification scheme based on human conversation patterns. It is robust to silence suppression and traffic dynamics due to network congestion and protocol design. 2) We evaluate the proposed scheme with extensive real-life traces and show that it achieves a high identification rate within a short detection time.

The remainder of this paper is organized as follows. In Section 2, we review related works. We discuss the data collection methodology and summarize our traces in Section 3. In Section 4, we describe the approach for inferring speech activity. In Section 5, we discuss the intuition behind our approach, and then present a detailed description of our identification scheme in Section 6. In Section 7, we evaluate the performance of the proposed scheme with extensive traces. Then, in Section 8, we summarize our conclusions.

2   Related Work

In recent years, there has been a great deal of research in the area of network traffic classification. One traditional approach identifies traffic based on port numbers, but it is becoming less effective because dynamic ports are currently used in many applications, especially peer-to-peer applications. Another widely used approach is based on payload matching, which analyzes a packet's payload to search for the specific signature of the application. However, the approach can only be used for applications whose signature is known and cannot be applied to encrypted traffic. Furthermore, examining payloads raises personal privacy concerns.

Flow statistics have also been used to classify network traffic. In [5], Moore et al. use a supervised machine learning technique, the naive Bayesian classifier, to categorize traffic by application types. In [6,7], an unsupervised clustering algorithm is proposed for traffic identification. These works focus on offline traffic classification for the purposes of traffic trend analysis and network planning. They do not consider online traffic identification, which is essential for real-time traffic management.

Another approach used to identify network traffic is based on the specific signature in packet exchanges between hosts. In [8], Dahmouni et al. modeled the sequence signature of TCP control packets with a first-order Markov chain. They first inferred the transition probabilities of a Markov model for each known application in the learning step, and then identified traffic based on the derived transition probabilities. Our scheme is similar to that in [8] as we also adopt Markov modeling; however, instead of relying on TCP control packets, our method is based on the conversation patterns between interacting hosts.

3   Data Description

We evaluated the proposed VoIP detection scheme on real-life Internet traffic traces obtained from five types of network applications: VoIP, TELNET, HTTP, P2P, and online games. Skype, a popular VoIP software, was chosen to represent VoIP applications. The collection procedures for our traces were as follows. 1) Skype traffic was captured according to the procedures detailed in [9]. 2) TELNET traffic was captured on a gateway router for all TCP flows with port numbers 22 (SSH) and 23 (telnet); all intra-campus traffic was removed. 3) We chose World of Warcraft, a popular MMORPG (Massively Multiplayer Online Role-Playing Game), to represent online games. The traffic was captured on a gateway router for all TCP flows with port number 3274; either the source or destination address is within the network 203.66 (where the World of Warcraft server is located in Taiwan). 4) P2P traffic was captured on a dedicated PC running BitComet, a variant of BitTorrent client [10]. As the BitTorrent protocol does not use a fixed port number, we recorded all the flows that used port numbers higher than 1024.

To ensure there were sufficient packet samples in each flow, we removed flows containing less than 2,000 packets. The collected traffic traces are summarized in Table 1.

Table 1. Trace Summary

Category	# Connections	Duration	# Packets	Packet Rate (1/sec)	Bytes
Skype	462	2,388 (min)	4,728,240	33	4,318 (MB)
TELNET	2,008	4,729 (min)	10,559,261	37	7,331 (MB)
WoW	1,406	1,537 (min)	2,528,359	27	680 (MB)
P2P	15,845	3,334 (min)	29,220,870	146	30,500 (MB)
HTTP	2,224	120 (min)	28,264,360	3,925	59,097 (MB)

4   Speech Activity Inference

The method used to infer speech activity from network traffic depends on whether or not *silence suppression* is employed. In this section, we discuss two methods (i.e., for applications with or without silence suppression), and present an algorithm that integrates them to detect speech activity in VoIP traffic.

4.1   Traffic with Silence Suppression

Some VoIP applications employ silence suppression, which reduces the packet sending rate when the user is not talking. The objective is to conserve network bandwidth and maximize the utilization of communication channels. We can infer the presence or absence of speech by the level of the packet rate during a short period. Specifically, a period is deemed a silence period if there are no packets longer than a threshold of 100 ms; otherwise, it is considered a speech period.

4.2   Traffic without Silence Suppression

Some VoIP applications, such as Skype and UGS [11], do not employ silence suppression. This design is intentional to ensure the UDP port bindings at the NAT and allow the background sounds to be heard all the time [12]. In this case, speech activity cannot be identified by simply observing the packet rate.

To infer speech activity from non-silence-suppressed VoIP traffic, we employ an algorithm adapted from [9], where the packet size is used to indicate whether a speech burst is present or not. The steps of the algorithm are as follows. First, we apply an exponential weighted moving average (EWMA) to remove high-frequency fluctuations in the packet size process and obtain a smoothed process. Second, we denote each peak and trough as (t_i, s_i), where t_i denotes the occurrence time of the peak or trough and s_i denotes the smoothed packet size. For each pair of adjacent troughs on the trough list, (t_a, s_a) and (t_b, s_b), if there is more than one peak on the peak list between these two troughs, we take the peak with the largest packet and denote its packet size as s_p. We then draw a line from $(t_a, (s_a + s_p)/2)$ to $(t_b, (s_b + s_p)/2)$ as an adaptive threshold. Finally, we determine the state of each voice sample as ON or OFF by checking whether the size of the smoothed packet is greater than any of the adaptive thresholds defined at the time the sample was taken.

4.3   Algorithm

We now present an integrated algorithm that can detect voice activity in VoIP flows in general, as shown in Algorithm 1. First, we observe the packet rate in either direction for a specific period, e.g., 1 second, to determine whether the flow is silence-suppressed. Because double-talk (i.e., both call parties talk at the same time) is normally short and infrequent, a period of continuous packets implies that the observed flow is not silence-suppressed. In this case, we infer voice activity in the VoIP flow based on the packet size. Otherwise, we assume the flow is generated by an application that employs silence suppression, and infer the conversation pattern embedded in the flow based on the packet rate.

Algorithm 1. Speech activity inference from VoIP traffic

---

for each flow **do**
    observe the size of packets for 1 second
    if an idle period in either direction **then**
        infer speech activity based on packet rate
    else
        infer speech activity based on packet size
    end if
end for

---

5   Motivation for the Proposed Scheme

In this section, we explain the intuition behind our approach. We consider that each type of network application possesses a unique conversation pattern. In addition, since *human interaction* is different to the interaction between computer applications, VoIP traffic can be identified based on the embedded human conversation activity. We also provide a graphical illustration of the conversation patterns of a number of applications to support our argument.

5.1   Application Behavior Analysis

To understand why human conversation patterns differ from the traffic patterns of other applications, in the following, we present a behavioral analysis of common applications.

- File transfer applications, such as FTP, are comprised of unidirectional flows. That is, downloading a file corresponds to a network flow containing only server-to-client packets, except for a few control messages from the client. On the other hand, if a client uploads a file, the traffic will contain only client-to-server packets. Moreover, a file transfer session often continues for a long period and achieves a stable bit rate in the long-term.
- In web browsing, when a user clicks on a URL, the browser sends a simple HTTP request message to the web server. The response message from the server normally comprises large objects, such as images, video clips, and document files. Therefore, HTTP traffic usually consists of small requests and large response messages.
- In TELNET applications, packets from a client to a server are normally small, as they only contain a few commands; in contrast, packets in the opposite direction often contain much more information. For example, if a client issues the command "ls," the server will reply with a list of files and directories that may contain hundreds of lines of text. Moreover, a TELNET user often spends time thinking about the next step or waiting for responses from the remote server, so the inter-packet time of the client traffic is likely to be highly variable.

- In real-time interactive online games, a client issues commands to direct the virtual avatar to move, chat, or perform other actions in the game. At the same time, the game server regularly sends out the latest game states to each client to maintain the state consistency of the virtual world. Because client packets are mostly generated according to player decisions and server packets are regulated by system timers and the dynamics of the virtual environment, the game traffic in either direction is likely to be *independent*.
- In video streaming applications, the traffic pattern is similar to that of bulk transfer. In other words, a client receives multimedia content continuously and seldom sends out packets, except for control messages.
- In video conferencing applications, participating computers send out video packets continuously to update the display on the remote hosts. At the same time, they send out audio packets independently of the video traffic. The audio packets can be sent at constant or variable intervals depending on whether silence suppression is enabled. Therefore, the traffic pattern of video conferencing is bidirectional, and the traffic in either direction is likely to be independent due to the relatively large volume of the video stream.

Table 2. Summary of application behavior

	File transfer	HTTP	TELNET	Online games	Video streaming	Video con.	VoIP
Unidirectionality	✓				✓		
Independence				✓		✓	
High interactivity							✓
Bulk transfer	✓	✓			✓	✓	
Large packet	✓	✓	✓	✓	✓		
CPR-like†				✓			✓

† constant packet rate

Table 2 summarizes the behavior of the applications analyzed in this study. We consider that the conversation pattern between two people is normally *highly interactive* and *highly interdependent*. According to our analysis, VoIP traffic is the only traffic type that exhibits both properties, which is the basis of our proposed VoIP flow identification algorithm.

5.2   Conversation Modeling

In some studies of human speech characteristics, conversation patterns have been modeled using *Markov chains* [13,14]. A 4-state model for generating artificial conversational speech is proposed in [15]. For two speakers, A and B, engaged in a conversation, the four states are as follows: state $\mathcal{A}$ represents that A is talking and B is silent; state $\mathcal{B}$ represents that A is silent and B is talking; state $\mathcal{D}$ indicates double-talking; and state $\mathcal{M}$ denotes mutual silence. We illustrate the definitions of the four states in Fig. 1, and the transitions between the four states in Fig. 2. Because of its simplicity, we employ this 4-state Markov chain for human conversation modeling in this study.

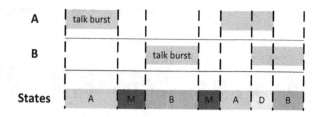

Fig. 1. Voice activity between two speakers and the conversation pattern

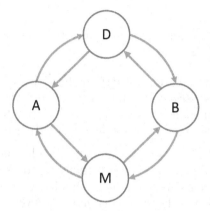

Fig. 2. Conversation model

5.3   Conversation Patterns: A Graphical Comparison

To verify our analysis of application behavior, we randomly select 10 flows from each of our traces and plot the conversation pattern of each flow, as shown in Fig. 3.

On the graph, each flow is divided into a number of periods and the conversation state in each period is determined by the traffic direction. The flows of HTTP, P2P and TELNET are assigned the state $\mathcal{M}$ most of time because their inter-packet times are normally large. On the other hand, VoIP flows consist mainly of states $\mathcal{A}$ and $\mathcal{B}$, as they reflect human conversations in which normally only one party speaks at a time. We also observe that the conversation pattern of WoW is more fragmented and disordered than that of VoIP because the interaction in online games is generally more frequent than in verbal conversations. In the following, we discuss the unique characteristics of each application.

HTTP: Normally, both the HTTP client and server remain silent for a while after a web page is downloaded, since the user needs time to read the page; this behavior is represented by state $\mathcal{A}$ or $\mathcal{B}$ followed by a long state $\mathcal{M}$. Because HTTP works in an *interactive and alternating* manner, the client and server never send packets simultaneously; thus, state $\mathcal{D}$ is not found in the pattern.

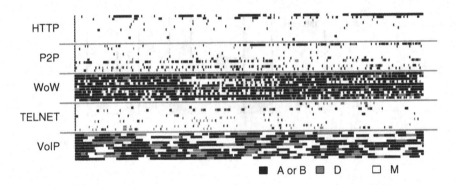

Fig. 3. The traffic patterns of the five applications considered in this study

P2P: In the conversation pattern of P2P applications, we observe a trend that single-talk states occur *periodically*. Intuitively, a host running P2P file-transfer applications must communicate regularly with its peers in order to send or receive the up-to-date block table for the files currently being transferred.

WoW: Although WoW is a real-time interactive application like VoIP, its traffic pattern is more *fragmented and chaotic* than that of VoIP for the following reasons: 1) the interaction in online games generally occurs in smaller time scales, where game actions are decided in *sub-seconds* and speech bursts usually last for a number of seconds; and 2) the commands from game clients and the responses from servers are nearly *independent*, so the traffic pattern of WoW frequently alternates between the four states.

TELNET: Like HTTP, the traffic pattern of TELNET applications consists mainly of state $\mathcal{M}$, which represents the time users spend reading information on the screen and thinking about the next action. However, the pattern of TELNET is different from that of HTTP because the length of consecutive non-$\mathcal{M}$ states is short and $\mathcal{D}$ states may occur in TELNET.

VoIP: We have identified the following unique characteristics in the VoIP conversation pattern: 1) each of the four states, tends to hold for a period, e.g., longer than one second; 2) the frequency and duration of single-talk states are often higher and longer than those of double-talk states; 3) there are two types of $\mathcal{M}$ states: short states, which may indicate gaps between words or sentences; and long states, which represent periods of silence when each speaker is thinking or waiting for the other to speak. To sum up, the VoIP traffic pattern accurately reflects human conversation patterns, i.e., *high interactivity, bi-directionality, and the interdependency between both directions*.

Through graphical comparisons, we show that the VoIP traffic pattern is very different from that of other applications. In addition, the 4-state model is effective for representing the differences between the applications' conversation patterns.

6   Methodology

In this section, we propose a VoIP flow identification scheme based on the unique human speech conversation patterns embedded in voice traffic. Our scheme comprises two phases: a training phase and an identification phase. In the training phase, we learn the parameters of a Markov model and train the classifier based on a set of existing traces. Then, in the identification phase, we use a supervised classification approach to detect VoIP flows.

6.1   Training Phase

In this phase, we use a 4-state Markov chain to model the human speech conversation pattern, and then apply a naive Bayesian classifier to distinguish VoIP flows from other flows.

Markov Chain: Given a set of known VoIP flows, we compute the initial probabilities of states $S_i \in \{\mathcal{A}, \mathcal{B}, \mathcal{D}, \mathcal{M}\}$ based on the proportion of their mean sojourn times, and compute the transition probabilities based on the empirical transition frequency between the states. We treat the trained Markov chain as representative of *typical* speech conversation patterns. Any conversation pattern that can be well-modeled by this approach is considered human-like and will be considered as a VoIP flow in the identification phase.

Naive Bayesian Classifier: To determine how well the model fit indicates that a traffic pattern is a human conversation, we employ a naive Bayesian classifier [5], which is a supervised machine learning tool. We use the flows from all the applications in our data set (Section 3) to train the classifier. For each training flow, we compute the likelihood of its conversation pattern generated by the trained Markov chain. Given a state sequence $S_1, S_2, \ldots S_n$, where $S_i \in \{\mathcal{A}, \mathcal{B}, \mathcal{D}, \mathcal{M}\}$, we compute the log-likelihood of the sequence as

$$\log(P_{1,2} \times P_{2,3} \times \ldots \times P_{(n-1),n}), \tag{1}$$

where $P_{i,j}$ is the transition probability of the state sequence $S_i S_j$. Since flows may vary in length, we define the *normalized log-likelihood value* as

$$\log(P_{1,2} \times P_{2,3} \times \ldots \times P_{(n-1),n})/N, \tag{2}$$

where N is the length of the sequence. For VoIP flows, the computed log-likelihood tends to be large as the Markov chain represents typical human conversation patterns. Because non-VoIP flows normally exhibit non-human-like behavior, such as being non-interactive, independent, and unidirectional, they likely lead to low log-likelihoods as their behavior does not fit the Markov chain well. Therefore, we use the computed log-likelihood value as one of features to train the naive Bayesian classifier.

In addition, based on the conversation pattern, we derive other features for each training flow, as shown in Table 3. We compute the mean and standard

Table 3. The features used in the naive Bayesian classifier

Features
Normalized log-likelihood value based on the Markov chain
Speech period of party A or B (mean, standard deviation)
Sojourn time in each states[†](mean, standard deviation)
Ratio of sojourn time in each states[†]
Alternation rate between states[†]

[†] states $\mathcal{A}$, $\mathcal{B}$, $\mathcal{D}$ and $\mathcal{M}$

deviation of the period that party A (resp. B) speaks each time, which reflects the bidirectional behavior of VoIP flows. To reveal the interactive behavior, we infer the summary of the sojourn time for four states $\mathcal{A}$, $\mathcal{B}$, $\mathcal{D}$ and $\mathcal{M}$. The last feature, the state alternation rate, which is the transition rate between the four states, reflects the fragmented and disordered level of traffic patterns. Since the VoIP traffic pattern is unique, these features and the log-likelihood values reveal the distinct behavior of VoIP applications; thus, we employ them to train the classifier that will be used in the classification stage.

6.2 Identification Phase

In the flow identification phase, we extract the conversation pattern from each flow, compute the normalized log-likelihood of the pattern, and determine whether the flow was generated by VoIP applications with the naive Bayesian classifier in the training phase.

7 Performance Evaluation

In this section, we first consider the effect of the order of the Markov model on the performance of flow identification, and compare the conversation patterns generated by different models to find the most appropriate order. Next, we evaluate the effect of detection time on the detection accuracy.

7.1 Effect of the Order of the Markov Model

Under our proposed scheme, the order of the Markov chain used to model human conversation patterns could affect the identification accuracy. In a first-order

Table 4. Transition probabilities of the 1st-order markov chain

	A	B	D	M
A	0.9022	0.0028	0.0380	0.0571
B	0.0029	0.9030	0.0391	0.0550
D	0.0607	0.0592	0.8763	0.0038
M	0.0465	0.0439	0.0019	0.9078

Table 5. Transition probabilities of the 2nd-order markov chain

	A	B	D	M
AA	0.9067	0.0034	0.0380	0.0519
AB	0.0000	1.0000	0.0000	0.0000
AD	0.0000	0.0781	0.9219	0.0000
AM	0.0000	0.0635	0.0000	0.9366
BA	1.0000	0.0000	0.0000	0.0000
BB	0.0032	0.9115	0.0346	0.0507
BD	0.0775	0.0001	0.9224	0.0000
BM	0.0641	0.0000	0.0000	0.9359
DA	0.9486	0.0000	0.0000	0.0514
DB	0.0000	0.9518	0.0000	0.0482
DD	0.0633	0.0678	0.8651	0.0037
DM	0.0000	0.0000	0.0000	1.0000
MA	0.9586	0.0000	0.0414	0.0000
MB	0.0000	0.9562	0.0438	0.0000
MD	0.0000	0.0005	0.9995	0.0000
MM	0.0549	0.0526	0.0025	0.8901

Fig. 4. Comparison of real human conversation patterns and artificial patterns generated by an nth-order Markov chain

Markov chain, the next state only depends on the current state, which implies a *memoryless* process. On the other hand, a second- or higher-order Markov chain considers the current state as well as the previous states. Finding an appropriate order for the Markov chain is essential to obtain a good fit of human conversation patterns and achieve high identification accuracy in our approach.

To examine the impact of the order of the Markov chain, we compare real human conversation patterns with patterns generated by different Markov models. Based on real human conversation traces, we first derive the transition probabilities, as shown in Tables 4 and 5. We then generate conversation patterns using the first- and second-order Markov chains respectively, as shown in Fig. 4. The *real* series shows the patterns of empirical conversations in our trace; the *2nd* and *1st* patterns are generated by the second- and first-order Markov chains, respectively. In addition, we generate a pattern with the *indep.* model, where the states are generated in an independent and identically-distributed (IID) manner.

Table 6. Summary of the mean sojourn times (sec.) for the pattern in Fig. 4

	A	B	D	M
real	1.03	1.15	0.75	0.86
2nd	1.21	1.17	0.66	0.88
1st	1.18	1.02	1.21	0.71
indep.	0.13	0.13	0.13	0.12

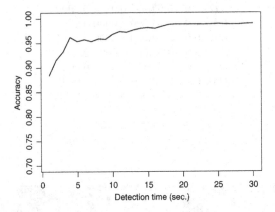

Fig. 5. Influence of the detection time on accuracy

Compared to the *real* case, the state alternation of the *indep.* model is rapid and disordered. Because of the large difference from true human behavior, the *indep.* model is clearly not suitable for describing human conversations. On the other hand, the patterns of the *1st* and *2nd* models are similar to those of the *real* case. For a detailed comparison, Table 6 lists the mean sojourn time for each state. Compared with the *1st* model, the mean state sojourn time in the *2nd* model is quite close to that of the *real* case, which indicates that the second-order Markov chain provides a better fit for human conversations. This also supports the intuition that a model with a larger memory can represent the evolution of a process more exactly.

While higher-order Markov chains generally provide better goodness-of-fit, the computational overhead is higher due to the model's complexity. In terms of the trade-off between computation time and identification accuracy, we consider that a second-order Markov chain provides the right balance. Thus, we adopt the second-order Markov chain in our proposed scheme.

7.2   Effect of Detection Time

Since our goal is to detect VoIP flows in real time, the detection time is a major concern. As shown in Fig. 5, the proposed scheme achieves a identification accuracy of 95% in the first 4 seconds of the detection time and 97% within 11

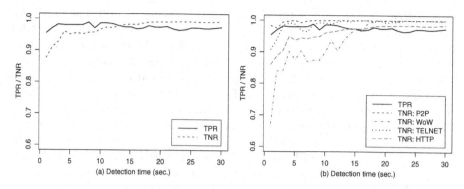

Fig. 6. Influence of the detection time on true positive rate (TPR) and true negative rate (TNR)

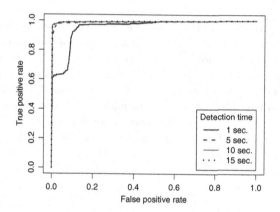

Fig. 7. ROC curves for four classifiers with different detection time

seconds. For a detailed identification performance, we plot the impact of the detection time on the true positive rate and true negative rate in Fig. 6. The true positive rate is estimated as

$$
\text{TPR} = \frac{\text{The number of VoIP flows correctly identified}}{\text{The number of total VoIP flows}}, \tag{3}
$$

while the true negative rate is

$$
\text{TNR} = \frac{\text{The number of non-VoIP flows correctly identified}}{\text{The number of total non-VoIP flows}}. \tag{4}
$$

As shown in Fig. 6(a), the true positive rate is 95% in the first seconds of the detection time. Specifically, the rate is higher than 97% for a detection time longer than 2 seconds. On the other hand, the true negative rate is 95% in the first 4 seconds of the detection time and 97% within 11 seconds. Fig. 6(b) shows the true negative rate for each non-VoIP application. We find that, among the non-VoIP applications, the flows of WoW tend to be mis-identified as VoIP. One possible explanation is that clients may be idle in some sessions so that the traffic consists mainly of server-to-client packets; therefore, the traffic pattern will be less disordered and close to that of VoIP. The true negative rate for WoW can achieve 90% with a detection time longer than 10 seconds.

In Fig. 7, we plot ROC curves for four classifiers that are based on different length of the detection time. The performance of a classifier is better than another while the true positive rate is close to 1 for a small false positive rate (i.e., TPR is higher and FPR is lower). From these curves, we observe that the classifier achieves a high TPR and an extremely low FPR with a short detection time (5 seconds). Therefore, the results evidence that our proposed scheme can identify VoIP fows in a short time with a high accuracy.

8   Conclusion

In this paper, we propose a real-time VoIP identification scheme based on human conversation activity. By analyzing the human conversation patterns of common network applications, we show that the pattern embedded in VoIP traffic is distinct; hence it can serve as a unique signature for VoIP flow identification. Based on this finding, we propose a Markov chain-based algorithm to detect VoIP flows in real time. Through a performance evaluation based on extensive Internet traces, we show that the proposed scheme is very effective in terms of classification accuracy and detection time. Specifically, the identification accuracy is 95% within 4 seconds and 97% within 11 seconds.

References

1. TelTel, http://www.teltel.com/
2. XMeeting, http://xmeeting.sourceforge.net/
3. Skype, http://www.skype.com/
4. iVisit, http://www.ivisit.com/
5. Moore, A.W., Zuev, D.: Internet traffic classification using bayesian analysis techniques. In: Proceedings of the ACM SIGMETRICS 2005, Banff, Alberta, Canada, pp. 50–60 (2005)
6. Erman, J., Mahanti, A., Arlitt, M.F.: Internet traffic identification using machine learning. In: Proceedings of the IEEE GLOBECOM 2006, San Francisco, California, USA, pp. 1–6 (2006)
7. Erman, J., Mahanti, A., Arlitt, M., Williamson, C.: Identifying and discriminating between web and peer-to-peer traffic in the network core. In: Proceedings of the 16th international conference on World Wide Web, Banff, Alberta, Canada, pp. 883–892 (2007)
8. Dahmouni, H., Vaton, S., Rossé, D.: A markovian signature-based approach to ip traffic classification. In: Proceedings of the 3rd annual ACM workshop on Mining network data, San Diego, California, USA, pp. 29–34 (2007)
9. Chen, K.T., Huang, C.Y., Huang, P., Lei, C.L.: Quantifying Skype user satisfaction. In: Proceedings of ACM SIGCOMM 2006, Pisa, Italy, pp. 399–410 (September 2006)

10. Qiu, D., Srikant, R.: Modeling and performance analysis of bittorrent-like peer-to-peer networks. In: Proceedings of ACM SIGCOMM 2004, Portland, OR, USA, pp. 367–378 (August 2004)
11. Hou, F., Ho, P.H., Shen, X.S.: Performance evaluation for unsolicited grant service flows in 802.16 networks. In: Proceedings of the 2006 international conference on Wireless communications and mobile computing, Vancouver, British Columbia, Canada, pp. 991–996 (July 2006)
12. Baset, S.A., Schulzrinne, H.G.: An analysis of the skype peer-to-peer internet telephony protocol. In: Proceedings of the IEEE INFOCOM 2006, Barcelona, Spain, pp. 1–11 (2006)
13. Brady, P.: A model for generating on-off speech patterns in two-way conversation. The Bell System Technical Journal 48(9), 2445–2472 (1969)
14. Stern, H.P., Wong, K.K.: A modified on-off model for conversational speech with short silence gaps. In: Proceedings of the 25th Southeastern Symposium on System Theory, Tuscaloosa, Alabama, USA, pp. 581–585 (1993)
15. International Telecommunication Union: Artificial conversational speech, ITU-T Recommendation P.59 (1993)

Template-Based Signaling Compression for Push-To-Talk over Cellular (PoC)

Andrea G. Forte and Henning Schulzrinne

Columbia University, New York, NY, USA
{andreaf,hgs}@cs.columbia.edu

Abstract. The Session Initiation Protocol (SIP) has been chosen as the standard signaling protocol for the IP Multimedia Subsystem (IMS). SIP is a text-based protocol with messages often exceeding 1000 bytes in size, thus causing high call set-up delays on low bit-rate links.

Signaling Compression (SigComp) is currently the only option cellular operators have for the compression of signaling messages. We study the performance of SigComp, showing that SigComp cannot achieve the level of compression required by Push-To-Talk over Cellular (PoC) services in the IMS. Furthermore, we propose an alternative compression mechanism, namely Template Based Compression (TBC), and show through measurements how we can achieve higher compression ratios than SigComp, satisfying the requirements for PoC on low bit-rate links.

1 Introduction

Push-To-Talk over Cellular (PoC) has seen a rapid growth in recent years. Various cellular carriers such as Nextel and Sprint offer PoC solutions usually combined with rich presence. PoC is a half-duplex technology that allows users to communicate with each other in a walkie-talkie fashion. Such communication can be point-to-point and point-to-multipoint.

The IP Multimedia Subsystem (IMS) represents the next evolution in fixed and mobile network access and it is currently being deployed in many cellular networks. In the IMS, different access technologies converge under one single architecture based on the Internet Protocol (IP). This convergence allows for the delivery of Internet services regardless of the access network used. We can think of the IMS as an abstraction layer between the service layer and the transport layer.

The IMS introduces many new network elements. For the purpose of this paper, however, we focus only on the User Equipment (UE) and the Proxy-Call Session Control Function (P-CSCF). The UE is the IMS end-point, while the P-CSCF represents the first point of attachment the UE has with the IMS. Once the UE connects to the IMS, its P-CSCF will remain the same for the whole duration of the IMS registration. The path between UE and P-CSCF usually includes a wireless link called the *air link*.

In order to facilitate the integration between IMS and the Internet, the protocols used in the IMS were chosen from protocols standardized by the Internet Engineering Task Force (IETF). In particular, the Session Initiation Protocol (SIP) [12] was chosen as the signaling protocol for the IMS and it has been mandatory since release 5. Using SIP

H. Schulzrinne, R. State, and S. Niccolini (Eds.): IPTComm 2008, LNCS 5310, pp. 296–321, 2008.
© Springer-Verlag Berlin Heidelberg 2008

terminology, the UE is the equivalent of a SIP user agent (UA) and the P-CSCF is the equivalent of a SIP proxy server.

SIP was designed as a text-based protocol to simplify building new SIP-based services, create new SIP extensions and debug implementations. Since SIP was designed for high bit-rate links, the size of SIP messages did not really matter. For high bit-rate links, the size of SIP messages does not introduce a significant delay in the call set-up process. Things, however, change when we consider IMS. In the IMS we have different access technologies such as UMTS and GPRS that have significantly lower bit-rates than, for example, IEEE 802.11 and IEEE 802.16. In such cases, the large size of SIP messages significantly contributes to the call set-up delay, making the call set-up time too big for real-time applications such as voice and PoC.

In order to address the large size of SIP messages and make SIP more "friendly" for low bit-rate links, the IETF standardized a general compression framework called Signaling Compression (SigComp) [11]. SigComp provides a high degree of flexibility in that it can support any type of dictionary-based compression algorithm, but it does so by sacrificing performance (see Section 4). By using SigComp, SIP messages are in many cases significantly shorter than their uncompressed version. This, however, is still not enough for applications such as PoC where the Post Dial Delay (PDD) has to be on the order of one second or less (see Section 6).

The main contributions of this paper are listed below.

- We study and evaluate SigComp performance for different SIP flows and show the call set-up delay for each.

- We show how SIP introduces the largest contribution to the call setup delay. In particular, in our measurements, the exchange of SIP messages took several seconds to complete.

- SIP affects only one component of the total call set-up delay, that is, the *air-link delay*. Because of this, a SigComp-based solution is limited since it does not improve on other components of the call set-up delay such as the *air-link setup delay*.

- SigComp has intrinsic limitations due to its architecture in order to achieve a high degree of flexibility. We analyze such limitations and show why SigComp is not suitable for achieving very high compression for smaller packets.

- We analyze compression techniques based on text substitution such as those of the Lempel-Ziv (LZ) family, pointing out limitations and shortcomings relevant to the present context.

- We introduce a new compression mechanism based on the concept of *templates* called Template Based Compression (TBC) that cellular operators can use in their network. We show how such mechanism makes it possible to achieve the delay requirements of the most time-critical applications such as PoC in the IMS. We compare the performance of the proposed compression mechanism with those of SigComp and show how the proposed compression mechanism always outperforms SigComp.

- Finally, we show how including our compression mechanism within the SigComp architecture is not desirable since SigComp becomes counter-productive as the size of messages becomes smaller.

The rest of the paper is organized as follows. In Section 2 we present current approaches for compressing signaling messages and Section 3 describes the delays in the IMS for call setup. In Section 4 we describe SigComp operations, pointing out advantages and disadvantages and in Section 5 we introduce TBC. Section 6 shows and compares performance of SigComp and TBC. Finally, Section 7 concludes the paper.

2   Related Work

The use of compression in network protocols is not new. Header compression such as Robust Header Compression (ROHC)[2] is used for the compression of protocol headers; Transport Layer Security (TLS)[3] and File Transfer Protocol (FTP)[10] have a compressed transmission mode and IP compression (IPComp)[13] is used to compress IP datagrams. All of these compression protocols, however, are not suitable for compression of application layer messages and while they can complement a compression mechanism at the application layer, they cannot replace it. In particular, TLS and IPComp use LZ-based compression for messages at the transport and IP layer respectively, without discerning between applications. This makes LZ-based compression less efficient since application-specific redundancy cannot be fully exploited.

Signaling compression, is relatively new and has attracted more interest in recent years, especially after SIP became the signaling protocol for the IMS. SigComp[11], a general framework for signaling compression, was standardized by the IETF in 2005. We present the SigComp architecture in Section 4 and compare it with our approach throughout the paper.

In [1], Akhtar et al. introduce a new entity called Encoding Assistant (EA) on both the UE and the P-CSCF. The EA is placed between the application layer and the SigComp layer and takes care of compressing some of the dynamic content of SIP messages such as SIP Uniform Resource Identifiers (URIs). Together with the EA, new SIP option tags and new SIP headers are introduced. The EA inserts new headers in the SIP message to be compressed. These new headers contain an index value that points to a particular entry in the Identity List. The Identity List is a list of maximum 16 entries containing identity information for a specific user. This list is used for indexing the content of the Via, From, Contact and P-Preferred-Identity headers. The use of an indexed list aims to reduce the size of the message by replacing a string with a number. This advantage, however, is not significant since the new headers added to contain this index are 14 bytes long or more. The performance of such mechanism have not been proven. Furthermore, SigComp Extended Operations [9] introduces the concept of User Specific Dictionary (USD) which offers similar functionalities to the ones of the EA in that it allows for a better compression of the dynamic content specific to each user, and this without the introduction of any new header or tag. Because of this, we see little or no use in adopting the proposal in [1].

Viamonte et al. in [14] introduce the concept of Session Description Protocol (SDP) template for reducing the session setup delay for streaming services using the Real-Time Streaming Protocol (RTSP). Here, the streaming server builds a template for the SDP part of the RTSP packet. This template contains all the SDP fields present in the packet and their values. Those SDP fields whose value is not known when the template is built, are still present in the template although empty. For those SDP fields that are empty in the template, their value is sent in the 200 OK answering the RTSP DESCRIBE request. In such case the order of the variables in the 200 OK has to be the same as in the template. Each field is not split in a variable part and a fixed part; it is either completely present in the template or it is sent later. The server sends to the client a URL where to download the template. When the template is no longer applicable because some parameters have changed, the server will send the client a new URL where to find the updated template.

The approach proposed in [14] can be seen as a specific case of our TBC, although with some important differences.

In [14] the way the template is built and used is specific to the characteristics of streaming sessions and it addresses only SDP content for RTSP messages. Many parameters that we consider as variable such as codecs and port numbers, are considered as constant and therefore part of the SDP template. Furthermore, new headers advertising the support of SDP templates and the URLs where to download such templates are included in packets exchanged during time-critical operations. This introduces the possibility of SDP templates negatively affecting the session setup delay. In TBC, information regarding templates is never sent during time-critical operations, hence TBC always improves the setup delay. Finally, the variable fields not included in the SDP template are sent in the 200 OK without any encoding. In TBC we encode variable content that is not included in the template to further improve compression.

3 Delays in the IMS

In terms of delay we look at the call setup delay and PDD. The call setup delay is the time between the INVITE request and the 200 OK. The PDD is the time from when users press the "call" button to when they receive the ring-back, that is, the 180 Ringing (see Fig. 1).

Generally speaking, users do not embrace a new service when this new service offers performance inferior to the service it replaces. This is the case of a GSM network and an IMS-based wireless network, for example. In a GSM network the typical call setup delay is 2 seconds for a mobile-to-PSTN call, 2.2 seconds for a PSTN-to-mobile call and about 4 seconds for a mobile-to-mobile call[1] [5]. As we show in Section 6, in the IMS, the air-link delay alone can be as high as 7 seconds. SigComp reduces air-link delay down to about 2 seconds. SigComp, however, improves only on the air-link delay, leaving other causes of delay unaffected. This makes a SigComp-only approach not sufficient for real-time applications such as PoC where PDD has to be on the order of one second or less.

Fig. 1 shows a typical call set-up flow for a SIP UA in the IMS. For each packet we have to consider the following delays: air-link setup delay, node processing delay, long distance and back-hauls delay, and air-link delay. The one-way end-to-end delay is given by:

$$\delta = N \cdot (T_{AD}^{up} + T_{AD}^{down} + T_{node} + T_{BH}) + T_{setup} \tag{1}$$

---

[1] GSM uses Signaling System No.7 (SS7), a bit-field-encoded signaling protocol.

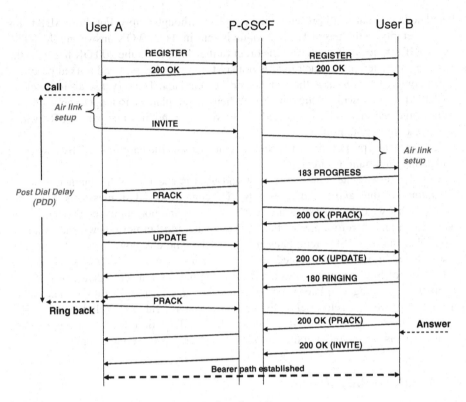

Fig. 1. SIP flow for call set-up

with

$$T_{AD}^{up} \equiv T_{AD}^{down} = \frac{L}{R} + \frac{RTT}{2} \qquad (2)$$

where N is the number of packets transmitted, T_{AD}^{up} is the air-link delay for the uplink, T_{AD}^{down} is the air-link delay for the downlink, T_{node} is the node processing delay, and T_{BH} is the back-hauls delay. Finally, T_{setup} is the air-link setup delay which is the time needed to setup the air-link before the first message can be sent and/or received on the *data* channel. T_{setup} is usually 1400 ms, that is 700 ms on the sender side and 700 ms on the receiver side (see Fig. 1). In Eq. (2), L is the message size, R is the link bit-rate and RTT is the Round-Trip Time. Throughout our calculations we assume the RTT to equal 140 ms [8].

SigComp helps in reducing the overall call set-up delay by reducing T_{AD}^{up} and T_{AD}^{down}. Other delays and in particular T_{setup} are not affected. We focus our attention on T_{setup} because T_{setup} is responsible for a significant part of the total delay. In particular, T_{setup} can be removed if at call set-up time the control channel can be used instead of the data channel. This, however, means that, for 1xEV−DO rev. A [7], the first INVITE and subsequent packets need to be no larger than 211 bytes for the uplink and no larger than 113 bytes for the downlink [1].

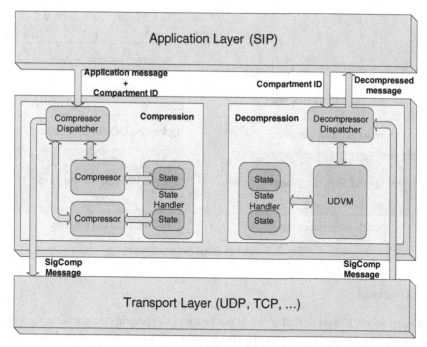

Fig. 2. Architecture of a SigComp end-point

As we show in Section 6.2, SigComp cannot compress the INVITE down to the required sizes, while TBC can.

4   Signaling Compression (SigComp)

Figure 2 shows the architecture of a SigComp end-point. We can consider SigComp as a new layer between application layer and transport layer. In particular, resources in SigComp are assigned based on *compartments*. A compartment is a particular grouping of messages that is specific to a particular application. In SIP, a compartment can be identified with a dialog. When an application wants to use SigComp, it has to provide the application message to compress and a unique compartment identifier. Messages belonging to the same SIP dialog have the same compartment identifier. This unique identifier is used by the SigComp layer to allocate resources such as state memory, Universal Decompressor Virtual Machine (UDVM) memory and compressor and also to access previous state.

The main component of the SigComp architecture is the UDVM which is a normal virtual machine, like the Java virtual machine, but optimized for decompression operations. The UDVM machine language is called *bytecode* and it is used to implement decompression algorithms that the UDVM has to run in order to decompress messages. Other components of the SigComp architecture are the Compressor Dispatcher, Decompressor Dispatcher, and the State Handler.

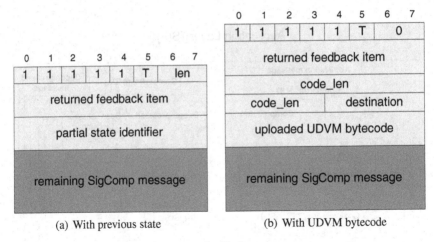

0	1	2	3	4	5	6	7
1	1	1	1	1	T	len	

returned feedback item

partial state identifier

remaining SigComp message

(a) With previous state

0	1	2	3	4	5	6	7
1	1	1	1	1	T		0

returned feedback item

code_len

| code_len | destination |

uploaded UDVM bytecode

remaining SigComp message

(b) With UDVM bytecode

Fig. 3. Format of a SigComp message

4.1 Overhead

SigComp was designed so that it would not be tied to a specific compression algorithm. This flexibility, however, introduces a cost in terms of complexity and packet size.

Aside from the performance of the particular compression algorithm used, SigComp has some significant drawbacks that do not make it the best choice when the size of the compressed packets needs to be very small. Fig. 3 shows the structure of a SigComp packet. All the fields other than the *remaining SigComp message* field form the packet header. Fig. 3(a) shows a SigComp message when a previous saved state is accessed on the remote end-point. Fig. 3(b) shows a SigComp message that does not point to a previous saved state but rather contains the UDVM bytecode. Also, SigComp uses a feedback mechanism to facilitate the exchange of state-related information and other parameters between compressor and UDVM.

As we can see, SigComp introduces various headers, adding to the total packet size. The feedback item can have a size of up to 128 bytes and the UDVM bytecode can be of variable length as specified in the *code_len* field. Its size can be anywhere between 0 and 4095 bytes.

All of this clearly shows how even one single feedback item may compromise any compression effort aimed to reach the size requirements specified in Section 3.

4.2 Compression

SigComp uses compression based on text substitution such as Lempel-Ziv 77 (LZ77) and Deflate[2]. Figure 4 shows the basic idea behind this family of compression algorithms. As we can see, the compression is based on the construction of an adaptive dictionary containing a number of unique strings. Every time a new string that is not

---

[2] Deflate uses LZ77 for the elimination of duplicate strings and Huffman coding for bit reduction.

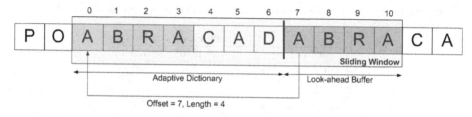

Fig. 4. Compression based on text substitution

present in the dictionary is found in the look-ahead buffer, it is added to the dictionary. Any occurrence of any string already present in the dictionary is replaced with an {offset, length} pair which points to the same string in the adaptive dictionary. In this way, string repetitions are replaced by {offset, length} pairs. The longer the string replaced and the more frequent the repetitions, the higher the compression.

Unfortunately, this kind of compression has several drawbacks.

- *The initial compression is low.* At the beginning of a sequence, the adaptive dictionary has yet to be built and the frequency of string repetitions is low. Static dictionaries such as the SIP static dictionary [6], can help in reducing this problem. Their use is however very limited due to the fact that the information they provide helps only for the very first stages of the compression process while consuming a significant amount of resources (see Section 4.3). Many SigComp implementations, such as Open SigComp [4], do not use static dictionaries for compression.
- *It is inefficient for smaller sequences.* Usually, short sequences have fewer string duplicates. The longer the sequence to compress, the higher the probability of finding string duplicates.
- *It is inefficient for short strings.* For very short strings, the pair {offset, length} can take more bytes than the actual string it is replacing. In Deflate, for example, string duplicates that are shorter than four bytes are ignored.

In order to find out the best possible compression achievable with compressors of the LZ family, we performed some preliminary measurements on two types of IMS flows, a short flow and a long flow. The short flow follows the basic SIP call setup flow (REGISTER→200→ INVITE→180→200→ACK), while the long flow is similar to the one shown in Fig. 1, but with multiple messages exchanged also before the INVITE request. We implemented the first phase of LZ-based compression, that is, identify if a string or sub-string had ever been encountered before in either the same packet or previous packets. In our implementation we use the same convention as in Deflate, that is, strings of three bytes or shorter are considered as *not found* in the adaptive dictionary. Furthermore, we do not limit the size of the adaptive dictionary, so that older state is not discarded because of newer state.

As we can see from Table 1, for the short flow we found that for the first INVITE request, 395 bytes out of 1350 bytes were not found in both previous lines of the same packet and in previous packets. For the long flow more repetitions were found and only 212 bytes out of 1253 bytes were not found. This shows that if we apply LZ to the first INVITE, in theory, we have at best a compressed size of 395 bytes for the short flow and

Table 1. First phase of LZ compression for the first INVITE request (All values in Bytes)

	Short Flow	Long Flow
Original size	1350	1253
From previous messages	790	989
From itself	577	596
Not found	395	212

212 bytes for the long flow. In reality, the compressed size is bigger for both flows since we have to consider the extra bytes that each {offset, length} pair takes, plus the size of the adaptive dictionary which is included in the compressed packet. Furthermore, in reality the adaptive dictionary is limited in size, eventually causing loss of older state, thus increasing the overall number of bytes not found.

Although Huffman coding might help to push compression a little further, it is clear that compressing a message that is 1300 bytes long to about 100 bytes or less is not possible with LZ-based compression.

4.3 SIP Static Dictionary

The use of the static dictionary improves the compression ratio for the initial messages by providing some initial content for the adaptive dictionary that would otherwise be empty. As we will see in Section 6.2, not using a static dictionary leads to a compression ratio above 100% for the initial messages. This happens until sufficient state is built. A compression ratio above 100% means that the size of the compressed messages is larger than the one of the original messages. Typically, however, this happens only for the initial REGISTER−200 OK handshake.

The SIP static dictionary has a size of 3468 bytes. After a few messages have been exchanged within the same dialog, most or part of the static dictionary is replaced in the state memory by more recent state and compression is performed according to the new state.

The added complexity and the fast aging of state based on the static dictionary make the use of static dictionaries very limited, with many implementations not supporting them at all. Furthermore, static dictionaries improve the compression of only the very first messages of a flow, typically the initial REGISTER−200 OK handshake, leaving time-critical messages unaffected. Because of all of these reasons, static dictionaries are not used in our experiments.

4.4 Extended Operations

SigComp Extended Operations are defined in RFC 3321 [9]. New mechanisms are proposed in order to further improve compression. All the proposed mechanisms try to improve on how state is created and destroyed so that unnecessary state deletions are avoided and new state is created more efficiently. Some of the mechanisms proposed in [9] are dynamic compression, shared compression, User Specific Dictionary (USD) and implicit deletion for dictionary update. Of all the proposed mechanisms, USD is the most relevant to the present context.

USD is a dictionary built on the assumption that a {user, device} pair produces, over time, the same content for those headers in a SIP message related to the capabilities of the device or to the user. USD, however, still uses the typical conventions of LZ-based compression algorithms. It just represents a different dictionary used in the LZ-based compression. Because of this, although USD improves on the compression of dynamic content, it still suffers from all the drawbacks previously discussed for LZ-based compression. This limits the improvements achievable with USD. Moreover, the way the USD is built and how it is exchanged between SIP entities is not standardized and as of the writing of this paper, SigComp implementations supporting Extended Operations are not available.

For all of these reasons, and because of the limited improvements that USD would introduce, we do not consider USD or any of the mechanisms proposed in [9] in the rest of the paper.

4.5   Advantages and Disadvantages

To summarize, the advantages in using SigComp are that it has already been standardized by the IETF, is mandatory in the IMS and there are already implementations available such as Open SigComp [4].

The disadvantages are that it is very complex and heavy, LZ-based compression is not enough for many delay sensitive applications such as PoC. Furthermore, SigComp introduces significant overhead regardless of the compression algorithm used.

5   Template-Based Compression (TBC)

As we have explained in Section 3, in order to significantly reduce the call setup time and PDD, we need to compress the messages so to achieve a maximum size of 211 bytes for the uplink and 113 bytes for the downlink. This is because we do not only want to reduce the air-link delay, but we also want to remove the air-link setup delay (see Eq. (1)) and in order to remove the air-link setup delay, we need to send the Data Over the Signaling channel (DOS).

As we show in Section 6, SigComp cannot satisfy the message size requirements for DOS while TBC can. In this section we describe how TBC works.

5.1   Overview

The basic idea behind TBC is that the content of many headers and SDP parameters in a SIP message does not significantly change over time. There are headers that do not change at all throughout different sessions, there are headers that do not change within a session and there are headers whose value changes on a per-call basis.

By using these characteristics of SIP headers and SDP lines, we build templates for SIP messages. A template contains the part of a message that is likely not going to change. In doing so, UE and P-CSCF need to exchange only the variable parts of a message so that the template can be "filled in" and the whole SIP message can be correctly re-constructed at both the UE and P-CSCF. By using templates we reduce the amount of information that needs to be exchanged between UE and P-CSCF. Also, in order to minimize the message size as much as possible, we encode such information.

Templates can be exchanged ahead of time-sensitive operations such as during registration. When the P-CSCF has to send an INVITE to a UE, it checks its outgoing-INVITE template for that particular UE. The P-CSCF extracts from the INVITE the variable content that is not present in the template and encodes it. The encoded values are then put in the final packet following a specific order and the final packet is sent to the UE. The ordering of the encoded values is very important since it allows the UE to know which value belongs to which header in the template. After receiving the encoded packet, the UE extracts the encoded values from the packet, decodes them and matches them to the corresponding headers in the incoming-INVITE template. In doing so, the INVITE has been successfully re-constructed.

The same process is performed in the other direction, from the UE to the P-CSCF.

TBC compresses a message in the following steps:

1. *Header Stripping.* Unnecessary headers are stripped from the message.
2. *Template.* The message is filtered according to a template so that only the dynamic content not present in the template is extracted from the message and eventually sent to the remote end-point.
3. *Shared Dictionary.* The Shared Dictionary (SD) is searched for matching strings among the ones present in the dynamic content extracted at step 2. If a match is found, the string is replaced by the corresponding index in the dictionary.
4. *Encoding.* The dynamic content is encoded so to occupy the minimum number of bytes.

Only after all of the above steps have been completed, the message is ready to be sent.

We now look in more detail at each one of the previous steps.

5.2   Header Stripping

Some SIP headers are present only in incoming messages while others are present only in outgoing messages. For example, headers such as Route, Security-Verify, P-Preferred-Identity, Proxy-Require are present in outgoing INVITE requests but not in incoming INVITE requests. On the other hand, headers such as Record-Route and P-Asserted-Identity are present in incoming INVITE requests but not in outgoing ones. This classification helps us in knowing what headers to expect when building a template for an outgoing or incoming SIP message. Furthermore, there are headers whose value is relevant only to SIP proxies and not to SIP UAs. If we assume SIP end-points to act as a SIP UA, for packets sent by the P-CSCF to the SIP UA we can safely ignore such headers. In order to exploit this behavior, before building a template, SIP headers that are not relevant to a SIP UA are removed from the message by the P-CSCF. Some of the headers that we strip from a SIP message are shown in Table 2.

Let us consider, for example, the case of the Via header for an incoming SIP IN-VITE. The Via header in this case is populated with all the SIP proxies the message has traversed in order to reach its destination. This is done so that the response to the SIP INVITE can follow the same path of the SIP INVITE itself. However, all the information the UA really needs is the first hop where to send its response, that is, the IP

Table 2. Actions on SIP headers

Header	Stripped (UA as receiver)	SW/HW dependent	Token	Typical values
Max−Forwards	X			
Via	X			
User−Agent	X			
P−Alerting−Mode	X			
Record−Route	X			
Session−Expires		X	X	1800, 3600
Supported		X	X	100rel, timer
Privacy			X	None, id
Require			X	Precondition
Allow		X	X	REGISTER, BYE, INVITE, . . .
Accept−Contact			X	*;+g.poc.talkburst; require;explicit
Content−Type			X	Application/sdp, mulitpart/mixed
Accept			X	Application/sdp, text/html

address of the P-CSCF the UA is currently attached to. The UA already has this information, therefore the P-CSCF does not need to send the content of the Via header to the UA. The response to the incoming INVITE sent by the UA will have a Via header containing only the address of its P-CSCF. The P-CSCF will then make sure to re-insert all the missing entries from the Via header received in the initial incoming INVITE into the UA response when re-constructing the packet for such response.

5.3   Templates

Generally speaking, we can classify SIP headers into four categories:

- *Variable*: headers that can change between calls.
- *Semi-variable*: headers that are session or registration dependent.
- *Semi-constant*: headers that are device dependent in either hardware, software or both.
- *Other*: all those headers that do not belong to any of the previous groups such as headers that change within a dialog.

Furthermore, there are headers that occur more frequently than others and there are headers that are present only in requests and headers that are present only in responses. All of these factors need to be taken into consideration when defining a TBC mechanism for SIP messages.

The construction of a template for a particular SIP message is based on the header classification that we have just introduced. In particular, headers belonging to the group of *semi-constant* and *semi-variable* are included in the template together with their value. Headers belonging to the group of *variable* and *other* are included in the template without any value. The content of those headers whose value is not included in the template represents the dynamic information that has to be sent on the air. Mixed situations are also possible where a semi-variable header, for example, can have a single parameter whose value is part of the dynamic content.

For semi-variable headers, templates can be updated between registrations to reflect a change in their value. Semi-constant headers allow us to tailor templates according to a particular hardware device or piece of software. In this last case, we can build templates specific to particular brands since order and header fields do not change for devices of the same brand. For example, if a device is running the Columbia University

Table 3. Classification of SIP headers

Header	Variable (call dependent)	Semi−var (session or registration dependent)	Semi−const (HW/SW dependent)	Other (variable within dialogue)	Occurrence
Accept			X		medium
Accept−Contact	X				high (PoC)
Accept−Encoding			X		low
Accept−Language			X		low
Alert−Info	X				low
Allow			X		high
Authorization		X			low
Call−ID	X				high
Call−Info		X			low
Contact		X			high
Content−Disposition	X				low
Content−Encoding			X		low
Content−Language	X				medium
Content−Length	X				high
Content−Type	X				high
CSeq				X	high
Date				X	low
Expires				X	medium
From		X			high
In−Reply−To		X			low
Max−Forwards			X		high
Record−Route	X				high
Route		X			high
Session−Expires			X		high
Supported			X		high
To	X				high
User−Agent			X		high
Via	X				high

SIP client, we know to use the templates for Columbia University or if a device is a Linksys device, we know to use the templates for the Linksys brand.

Without the notion of software/hardware-dependent headers we would not be able to consider as constant many headers that indeed can be considered as such.

Table 3 lists a sample number of SIP headers and their classification as discussed above. Their frequency of use is also shown.

Templates for outgoing messages and incoming messages are different even though the type of message is the same. This is because for an outgoing INVITE request, for example, the number of headers whose value is known is much higher than for an incoming INVITE request. An incoming INVITE request can come from anywhere and anyone, therefore the *a priori* knowledge we have on such INVITE request is small.

5.4 Shared Dictionary (SD)

A dictionary is an ordered collection of strings. The use of a dictionary is very convenient for compression because by using a dictionary we can replace a string with its corresponding index in the dictionary. Naturally, for things to work correctly at decompression time, the dictionary used for decompression needs to be an exact copy of the one used for compression so that the same index corresponds to the same string. If this does not happen, we have a decompression failure. Decompression failures are discussed in Section 5.7.

As we can see from Table 3, many of the SIP headers belong to the group of *variable* headers. Many of these contain a URI. This URI can be related to one of the UA public identities (i.e., P-Called-Party-ID) or to another user. Other sources of variable headers comprise the codecs included in the SDP part of the SIP message together with rtpmap lines and the codecs' fmtp parameters. Here, we use a dictionary in order to reduce the amount of bytes that URIs and codec-related parameters take.

As we said earlier, a dictionary is simply an ordered list of strings containing all the URIs known to the UA or P-CSCF (i.e., own URIs and URIs of other SIP entities), the list of codecs with both static and dynamic payload types and all known rtpmap and fmtp lines.

If a match is found in the dictionary, the corresponding string is replaced by its index in the dictionary; if no match is found then the string is left as is. In the latter case, such string would be added to the dictionary by both UA and P-CSCF, as the last entry in the dictionary. In this way, this new entry can be used for future packets.

There are many possible ways to build such an SD. In a typical scenario, users want to start a PoC session with contacts present in their presence "buddy list", that is, people they already know. In order to build a dictionary containing URIs of other end-points, such as a shared address book, we could think of the following. When the P-CSCF has an INVITE request to send whose URI in the From header is not present in the dictionary, it adds the URI to its dictionary and replaces it with its index. When the UA receives such INVITE, it does not find that particular index in its dictionary, so it associates the index received in the From header to that SIP dialog. When the P-CSCF sends the ACK in response to the 200 OK, the UA extracts the URI from the From header of the ACK and associates it to the index previously saved for that dialog. In doing so, the UA has added a new entry to its dictionary.

Further details on how to build synchronized dictionaries is reserved for future study.

5.5   Encoding

By using templates, UA and P-CSCF need to exchange only the content of those headers that are without a value in the template, that is, the dynamic content of a SIP message. However, as we show in Section 5.6, even exchanging only the dynamic content of a message is not enough to achieve the requirements for DOS. In order to achieve such requirements the dynamic content needs to be encoded to further reduce the size of messages exchanged between UA and P-CSCF.

Variable content can be encoded using integer and bitwise representations. We can apply the latter to all those headers whose values belong to a finite set of known elements (see *Token* column in Table 2). In order to encode strings such as IP addresses, port numbers, and clock rates, we encode these as fixed and variable length integers. For example, an IP address can be encoded as a four byte integer and a port number can be encoded as a two byte integer. Dictionary indexes can be encoded as variable-length integers depending on the cardinality of the number to encode.

One other important aspect to take into consideration is the structure of the final packet. Once all the content has been encoded, the way such content is organized in the final packet also affects the size of the packet. In particular, we divide the packet in two parts. In one part we put all the encoded content of variable length and in another part we put all the encoded content of fixed length. The fixed-length content forms the last line of the packet. Each line in the packet has the first byte representing its length. The byte representing the length is also encoded. In particular, only 7 bits are used to represent the length of a line which limits the maximum length to 127 bytes. The most significant bit (MSB) is used to indicate if the following line is of the same type of the current line. This, for example, is useful if we have a SIP message with two or more c= lines in the SDP part.

Since the order of variables in the packet has to be preserved, we need to explicitly mark those variables not present in the message but whose header is present in the template, as empty. In order to do this, we reserve one value of the byte representing the length of the line to indicate a length value of zero. Such value is given by the MSB set to one and all the remaining 7 bits representing the length, set to zero.

5.6   Contributions to Compression

Table 4 shows how each of the mechanisms described above contributes to the overall compression. As we can see, each one of them has a significant role in the overall compression. In particular, the table shows the results for an incoming INVITE request. In the experiments all heuristics were applied so that, for example, the size shown for *Template* reflects the size of the packet after both *Stripped Headers* and *Template* have been applied. The *Removed* row shows how many bytes were removed from the message after applying the corresponding technique.

Table 4. Contributions to TBC for an INVITE request

	Original Packet	Stripped Headers	Template	SD	Encoding	Packet Order
Packet size [Bytes]	1182	1008	343	284	137	81
Removed [Bytes]	–	174	665	59	147	56

In conclusion, from Table 4 we can see that with TBC, we can satisfy the requirements for DOS, but in order to do this all the proposed techniques need to be applied.

5.7   Decompression Failures

TBC relies on the use of a shared dictionary in order to achieve maximum compression. In order for this to work, it is important that UE and P-CSCF keep their dictionaries synchronized at all times. A loss in dictionary synchronization almost certainly translates in a decompression failure at either end-point. A decompression failure is a very expensive event. When it happens, it requires the packet to be re-transmitted uncompressed and subsequent packets to be transmitted without compression until the cause for the decompression failure has been resolved. Because of this, a sanity check should be performed periodically in order to validate the synchronization of the dictionary. In any event, if a loss in synchronization happens, it has to be detected in a timely manner so that it can be quickly resolved.

Loss in synchronization between dictionaries can happen for various reasons. For example, when using non-reliable transport, we have to be careful to the way the shared dictionary is built. If packets used to build the dictionary are lost or end up out of sequence, we might end up with dictionaries that are not synchronized. It is important to notice that this problem is not present when we use the INVITE−ACK procedure described earlier for building the dictionary. In such a case, if an ACK is lost, the 200 OK would be re-transmitted thus triggering another ACK.

In order to verify the synchronization of the shared dictionary we can use a short checksum such as Cyclic Redundancy Check 16 (CRC−16). This checksum is calculated on the message to send, after stripping the unnecessary headers but *before* applying the template. Once the message is received and re-constructed at the other end-point, the UE or P-CSCF can re-calculate the checksum and see if it matches with the checksum received with the message. If there is a mismatch it means that the reconstructed message is different from the original message, which means that the dictionaries have lost synchronization.

Another way to verify the synchronization of the shared dictionary is to compute an hash of the dictionary and have UE and P-CSCF periodically exchange it during non-time-sensitive operations. If the two hash values do not match, the shared dictionaries are not synchronized. In order to identify which part of the dictionary is out of sync, a binary search can be performed on the dictionary, recursively hashing smaller parts of it until the one or more entries responsible for the mismatch are found.

Once a loss in synchronization has been detected and the non-aligned entries have been identified, the dictionaries can be re-synchronized by having UE and P-CSCF exchange such non-aligned entries.

6   Experiments

In this section we present the results of our experiments for SigComp and TBC. We consider both Mobile Originated (MO) calls and Mobile Terminated (MT) calls. An MO call is a call initiated by the mobile node, that is, by a mobile SIP UA. For such call, the first INVITE request is sent by the mobile SIP UA to the P-CSCF and then forwarded to the remote SIP UA. An MT call is a call initiated by a remote SIP end-point. In this case, the first INVITE request is sent by remote SIP UA and forwarded to the appropriate P-CSCF which sends it to the mobile SIP UA.

6.1   Experimental Setup

For our experiments, we used an IBM T42 Thinkpad laptop with a 1.7 GHz Pentium Mobile processor and 1 GB of RAM and an eRack server with a 3 GHz Pentium 4 processor and 1 GB of RAM. The T42 runs Linux kernel version 2.6.3–25 and the eRack runs Linux kernel version 2.6.9-42. The T42 behaves as an UE and the eRack as a P-CSCF. Both, UE and P-CSCF, read a SIP flow from a text file and exchange the compressed messages respecting the order of the packets in the flow. In order to test TBC and SigComp in realistic scenarios, all the IMS SIP flows used in the experiments were captured from a real IMS testbed and provided to us by Nortel. We used Open SigComp [4], an open-source SigComp stack and implemented a TBC compressor and decompressor. Compression for both MO and MT calls was measured and delays were later calculated according to Eq. (1).

6.2   Measurement Results

In the following measurements we focus our attention only on SIP messages and do not consider lower-layer protocol headers (e.g., UDP, IP). Such headers are not really relevant for PoC purposes and protocols like ROHC can help in their compression.

SigComp. As explained in Sections 4.3 and 4.4, in analyzing SigComp performance we do not use the SIP static dictionary and also, do not consider any of the mechanisms specified in [9]. Furthermore, we perform measurements for the most common values of *state memory size* (SMS), *CPU cycles* (CC) and *UDVM memory size* (UMS). Figs. 5 and 6 and Figs. 7 and 8 show the compression ratio that SigComp can achieve for an MO call and an MT call, respectively. Figs. 5 and 7 show the results for SMS, CC and UMS equal to 4096 bytes, 64 cycles and 4096 bytes, respectively. Figs. 6 and 8 show results for SMS, CC and UMS equal to 8192 bytes, 64 cycles and 8192 bytes, respectively.

The compression ratio is calculated as:

$$\rho = \frac{\text{size of } compressed\ packet\ [bytes]}{\text{size of } uncompressed\ packet\ [bytes]} \tag{3}$$

so that the smaller the compression ratio, the better. As we can see from Figs. 5, 6, 7 and 8, ρ for the first two messages is above 100%. This happens because the size of the compressed packet is larger than the size of the original uncompressed packet.

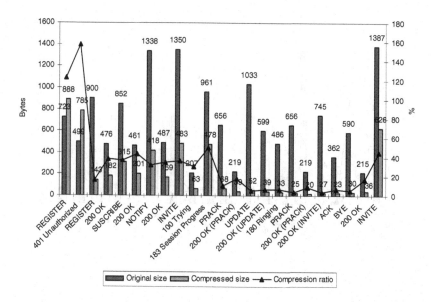

Fig. 5. SigComp performance for an MO call - long flow (SMS: 4096, CC: 64, UMS: 4096)

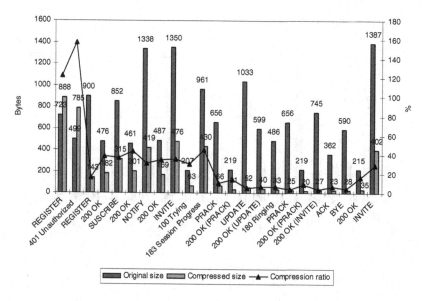

Fig. 6. SigComp performance for an MO call - long flow (SMS: 8192, CC: 64, UMS: 8192)

Such a behavior is expected since for the first packets there is no previous state to compress against, that is, the adaptive dictionary is empty (see Section 4.3). As the number of compressed messages grows, so does the adaptive dictionary, allowing for a better compression ratio as more messages are exchanged.

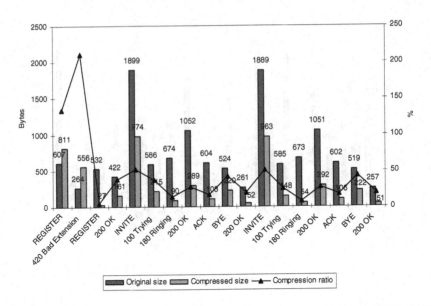

Fig. 7. SigComp performance for an MT call - short flow (SMS: 4096, CC: 64, UMS: 4096)

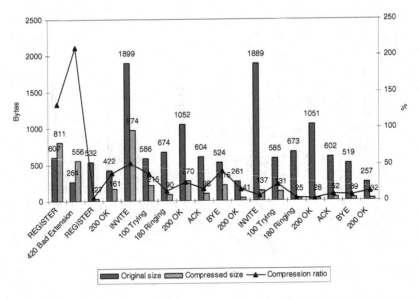

Fig. 8. SigComp performance for an MT call - short flow (SMS: 8192, CC: 64, UMS: 8192)

In Fig. 5 we can see that the first INVITE request is compressed from 1350 bytes to 483 bytes, while the second INVITE is compressed from a size of 1387 bytes to a size of 626 bytes. This is the case when using SMS and UMS of 4096 bytes each. On the other hand, when we increase SMS and UMS to 8192 bytes (see Fig. 6), the first

INVITE is compressed to 476 bytes and the second INVITE is compressed to 402 bytes. This improvement in compression is due to the fact that we have increased SMS and UMS, which means that the adaptive dictionary is larger. In doing so, when the second INVITE has to be compressed, the adaptive dictionary still contains some information relative to the first INVITE, thus allowing for higher compression. If we further increase SMS and UMS, the second INVITE can be further compressed to a size of 193 bytes. This, however, is the maximum compression that can be achieved since, at this point, all available state has been used and increasing SMS and UMS even more, would not provide more state.

In Figs. 7 and 8 we show SigComp performance for an MT call when using a shorter call flow than the one used for the MO call. Shorter call flows have been proposed in the past in order to reduce the call setup delay. As we can see, in Fig. 7 the first INVITE is compressed from 1899 bytes to 974 bytes and the second INVITE from 1889 bytes to 963 bytes. As before, when we increase SMS and UMS from 4096 bytes to 8192 bytes (see Fig. 8), the first INVITE is about the same while the second INVITE is compressed from 1889 bytes to 137 bytes. The reason for this big improvement in the compression of the second INVITE is that not only have we increased SMS and UMS but we are also exchanging fewer messages which means that new states created after the first INVITE are not enough to expunge state information regarding the first INVITE from the adaptive dictionary. In other words, when the second INVITE needs to be compressed, the adaptive dictionary still contains all the information regarding the first INVITE, hence achieving higher compression. If we further increase SMS and UMS, the compression of the second INVITE does not improve. This is because all available state has already been used and larger SMS and UMS do not correspond to an increase of state for that INVITE.

To summarize, SigComp can achieve significant compression ratios only for INVITE requests following the first one and only if enough state is available. The size of the first INVITE request remains significantly high also after compression. Furthermore, it is important to notice that in Figs. 7 and 8, the first and second INVITE are extremely similar, with the second INVITE having only 91 bytes that differ from the first INVITE. Still, we can see that the best compression achievable with SigComp, gives us a final size of 137 bytes which still does not satisfy the DOS requirements. In particular, since Open SigComp uses Deflate, the 137 bytes are an Huffman representation of the {offset, length} pairs plus strings not found in the dictionary.

Fig. 9 shows the call setup delay only in terms of one-way air-link delay for bit-rates typical of a control channel. As we can see, for the uncompressed flow the one-way air-link delay alone is significantly larger than the whole call setup delay for a GSM call (see Section 3). Such delay decreases below 2 seconds if we either use higher bit-rates or if we compress the flow. By using SigComp, the one-way air-link delay is below 2 seconds also for lower bit-rates. We have to keep in mind, however, that the air-link delay is only one of the many components of delay contributing to PDD and call setup delay (see Eq. (1)). Unfortunately, the air-link delay is the only component of the overall delay that can be improved by SigComp. Any other component of delay remains completely unaffected.

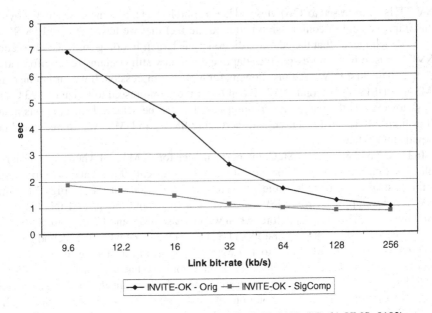

Fig. 9. One-way air-link delay for an MO call (SMS: 8192, CC: 64, UMS: 8192)

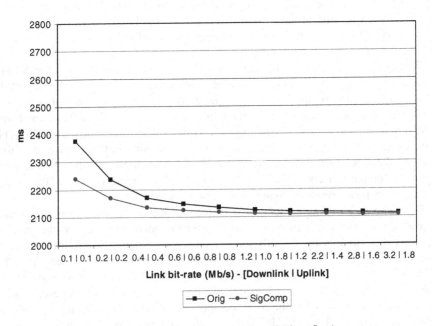

Fig. 10. PDD for mobile-to-mobile call (short flow)

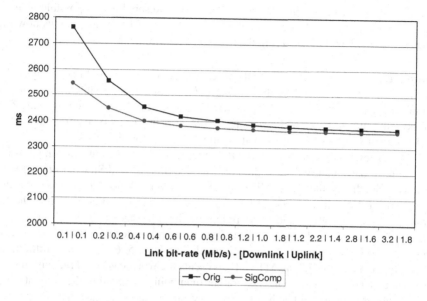

Fig. 11. Call setup delay for mobile-to-mobile call (short flow)

Table 5. Parameters used in delay calculation (source Nortel)

T_{setup}	1400 ms
T_{node}	150 ms
T_{BH}	100 ms
RTT	140 ms

A more realistic scenario in terms of PDD and call setup delay is shown in Figs. 10 and 11, respectively. Here we consider all the contributions to the overall delay. Table 5 shows typical values for all the other components of delay that need to be added to the air-link delay (see Eq. (1)). These values are for 1xEV−DO rev. A networks. As we can see, when we consider both wireless links at each end-point and all the contributions to the overall delay, PDD and call setup delay are above 2 seconds, regardless of SigComp. This is still too high for delay-sensitive applications.

The delays shown in Figs. 10 and 11 represent the best-case scenario for the higher bit-rates. In Figs. 10 and 11 we are assuming that the bit-rates shown on the x-axis are fully available to each user, including the highest ones. In reality, the available bit-rate decreases as users move further away from their Base Station (BS) and also, it has to be divided between all users belonging to the same sector. So, for example, if a client is far from its BS, then the maximum available bit-rate is more likely 1.2 Mb/s for download and 0.9 Mb/s for upload. This is a drastic reduction from a download bit-rate of 3.2 Mb/s and an upload bit-rate of 1.8 Mb/s. Furthermore, this maximum available bit-rate has to be divided among all the users in the same sector. So, if each user uses 0.12 Mb/s, for example, only 10 users can be supported in the same sector.

Although the higher bit-rates in Figs. 10 and 11 represent the best possible scenario, the call setup delay is still too high, above two seconds. This clearly shows how Sig-Comp is not sufficient in satisfying the necessary requirements.

Templates. In order to achieve a PDD of less than two seconds and PoC delays below one second, we need to reduce the *air-link delay* as much as possible and we need to completely remove the *air-link setup delay*. The latter can be achieved by using DOS for the call setup. As explained earlier, for 1xEV–DO rev. A, DOS requires a maximum packet size of 113 bytes for the downlink and 211 bytes for the uplink.

Table 6 shows the performance of TBC in terms of compression and compares it to SigComp. In particular, we show the performance of TBC and SigComp in the worst case scenario, that is, the first INVITE request of an MT call flow. This message is usually the most difficult to compress because of its large size and because it is the first message of the call-setup handshake. Being the first message of the handshake means that prior state is limited and therefore, SigComp, and in general any LZ-based compression mechanism, cannot compress it much (see Figs. 5, 6, 7 and 8). Furthermore, as explained in Section 5.3, an MT call represents the worst case for TBC with most of the content sent over-the-air encoded, rather than being included in the template. This is because the *a priori* knowledge that we have on an incoming message is very small since such message can come from anywhere and anyone.

Also for TBC experiments we consider two types of flows, a long flow and a short flow. In particular, flows 1 and 2 are long and flows 3 and 4 are short (see Table 6). The flows used here are extremely similar to the ones shown in Figs. 5, 6, 7 and 8.

As we can see from Table 6, when all entries are found in the SD, with TBC we achieve the packet size requirements of DOS for both PoC calls and normal SIP calls. Furthermore, SigComp performs consistently worst than TBC and if we try to apply SigComp compression on top of TBC, the size of the final packet is larger than if only TBC is used (see Section 4.2). From this we can conclude that TBC can satisfy the requirements for DOS and therefore satisfy the requirements for SIP calls and PoC. Also, it is clear how incorporating TBC in the SigComp framework would affect compression negatively.

In Table 6, flow 3 represents the particular case in which no packets are exchanged previous to the first INVITE. This can simulate, for example, a decompression failure or loss of state in SigComp. In such case, with SigComp, the compressed packet has a size larger than its uncompressed size (see Section 4.2). TBC, however, has performance that are consistent with the compression of other flows since it does not rely on state saved from previous messages. The compressed packet size with TBC in flow 3 is significantly larger than in flow 4 because in flow 3 the Call–ID header alone was 46 bytes long.

When only few entries or none at all are found in SD (see Table 6), TBC still outperforms SigComp although it might not achieve the requirements for DOS any longer. This depends very much on the particular packet to compress and the values of its SIP headers and SDP lines. In particular, headers whose value is a random string such as the content of Call–ID[3] or the content of the tag parameter, significantly affect the size of the compressed packet since templates and other forms of compression cannot help much.

---

[3] Call-ID is usually in the form *name@host* where *name* is a random string.

Table 6. Size in bytes of first INVITE for different MT calls

Flow	PoC	Entries found in SD	Original	SigComp	TBC	TBC + SigComp
1	Y	all	1244	629	**100**	110
		few	1244	629	168	138
		none	1244	629	210	177
2	Y	all	1181	591	**94**	104
		few	1181	591	162	132
		none	1181	591	187	156
3	N	all	795	934	**110**	449
		few	795	934	139	466
		none	795	934	163	488
4	N	all	900	535	**87**	93
		few	900	535	127	114
		none	900	535	157	140

All of this shows that a well synchronized and up-to-date Shared Dictionary is crucial for TBC to achieve the required packet sizes.

For MO calls, TBC can significantly reduce the packet size since most of the parameters are known by the UE and P-CSCF prior to the establishment of a call. For example, the first INVITE request of an MO call can be compressed from 1253 bytes to about 20 bytes when all entries are found in the SD and to about 40 bytes when no entries are found in the SD. With SigComp the same INVITE is compressed to 639 bytes. TBC satisfies the size requirements of DOS for MO calls and consistently outperforms SigComp.

The extremely large compression achieved for MO calls is possible because the only information we need to send is the content of the request line, To header, Call-ID and the value of the utran-cell-id-3gpp parameter in the P-Access-Network-Info header. Everything else is included in the template.

7   Conclusions

We have examined the performance of SigComp for IMS call flows and shown through measurements that although SigComp can achieve significant compression ratios, it cannot satisfy the requirements for DOS and therefore cannot be used for PoC in the IMS. SigComp is based on text-substitution compressions. Because of this, it becomes counter-productive when the size of the packets becomes smaller. Furthermore, Sig-Comp adds its own overhead to compressed packets and such overhead can significantly limit the benefits of its compression.

In order to satisfy the delay requirements for PoC in the IMS, SIP messages need to be sent over the control channel. This imposes a limit to the size of such messages. In particular, for 1xEV−DO rev. A, messages on the downlink cannot be larger than 113 bytes and messages on the uplink cannot be larger than 211 bytes. We have shown how SigComp cannot satisfy such requirements. At the same time, we have introduced a novel compression technique, namely TBC, based on the concept of *templates*. TBC can be used by cellular operators to deploy voice and PoC services in the IMS instead of SigComp. By using templates we can satisfy the requirements for data over signaling and send SIP messages on the control channel. In particular, TBC can reduce the size of the first INVITE in the flow, for an MT call, to about 100 bytes and can reduce the size of the first INVITE in the flow, for an MO call, to about 20 bytes. By doing so, we can satisfy the delay requirements for PoC, voice and any other delay-sensitive application.

We will look at ways to further improve compression with TBC. In particular, we will study the use of pointers as a way to avoid string duplication in the encoded content sent over the air. Also, other options will be studied in order to improve compression. In order to address the problem of headers containing long random numbers, the P-CSCF could substitute long random numbers with shorter ones for the downlink (P-CSCF→UE) since the P-CSCF has a clear view of all ongoing sessions and can therefore provide shorter unique identifiers. Replacing long random strings such as the ones used for Call-ID with shorter ones would further improve the overall compression.

Acknowledgments

This work was supported by Sprint and FirstHand Technologies.

References

1. Akhtar, H., Brombal, D., Jones, A.: New SIP Headers for Reducing SIP Message Size. Internet Draft: draft-akhtar-sipping-header-reduction-01.txt (work in progress) (September 2006)
2. Bormann, C., Burmeister, C., Degermark, M., Fukushima, H., Hannu, H., Jonsson, L.-E., Hakenberg, R., Koren, T., Le, K., Liu, Z., Martensson, A., Miyazaki, A., Svanbro, K., Wiebke, T., Yoshimura, T., Zheng, H.: RObust Header Compression (ROHC): Framework and four profiles: RTP, UDP, ESP, and uncompressed. RFC 3095 (July 2001)
3. Dierks, T., Allen, C.: The TLS Protocol Version 1.0. RFC 2246 (January 1999)
4. Estacado Systems. Open SigComp (2006)
5. Foster, G., Pous, M.I., Pesch, D., Sesmun, A., Kenneally, V.: Performance Estimation of Efficient UMTS Packet Voice Call Control. In: Proc. IEEE Vehicular Technology Conference (VTC 2002), Birmingham AL, USA, pp. 1447–1451 (september 2002)
6. Garcia-Martin, M., Bormann, C., Ott, J., Price, R., Roach, A.B.: The Session Initiation Protocol (SIP) and Session Description Protocol (SDP) Static Dictionary for Signaling Compression (SigComp). RFC 3485 (February 2003)
7. 3GPP2 TIA-856-A-1. cdma2000 High Rate Packet Data Air Interface Specification (March 2004)
8. Hannu, H.: Signaling Compression (SigComp) Requirements and Assumptions. RFC 3322 (January 2003)
9. Hannu, H., Christoffersson, J., Forsgren, S., Leung, K.-C., Liu, Z., Price, R.: Signaling Compression (SigComp) - Extended Operations. RFC 3321 (January 2003)
10. Postel, J., Reynolds, J.: File Transfer Protocol (FTP). RFC 959 (October 1985)

11. Price, R., Bormann, C., Christoffersson, J., Hannu, H., Liu, Z., Rosenberg, J.: Signaling Compression (SigComp). RFC 3320 (January 2003)
12. Rosenberg, J., Schulzrinne, H., Camarillo, G., Johnston, A.R., Peterson, J., Sparks, R., Handley, M., Schooler, E.: SIP: Session Initiation Protocol. RFC 3261 (June 2002)
13. Shacham, A., Monsour, B., Pereira, R., Thomas, M.: IP Payload Compression Protocol (IPComp). RFC 3173 (September 2001)
14. Viamonte, D., Calveras, A., Paradells, J., Gómez, C.: Evaluation and optimisation of session setup delay for streaming services over 3G networks with quality of service support. In: Proc. IEEE Wireless Communications and Mobile Computing (WCMC 2006) (2006)

Providing Content Aware Enterprise Communication Services

Xiaotao Wu, Krishna Dhara, and Venkatesh Krishnaswamy

Avaya Labs Research, 307 Middletown Lincroft Rd., Lincroft, NJ 07738, USA
{xwu,dhara,venky}@avaya.com
http://www.research.avayalabs.com

Abstract. Intelligent communication often requires context information to trigger proper communication services. In many cases, names, locations, as well as activities and status of communication participants are used to enable context-aware communication. In this paper, we propose a new context-aware communication paradigm, namely content-aware communication, which infers context information based on the content of ongoing conversations. New communication services can then be introduced by utilizing the content and the inferred information.

Content-aware communication employs Automatic Speech Recognition (ASR) to acquire conversation content, Information Extraction (IE) to help identify useful context information, and Information Retrieval (IR) to find related information. The existing ASR and IR technologies can already provide applicable approaches to enable content-aware communication for a single user on his or her personal computer. However, there are still very few existing content-aware voice communication services and also lacks a secure and scalable way to integrate different technologies and resources for enterprise wide deployment of the services. In this paper, we first categorize enterprise content-aware communication services and illustrate some new content-aware services. We then define an architecture with distributed media processing and centralized call control to manage enterprise content-aware communications. This architecture also helps manage feature interactions when integrating content-aware services with other enterprise communication features. In addition, we allow enterprise users to experience content-aware communication on different devices and in different modalities.

1   Introduction

The existing context-aware communication services often use people's location, presence status, calendar, as well as ongoing activities to help improve enterprise employees' communication efficiency. In most cases, they ignore the voice content of the conversation. In other words, they are not content-aware. However, the content of conversations can introduce many interesting services that can greatly improve employees' productivity and help better serve customers.

Content-aware is not a new idea in some other communication means. For example, the email service provided by Google, the Gmail, can display related

H. Schulzrinne, R. State, and S. Niccolini (Eds.): IPTComm 2008, LNCS 5310, pp. 322–341, 2008.

advertisements in a side frame based on the content of an email. However, there are very few content-aware services in voice communication for several reasons.

First and the foremost, the content of a voice communication cannot be acquired as easily as that for an email. It requires Automatic Speech Recognition (ASR) over continuous speech, which is a computation intensive task and usually cannot be handled by phones. It is also not scalable if we handle ASR for continuous speech at a centralized server. To achieve content-aware voice communication, there must be pairing entities of phones that have sufficient computation power and are able to monitor conversation audio streams. In addition, the low accuracy of ASR on arbitrary voice content also prohibits the deployment of content-aware voice communication. There must be an applicable way to ensure reasonable ASR accuracy for content-aware services.

Secondly, voice content-aware services need to support various end devices. End devices for voice communication may vary from very old phones without any display to softphones running on personal computers. The variation of computational as well as display capabilities requires different rendering and sometimes different modalities in presenting content related information to users. This is very different from text-based content-aware communication, which usually presents information on computer screens and can easily render content related information in a user friendly way.

Last, but not the least, legal and privacy concerns may also hinder the deployment of content-aware voice communications. In many cases, voice content may be saved and recognized offline for better ASR accuracy. However, different from saving text messages, audio recording requires one or all party consent, which is required by federal laws. It requires a user friendly way to acquire the consent for audio recording.

To provide content-aware services for voice communications, we need to address all the above issues and identify novel services to prove the value of content-aware voice communication, and this is the focus of the paper. The main contributions of the paper are:

1) We group enterprise content-aware services into four categories and define new services for each category.
2) We study the feasibility of the proposed new services and define an architecture with centralized call control, distributed ASR processing, and sharable information retrieval for scalable and secure enterprise content-aware communication.
3) We introduce our prototype implementation of the architecture and illustrate several practical approaches to handle different technical issues in providing content-aware services, such as choosing an appropriate host for ASR, handling feature interactions, and negotiating audio recording consent.

This paper is organized as follows: We first discuss some related work in Section 2 and discuss the categorization of content-aware enterprise services in Section 3. We then provide an overview of content-aware communication for a single user in Section 4. We illustrate our architecture to provide enterprise scale content-aware voice communication services in Section 5. Section 6 shows our prototype implementation and Section 7 concludes this paper and discusses our future work. Because we build our prototype based on the Session Initiation Protocol (SIP) [15], in this paper, we use SIP in all of our discussions.

2   Related Work

There are several unified communication tools and services developed by Microsoft, Google, and other enterprises to provide context-based services. As discussed earlier, most of these tools are limited to services like click-to-call or click-to-conference that are embedded in the results of a search. New versions of these tools, such as Microsoft Office tools, go further by embedding presence information of co-workers, whose names appear in various documents. While these attempts unify various communication tools of enterprise users and employs some context information for communication, they are not aware of the content of conversations and are not dynamic in nature.

The main component of content-aware communication is an ASR engine that can recognize voice communication content in real-time. Various aspects of ASR, such as accuracy and speed, have been extensively studied over the years. NIST [5] conducts extensive benchmark speech recognition for conversational speech and is quite useful in selecting appropriate ASR technologies for content-aware voice services. Several classes of applications based on ASR have been developed to assist end user communications. There are two classes of applications that are related to our usage of ASR. One is the multimedia indexing applications such as Speechbot [8]. Speechbot uses ASR to index documents on the world wide web when no transcriptions are available. They use these index techniques along with several other multimedia indexing methods to build a multimedia retrieval system [12]. While some of the research done on these applications, especially on error rates and document rankings, are applicable to our system, the scope of the two applications is different. Speechbot focuses on web content searching, while our system focuses on using the search result to infer context and augment enterprise communications. Another class of ASR applications is voice based search, such as spoken queries [6]. The query keywords are spoken instead of being typed by people to search the web. In our system, this technique can be an alternative option if the accuracy of continuous speech recognition is very low. It can also be enhanced in our system by using Information Extraction (IE) to identify a fixed vocabulary based on users' previous conversation and existing documents.

3   Content-Aware Communication Services

The goal of providing communication services in enterprises is to improve productivity as well as better serve customers. Based on the serving targets, we categorize the content-aware services into four groups: individual services, group

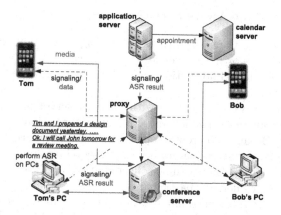

Fig. 1. Content-based information retrieval and reminder

services, enterprise services, and customer support services. Individual services can help improve individual efficiencies; group services can help coordinate group members; enterprise services can help create more agile, responsive enterprises; and customer support services can help improve customer satisfaction. For each service category, we illustrate one or several use cases below, then analyze how to achieve the services.

3.1   Individual Content-Aware Services

Use case 1: Figure 1 shows a way to achieve the content-based information retrieval and reminder. Tom and Bob talk over their mobile phones on the road. During the conversation, Tom mentions a document and plans to make a call to John. The ASR server recognizes the conversation, the application server then finds the document on Tom's PC and displays the link on Tom's phone. Tom clicks a *Send* button and Bob clicks a *Confirm* button on their phones, a file transfer session is established and the document is sent from Tom's PC to Bob's PC. After the conversation, the application server asks Tom to confirm a phone conference appointment with John. The reminder is then saved in the calendar server. In this use case, the content-aware service acts as a personal assistant helping users to intelligently handle conversation related issues.

The use case shows that individual content-aware services can be tightly bound to other resources people use often in their daily work, e.g., their PCs. Indeed, users' PCs can serve as both information sources and computing resources for content-aware services, especially for computation intensive tasks, such as ASR. For a large enterprise, it is not scalable to use a centralized media server to handle continuous speech recognition for all the employees. It is desirable to distribute ASR on users' PCs for individual content-aware services.

3.2   Group Content-Aware Services

Use case 2: Following the same idea as employing a *"personal assistant"* for a single user during his or her conversations, there can also be a group assistant to coordinate and share information among group members e.g., based on the content of a conference.

Figure 2 shows a web conference with an ASR server notating the conversation. All the conference participants perform information retrieval based on the ASR result. Because different people have different information sources for searching and different accessing privileges, the searching results can be very different. Those searching results can be collected at the application server, filtered, and shared among conference participants.

Use case 3: Content based communication services can also be integrated with existing group productivity tools, such as version control tools, like *Concurrent*

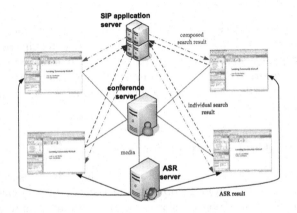

Fig. 2. Content-based information retrieval for a conference

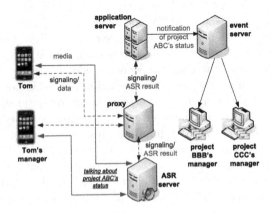

Fig. 3. Conversation content as an input for CEBP

Version System (CVS), and bug management tools, like *Bugzilla*. For example, for a project discussion, based on the content of the conversation, the group assistant can find the source files related to the conversation, then attach the link of the recorded discussion audio clips or the recognized text as the check-in comments into a version control system.

In group content-aware communication, the most important task is to enable information and resource sharing among group members. For example, group members may use their own PCs and speech profiles to recognize their own voices, then share the recognized speech among group members. In addition, the searching can be performed in a distributed way by each group member, and results then be shared among the group members as discussed in use case 2.

3.3   Enterprise Content-Aware Services

Use case 4: To create more agile, responsive organizations, Communication Enabled Business Processes (CEBP) is proposed, which can minimize the latency of detecting and responding important business events by intelligently arranging communication resources and providing advisory and notifications. The content of conversations can be treated as an input of CEBP solutions. For example, as shown in Figure 3, a developer is reporting the progress of a project to his manager. Based on the conversation, the content-aware service application can notify other managers on related projects.

Use case 5: In enterprises, the content of conversations can also help analyze social network maps and project relationships. There are many existing research on analyzing social networks based on email achieves [19], the same techniques can also be applied to the recognized voice conversation contents. The social network map can then help to improve the overall productivity of an enterprise, e.g., better identifying correct contacts for business events.

As shown in use case 4 and 5, conversation content can not only serve as the event to trigger service actions, it can also help to build communication intelligence.

3.4   Customer Support Content-Aware Services

Use case 6: To better serve customers is the most important thing for enterprises. Content-aware services can help ensure customer satisfaction in many different ways. For example, Figure 4 shows a service to detect foul language in customer support conversations. If a customer support person speaks a foul word, the service may notify his manager and conference the manager into the conversation. The foul language detector can also help detect customer's attitude and decide whether to leverage the call.

Use case 7: Content-aware services can also help to identify the most frequently asked questions and provide answers, e.g., by recording, recognizing, and analyzing customer support conversations. This can help build a better IVR system. In addition, recorded conversation content can also be used for training.

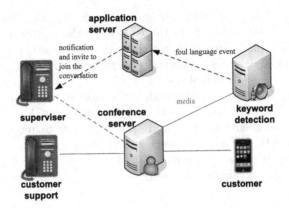

Fig. 4. Foul language detection service

Customer support content-aware services can also be part of CEBP to provide more responsive customer services. Different from the other three categories of content-aware services, customer support content-aware services need to support a large variety of end devices, and handle untrained voices for ASR.

In the above sections, we proposed several new content-aware services. To support the above proposed new services, we need to handle the following challenges:

1) Design a scalable architecture that can properly integrate enterprise users' PCs for ASR.
2) Ensure appropriate security and privacy handling in the architecture.
3) Find a practical approach to provide sufficient ASR accuracy by using the commercially available ASR engines.
4) Allow users to experience content-aware services on different devices with different modalities.
5) Define a user-friendly method to legally record conversations.
6) Identify a viable way to handle potential feature interactions.

4   Content-Aware Communication for a Single User

We have built a content-aware communication project called *Connote* that can monitor ongoing conversations and provide content-aware services for a single user. The key idea of *Connote* is to monitor a user's conversation by pairing the user's PC with his or her phone. There are several ways to achieve the pairing. A simple way is to use a phone headset switcher, e.g., Avaya's MX10 headset switcher multimedia amplifier as shown in Figure 5(a), to convert audio signals from a phone line to the microphone input of a PC. This way, users can talk over the phone while the PC performs ASR, conducts content-based searching, and presents related information on the PC's screen. The drawback of this approach is that the PC only handles audio streams without the knowledge

Fig. 5. Content-aware voice communication for a single user

of the call session, e.g., the participants of the call. Therefore the PC application cannot automatically share content-related information with other users and perform more features.

An improved way is to build a softphone on the user's PC which registers as the user's contact point. The softphone then acts as a back-to-back user agent (B2BUA) to bring the user's phone into conversations, and relay audio streams to the user's phone as shown in Figure 5(b). Since both audio streams and call signaling going through the softphone, the softphone has the complete knowledge of call sessions and can perform more content-aware services, e.g., conferencing other people into a call session. The drawback of this method is that the PC has to be always on for call handling.

In addition, simply pairing users' PCs with their phones is not sufficient to handle other kinds of content-aware services, such as group, enterprise, and customer support services. Neither of the above mentioned methods can share available resources among group members. For example, if a user's PC is unavailable to handle ASR, the above approaches cannot employ another available machine in the user's group for ASR. In addition, it is difficult to incorporate the content-aware services running on users' PCs with other services running on application servers. For example, users may not want to apply content-aware services for call coverage handling, such as recognizing audio streams from an Interactive Voice Response (IVR) system. Third, sometimes, a centralized media server is sufficient and more reliable to handle ASR and other media processing tasks, e.g., for isolated keyword recognition, a VoiceXML server may be better than a user's PC, even for a large number of ASR tasks. To overcome these drawbacks, we proposed an architecture that can be easily customized to handle all the four categories of content-aware communication services.

5 Enterprise Content-Aware Voice Communication Architecture

Figure 6 shows the enterprise content-aware voice communication architecture. The left hand side of the figure shows endpoints and the right hand side shows servers and available resources (outlined in a circle). In the architecture, the *communication server* serves as the central point to coordinate signaling, media, and data sessions. The security and privacy issues are handled by the communication server. The *application server* hosts enterprise communication services, including content-aware communication services. The *content server* represents

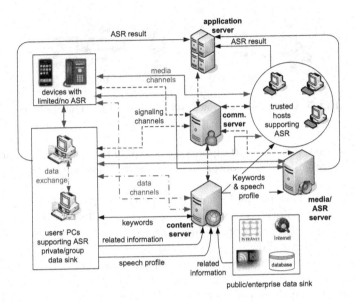

Fig. 6. Enterprise content-aware voice communication architecture

an enterprise repository for information aggregation and synthesization. The *media/ASR server* is a central place for media handling, such as ASR and IVR. In our architecture, media handling can be distributed to different entities, such as users' PCs and trusted hosts in the intranet. For an enterprise employee, the trusted hosts can be computers of his or her team members, or shared computers in his or her group. Which entity to use for media handling is determined by the application server. Below we discuss how this architecture addresses all the issues raised in Section 1, deals different categories of content-aware services, and overcomes the drawbacks discussed in Section 4.

5.1   Scalable ASR Handling

In the architecture, ASR can be handled by different entities. The application server decides which entity to use based on the computation capability, expected ASR accuracy, network bandwidth, audio latency, as well as security and privacy attributes of each entity. In general, ASR should be handled by users' own PCs for better scalability, ASR accuracy, and easier security and privacy handling. If users' own PCs are not available, trusted hosts should be employed. The last resort is the centralized media server. We first introduce how we incorporate different resources for ASR, then explain the rational of how we choose a resource for ASR.

In the architecture, the application server can monitor an ongoing call session through the communication server, e.g., by using SIP event notification architecture [14] and SIP dialog state event [16] package. The application server then creates a conference call based on the dialog information and bridge an

ASR engine into the conference for receiving audio streams. The conference call can be hosted at enterprises' Private Branch eXchanges (PBXs), a conference server, or at a PC in the enterprise depending on the capabilities of the PC. The capability information can be retrieved by using SIP OPTIONS methods [15], and the conference call can be established by using SIP REFER methods [10]. In general, a PC with a moderate configuration can easily handle a 3-way conferencing and perform ASR simultaneously. Which we discuss in detail in the following section.

Computational capability consideration. Based on our experience of Connote for a single user, a modest PC with a 3.0 GHz Intel processor and 2.0 GB of memory, while handling a 3-way conference with G711 codec, takes a reasonable $10 \sim 20$ seconds to recognize a 20 second audio clip, or $700ms$ to recognize a keyword in a continuous speech by using Microsoft speech engine. The ASR time can be reduced to $3 \sim 5$ seconds for a 20 second audio clip on a better dual core PC with Intel Core 2 Duo 1.86 GHz processors and 1.0 GB of memory. However, if there are other processes occupying CPU cycles, the ASR time will increase. Figure 7 shows a test of running multiple ASR processes on the modest PC we mentioned earlier. During the test, the memory usage of each ASR process is constantly around 30MB. The audio clip we used in the test is a 23 second length, single channel, 16 bits, 20ms sample rate, PCM-encoded WAV file. The figure shows that ASR time increases in linear with the number of ASR sessions, and that is mainly caused by sharing CPU cycles among multiple ASR sessions.

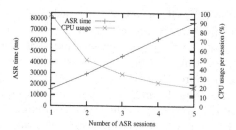

Fig. 7. ASR time and CPU usage

The test suggests that when the communication server tries to employ a PC to handle ASR for a conversation, it must check available CPU cycles of that PC for the duration of the conversation. In general, it is hard to predict CPU cycle consumption over a relatively long period of time. However, by checking people's calendar and ongoing activities, in some circumstances, we may predict CPU usage for a certain period of time. We detail how to choose an entity for ASR based on CPU usage in our prototype in Section 6.1.

Bandwidth and audio latency consideration. Network bandwidth and transmission delay can greatly affect audio quality and in turn affect ASR accuracy. In our architecture, due to security and privacy concerns, the candidate PCs that are suitable to perform ASR for a user are usually very limited, e.g., to only the user's team members' PCs or the PCs with an explicit permission granted. The application server can retrieve the information of those PCs from the communication server based on registration information, then determine which machine to use for audio mixing and ASR based on network proximity. For example, if an employee, whose office is in New York City, joins a meeting at Denver, his audio streams should be relayed to his Denver colleague's PC for ASR, instead of his own PC in New York City. We discuss how to handle content-aware services based on the end-to-end transportation latency in detail in Section 6.1.

5.2   Security and Privacy Consideration

As we discussed in Section 5, the communication server serves as the central point to coordinate all the components in our architecture, and handles security and privacy issues. The content server, application server, and media server can be treated as trusted hosts to the communication server and no authentication needed. All the other components in the architecture must be authenticated. The application server can authorize which entity should perform ASR for a user based on hierarchical structure of an enterprise. For example, team members may share their machines. Sharable resources of a department, such as lab machines, can be used by all department members. We will illustrate how to handle the trust relationship in our prototype in Section 6.2.

5.3   ASR Accuracy Consideration

Table 1 [3] shows the difficulty levels of ASR tasks related to vocabulary size and the type of the speakers with a score from 1 to 10, where 1 is the simplest system. The table suggests two approaches to improve ASR accuracy without extensive update on existing ASR engines. Below we show that our architecture can help achieve both approaches.

The first approach is to perform ASR with a trained speech profile. In general, users can easily train their voices on their own computers. In our architecture, we use users' own PCs for ASR can easily access the trained speech profile and improve ASR accuracy. The ASR can also be handled by trusted hosts. In this case, the speech profile of the user should be transferred to the machine that handles ASR. Users can also store their trained profile on the content server.

Table 1. Vocabulary size and ASR difficulties

	Isolated	Spotting	Continuous
Speaker Dependent (small voc)	1	3	5
Speaker Dependent (large voc)	4	6	7
Multi-Speaker (small voc)	2	4	6
Multi-Speaker (large voc)	4	6	7
Speaker Independent (small voc)	3	6	8
Speaker Independent (large voc)	5	8	10

The second approach is to limit the size of vocabulary for ASR. In an enterprise, most conversations of a user usually revolve around one or several specific intents during a certain period of time. By applying Information Extraction (IE) technologies upon existing users' conversations, we can greatly reduce the size of vocabulary for ASR and improve ASR accuracy. We will further discuss applying IE on users' email achieves to improve ASR accuracy in Section 6.3.

5.4 Presenting Content-Aware Information on Different Devices

A critical factor that may determine whether people will use a communication service highly depends on the ability of the service to run on both PCs and on portable devices with limited input/output capabilities, such as PDAs, desk phones, and mobile phones. In our architecture, the content server is responsible to aggregate information from different sources and render them in an appropriate format and present to users based on the devices the users are using. In Section 6.4, we will show the interfaces we implemented on IP phones and on users' PCs.

5.5 Dealing with Legal Issues Related to Audio Recording

Federal law requires the parties of a conversation to consent to media recording. In addition, the FCC requires the recorded parties be notified before the recording. These requirements make automatic recording illegal without consent among conversation participants. In one method, after ASR, we can discard the original recorded audio clips, or we can simply perform ASR based on real-time RTP streams without any recording. In another method, we propose to use a private SIP header "*P-Consent-Needed*" to request recording consent. The consent can be represented in an XML format and carried in Multipurpose Internet Mail Extensions (MIME) using SIP requests or responses, e.g., SIP MESSAGE requests [1]. Figure 8 shows the message flow for a recording consent negotiation.

5.6 Feature Interaction Handling

In enterprises, there usually are hundreds of communication services. Any new introduced services should not interact with the existing services in an unexpected manner. For example, a user can provision his services as *"if a callee has a call coverage service invoked and the service redirects the call to an IVR system, the content-aware service should not be invoked"*. Another example is *"on a menu-driven phone display, an emergency message should override the content-related information screen, but a buddy presence status notification should not"*. Unlike the *Connote* service we introduced in Section 4, our architecture enables feature interaction handling for enterprise content-aware services.

The application server in our architecture uses the mechanisms defined in SIP Servlet v1.1 (JSR 289) [13] for application sequencing. The application router in JSR 289 application framework will decide when and how a content-aware service should be invoked. Since some application logic can also be executed at users' PCs, we have to decide how to coordinate users' PCs into application

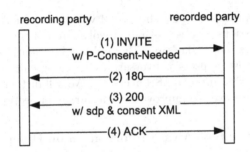

(1) P-Consent-Needed: sip:tom@example.com;
    purpose=recording;audio;mode=all-or-none

(3) <xml version="1.0"?>
      <consent id="a7b8c65a">
       <sender uri="sip:tom@example.com"/>
       <recipient uri="sip:bob@example.com"/>
       <purpose purpose="session-recording">
        <session-recording id="123456" mode="mixed">
         <call-leg uri="sip:bob@example.com"
               call-id="a1b2c3d4@10.1.2.3">
          <media type="audio" mid="mid:1"/>
         </call-leg>
         <call-leg uri="sip:tom@example.com"
               call-id="a1b2c3d4@10.1.2.3">
          <media type="audio" mid="mid:1"/>
         </call-leg>
        </session-recording>
       </purpose>
      </consent>

Fig. 8. Consent negotiation for audio recording

sequencing. Theoretically, each application host can have an application router to coordinate its hosted applications, and application routers can communicate with each other to exchange call state information and handle overall feature interactions. For example, each user's PC can have an application router that can communicate with other application routers running on other PCs or on the centralized application server. However, practically, the distributed application routers would make feature interaction intangible. Therefore, in our architecture, the content-aware service logic are completely centralized at the application server with users' PCs only serving as information sources and computation resources. We will detail how to centralize the service logic in Section 6.5.

6   Prototype Implementation

We have developed a prototype of our architecture by using Ubiquity SIP A/S as the application server, Avaya's SIP Enablement Services (SES) and Communication Manager (CM) as the communication server, Avaya Voice Portal as the media server. Ubiquity SIP A/S can support JSR 289. The content server is co-located with the Ubiquity server for simplicity. The content server uses Apache Tomcat 5.5 as a web server for VoiceXML retrieval. We also use Microsoft Office Communicator (MOC) and Avaya's MOC gateway for desktop call control, Microsoft Speech SDK for ASR on PCs, Nuance's Dragon NaturallySpeaking server for ASR on Avaya's Voice Portal, and Google Desktop API (GDK) for indexing and searching documents on PCs.

At users' PCs, we developed a SIP-based user agent running as a Windows service. We call it *Desktop Service Agent (DSA)*. DSA registers to the communication server and notifies the communication server of its capabilities, such as its computation and audio mixing capabilities. DSA can accept incoming calls to perform ASR and IR and send the ASR and IR results to the communication server.

In the prototype, phone control is achieved by using an XML-based protocol called the IP Telephony Markup Language (IPTML) [4]. We also allow MOC to control phones through the Computer Supported Telecommunications Applications (CSTA) Phase III (ECMA-323) [9]. With phone control functions, users can easily click-to-dial and bring related people into a conversation. In addition, we use a proprietary XML-based protocol called Desktop Service Query (DSQ) to control DSAs running on users' PCs. All the control protocols can be transported over SIP. IPTML and DSQ are carried by SIP MESSAGE requests. CSTA sessions are established by using SIP INVITE requests and CSTA messages are carried by SIP INFO requests. Therefore, the control channels follow the same path as the call signaling channels. Below we illustrate the implementation details of handling the considerations in Section 5.

6.1 Capability Notification and ASR Host Pickup

In our prototype, we simply use the ongoing CPU and memory usage, as well as end-to-end network latency to decide which entity should be used to handle ASR and audio mixing. On a Windows machine, Microsoft Speech engine only needs 30 MB for ASR, so in most cases, the size of memory will not affect which entity to choose.

The relationship between available CPU cycles and the latency of ASR can be acquired by following the same test as we discussed in Section 5.1 and get a map as shown in Figure 7. The test should be done when a user installs a DSA on his or her PC. Based on the test and the ongoing available CPU cycles, we can then roughly calculate the estimated time to recognize a 1 second audio clip.

$$T_{estimate} = T_{min} + \alpha * CPU_{available-percentage}$$

$$\alpha = ((T_{max} - T_{min})/(CPU_{max} - CPU_{min}))/L_{audio-clip}$$

In the equation, $L_{audio-clip}$ represents the length of the audio clip used in the test. CPU_{min} represents the lowest CPU percentage in the test and T_{min} represents the according ASR latency. CPU_{max} represents the highest CPU percentage in the test and T_{max} for the according ASR latency. The estimated time will be sent to the application server for picking up an appropriate ASR host. Based on our observation, using less than 2 seconds to recognize a 1 second audio clip is acceptable, considering that usually it is not necessary to notate the complete conversation.

We simply use `ping` to acquire end-to-end network latency. This is not accurate for real time audio communication because audio streams are usually sent over UDP and with relatively big throughput. But the result of `ping` can still help to decide whether to choose an entity for ASR or not.

In our prototype, we use SIP event notification architecture [14] for sending capability information from PCs to the communication server. The application server subscribes to candidate PCs for capability information. The capability information can be represented in the similar format as those defined in the Session Initiation Protocol (SIP) User Agent Capability Extension to Presence Information Data Format (PIDF) [11].

6.2   Trust Relationship Handling

As we discussed in Section 5, the trust relationship should be handled in centralized servers. In our prototype, the application server and the communication server has a trust relationship. The content-aware service application residing on the application server registers a URI for each user at the communication server. We call this URI the user's personal assistant (PA)'s URI. All the other entities of the user must trust the user's PA that runs on the centralized application server. Each user's PA can receive the user's primary contact's dialog state events. The PA can then control the user's call sessions. The DSA running on the user's PC also trusts the requests sent from the according PA. For single user content-aware services, all the service logic is handled at the user's PA. For group and enterprise services, we can define the trust policies between different PAs at the application server. For customer support services, a customer support's PA will always participate into calls to monitor conversations.

6.3   IE and ASR

As we discussed in Section 5.3, reducing the size of vocabulary and using keyword spotting can have better accuracy than recognizing the complete continuous speech over a large vocabulary. In our prototype, we extract the vocabulary for ASR from users' emails.

Figure 9 shows the number of unique words and key phrases extracted by IE technologies in two email archives. One is from a personal email archive and the other is from IETF sipping working group email archive. In general, the vocabulary size of a general ASR engine can be 100,000 or more. The vocabulary retrieved from email archives or obtained by IE has a much smaller size. Note that even though the vocabulary generated from email archives is smaller, it contains names and acronyms that are not in general vocabulary, but important to users. In our initial tests for a non-native English speaker, the accuracy of recognizing a keyword in a sentence by using Microsoft speech engine without limiting the vocabulary size is just around 30 ~ 40%, but increased to 80 ~ 90% with the

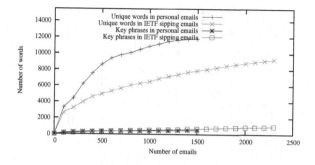

Fig. 9. The size of vocabularies generated from email archives

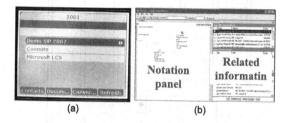

Fig. 10. Connote user interface on IP phone and on PC

vocabulary size limited to 100 keywords. We are still working on providing a complete evaluation of improving ASR accuracy by reducing the size of vocabulary with applying IE on users' email archives for the existing commercially available ASR engines (Microsoft Speech engine and Nuance's NaturallySpeaking engine).

6.4   Multimodal User Interactions

In our prototype, a PC user will have a graphical user interface (GUI) for content-aware services, as shown in Figure 10(b), and a phone with a LCD display will have a menu-driven interface, as shown in Figure 10(a). For a device that does not have the menu-driven interface or even no LCD display, the content server can generate a VoiceXML page, and the application server can then bridge the media server, and provide a voice menu for the user.

6.5   Handling Feature Interactions of Displaying Phone Menus

As we discussed in Section 6.2, the DSAs running on users' PCs are completely controlled by its according PAs running on the application server by using DSQ. The users' PCs only serve as computation resources or information sources. In addition, users' phones are also controlled by the PAs by using IPTML. Therefore, in our prototype, feature interactions can be completely handled at the application server, though, logically there can be feature interactions among

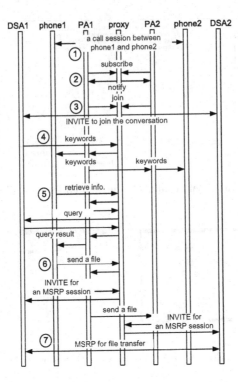

Fig. 11. File sharing between two DSAs

multiple PAs. One interesting feature interaction in our prototype is to handle
menu display on phones. Because a phone usually has a very limited display, it
can only display one menu at a time. If there are multiple applications want to
show their menus on the phone, those applications conflict. For example, during a call, a user presses a phone control menu item to check his or her missed
calls, while at the same time, the ASR recognizes a keyword and the content-
aware application wants to display related information on the phone, and at the
mean time, an emergency alert also wants to show some warning messages on
the phone, these services conflict. In our prototype, we simply define user invoked menu has higher priority than content-aware application generated menu,
and assume other services should also have priority information and let application router decide the application sequencing. The more granulated feature
interaction handling method is in our future work.

6.6   Use Case Implementation

We implemented the services we presented in use case 1 and use case 2 in our
prototype. Figure 11 shows the call flow for content based searching and file
transfer. In the figure, the file transfer operation can be initiated at users' phones.
The PAs get the request and serve as a B2BUA to establish a file transfer session

by following the SDP offer/answer mechanism for file transfer [7]. The real file transfer is then handled by two DSAs using MSRP [2]. Notice that *PA1* and *PA2* are logically separated, but are part of the same application. They can communicate by function calls. In the service, *PA2* allows messages from *PA1* only if *phone1* and *phone2* are in the same communication session.

Sharing content-aware searching results. Once the content of a conversation is obtained, the immediate usage of the content is to find content-related information so users can bring related people into the conversation and share useful documents. In general, not all the related documents are publicly available to all users. For example, the result of the desktop search of a PC are only available to the owner of the PC. In a conversation, in many cases, it is desirable to grant permission to the other conversation participants to access desktop search result and retrieve related documents. In our prototype, the content server handles the aggregation and synthesization. The synthesized results can be ordered based on the following method.

Each search has a search sequence number r with initial value as 1 for the first recognized keyword during a conversation. The search sequence number increases 1 for each new search. Each search result is a list that contains multiple items. In the list, each item has a position number i started at 1. The smaller the position number, the higher the relevance of the item is for the searching keyword. Each search result item will be integrated into a overall return list that will be presented to the user based on the importance value of the item. For information retrieval based on continuous speech, the topics may keep changing but most likely are relevant. Therefore, the consecutive searches should be processed in a correlated manner. Based on the above observation, we define the importance of an item I in a search result with respect to its search sequence number r and its position i as follows:

$$I_{(r,i)} = C_r * R_i * A_r$$

C_r represents the speech recognition confidence value of the keywords that are used to perform the search, which can be obtained from the result of ASR. R_i represents the relevant factor of the ith item to the keywords. Ideally, the search engine should provide the relevance value of each search result item. But in our prototype, we use Google desktop search API which does not provide such a value so we simply set $R_i = 1/sqrt(i)$. A_r represents the aging factor of the rth search, the bigger the r, the smaller the A_r. The return list contains all the searching result items in the descending order of the $I_{(r,i)}$.

Recorded conversation tagging. If we can acquire required conversation participants' consents for audio recording, the recorded audio clip can be saved on users' PCs for offline analysis. Offline analysis can usually achieve higher ASR accuracy. The recorded audio clips can be tagged based on the recognized scripts. The content server can then coordinate distributed searching on saved audio clips.

Further actions for searching and tagging results. Finding related information is just the first step for content-aware services. The more important task is to best use the acquired information. In our prototype, we can easily allow users to share documents, click-to-call related people, as well as interacting with other Internet services. Note that all the services performed in this use case are not independent to each other. Rather, the service logic runs on Ubiquity SIP A/S so they fell into a unified application framework and feature interactions can be well handled.

6.7 Performance Evaluation

We have conducted several performance tests on a PC with 3.0 GHz Intel processor, 2.0 GB memory, and using Microsoft Speech engine as the ASR engine. Based on our tests, in local network, the introduced delay by audio relay $((mouth\text{-}to\text{-}ear)_{with\_audio\_relay} - (mouth\text{-}to\text{-}ear)_{no\_audio\_relay})$ is less than $5ms$ and the quality downgrade by audio relay $(PESQ_{no\_audio\_relay} - PESQ_{with\_audio\_relay},$ $PESQ$ stands for *Perceptual Evaluation of Speech Quality*) is not observable.

We also tested ASR for keyword spotting on Nuance's Dragon NaturallySpeaking server and on Microsoft Speech engine. Both ASR engines take less than 1 second to recognize a keyword. In addition, it takes about $200ms \sim 3s$ to get the first 10 IR results of the keyword in Google Desktop search. Therefore, it takes $1 \sim 4$ seconds to retrieve related information of an ongoing conversation when the PC is not heavily loaded.

7 Conclusion

One of the biggest advantages of Internet telephony is to easily integrate computer applications and services into people's communications. In this paper, we design and present an architecture for providing content-aware services for enterprises. The architecture extends the current efforts in unifying various communication tools by augmenting user communication with a context that is dynamically inferred. We evaluated several issues to meet the challenges of providing enterprise content-aware services. Our prototype implementation shows that the performance provided by this architecture is acceptable and the new content-aware services can be easily incorporated into the architecture. For future work, we will investigate how to further improve the information retrieval accuracy based on ASR on continuous speech.

References

1. Campbell, E.B., Rosenberg, J., Schulzrinne, H., Huitema, C., Gurle, D. (eds.): Session Initiation Protocol (SIP) extension for instant messaging. RFC 3428, Internet Engineering Task Force (December 2002)
2. Campbell, E.B., Mahy, R., Jennings, C. (eds.): The Message Session Relay Protocol (MSRP). RFC 4975, Internet Engineering Task Force (September 2007)

3. Deroo, O.: A short introduction to speech recognition,
   http://tcts.fpms.ac.be/asr/intro.php
4. Dhara, K., Krishnaswamy, V.: A SIP-based application framework for intelligent end-points. In: The International SIP Conference 2003, January 14-17 (2003)
5. Fiscus, J., Fisher, W., Martin, A., Przybocki, M., Pallett, D.: NIST evaluation of conversational speech recognition over the telephone: English and Mandarin performance results. In: DARPA Broadcast News Workshop (2000)
6. Franz, A., Milch, B.: Searching the web by voice. In: 19th International Conference on Computational Linguistics (COLING), pp. 1213–1217 (August 2002)
7. Garcia-Martin, M., Isomaki, M., Camarillo, G., Loreto, S.: A Session Description Protocol (SDP) offer/answer mechanism to enable file transfer. Internet draft, Internet Engineering Task Force, Work in progress (December 2006)
8. Gauvain, J.L., Lamel, L., Adda, G., Adda-Decker, M., Barras, C., Chen, L., de Kercadio, Y.: Processing broadcast audio for information access. In: 39th Annual Meeting on Association for Computational Linguistics (ACL) Morristown, NJ, USA, pp. 2–9 (2001)
9. Ecma International. XML protocol for computer supported telecommunications applications (CSTA) phase III. Standard 323, Ecma International (December 2006)
10. Johnston, A., Levin, O.: Session Initiation Protocol (SIP) Call Control - Conferencing for User Agents. RFC 4579, Internet Engineering Task Force (August 2006)
11. Lonnfors, M., Kiss, K.: User agent capability presence status extension. Internet Draft draft-ietf-simple-prescaps-ext-08, Internet Engineering Task Force, Work in progress (September 2007)
12. Moreno, P.J., Van Thong, J.M., Logan, B., Jones, G.J.F.: From multimedia retrieval to knowledge management. Computer 35(4), 58–66 (2002)
13. Java Community Process. SIP servlet API v1.1. Java Specification Requests 289, Java Community Process (December 2007)
14. Roach, A.: Session initiation protocol (SIP)-specific event notification. RFC 3265, Internet Engineering Task Force (June 2002)
15. Rosenberg, J., Schulzrinne, H., Camarillo, G., Johnston, A.R., Peterson, J., Sparks, R., Handley, M., Schooler, E.: SIP: Session Initiation Protocol. RFC 3261, Internet Engineering Task Force (June 2002)
16. Rosenberg, J., et al.: An INVITE inititiated dialog event package for the session initiation protocol (SIP). RFC 4235, Internet Engineering Task Force (December 2005)
17. Witbrock, M., Hauptmann, A.: Speech recognition and information retrieval. In: Proceedings of the 1997 DARPA Speech Recognition Workshop, Chantilly, February 2-5 (1997)
18. Wu, X., Krishnaswamy, V.: Using SIP event package and consent request for media recording. Internet draft, Internet Engineering Task Force (June 2006) (Expired)
19. Email Archive Visualization Workshop (June 2005),
    http://www.cs.umd.edu/hcil/emailviz/workshop/

Author Index